"The Ticket to Freedom"

New Perspectives on the History of the South

Florida A&M University, Tallahassee
Florida Atlantic University, Boca Raton
Florida Gulf Coast University, Ft. Myers
Florida International University, Miami
Florida State University, Tallahassee
University of Central Florida, Orlando
University of Florida, Gainesville
University of North Florida, Jacksonville
University of South Florida, Tampa
University of West Florida, Pensacola

New Perspectives on the History of the South
Edited by John David Smith

"In the Country of the Enemy": The Civil War Reports of a Massachusetts Corporal,
edited by William C. Harris (1999)

The Wild East: A Biography of the Great Smoky Mountains, by Margaret L. Brown (2000);
first paperback edition, 2001

*Crime, Sexual Violence, and Clemency: Florida's Pardon Board and Penal System in the Progressive
Era,* by Vivien M. L. Miller (2000)

*The New South's New Frontier: A Social History of Economic Development in Southwestern North
Carolina,* by Stephen Wallace Taylor (2001)

Redefining the Color Line: Black Activism in Little Rock, Arkansas, 1940–1970, by John A. Kirk
(2002)

The Southern Dream of a Caribbean Empire, 1854–1861, by Robert E. May (2002)

Forging a Common Bond: Labor and Environmental Activism during the BASF Lockout,
by Timothy J. Minchin (2003)

*Dixie's Daughters: The United Daughters of the Confederacy and the Preservation
of Confederate Culture,* by Karen L. Cox (2003)

The Other War of 1812: The Patriot War and the American Invasion of Spanish East Florida,
by James G. Cusick (2003)

"Lives Full of Struggle and Triumph": Southern Women, Their Institutions, and Their Communities,
edited by Bruce L. Clayton and John A. Salmond (2003)

German-Speaking Officers in the United States Colored Troops, 1863–1867, by Martin W. Öfele
(2004)

Southern Struggles: The Southern Labor Movement and the Civil Rights Struggle,
by John A. Salmond (2004)

Radio and the Struggle for Civil Rights in the South, by Brian Ward (2004)

Southern Ladies, New Women: Race, Region, and Clubwomen in South Carolina, 1890–1930,
by Joan Marie Johnson (2004)

Fighting against the Odds: A Concise History of Southern Labor since World War II,
by Timothy J. Minchin (2004)

"Don't Sleep with Stevens!": The J. P. Stevens Campaign and the Struggle to Organize the South,
1963–80, by Timothy J. Minchin (2005)

"The Ticket to Freedom": The NAACP and the Struggle for Black Political Integration,
by Manfred Berg (2005)

"War Governor of the South": North Carolina's Zeb Vance in the Confederacy, by Joe A. Mobley (2005)

Planters' Progress: Moderning Confederate Georgia, by Chad Morgan (2005)

"The Ticket to Freedom"

The NAACP and the Struggle for Black Political Integration

Manfred Berg

Foreword by John David Smith, Series Editor

University Press of Florida

Gainesville/Tallahassee/Tampa/Boca Raton

Pensacola/Orlando/Miami/Jacksonville/Ft. Myers

10 09 08 07 06 05   6 5 4 3 2 1

A record of cataloging-in-publication data is available from the Library of Congress.
ISBN 0-8130-2832-9

The University Press of Florida is the scholarly publishing agency for the State University
System of Florida, comprising Florida A&M University, Florida Atlantic University, Florida
Gulf Coast University, Florida International University, Florida State University, University
of Central Florida, University of Florida, University of North Florida, University of South
Florida, and University of West Florida.

University Press of Florida
15 Northwest 15th Street
Gainesville, FL 32611-2079
http://www.upf.com

To Anja and Charlotte

Contents

List of Tables xi
Series Foreword xiii
Preface xvii
List of Abbreviations xix
Introduction: Writing the History of the NAACP 1
1. The Making of an Integrationist Civil Rights Organization 10
2. Educating Black Voters and White Politicians 40
3. Chasing the Rainbow? Black Voting Rights in the Courts 69
4. Protest and Loyalty: The NAACP in the Second World War 94
5. Civil Rights and Liberal Anticommunism 116
6. "Aren't You an American Citizen?" The NAACP Voter Registration
   Campaigns in the South, 1940–1962 140
7. Voter Registration or Nonviolent Direct Action? 166
8. The Politics of Civil Rights 191
9. Black Power—White Backlash 221
   Conclusion: The Ticket to Freedom? 250
   Notes 265
   Bibliography 323
   Index 343

Tables

1. NAACP Members and Branches, 1912 to 1919   23
2. Black Registration in the South, 1940–1952   141
3. Black Registration in Eleven Southern States, 1960 to 1970   188
4. Percentage of Eligible Blacks Registered, 1960 to 1971   189

Foreword

Historians and writers from Ulrich Bonnell Phillips, C. Vann Woodward, and Howard Zinn to Wilbur J. Cash, William Faulkner, and Lee Smith have underscored the South's distinctiveness. For many persons the South signifies more than a region. For them it represents an idea, an abstraction, even an ideology. For some the South has become an obsession. Since the colonial period, the South has been both connected to and distanced from the rest of North America. Its settlement pattern, its crops, and, most significantly, its commitment to racial slavery earmarked the Old South as different from the rest of the nation. As Woodward noted in 1960, the South has many "burdens." Its defeat in the Civil War and its experiences during and after Reconstruction left an indelible blot on the fabric of southern history. Yet in the twenty-first century, the South seems very much "American"—more like the rest of the country, not some mythic land apart.

Dating back to the 1880s, historians and critics have defined and redefined southern history in innumerable ways. The "Nationalist" historians, the "Dunning School," the "Agrarians," the "Revisionists," the "Post-Revisionists," the Marxists, and, today, all manner of postmodernists have tried to squeeze some contemporary meaning from southern history. Historians and others regularly interpret the region's history and culture in such varied journals and magazines as the *Journal of Southern History, Southern Review, Southern Humanities Review, Southern Living, Southern Exposure*, and *Southern Cultures*. In 1979 the *Encyclopedia of Southern History* appeared, followed ten years later by the *Encyclopedia of Southern Culture*. Both within and beyond the region, there seems to be an insatiable appetite for information on the South and its people.

In fact, no region in America, including New England and the West, has received as much in-depth analysis and reflection as has the American South.

Insiders (native southerners) and outsiders (non-southerners, including an unusually large number of northern and European specialists on the South) agree that the Southland has a particular *Weltanschauung*, one loaded with irony, pathos, paradox, and racial and class conflict. In some universities southern history long has reigned as a major research specialty. They confer doctorates in the field. Many academic publishers consider "southern studies" a strong part of their list. Books about the South sell on both sides of the Mason-Dixon line and overseas. Associations and institutions sponsor regular symposia and conferences regionally, nationally, and internationally on the South's past.

In the last century, when the South ranked as "the nation's economic problem No. 1," sociologists dissected the region's pathologies, especially its historic race problem and poverty. Today, social scientists and economists marvel at the "Sun Belt"—its thriving and alluring prosperity built atop long-standing antiunion sentiment, its daunting skyscrapers, its rapid transit systems, its social and racial progress. Atlanta, the region's bourgeois Mecca, has numerous lesser rivals throughout the former Confederacy—Dallas, New Orleans, Miami, Nashville, Charlotte, Raleigh, and Richmond. Cable television, chain restaurants, New York department stores, "malls" and their accompanying outlet shops—even the *New York Times'* "national edition" (printed in several southern cities and delivered to the doorsteps of thousands of southerners)—dot the southern landscape like the proverbial cotton plants of old.

An appreciation of the South's distinctiveness and its diversity lies at the heart of the University Press of Florida's New Perspectives on the History of the South series. This broadly based series publishes the highest quality new scholarship on the history of the American South. The books cover all aspects and periods of the southern past, with special emphasis on the region's cultural, economic, intellectual, and social history.

Manfred Berg's *"The Ticket to Freedom,"* the latest volume in the series, is a landmark study of the National Association for the Advancement of Colored People (NAACP). Berg, one of Europe's leading American historians, has written a comprehensive yet compact, analytical yet fast-paced, balanced and objective history of the NAACP. This veteran biracial organization, founded in 1909, merged the neoabolitionist tradition of the late nineteenth century and early twentieth century progressivism. In establishing the NAACP, blacks and whites, including Oswald Garrison Villard, W.E.B. Du Bois, and Moorfield Storey eschewed Booker T. Washington's accommodationism. Instead the new organization openly challenged white racism through public protest, demands for political participation, and legal campaigns that focused on lynching and the redress of other racial grievances. As Berg argues elegantly but without hyperbole, throughout its long history no racial organization has played as salient a role in the political fight for true freedom for all Americans as the NAACP.

Berg carefully and thoroughly charts the NAACP's growth, successes, and failures as an integrationist and interracial civil rights organization. He examines the group's national organization and its activities on the local level, especially its aggressive voter registration drives. While many whites, especially southerners, considered the organization radical, Berg notes that it "remained firmly committed to the institutional and normative framework provided by the U.S. Constitution and the American political system." He credits the group's lobbying and propaganda efforts before, during, and after World War II with "politicizing the black population." This was essential to southern blacks because in the 1940s more than three-quarters of all African-Americans lived in Dixie.

Rescuing the NAACP from relative historiographical obscurity, Berg focuses incisively on the organization's determined efforts to win African-Americans the right to vote. Voting rights, he explains, "took center stage in the NAACP's strategy to win freedom and equality for blacks both as the symbol of first-class citizenship and as the crucial weapon for advancing collective interests." Berg frames the NAACP's successful role in the landmark *Brown v. Board of Education of Topeka, Kansas* around "the broader and widely debated question whether political and social movements should resort to legal options at all."

Berg's graceful study underscores the long struggle by African-Americans and their white allies to integrate blacks fully into American life. Given the South's long record of slavery, neoslavery, and racial proscription, this timely book reminds us of the continuing quest by black southerners not just for legal equality, but for economic and social equality as well. The NAACP has played no small role in the evolution of today's decidedly distinctive and diverse South.

John David Smith
Series Editor

Preface

This book traces the struggle of the National Association for the Advancement of Colored People for political rights and the full integration of African-Americans into the political life of the United States throughout the twentieth century. It was written for both specialists in the history of the black civil rights movement and general readers interested in America's oldest and most important civil rights organization. While I hope that the readers will appreciate my effort at maintaining a critical and scholarly perspective, they will also notice that I have taken the liberal creed and the political realism of the NAACP seriously and tried to avoid presentist judgment as much as is possible for a historian writing contemporary history. Obviously, I believe that the NAACP's contributions to the black struggle for rights, freedom, and equality have been underrated—and sometimes misrepresented—by much of the recent scholarship. This book, I hope, offers a more nuanced and balanced account of the NAACP and its role in the civil rights movement.

In researching and writing the history of the NAACP, I was privileged by the opportunity to spend the five years from 1992 to 1997 as a research fellow at the German Historical Institute in Washington, D.C. Without the generous support of this fine institution my work would have been much more difficult. I wish to thank the members of the Institute's academic advisory council and, in particular, its former directors Professor Hartmut Lehmann and Professor Detlef Junker for their support and encouragement. In addition, many colleagues and friends at the Institute encouraged my work with empathy and numerous valuable suggestions. I would also like to express my appreciation for the help I received from countless archivists and librarians in both the United States and Germany, first and foremost the magnificent staff of the Manuscript Division at the Library of Congress, who made the voluminous NAACP Records as accessible as possible for me.

I first wrote this book in German as a *Habilitationsschrift*—a second dissertation required by the German academic system—and it was subsequently published in 2000. I had always wanted to make it available to American readers, and when John David Smith suggested several years ago that I should write an English-language version for the University Press of Florida, I enthusiastically accepted his offer. Of course, it turned out to be an effort that took much more time and energy than I had anticipated, but I enjoyed it anyway and I hope that the readers will agree that the work has been worthwhile. Through these years, John David Smith has been a great editor and a dear friend whose incessant encouragement, prudent advice, and scholarly accomplishment has done more for this book than he will ever acknowledge. Meredith Morris-Babb kept the faith in my finishing the manuscript despite the delays. I would also like to thank the two anonymous readers for the University Press of Florida for their thoughtful critiques. Carsten Hummel has done a great job in helping to prepare the manuscript.

Since I first became interested in the history of the civil rights movement and of American race relations, many teachers, friends, colleagues, and students have influenced my work and challenged my thought and approach. I would like to mention especially Detlef Junker, Knud Krakau, the late Willi Paul Adams, the late Jürgen Heideking, Martin Geyer, Terry Anderson, Paul Finkelman, Genna Rae McNeil, David Thelen, Simon Wendt, Britta Waldschmidt-Nelson, Axel Schäfer, Ruben Rumbaut, Peter Rose, Gerald Horne, Tony Badger, Harvard Sitkoff, the late Hugh Davis Graham, Hartmut Keil, Susan Strasser, Kitty Sklar, James and Lois Horton, Roger Daniels, Hasia Diner, Michael Dreyer, Dietrich Herrmann, Maria Höhn, and Claire Bortfeldt. While some of them will surely disagree with much of what I say in this book, I have benefited enormously from all of our debates on race and rights in America. A special debt extends to Georg Iggers, professor emeritus at SUNY Buffalo, who shared with me his rich experiences as a white NAACP activist in the Jim Crow South, where he lived and taught as a young man after his family had been expelled from his native Germany because of their "race." Finally and most importantly, I cannot possibly express the depth of my gratitude for the encouragement, support, and love I have received from my wife, Anja Schüler, an accomplished historian and the mother of our daughter, Charlotte, who was born and raised in the midst of my travail with the NAACP.

Abbreviations

ACLU	American Civil Liberties Union
ADA	Americans for Democratic Action
BWC	Birmingham World Correspondence
CIO	Congress of Industrial Organizations
CORE	Congress of Racial Equality
COFO	Council of Federated Organizations
CRC	Civil Rights Congress
CRJFK	Civil Rights During the Kennedy Administration
CRLBJ	Civil Rights During the Johnson Administration
CRRN	Civil Rights During the Nixon Administration
CPUSA	Communist Party of the United States of America
DoJ	U.S. Department of Justice
FBI	Federal Bureau of Investigation
FEPC	Fair Employment Practices Committee
HUAC	House Un-American Activities Committee
ILD	International Labor Defense
LCCR	Leadership Conference on Civil Rights
LCFO	Lowndes County Freedom Organization
MFDP	Mississippi Freedom Democratic Party
NAACP	National Association for the Advancement of Colored People
NAACP LDF	National Association for the Advancement of Colored People Legal Defense and Educational Fund
NAWSA	National American Woman Suffrage Association
NCAPT	National Committee to Abolish the Poll Tax
NNC	National Negro Congress
NUL	National Urban League
NWP	National Woman's Party

RJBOHC	Ralph J. Bunche Oral History Collection
SCHW	Southern Conference for Human Welfare
SCLC	Southern Christian Leadership Conference
SNCC	Student Nonviolent Coordinating Committee
SRC	Southern Regional Council
UNIA	Universal Negro Improvement Association
VEP	Voter Education Project
WPA	Works Progress Administration

Introduction

Writing the History of the NAACP

The National Association for the Advancement of Colored People, known as the NAACP, is America's largest and oldest civil rights organization. Founded in 1909 by a small band of white social reformers and black intellectuals, by mid-century the association had grown into a large membership organization with roughly a half million dues-paying members and more than a thousand branches all over the United States. For millions of African-Americans, the five capital letters NAACP signified black America's determination not to be content with "second-class citizenship." For the guardians of white supremacy, particularly in the South, the association became synonymous with the "radicals" and "outside agitators" that disturbed the allegedly harmonious race relations based on black subordination. Although the NAACP at times seemed to fall back into the rearguard of the civil rights struggle, it remains one of the most important African-American organizations as it approaches its centennial anniversary.

As the late August Meier, one of the foremost scholars on the history of the association, once observed, it is almost impossible to exaggerate the importance of the NAACP in the history of the black struggle for freedom and equality.[1] Nevertheless, for many years the NAACP has been the stepchild of civil rights historiography. In a recent review article, Charles Eagles noted with some astonishment that no historian had yet written a major work on the NAACP, while general histories of other black advancement groups, such as the Student Nonviolent Coordinating Committee (SNCC), the Congress of Racial Equality (CORE), the National Urban League, and the Southern Christian Leadership Conference (SCLC), were readily available.[2] Charles Kellogg's projected multivolume history of the association never proceeded beyond the first volume and the NAACP's first decade. And although August Meier and Elliott Rudwick made numerous valuable contributions to writing the history of the NAACP, they never published a book-length study.[3] Until the early 1990s, we only had a small number of case studies on specific aspects of the NAACP's history, plus a few outdated overviews of little historio-graphical significance.[4] In addition, several autobiographies of NAACP leaders were published over the years.[5]

No scholar who has worked in the NAACP Records held by the Library of Congress in Washington, D.C., will be surprised by the want of a comprehensive history of the association. Their sheer volume of several million documents—the largest single archival holding of the LoC—make this a daunting task that perhaps goes beyond the power of an individual researcher.[6] But there are other reasons as well why the NAACP has been neglected by civil rights scholars. To begin with, the history of the civil rights movement was long dominated by the political biography of Dr. Martin Luther King Jr., undoubtedly the most charismatic black leader of the twentieth century.[7] While there is no shortage of King biographies, the leaders of the NAACP were largely ignored. Its two most important executive secretaries, Walter Francis White and Roy Wilkins, were not even included in the standard biographical volume *Black Leaders of the Twentieth Century*, published in the early 1980s.[8]

Perhaps the most important reason for the relative lack of interest in the NAACP has been the association's image as legalistic, bureaucratic, wedded to the liberal establishment, and out of touch with the true aspirations of the black masses, which was projected by historians who emphasized the grass-roots origins and mass-action character of the black struggle. Clayborne Carson's 1983 essay on the civil rights movement in the *Encyclopedia of American Political History*, for example, barely mentions the NAACP. Carson and other historians called for a paradigm shift away from what they saw as a "top-down" approach focusing on national leaders and organizations and toward the history of local activists and movements who represented the true backbone and essence of the black freedom struggle.[9]

Local history, to be sure, has opened up inspiring new perspectives and yielded a rich empirical harvest, especially when the focus of these studies was extended to entire states rather than confined to individual communities. Moreover, local history has demonstrated, among other things, the importance of the NAACP branches and state conferences.[10] Unfortunately, though, the paradigm shift toward the local occurred before the national leadership and policies of the NAACP had been adequately researched. In this context, it is important to emphasize that the association's leaders and decision-making bodies were basically guided by the belief that the struggle for civil rights could only be victorious if it were placed on the national agenda of American politics. Although the local branches were "the lifeblood of the association," according to Ella Baker, who served as the director of branches from 1943 to 1946, the political perspective of the NAACP was a national one.[11] Moreover, it would be misleading to separate the NAACP's leadership from the membership at large along the patterns of "bureaucrats versus activists" or "new crowd" versus "old guard."[12] As this book will demonstrate, the association's New York headquarters did not usually stand in the way of local activism but often initiated and supported activities at the local level, particularly in the field of voter registration.[13] It is also noteworthy that, by and large, the membership backed the policies of the national secretariat and the board of directors, even though there never was a shortage of internal dissenters.

During the last ten years, however, the historiographical neglect of the NAACP has clearly come to an end and a reassessment of its role in the civil rights movement is clearly underway. British historian Adam Fairclough has given much attention to the association both in his book on the civil rights movement in Louisiana and in his recent synthesis of the black struggle for equality in the twentieth century.[14] Mark R. Schneider's *The Civil Rights Movement in the Jazz Age* covers much of the NAACP's history in the 1920s and contests the "myth" that the association was a white-dominated middle-class group without a mass following.[15] Kenneth R. Janken has published an admirable, full-scale biography of Walter White, a key figure in the NAACP from 1916 to his death in 1955, that is critical of its protagonist's penchant for self-promotion and personal vanity, but always empathetic and judicious.[16] In her book on the black struggle during the early Cold War, Carol Anderson harshly criticizes the NAACP for allegedly succumbing to anticommunism and for abandoning the progressive vision of human rights in favor of a narrow civil rights agenda. But while Anderson finds much fault with the association, she does not question its historical significance. To the contrary, the decisions of the NAACP leaders in this crucial period were so fateful, she argues, precisely because the NAACP was the leading black political organization of the time.[17]

This book was researched in the mid-1990s and first published in German in 2000. Although some of its findings and arguments have already been published in English, I am grateful for the suggestion by John David Smith to make the whole book available to American readers.[18] This involved more than just translation. It meant rewriting and rearranging for American scholars and general readers a book that was first conceived as a study addressed to a German academic audience. Despite the laudable and increasing efforts at international cooperation among historians, there are still distinct national differences in shaping arguments and narratives. I have tried to make the transition to what I see as a more narrative-oriented American style of writing historical monographs without trying to conceal my position and perspective as a non-American observer. In all candor, I also accepted the challenge to spend several more years with the NAACP and write an English version of my earlier book because American scholars of U.S. history generally ignore all publications not written in English.[19]

I do not claim, however, to have written a comprehensive—let alone a definitive—history of the NAACP. As Adam Fairclough has aptly observed, "the history of the NAACP is so long, rich, and diverse that it is impossible to set down between two covers."[20] My topic is the association's struggle for the right to vote, from its founding in the early twentieth century to about 1970, when the right to cast a ballot and have it fairly counted was reasonably secure for all African-Americans.[21] The suffrage, I argue, took center stage in the NAACP's strategy to win freedom and equality for blacks, both as the symbol of first-class citizenship and as the crucial weapon for advancing collective interests. As a flyer issued by the Baltimore, Maryland, NAACP branch for a 1965 voter registration drive, from which I borrow the title of this book, put it confidently: "The Ballot is Our Ticket to Freedom!"[22] This struggle for the ballot involved the five levels that I have tried to trace throughout the following chapters.

- The disfranchisement of African-Americans, as it was practiced almost everywhere in the southern states, constituted a flagrant violation of America's egalitarian and democratic ideology. In order to challenge this fundamental flaw of American democracy, the NAACP needed to initiate national discourses about racial disfranchisement, discrimination, and violence. In following these efforts, I look at the historical contexts that favored or inhibited the association's claims to black rights. It was no coincidence, for example, that the two World Wars and the Cold War, when the American creed was taken to task before world opinion, each had a profound impact on the NAACP's work.

- The NAACP leaders firmly believed in the American system of representative government and worked hard for the passage of national civil rights laws. From the 1910s on, the association lobbied for a federal antilynching bill, and since 1942 it maintained a bureau in Washington, D.C., whose longtime head, Clarence Mitchell, was hailed as one of the most effective lobbyists in the nation's capital. Although the segregationist southerners invariably succeeded in thwarting all national civil rights legislation until the late 1950s, including several bills to prohibit the use of the poll tax as a qualification for voting, the lobbying effort eventually paid off when Congress passed two historic civil rights laws in the mid-1960s that ended racial segregation and disfranchisement. Still, the NAACP paid a price for its alliance with liberal lawmakers and administrations. Working the halls of Congress involved compromises that many civil rights activists found hard to stomach. Because of its close relationship with the liberal establishment, critics viewed the association more like a traditional lobbying group than as part of a social movement, especially when the civil rights struggle entered the phase of nonviolent mass protests.[23]

• Because the NAACP won a good number of legendary court victories, most famously the 1954 desegregation ruling of the U.S. Supreme Court in *Brown v. Board of Education of Topeka, Kansas,* it has often been consigned to the role of the civil rights movement's legal branch. And indeed, the association attracted the elite of black lawyers in the United States. Most prominent among them was its longtime chief counsel, Thurgood Marshall, who later became the first African-American Supreme Court justice, and who was widely praised as an outstanding legal mind and a skillful litigator. However, as early as 1940, the NAACP's legal department began to assume an organizational life of its own, as the NAACP Legal Defense and Education Fund, also known as the LDF or Ink Fund, eventually leading to a total separation between the two groups. The legal campaigns for civil rights thus are only one part of the association's history.[24] In this book I will not repeat the well-known story of *Brown.* Instead, I focus on litigation to secure the right to vote, most importantly the fight against the white primary.[25] My interest, moreover, is less in the details of litigation than in the broader and widely debated question of whether political and social movements should resort to legal options at all.[26]

• The key task in regaining the vote was inducing eligible African-Americans to assert their citizenship rights by trying to register as voters. In the South, this meant challenging head-on the institutional and cultural barriers of white supremacy, often at considerable personal risk. In the North, blacks had to be convinced that their votes could actually make a difference, given that neither of the major parties was really interested in representing black constituencies. Organizing voter registration drives was a task that the local NAACP branches performed incessantly from the early days of the association's history. After the Second World War, the national secretariat became heavily involved and made registration into a major focus of NAACP work. During the nonviolent protests of the 1950s and 1960s, voter registration developed into an area of both cooperation and competition with other civil rights groups. In responding to nonviolent direct action and militant protest, the NAACP leadership emphasized registration campaigns as the "unglamorous" but politically most effective strategy of mass mobilization.[27]

• If racial discrimination was to be ended by the ballot, voter registration was but a first step. Black voters had to be educated to use their power "intelligently," while white politicians needed to be taught to respect this power. For decades, the NAACP preached the theory that the black electorate, although relatively small in number, could hold the balance of power in local, state, and national elections, if only blacks realized the potential impact of their ballots. Its official commitment to nonpartisanship notwithstanding, the association tried to mobilize black voters in order to reward friends and punish enemies at the polls, albeit with limited success.

In chapter one, I describe the origins, program, and organizational growth of the NAACP and discuss the issue of internal race relations. The chapter then analyzes the association's constitutional discourse and its attempts to enforce the Fourteenth and Fifteenth Amendments to the U.S. Constitution. At the end of its first decade, the NAACP's membership and prestige had reached a temporary peak, but it also painfully experienced the limits to interracial coalition building when its advances were coldly rejected by the woman suffrage movement. Still, the association did not waver in its integrationist outlook when challenged by Marcus Garvey's competing vision of black separatism.

Chapter two tells the story of the NAACP's efforts to establish black voters as a political factor in a two-party system that had virtually shut them out. In a political culture of racism, the association tried to enlighten both black voters and white politicians about the power of black votes. Campaigns to punish hostile politicians at the polls yielded at least some encouraging results. During the Great Depression, the NAACP was shattered by ideological debates over the wisdom of integrationism and the necessity to take a more class-based perspective on the race question. While the association retained its character as a civil rights organization, it also adopted a new economic program embracing the liberal welfare state and entered into alliances with the labor movement. As black voters shifted their allegiance from the GOP to the Roosevelt Democrats, the NAACP for all practical purposes became part of the New Deal coalition.

In chapter three, my account of the NAACP's voting rights litigation takes up recent debates about the effectiveness of pursuing legal strategies to bring about social and political change. The chapter describes the external constraints of legal action to enforce civil rights during the first half of the twen-tieth century and offers an in-depth discussion of the white primary cases and a reinterpretation of their meaning and historical significance.

Chapter four deals with the NAACP's organizational, political, and ideo-logical development during the Second World War. The war triggered far-reaching social and cultural changes that, on the whole, were conducive to the cause of black rights and advancement. In contrast to its patriotic quiet-ism in World War I, the association struck a successful balance between loy-alty and protest. The campaign against the poll tax broadened its political base and yielded some encouraging results in the struggle for reenfran-chising southern blacks. Perhaps most important, the association benefited from the politicization of African-Americans during World War II by spec-tacularly expanding its membership and branches. In the aftermath of the war, it was undoubtedly the strongest black political organization in America.

Chapter five deals with the impact of the Cold War and its concomitant anticommunist hysteria on the civil rights movement. The exuberant mood among black activists during the immediate aftermath of World War II soon gave way to a repressive climate that put black rights on the defense. Some historians have harshly criticized the NAACP's embrace of liberal anticom-munism for allegedly having retarded the black struggle for decades to come. In contrast, I argue that much of this criticism is exaggerated, inconsistent, and misleading. In particular, my research reveals that the NAACP did not conduct large-scale "purges" of leftists among its members, as several schol-ars have stated without providing empirical evidence.

In chapter six, I describe the NAACP's voter registration campaigns in the South from the Second World War to the early 1960s. This grassroots work played an important part in the considerable increase of black registration during these two decades. The chapter discusses the goals and methods of the association's registration drives and the obstacles and hazards its activists faced. In the late 1950s, the national office created the NAACP Voter Regis-tration Committee, charged with organizing and coordinating campaigns throughout the entire South. The NAACP did not limit itself to legal action and adopting a defensive mind-set, as some historians have argued. My analysis of the association's southern registration work shows a vibrant, ac-tive, and highly political organization.

Chapter seven probes into the association's response to the wave of non-violent direct action that began to build a new momentum for the civil rights struggle at the end of the 1950s. The new approach, along with the founding of new civil rights organizations, posed a considerable strategic and organiza-tional challenge to the NAACP. There was much bickering and rivalry with

Martin Luther King's SCLC and with SNCC and CORE, respectively, but the association also developed a constructive response to the new situation. In particular, it stepped up the voter registration campaigns that it offered as an alternative to nonviolent protest and as a constructive way to channel mass participation into the political process. In the joint Voter Education Projects of the 1960s, the NAACP vigorously asserted its leadership role as the largest and most efficient civil rights organization.

In chapter eight, I analyze the involvement and role of the NAACP in the national politics of civil rights during the 1950s and 1960s. The long and hard quest for civil rights legislation often involved painful compromises and almost infinite patience. However, it was not primarily patient and skillful lobbying that put civil rights on the congressional agenda, but the crises created by nonviolent protest provoking violent responses from white supremacists. When the crucial breakthrough came within reach, the NAACP made every effort to mobilize the necessary electoral support for the liberal coalition and to communicate the imperatives of a "responsible" civil rights strategy to the black community.

Chapter nine explores the association's reaction to the racial polarization in the second half of the 1960s, signified by the catchphrases "Black Power" and "white backlash." While the NAACP leaders were not altogether unhappy with the split of the civil rights movement, which freed them from the uneasy alliance with its radical rivals, they viewed the growing militancy among African-Americans as a dangerous threat to the Johnson administration's agenda of civil rights and social reforms. Viewing the "Great Society" as the grand prize for blacks, the NAACP's support for the president also included backing Johnson's Vietnam policy. In its response to the ideological challenges from the Black Power militants, the association reasserted its traditional goals, methods, and ideals and continued to rely on its organizational strength. As the liberal consensus unraveled in the late 1960s and the white backlash seemed to threaten the achievements of the Second Reconstruction, the NAACP remained a strong political force for civil rights.

In the conclusions, I restate my argument and ponder the historical achievements of the NAACP's struggle for black voting rights and political integration. I also sketch the development of the association in the post–civil rights era. Going beyond the history of the NAACP, I discuss the evolution of the American voting rights discourse from racial disfranchisement to minority vote dilution, arguably one of the most contentious racial issues in American politics today.

This book emphasizes the eminently political character of the NAACP. Throughout its history, the association pursued social and racial change predominantly by political means. It worked hard prodding the federal government to intervene against racial discrimination and sought the support of parties and candidates for black civil rights as well as for advancing the social and economic interests of African-Americans.[28] It entered into alliances and coalitions, opposed powerful political forces, and quarreled over strategic issues with other organizations dedicated to black rights. At times, the differences of opinion escalated into intense rivalries and outright conflict. In tracing the NAACP's political history, I wish to contribute to a richer and perhaps more nuanced picture of America's veteran civil rights group.

The historiographical debates over the NAACP's role in the black struggle have centered around the historical and political legitimacy of racial integration, the chief goal proclaimed by the association from its beginnings to the aftermath of the civil rights era. At all times, there were critics who ridiculed and condemned this goal as illusionary or even treacherous, and modern historians have echoed much of this criticism. In a fundamentally racist society, it is said, the concept of integration may easily become an ideological subterfuge for concealing white privilege and black exclusion behind a masquerade of tokenism. Desegregation and civil and political rights within the confines of liberal individualism are seen at best as a first step in a much broader and ongoing struggle for black liberation that would involve nothing less than a full-scale political, economic, and cultural transformation of American society.[29]

I refrain from discussing the future prospects for such sweeping social change here. However, I wish to remind the readers of the fact that during most of the time span covered in this book the notion of racial integration was viewed as distinctly radical, even revolutionary, by most white Americans. Simultaneously, equality of justice, rights, and opportunity, freedom in the pursuit of happiness, personal respect, political representation, and full inclusion and participation as citizens of the American Republic were goals that most African-Americans considered as highly important and worth fighting for. In assessing the historical achievements and failures of the NAACP, I propose to take its agenda of civil and political integration seriously.

The Making of
an Integrationist Civil Rights Organization

Origins

On the evening of August 15, 1908, William English Walling, a young journalist and social reformer, and his wife boarded the night train from Chicago
to Springfield, Illinois, to investigate the news about a race riot that had
erupted in the state capital the day before. When the couple arrived, thousands of militia troops had finally succeeded in quelling the violence. The
two-day riot left six persons dead. Two black men had been lynched and four
whites killed by gunfire from blacks trying to defend themselves. Hundreds
more suffered injuries. Forty houses in which blacks lived had been burnt to
the ground. Most of Springfield's roughly twenty-five hundred African-
American residents had fled the city or sought shelter in the state arsenal. No
wonder that the scene reminded Walling's Jewish wife, Anna Strunsky, of the
anti-Semitic pogroms in her native Russia. The following month, Walling
published his firsthand account of the events in the liberal magazine *The
Independent.*[1]

The Springfield riots were no isolated aberration. During the preceding
decade similar outbreaks of racist mob violence had occurred in Wilmington,
North Carolina (1898), New Orleans (1900), Pierce City, Missouri (1901),
Atlanta, Georgia (1906), and Meridian, Mississippi (1906), to mention only
the most deadly ones. Although somewhat in decline from its peak in the
early 1890s, the lynching of African-Americans continued on a weekly basis.[2]
Like many other acts of collective racist violence, the Springfield riots were
triggered by allegations that a white woman had been raped by a black man.
After a suspect had been arrested, a lynch mob formed in front of the county
jail. Finding that the police had already rushed the alleged rapist and another
black prisoner charged with the murder of a white man out of town, the mob

descended on Springfield's black community. In keeping with the racist spirit of the time, Springfield's white newspapers blamed the violence on the victims, insinuating that it was the inevitable consequence of mounting black crime and vice. Editorials claimed that the rioters by no means represented the good citizens of Springfield but a tiny fraction of undesirable riffraff. Walling, however, came away with a very different impression from talking to numerous white residents immediately after the riot. "We at once discovered, to our amazement," he wrote, "that Springfield had no shame. She stood for the action of the mob. She hoped that the rest of the negroes might flee."[3]

This tacit approval was confirmed by the criminal proceedings brought against the rioters later in the year. Few whites were willing to take the witness stand, and the local juries simply refused to convict rioters on any charges whatsoever. All that the prosecution could eventually obtain out of more than one hundred indictments was a single conviction for petty larceny resulting in a twenty-five-dollar fine and a thirty-day jail sentence. In contrast, the black defendant who was accused of having murdered a white man and whom the mob had demanded from the sheriff at the onset of the riot was speedily tried and convicted with the mob spirit still hovering over the city. He died on the gallows two months after the riot, a convenient scapegoat for the sake of racial peace.[4]

While the patterns of the Springfield riot were in many ways typical of collective racial violence in the early twentieth-century United States, the city stood out in one important symbolic respect. It was the longtime residence and the burial site of Abraham Lincoln, the Great Emancipator. This fact was not lost on the rioters, many of whom had shouted: "Lincoln freed you, we show you where you belong." As Walling noted in alarm, southern demagogues immediately seized the opportunity to demand that the North show more toleration for the southern way of dealing with the race question. If these methods were transferred to the North, Walling warned his readers, "every hope of political democracy will be dead." The only alternative was to revive "the spirit of the abolitionists, of Lincoln and of [martyred abolitionist Elijah] Lovejoy." "Yet who realizes the seriousness of the situation," the journalist ended his grim account, "and what large and powerful body of citizens is ready to come to their [the black minority's] aid?"[5] Walling's passionate plea reflected the desperation many racial liberals felt in the face of growing indifference or outright hostility toward African-Americans. Unlike the civil rights revolution of the 1960s, which reflected a bold sense of grand expectations, the prevailing mood among racial reformers in the early twentieth century was largely defensive. How could the rising tide of segregation, disfranchisement, and violence be stemmed?

William Walling's appeal was answered by Mary White Ovington, a descendant of New England abolitionists, who lived as a settlement worker among poor blacks in Brooklyn, New York. After several letters had been exchanged between the two, a meeting was arranged for early 1909 in Walling's New York home. They were joined by Henry Moskovitz, a Jewish social worker. The group conceived of a plan to call for a national conference on the race question and decided to involve both white and black associates. Among the first to be contacted were Bishop Alexander Walters and Reverend William Henry Brooks, two prominent African-American clergymen, and W.E.B. Du Bois, a professor at Atlanta University and the leading intellectual voice of black protest in America. Oswald Garrison Villard, the grandson of the abolitionist hero William Lloyd Garrison and owner of both the *New York Evening Post* and *The Nation*, was asked to write a statement to be published on February 12, 1909, the centenary of Abraham Lincoln.[6]

Villard's *Call* was issued on the same day that the city of Springfield, Illinois, celebrated Lincoln's birthday with a lavish banquet—from which African-Americans were of course excluded. Cloaked in the allegory of the martyred president returning to earth to review the progress of African-Americans since his Emancipation Proclamation, *The Call* was a scathing indictment of racial discrimination, disfranchisement, and lawlessness in America. It did not bother to attack southern racists at great length but squarely put the blame on the collusion and indifference of the North and the nation at large. Because "silence under these conditions" meant "tacit approval," the initiators called upon "all believers in democracy to join in a national conference for the discussion of present evils, the voicing of protests, and the renewal of the struggle for civil and political liberty." *The Call* was signed by sixty leading social reformers, including such progressive luminaries as Jane Addams, John Dewey, Florence Kelley, and Lincoln Steffens. Among the African-American signers were the names of the antilynching crusader Ida Wells-Barnett, W.E.B. Du Bois, the Reverend Francis J. Grimke, and woman's rights activist Mary Church Terrell.[7]

Although the response to *The Call* in both the white and the black press was somewhat disappointing, the National Negro Conference was held in New York City on May 31 and June 1, 1909. The vast majority of the roughly three hundred participants were white philanthropists and social reformers, but with Du Bois, Wells-Barnett, Terrell, and William Monroe Trotter, the radical editor of the *Boston Guardian,* the spearheads of African-American protest were also present. Still, it was indicative of the cultural hegemony of racism in early twentieth-century America that the conference started out with two prominent scientists refuting the doctrines of innate black inferiority. True to the spirit of progressivism, the demand for civil and political equality was first put on the solid ground of scientific, social, and historical evidence. At the end of the conference, resolutions were passed that demanded the strict enforcement of the civil and political rights guaranteed to African-Americans under the Fourteenth and Fifteenth Amendments to the U.S. Constitution. However, more important than solemn appeals was the determination "that some permanent body should grow out of this gathering," as Villard put it. In its final session, the conference selected a committee on permanent organization numbering forty persons and charged with the incorporation of a national Committee for the Advancement of the Negro Race and with preparing another convention in 1910. Although the name National Association for the Advancement of Colored People was only adopted at this second conference, the National Negro Conference of 1909 was the founding act of the NAACP and would henceforth be counted as its first annual meeting.[8]

After some organizational difficulties, the second conference was held again in New York City in May 1910. At this meeting the new group began to take shape. An executive committee was elected, with Walling as its chairman, New York industrialist John Milholland as the treasurer, and Villard the assistant treasurer. Moorfield Storey, a prominent Boston lawyer and former president of the American Bar Association, was made the first national president of the NAACP. Membership dues were set from $1 per year for ordinary members to $500 for a life membership. Shortly after the conference, the NAACP established an office in the building of Villard's *Evening Post*. Upon its incorporation in June of 1911, the association adopted its permanent organizational structure. The executive committee was replaced by a board of directors headed by a chairman and designated as the highest decision-making body in between the annual conferences. At its first meeting the board of directors elected Villard as its chairman. In addition, the position of a secretary responsible for carrying out the day-to-day business was created and filled with Mary White Ovington until a more permanent solution could be found. This new position formed the nucleus of an expanding executive secretariat that would assume most of the practical leadership tasks throughout the following two decades.[9]

Programmatically, the NAACP pledged itself to "active opposition" against the evil of racial hatred and prejudice. It hoped to accomplish its objectives primarily through "the argument of the printed and the spoken word" and "by individual relief of the wretched," which first of all meant legal assistance to the victims of racial injustice.[10] Since the dominant racial discourse held that the relations between blacks and whites were "harmonious" as long as they remained undisturbed by irresponsible "agitation," the new group felt the need to justify its approach. Its newly established organ, the magazine *The Crisis*, edited by W.E.B. Du Bois, explained: "[C]ritics mistake the function of agitation. A toothache is agitation. Is a toothache a good thing? No. Is it therefore useless? No. It is supremely useful, for it tells the body of decay, dyspepsia and death. . . . The same is true of the Social Body. Agitation is a necessary evil to tell of the ills of the Suffering. . . . The function of this Association is to tell this nation the crying evil of race prejudice. . . . Agitation does not mean Aggravation—Aggravation calls for Agitation in order that Remedy may be found."[11]

The metaphor of racism as a social disease implied that both the minority and the majority had a vital interest in "healing." Such organicist language reflected the impulse of progressive reform, which did not aim at the overthrow of the American social and political order, but at curing the "social ills" that came with industrialization, urbanization, and mass migration. Leading progressive reformers had signed *The Call* and attended the National Negro Conference in 1909. With one exception, each of the five white employees who held the position of the NAACP secretary until 1920 had their roots in the settlement house movement. Progressivism at large, however, was deeply ambiguous about the race question. Southern progressives advocated segregation and disfranchisement as benevolent reforms, while most northerners cared more about immigrants than about blacks. Even reformers with impeccable antiracist credentials tended to emphasize the need for the social control of lower-class blacks. Jane Addams, for example, opposed segregation because, among other reasons, it prevented the assimilation of the black urban proletariat to the values and culture of the white middle class.[12]

Although the NAACP was conceived in the spirit of progressive reform, practical social work to improve the lot of poor blacks was not part of its agenda. The 1911 founding of the National Urban League, which dedicated itself to this task, allowed for a fortunate division of labor, as Mary Ovington observed in retrospect. But there were more fundamental reasons behind the decision to focus on civil and political rights.[13] Most of the association's founders, and especially those who, like Walling, Du Bois, and Ovington, cherished socialist ideas, agreed that economic improvement was essential to the advancement of African-Americans. Yet they were also fully aware that the discourse of economic progress was closely linked to the dominant ideology of accommodation, which held that material self-improvement had to come first before blacks could claim full citizenship. In contrast, the radicalism of the NAACP manifested itself in separating civil rights from economic progress.

The founding of the NAACP and the new group's insistence on the priority of civic and political equality over economic issues posed a deliberate challenge to Booker T. Washington, the most prominent black leader in the United States and the leading spokesman of accommodation. Born as a slave five years before the Civil War, Washington had worked his way "up from slavery," as the title of his autobiography read. In 1881, he became the principal of the Tuskegee, Alabama, Normal and Industrial Institute, which was dedicated to providing agricultural, vocational, and academic training for black students. In his famous 1895 speech at the Cotton States and International Exhibition in Atlanta, Georgia, Washington conceded that blacks must begin "at the bottom of life, and not at the top." His "Atlanta Compromise," as the speech became known, held that they should follow the lead of their southern white neighbors and join hands with them for the sake of mutual progress, while "in all things that are purely social, we can be as separate as the fingers." Although Washington did not counsel African-Americans to refrain from voting or approve of discriminatory election laws, he believed that "the opportunity to freely exercise such political rights will not come in any large degree through outside or artificial forcing, but will be accorded to the Negro by the southern white people themselves."[14]

The Atlanta Compromise propelled Washington to national fame and made him the favorite of white philanthropists, North and South. Under his leadership, the Tuskegee Institute developed into both a successful educational institution and a political machine, which the "Wizard," as Washington was called for his political wits, skillfully employed to control the black press and organizations such as the Afro-American Council and the National Negro Business League. Washington considered himself a role model of black advancement and was sincerely convinced that his program of accommodation and gradualism would lead to civil and political equality much more quickly and much more safely than would open protest. It is true that he also secretly supported lawsuits against disfranchisement and segregation. Nevertheless, his public message of hard work and self-discipline as the key to full citizenship and his reluctance to speak out on lynching made him into a witness for "the alleged inferiority of the Negro races," as W.E.B. Du Bois charged in *The Souls of Black Folk*, first published in 1903.[15]

Du Bois had at first supported Washington's approach but then became increasingly disillusioned with both the philosophy of accommodation and the Wizard's autocratic style of leadership. For all of Washington's accomplishments, the price of timid self-denial seemed too high. "Manly self-respect," Du Bois declared, "is worth more than lands and houses." Since 1905, he had tried to rally the opposition against Washington in the so-called

Niagara Movement, named after its first meeting place on the Canadian side of the waterfalls. The group's Declaration of Principles demanded manhood suffrage, civil rights, equality of economic and educational opportunity, impartial courts, and an end of all discrimination based on race or color. "We refuse to allow the impression to remain," it emphatically proclaimed, "that the Negro-American assents to inferiority, is submissive under oppression and apologetic before insults. Through helplessness we may submit, but the voice of protest of ten million Americans must never cease to assail the ears of their fellows, as long as America is unjust." The impact of the Niagara associates, however, remained limited. In fact, the "movement" was little more than a band of black intellectuals who were united in their opposition to Booker T. Washington but otherwise torn by internal feuds to which the Wizard himself made no small contribution. By the end of the decade, the Niagara group was financially broke and disintegrating, when *The Call* for the National Negro Conference offered a chance for creating a radical and biracial civil rights coalition.[16]

As the intellectual spearhead of the anti-Washingtonians, Du Bois had a quasi-natural claim to a leading position in the new organization. In July 1910, he was made the director of publications and research of the NAACP, and in November he began publishing its official journal, *The Crisis*. Protest, the magazine argued with a clear edge against Tuskegee, was imperative, because silence meant consent: "Agitate then, brother; protest, reveal the truth and refuse to be silenced." Such uncompromising rhetoric struck a sympathetic chord with many African-American readers. *The Crisis* started out with one thousand copies in November 1910, and six months later it was selling ten thousand copies. By the end of 1915, the magazine reached an average monthly circulation of more than thirty-two thousand and had sold a grand total of roughly 1.4 million copies.[17]

Not surprisingly, Booker T. Washington watched the founding of the NAACP with displeasure. It was perfectly clear that the new organization posed a serious challenge to his leadership position within the black community. But the Wizard's attacks and intrigues against the fledgling association did not prevent more and more black leaders and white liberals from distancing themselves from him and his approach. It had simply become too obvious that his message of accommodation and racial harmony amounted to little more than rhetoric and accomplished next to nothing in stemming racial violence and the spread of Jim Crow laws. Villard, a longtime supporter of Tuskegee, had sent Washington an invitation to the National Negro Conference but implied that he would feel uncomfortable with the thrust of the whole affair. The Wizard politely declined. Although the relationship between the NAACP and Booker T. Washington softened after the latter had been assaulted and severely injured by an unidentified white man in New York in March 1911, tensions remained until the Wizard's premature death in 1915, which paved the way for a rapprochement between Tuskegee and the association.[18]

While the radicalism of the black NAACP founders manifested itself in their opposition to Washington, their white associates sought to revive the abolitionist tradition to which several of them had a strong biographical claim. As mentioned above, Villard was the grandson of William Lloyd Garrison and considered himself the legitimate heir to his famed grandfather. Mary White Ovington also prided herself of parents and grandparents who had been active in the abolitionist movement. The association's first president, Moorfield Storey, had once been the personal secretary of the antislavery senator Charles Sumner of Massachusetts. Not surprisingly, the paternalist attitude that the old abolitionists had shown toward blacks lingered on among some of their successors. However, the strong religious impetus of abolitionism did not carry over to the NAACP, which was conceived as a strictly secular association.[19]

The second major group of white supporters that felt attracted to the NAACP's struggle were Jews. For many years, the Jewish element in the leadership of the association was represented by Joel Elias Spingarn, a wealthy writer, publisher, and former Columbia professor, and his younger brother Arthur, a prominent lawyer. Between 1913 and his death in 1939, Joel Spingarn served as the treasurer, the chairman of the board of directors, and the president of the association with only a few brief interruptions. Arthur Spingarn headed the legal committee of the board of directors and succeeded his brother as president, a position he retained until 1965. Other Jewish supporters of the NAACP included Louis Marshall, a well-known constitutional lawyer, the famous anthropologist Franz Boas, and Julius Rosenwald, the president of Sears, Roebuck. In the various leadership committees of the early NAACP, historian Hasia Diner has written, Jews were represented "far out of proportion to their numbers in the population." Many Jewish Americans felt a general empathy for an oppressed minority whose fate resembled that of Jews in the diaspora. In addition, David Lewis has argued that the well-established Jewish elite of central European descent was concerned about the rise of anti-Semitism in the wake of Jewish mass immigration from Eastern Europe just as the northern black middle class was afraid that the influx of southern black migrants would trigger movements for segregation and disfranchisement in the North. These parallel interests, according to Lewis, formed the cornerstone of the longtime "defensive alliance" between Jews and African-Americans in the civil rights movement.[20]

Race Relations

Proclamations on racial equality and justice did not answer the question of on whose terms the races would work together within the association. If the NAACP wished to avoid ending up as another debating society dominated by white philanthropists, a common ground acceptable to both blacks and whites had to be established. In the wake of the National Negro Conference, both black radicals, including William Monroe Trotter and Ida Wells-Barnett, and the accommodationists of the Tuskegee camp had voiced their distrust of an initiative that came from white reformers.[21]

In the early years of the association, white dominance was an indisputable fact. Financially, the NAACP depended on the donations and pro bono services of wealthy whites, while virtually all unpaid leadership positions were held by whites as well. As the director of publications and research, W.E.B. Du Bois was the only black person among the association's executive officers. The fact that he was also a paid employee, however, led to numerous clashes with the board of directors and the executive secretaries. Although these quarrels were ostensibly about Du Bois's alleged neglect of the finances of *The Crisis* and his claim to complete editorial autonomy, race inevitably figured in.[22] Villard, in particular, displayed a good measure of the paternalist attitudes that had characterized the old abolitionist movement. Mary Childs Nerney, a white social worker who served as the NAACP secretary from 1912 to 1916, personified the social reformer who easily lost patience with the objects of her benevolence. Du Bois, on the other hand, was as sensitive as a Geiger counter to white condescension and quick to charge his antagonists with racism. Behind these personal differences, however, loomed the larger question of race and power. When Villard resigned as chairman of the board of directors in late 1913, Mary Ovington, who constantly tried to mediate between her friend Du Bois and Villard, saw this as "a confession to the world that we cannot work with colored people unless they are our subordinates."[23] This, indeed, was the key question: Did the interracialism of the NAACP extend to blacks exerting authority over whites?

Despite their residual paternalism, the white NAACP founders knew perfectly well that if the association were to survive and to thrive it had to become a broad-based black organization under black leadership. Not only was Du Bois's prestige indispensable, the number and visibility of African-Americans in the NAACP needed to be increased. The stage for such a transfer of leadership was set in the summer of 1916 at a conference in Amenia, New York, where Joel Spingarn, who had succeeded Villard as the chairman of the board of directors, had gathered several hundred leading black and white racial reformers at his country home. The meeting not only brought a rapprochement between the NAACP and the followers of the late Booker T. Washington, it also paved the way for the appointment of James Weldon Johnson, an African-American writer and diplomat, as a field secretary of the association. This marked the beginning of the transition to a predominantly black secretariat. In 1920, Johnson became the first black executive secretary of the NAACP. By then, two other African-Americans, the journalist and insurance agent Walter White and the educator William Pickens, had already been appointed assistant executive secretary and field secretary, respectively. At the end of the association's first decade, the NAACP board of directors was made up about equally of black and white members.[24]

These changes reflected the important fact that the association had successfully established itself as a predominantly black membership organization. The exact ratio between black and white members cannot be gauged, however. True to its integrationist creed that skin color was irrelevant in the struggle for human rights, the association did not keep records on the race of its members or the proportion of its white membership in particular. Since white neoabolitionists and social reformers were instrumental in its founding, it is not surprising that several of the early NAACP branches were dominated by whites. Until 1918, the branch of Boston, Massachusetts, the cradle of abolitionism, not only was the largest NAACP unit, it also had a majority of white members. Its leaders were prominent citizens with famous names from the abolitionist tradition, including the first branch president, Francis Jackson Garrison, the youngest son of William Lloyd Garrison. Successful membership drives in 1918 and 1919, however, brought about two thousand new members into the branch and reversed its racial makeup. By then, the treasurer of the branch had become worried that too few whites were participating in the association and proposed that all NAACP units should be committed to strive for at least 10 percent white membership. In Chicago, white progressives, such as Jane Addams and Sophonisba Breckenridge, played a visible, if limited, role in the founding of the local NAACP. Wealthy businessman and philanthropist Julius Rosenwald, who has been depicted as a dominating influence on the branch, was apparently only marginally involved, according to a recent study of the branch's history.[25]

The NAACP board of directors had advised branches to include white members as early as 1913, but no fixed racial quotas were adopted. By 1914, the annual report proudly claimed a black membership of 80 percent to demonstrate that the association had struck firm roots within the black community. In 1920, blacks made up 90 percent of the total membership, according to an estimate by The Crisis. Subsequently, NAACP officials uniformly cited the magic number of an overall 10 percent, when asked to estimate the proportion of white members.[26] It is doubtful, however, whether integrationism alone accounts for this internal color-blindness. As an organization committed to interracialism in its own ranks, the NAACP had to maintain a certain level of white membership. Although it was never publicly admitted, the NAACP leadership might have viewed 10 percent as a minimum that was not to be discredited by any detailed accounts. Still, it is very likely that in states with a small African-American population there were quite a few NAACP branches with a considerably higher share of white members than merely 10 percent, while in the South there were hardly any white members at all.

Nevertheless, criticism that the association was controlled by whites never died down and became especially vocal in times of increased rivalry for the political leadership of the African-American community at large. In retrospect, however, it appears incontrovertible that the social prestige, the financial resources, and the political connections of the white NAACP founders were essential for its survival and consolidation. There were simply no African-Americans who could afford to work pro bono as organizers and lawyers, or who could underwrite the deficits of The Crisis or the national secretariat. The crucial question was not whether whites had power, but how they used it. During the first three decades, when white influence was at its peak, there is no evidence of racial polarization within the organization. Not a single vote by the board of directors was divided along racial lines; no internal conflict followed a pattern of whites versus blacks.[27] In his autobiography, published in 1940, W.E.B. Du Bois advanced a remarkably positive assessment of race relations in the early NAACP:

> There was one initial difficulty common to all interracial effort in the United States. Ordinarily the white members of a committee formed of Negroes and whites become dominant. Either by superior training or their influence or their wealth they take charge of the committee, guide it and use the colored membership as their helpers and executive workers in certain directions. Usually if the opposite policy is attempted, if the Negroes attempt to dominate and conduct the committee, the whites become dissatisfied and gradually withdraw. In the NAACP, it was our primary effort to achieve an equality of racial influence without

stressing race and without allowing undue predominance to either group. I think we accomplished this for a time to an unusual degree.[28]

The transition from white to black leadership was carried out on a gradual and consensual basis without forcing the white leaders out or breaking the ties with white allies of the liberal establishment. This was no small achievement. It was possible because white leaders basically acted out of a genuine commitment to racial justice and did not seek any personal or political gains from their NAACP work. They were mostly wealthy and influential people without political ambitions in a narrow sense. Besides, working for black rights was hardly an asset in early twentieth-century American politics. African-Americans in the NAACP, usually members of the small black middle class, were fully aware of the key importance of white participation as a source of material support and political legitimacy. The early NAACP leadership thus has been aptly described as an alliance of white and black elites.[29] This social affinity alone, however, did not insure cooperative race relations. It was necessary that both groups maintained a strong ideological commitment to interracialism, equality before the law, and a color-blind democracy that worked as a safeguard against both white paternalism and black nationalism.

Organizational Growth

In addition to creating a common ground for both white philanthropists and black radicals, the NAACP faced the challenge of building a stable and efficient organizational structure. As Du Bois put it, the association had to find a middle ground between "too great concentration of power, leading our members to feel that they . . . cannot be effective parts and workers in the organization" and "so great a decentralization of power as would fritter away efficiency, leading to local bickering and lack of concentrated action."[30] As early as November 1910, the executive committee had authorized the founding of NAACP branches and paved the way for building a national membership organization with a top-down structure. The 1911 articles of incorporation stipulated that local affiliates had to adopt the official name National Association for the Advancement of Colored People and submit their constitutions to the board of directors for approval. Members of the local branches were also members of the national organization, which claimed three-fifths of the membership dues. The branches were obliged to send monthly reports on their activities to the national secretary and were bound by the policy decisions of the national leadership. If a branch violated national rules and decisions or became inactive, its charter could be revoked or suspended and its membership would be retained as at-large members of the association. In 1918 a department of branch affairs was established, with Mary Ovington at its head.[31]

The first branches outside of New York City were organized by members of the executive committee in Boston, Chicago, and Philadelphia, followed by Washington, D.C., and Baltimore. After the NAACP had become operative, its field secretary was expected to facilitate the founding of new branches, which often happened upon the request of the local black population. In addition, NAACP members who moved to a different town or city might initiate the establishment of a new affiliate. As the link between the national organization and the local black communities, the NAACP branches, to which later youth councils and student chapters were added, formed the backbone of the association. Its prestige and efficacy largely depended on the activism of its local members.[32]

After the difficulties of getting organized had been overcome, the NAACP began to grow impressively. In 1913, two years after its incorporation, there were ten branches, with a total of 1,100 members. Three years later, the number of branches and members had increased to seventy and 8,785, respectively. Not surprisingly, the strongholds of the NAACP were concentrated in the northern metropolitan areas, the destination of many southern blacks in the Great Migration during the First World War. In the South, however, there were only three NAACP branches so far, located in New Orleans, Shreveport, Louisiana, and Key West, Florida, with a combined membership of 348 persons. In view of the oppressive racial climate, it seemed doubtful whether the association could successfully expand into Dixie at all. However, the vigor and determination of field secretary James Weldon Johnson made it possible to launch such a project in early 1917. After drafting a manual for branches and contacting a host of local black leaders, Johnson embarked on a trip to twenty southern cities. Almost everywhere, his visits resulted in the establishment of new branches. By the end of the decade, 131 of the 310 NAACP branches were located in the South. It attested to the NAACP's new assertiveness that it held its 1920 annual conference in Atlanta, Georgia. Despite some misgivings among northern members about possible harassment, the mayor of the city gave a short welcome speech and made sure that the local segregation ordinances were handled with some flexibility.[33]

The NAACP's organizational work was accompanied by active protest against racism and racial violence. In 1915, the association launched a propaganda campaign against D. W. Griffith's sensational motion picture *The Birth*

Table 1. NAACP Members and Branches, 1912 to 1919

Year	Members	Branches
1912	329	3
1913	1,100	10
1914	3,000	24
1915	6,000	50
1916	8,785	70
1917	9,282	80
1918	43,994	165
1919	91,203	310

Note: Figures according to the 1919 NAACP *Annual Report*, in *Crisis* 19 (March 1920): 241; see also memorandum by R. Williams to Gloster Current, 15 June 1954, NAACP Records II A 202.

of a Nation, which, based on Thomas Dixon's novel *The Clansman,* glorified the Ku Klux Klan and portrayed African-Americans either as good-natured fools or lecherous beasts. The success of these protests was rather limited, however. In the aftermath of the East St. Louis, Illinois, race riots in July 1917, which cost the lives of at least forty blacks, the association assisted in the legal defense of African-Americans accused of murder and initiated a silent protest march of ten thousand participants along New York City's Fifth Avenue. Lynchings were investigated and publicized, often at considerable personal risk to the investigators. Extensive documentary materials were collected and a campaign was launched to make lynching a federal crime.[34]

While these activities underscored the NAACP's reputation as a militant civil rights group, the crucial organizational breakthrough occurred as a result of World War I and its aftermath, when the high hopes black Americans had associated with the crusade for democracy were bitterly disappointed and a wave of racist violence swept through America. Between early 1918 and late 1919, membership in the NAACP skyrocketed from nine thousand to ninety thousand.

At the same time, American entry into the Great War caused considerable strain within the association. Pacifists, such as Villard, Jane Addams, and Mary Ovington, opposed American participation, while the two Spingarn brothers and NAACP executive secretary Roy Nash enthusiastically volunteered for the army.[35] More important, however, was the question whether African-Americans should fight in a rigidly segregated military that made every effort to reduce them to the status of menial laborers. Shortly before the American entry into the war, Joel Spingarn had privately advocated a separate training camp for black officers in order to insure that African-Americans could rise to higher ranks at all. Predictably, this compromise with segregation drew heavy criticism from the black press and caused much controversy within the NAACP. In May 1917, the board of directors grudgingly approved of separate training camps but maintained its principled opposition to all forms of racial segregation. Five months later, more than six hundred black candidates received their commissions as officers at the training camp in Des Moines, Iowa.[36]

Du Bois had supported Spingarn's plans because he believed that no practical alternative existed. African-Americans, he argued, were not responsible for the "damnable dilemma" of having to choose between segregation and complete exclusion. Hoping that loyalty might pay off after the war, the editor even went a step further and in July 1918 called upon black Americans "to forget our special grievances and close our ranks shoulder to shoulder with our own white fellow citizens" for the duration of the war. Because the appeal coincided with a proposal by Joel Spingarn to appoint Du Bois as a liaison officer for African-American affairs in the Military Intelligence Branch of the War Department, the "close ranks" editorial smacked of outright opportunism and exposed its author to sharp rebukes from black leaders and NAACP members. Both the War Department and the editor quickly retracted the plan. Even if Du Bois did not seek personal advancement, he certainly was much too optimistic about his potential influence as a military officer in particular and the benign consequences of black wartime loyalty in general.[37]

African-American soldiers who served in the war to make the world safe for democracy experienced segregation, discrimination, chicanery, and defamation in many forms and shapes. Despite its professed patriotism, the NAACP did not remain silent. It protested Jim Crow practices in the military and the defense industries and provided legal aid to black soldiers who had rioted in Houston, Texas, in August 1917 after having been provoked by continued police brutality. Immediately after the armistice, the NAACP board of directors sent Du Bois to France to investigate the treatment of black troops. Firsthand information of the discrimination and defamation suffered by African-American soldiers led him to the conclusion "that American white officers fought more valiantly against Negroes than they did against the Germans." Among the materials Du Bois brought home, the most explosive documents were the "Secret Information Concerning Black American Troops," which the American High Command had distributed to French military and civilian authorities. This "information" denounced black soldiers as potential rapists and warned the French against too much "indulgence and familiarity," lest this might inspire aspirations that were intolerable to white Americans. When *The Crisis* published the "Secret Documents" in May 1919, it sold an unprecedented one hundred thousand copies within a few days. Thoroughly disabused of his earlier hopes for a postwar era of good feelings among the races, Du Bois proclaimed that the struggle against racism would resume without delay: "We return from fighting. We return fighting!"[38]

By the end of its first decade, the NAACP, despite its vigorous efforts, had not yet won any major battles against racial discrimination. However, it had created a stable organizational structure and a nationwide network of branches that would be able to withstand both external pressures and internal quarrels. Also the association had established a reputation as a militant civil rights group with firm roots in the black community. By its own account, nine-tenths of its income came from small individual dues and contributions by African-Americans, mostly between one and five dollars.[39] The danger that the NAACP might deteriorate into a debating circle of high-minded philanthropists and intellectuals had been effectively averted.

Black Suffrage and Constitutional Discourse

While its outspoken protests against the pervasive racism of American society made the NAACP a radical organization in the eyes of most white Americans, the association remained firmly committed to the institutional and normative framework provided by the U.S. Constitution and the American political system. Its "Declaration of Principles and Purposes," passed by its third annual conference in 1911, proclaimed: "We insist that the colored citizen of the United States is entitled to every right, civil and political, that is accorded to his white neighbor. We hold as a self-evident political truth that no men who are deprived of the right to vote can protect themselves against oppression and injustice. They cannot influence legislation or have a voice in selecting the tribunals by which their rights are determined, and the first step toward the advancement of the colored race is the recognition and protection of their right to vote."[40]

At the time of this resolution, the white South had just about completed the nullification of the Fifteenth Amendment, which had been ratified in 1870 to insure suffrage for black men. Between 1890 and 1910, the southern states had enacted a variety of devices to insure the "orderly" exclusion of black voters. Although not racially discriminatory in their language, voting requirements such as the poll tax and literacy tests were administered in a way that made sure that most African-Americans were barred from registering and voting. These "reforms" resulted in a peculiar political system characterized by the monopoly of the Democratic Party, the dominance of a well-to-do planter and business elite, widespread apathy, and unabashed racial demagoguery.[41]

Ironically, the disfranchisement of southern blacks was accomplished during a period in American history that otherwise saw the expansion of participation rights. To be sure, the electoral reforms of the Progressive Era that were targeted against urban machines and corrupt bosses clearly betrayed an anti-immigrant bias, but whatever discrimination occurred was a far cry from southern practices. In general, the introduction of direct primaries and plebiscites, especially in the western states, the direct election of U.S. senators, and the successful conclusion of the stride toward woman suffrage in 1920 testify to a strong democratic current in the American political culture in the early twentieth century.

Black voters, however, were clearly not included. The disfranchisement of African-Americans met with little protest outside of the South. In his *History of Suffrage in the United States,* published in 1918, historian Kirk Porter summarized the prevailing opinion, arguing that experience had exposed black suffrage as a grave historical mistake. African-Americans neither desired the vote nor knew how to use it intelligently. The fact that blacks had passively watched their "own political funeral," Porter wrote, had brought more and more of the former advocates of black suffrage to their senses. At last, northern public opinion had conceded that federal action to protect the voting rights of southern blacks was a misguided idea.[42]

The NAACP had to operate in a racist political culture that assumed black people to be incapable of articulating and pursuing any common interests independently of whites. This situation required a difficult balancing act. On the one hand, the advancement of colored people could only be achieved if the association encouraged African-Americans to assert their rights and interests as a group. On the other hand, the white majority had to be reassured that such assertiveness did not pose a threat to their own interests. Like other reform movements, the NAACP wrapped itself in the flag to persuade the American public that political rights for blacks were in the best interest of the nation.

The discursive strategy that the NAACP adopted in its early days and maintained throughout the next six decades perhaps can be characterized best as democratic nationalism. The association tried to combine the universalist principles and language of the Declaration of Independence and the U.S. Constitution with traditional patriotism. In order to redeem her promise of freedom, equality, and democracy, America had to liberate herself from the blemish of racism. Thus the struggle against the oppression of black Americans was a service to the entire nation, including the oppressors. "As much as anybody in the country the Negro wants to be a good American," wrote the NAACP executive secretary, James Weldon Johnson, in 1929 for the *American Mercury*, ". . . he is also determined to wear the rights as well as bear the burdens of American citizenship. . . . He must win not only for himself but for the South. . . . He must win for the nation, because if he fails, democracy in America fails with him."[43]

Obviously, it made little sense to preach the gospel of democracy to white supremacists in the South. The NAACP had to address its protests and demands to national audiences and, most importantly, to the federal government. The large majority of Americans who had no personal stake in racial discrimination had to be convinced of its irrationality and corruption. One way to approach this challenge was to demonstrate that white supremacy was not a benevolent and paternalistic system, as its apologists claimed, but based on naked force. Next to the association's antilynching campaign, violence against black voters was a major topic of its agitation.

In the fall of 1920, the Ku Klux Klan waged a campaign of terror in Florida against African-Americans who might dare to vote in the forthcoming elections. An altercation in the small township of Ocoee, Orange County, in which a black farmer killed two white attackers in self-defense resulted in a three-day pogrom with dozens of black residents killed and almost all black homes burnt to the ground. Walter White, the NAACP's assistant secretary, whose light complexion, blondish hair, and blue eyes allowed him to approach white witnesses without being identified as a person of African-American descent, investigated the facts on site. In late December, White and other NAACP leaders were given the opportunity to present their case to the Committee on the Census of the U.S. House of Representatives. The testimony marshaled by the NAACP caused considerable embarrassment to the southern committee members, who obstructed the presentation of evidence and even tried to intimidate witnesses. Indeed, a few days after the hearings White learned that several local blacks had withdrawn their affidavits or denied the charges made by the NAACP. Its demand for a congressional investigation of the election in the southern states, never very realistic in the first place, came to no avail.[44]

The testimony before the House Census Committee was part of a larger NAACP campaign for the enforcement of Section Two of the Fourteenth Amendment to the U.S. Constitution, which stipulates that the congressional representation of states that deny the vote to any number of their adult (male) inhabitants for reasons other than rebellion or crime shall be reduced in proportion to the number of disfranchised voters. The clause, passed by Congress in 1866, had been intended to prevent the reconstructed Confederate states from benefiting from the emancipation of their former slaves who would henceforth be fully counted in the apportionment of congressional seats. If states wanted to deny the vote to the freedmen, they had to pay a political price. Yet neither this penalty, which was never imposed, nor the Fifteenth Amendment of 1870, which prohibits disfranchisement "on account of race, color, or previous condition of servitude," deterred the South from excluding almost all black voters while enjoying full congressional representation.[45]

As a consequence, significantly fewer votes were needed below the Mason-Dixon line to win a seat in Congress or to carry a state in a presidential election than in the North. For example, *The Crisis* demonstrated that in 1908 Republican candidate William Howard Taft had received almost two hundred thousand votes to win the eleven electoral votes of Minnesota, while his Democratic rival, William J. Bryan, needed fewer than seventy-five thousand votes to pocket an equal number of presidential electors in Alabama. In the congressional elections of 1910, the victorious candidate in the 19th congressional district of Illinois received about as many votes (23,000), as all winners in Mississippi's eight congressional districts combined.[46] Southern congressmen represented far fewer voters than their northern colleagues, and the individual ballots of southern voters counted for many times more than those of their fellow citizens in the rest of the nation. As former Massachusetts attorney general Albert Pillsbury put it at the 1909 National Negro Conference, racial disfranchisement was "not merely a question of Negro suffrage, or Negro equality" but "a question of the equality of white men."[47]

Because southern Democrats wielded congressional power vastly in excess of their electoral base, the exclusion of black voters also had a distinctly partisan dimension. After the Democratic Party had captured the White House and the majority of both the House and the Senate in the 1912 elections, it was hoped the Republicans might be tempted to invoke Section Two of the Fourteenth Amendment. "The dominant power of the south is now so great," NAACP president Moorfield Storey speculated in 1915, "that perhaps the Republican party will see its advantage in passing a statute . . . which will force the south in the long run to repeal its restrictive laws." Storey rejected the argument that the Fifteenth Amendment had superseded Section Two of the Fourteenth. Racial disfranchisement was patently illegal under the former clause, but all legal voting restrictions, such as literacy tests and poll taxes, were still covered by the latter and should trigger a reduced representation in Congress.[48]

Enforcing Section Two of the Fourteenth Amendment was not exactly a new idea. Republican congressmen had introduced several bills to this end in

1900 and 1904, but the proposals had never made it to an official vote.[49] In 1920, however, the presidential election coincided with the decennial census for the first time in twenty years, providing an opportunity to link the issue of racial disfranchisement to the forthcoming reapportionment of congressional representation. Immediately after the election, the NAACP board of directors offered to present evidence of the "open and flagrant disfranchisement of colored voters" to the House Census Committee during the impending hearings on the new congressional reapportionment bill. In early December, Republican representative George H. Tinkham of Massachusetts introduced a resolution demanding a congressional inquiry as to "the extent to which the right to vote is denied or abridged to citizens" and calling for appropriate legislation. In late December and early January, both the representatives of the NAACP and George Tinkham appeared before the committee.[50]

In addition to evidence of violence and intimidation, the NAACP submitted statistical material documenting the gross overrepresentation of the South in relation to the actual number of voters. While in the rest of the nation between 50 and 70 percent of all eligible voters had cast their ballots in the recent election, the average turnout in the southern states was lower than 20 percent; in South Carolina, Mississippi, and Georgia it did not even reach 10 percent. To illustrate the distortion of political power between the sections, Du Bois had drawn a map of the United States based on the ratio between voter turnout and congressional seats that showed the South as almost twice as large as all other regions combined.[51]

Tinkham repeated his demand for a congressional investigation and even threatened to take the enforcement of the Fourteenth Amendment to the Supreme Court. Unimpressed, the Census Committee took no action. When the reapportionment bill came to the House floor in May, Tinkham once again tried to introduce his resolution, but the Speaker of the House tabled this motion and a subsequent appeal was voted down by a large majority.[52] Neither the NAACP nor Tinkham had been able to convince lawmakers of the need for a congressional investigation, let alone for legislation to enforce Section Two of the Fourteenth Amendment.

Although the Amendment seemed to provide promising leverage against disfranchisement, its enforcement involved too many controversial constitutional and political issues that touched directly upon the balance of power between the sections and the two major parties. For starters, low voter turnout alone was hardly sufficient for reducing a state's congressional representation. Not only would it have been necessary to demonstrate that the low level of participation was the direct consequence of restrictive suffrage laws, but it would also have required a reliable method to determine how much nonvoting was voluntary and how much was the result of legal and illegal disfranchisement. While nobody could earnestly deny that the southern suffrage reforms had been devised to exclude as many blacks as possible, the majority of the white electorate also abstained from voting, at least in the general elections. Moreover, the South and the other predominantly rural states pointed to the large alien immigrant population in the urban North that counted in the apportionment of congressional representation but could not vote either. After the 1920 census, the conflict between urban and rural states became so deadlocked that Congress failed to pass any reapportionment bill at all. Few lawmakers were inclined to complicate this controversial issue by invoking a constitutional clause widely viewed as a holdover from Reconstruction. As the scant support for Tinkham's resolution even among his own party clearly indicated, the Republicans had lost interest in pressing the issue of southern representation after having recaptured both houses of Congress and the White House.[53]

The NAACP continued to demand the enforcement of Section Two of the Fourteenth Amendment after 1920, albeit with little dedication. Obviously, the history and language of the Fifteenth Amendment offered the stronger constitutional leverage against racial disfranchisement. However, by the early twentieth century an extremely narrow construction of this instrument had become dominant. In a series of decisions on the validity of southern literacy tests, the U.S. Supreme Court had made it perfectly clear that it accepted at face value all suffrage qualifications imposed by the states, as long as they did not explicitly discriminate by race and a few token blacks were permitted to vote.[54] A strict textual interpretation also characterized the NAACP's voting rights discourse during its early decades. According to Albert Pillsbury, the Fifteenth Amendment entitled blacks "to be treated, in respect of the suffrage, only as other men of the same standing or character are treated, and nothing more. The federal law does not make a single Negro a voter, in any state of the union." NAACP president Moorfield Storey deemed it utterly pointless to go back to the original intent of the Reconstruction Amendments, because "[i]t is what the constitution says which determines what it means."[55]

The view that the Fifteenth Amendment was a mere prohibition against open racial discrimination that otherwise left the states free to impose all kinds of ostensibly color-blind restrictions on voting was by no means confined to prominent white lawyers, such as Pillsbury or Storey. In *The Souls of Black Folk*, Du Bois had conceded that "reasonable restrictions in the suffrage," even if applied impartially, would disfranchise many African-Americans because of "the low social level of the mass of the race." In 1921, he wrote in *The Crisis*: "As long as the 15th Amendment stands, it is absolutely illegal to disfranchise a person because of 'race, color, or previous condition of servitude.' But it is absolutely legal to disfranchise persons for any number of other reasons. Indeed a state might legally disfranchise a person for having red hair." Du Bois may have referred to hair color as a figure of speech, but he clearly acknowledged a broad discretion of the states to impose suffrage qualifications. "If the[se] qualifications are reasonable," he continued, "it is only a matter of time when Negroes will meet them. . . . If they are disfranchised by unreasonable qualifications or by the unfair administration of the law, they can continue to attack these in the courts and before the public opinion of the nation. . . . In such a case they cannot in the long run fail to triumph."[56]

Such language reflected the unwavering faith of the NAACP leaders, white and black, in the inexorable historical force of the Constitution. But the NAACP's rhetorical celebration of color-blind fairness also served the purpose of demonstrating to the American public that African-Americans neither needed nor sought special privileges. In particular, this mind-set governed the association's attitude toward the most important of nonracial voting qualifications, the literacy test. It is remarkable that the NAACP never attacked the literacy test directly, but merely insisted on its impartial, color-blind administration. Surely, it was difficult enough to prove the discriminatory intent of registrars in court. Legal considerations, however, cannot fully explain why the association remained acquiescent toward educational tests in its discursive strategy. Evidently, broader cultural considerations also played a role. The notion that the responsible exercise of the suffrage is predicated on the ability to read and write had always enjoyed a high degree of legitimacy in the American political culture. Literacy tests as a qualification for voting were also required in many non-southern states.[57]

In this cultural context the demand for the abolition of educational tests could easily be construed as an admission of black intellectual deficiency. The frequent use of the phrase "intelligent Negroes" in the NAACP's rhetoric betrays a deep-seated inferiority complex that inadvertently played into the hands of racism. By accepting educational deficits as a legitimate reason for disfranchisement, the NAACP ignored the fact that the high ideal of the "intelligent voter" served to justify the exclusion of marginalized groups. This attitude also mirrored the pride of the association's black middle-class leaders in their own educational achievements. As late as 1938, Walter White wrote to U.S. senator Carter Glass, a member of the archconservative Virginia oligarchy: "[A]n increasing number of intelligent southerners, both white and Negro . . . realize that the only way to solve the problem of disfranchisement in southern states is to grant use of the ballot to all persons, regardless of race, who are qualified by tests fairly and honestly applied. We do not care how rigid these tests are, all we insist upon is that they be applied without restriction of race, creed, or color."[58] White ignored, of course, that even if "rigid tests" were administered in a perfectly impartial manner, large numbers of blacks would still be excluded as a result of the blatant racial discrimination in education.

To be sure, the NAACP vigorously fought for equal opportunity in education, which was expected to do away gradually with the racial imbalance of literacy tests as a qualification for voting.[59] As will be shown in the next chapter, the association also worked diligently for the political education of black voters. Its discourse on black voting rights, however, remained largely within the confines of a color-blind administration of existing laws. As a legal strategy this may have been the only promising approach, but politically it was hardly a visionary strategy. Rhetorically, the concept of the "intelligent Negro" came perilously close to the racist claim that blacks as a group were unfit for voting and could only qualify on the basis of individual achievement. As the *Charleston News and Courier* once put it: "We Southerners know that there are intelligent Negroes . . . of character and information qualifying them for the suffrage. But we know that they are extremely few."[60]

Woman Suffrage—A Question of Cold, Hard Politics

At the same time that the Fifteenth Amendment had been rendered a dead letter for most African-Americans, the American people were embracing the instrument of constitutional amendments to enact far-reaching measures of public policy and the largest expansion of participation rights in all of their history. The Eighteenth Amendment, adopted in 1919, started the unprecedented social experiment of a near total national prohibition of alcohol. While the U.S. Congress showed no intention to make use of its power to enforce the Fifteenth Amendment, the Eighteenth was immediately enacted into a law, passed over a presidential veto, which made the sale of alcoholic beverages a federal offense. Prohibition was extremely unpopular in the urban North, where it could never be fully enforced. Its opponents were especially galled that southern drys lamented over the "nullification" of the Eighteenth Amendment, and they warned "that the man who lives in a glass house should not throw stones," lest the North might also press for the strict enforcement of the Reconstruction Amendments. Hopes by NAACP leaders to link prohibition to the issue of black suffrage came to no avail, however.

Northern wets did not care much about black voting rights but wanted the repeal of the Eighteenth Amendment, which was finally accomplished in 1932.[61]

Woman suffrage, however, was a different matter. The language of the Nineteenth Amendment, ratified in 1920, followed the Fifteenth, forbidding the United States and the individual states to deny or abridge the right to vote on account of sex. Historically, the struggle for women's rights had had close ties to the struggle for the abolition of slavery. In the aftermath of the Civil War, woman's suffragists had hoped, in a famous phrase coined by Elizabeth Cady Stanton, "to avail ourselves of the strong arm and the blue uniform of the black soldier to walk in[to the voting booth] by his side." Although many feminists were enraged that black manhood suffrage had been given precedence over the political rights of educated white women, and had divorced themselves from the cause of racial equality, this legacy carried over into the NAACP. Leading white feminists such as Jane Addams and Florence Kelley worked for the association, while black woman's activists such as Ida Wells Barnett and Mary Church Terrell vigorously defended the vote for all women against the male chauvinism of African-American men. It was "absurd" for black men to oppose woman suffrage, Terrell maintained in an article for *The Crisis*, "[f]or the very arguments which are advanced against granting the right of suffrage to women are offered by those who have disfranchised colored men."[62] Du Bois willingly opened the pages of the NAACP organ to the advocates of woman suffrage, declaring it a "great human question" and predicting that "any agitation, discussion or reopening of the problem of voting must inevitably be a discussion of the right of black folk to vote in America and Africa." Although the editor harbored no illusions that the majority of white women in the South supported white supremacy, he did not waver in his support for the political equality of men and women.[63]

By 1918, eleven states, mostly in the West, had given women the vote, but a constitutional amendment ran into the hard-nosed opposition of conservative southerners who feared that woman suffrage might resurrect black voting. If ratification was to be secured, the South had to be placated on the race issue. With the First World War offering a splendid opportunity to sell woman suffrage as a "war measure" supported by President Woodrow Wilson, suffragist leaders did not hesitate to pay that price. When the struggle for the suffrage amendment entered a critical phase in early 1919, Carrie Chapman Catt of the National American Woman Suffrage Association (NAWSA) blocked the admission of the African-American Northeastern Federation of Women's Clubs to her organization in order not to offend southern senators whose votes would be needed to achieve the necessary two-thirds majority.

NAWSA's enduring commitment to universal suffrage notwithstanding, appeasing the South had become "a question of cold, hard politics," as one of Catt's associates explained to the black women of Massachusetts.[64]

In response to concerns from South Carolina, Alice Paul, the leader of the radical National Woman's Party (NWP), allegedly stated in a press interview that "Negro men cannot vote in South Carolina and therefore negro women could not if women were permitted to vote in the Nation." When the NAACP board of directors sent her a sharp letter of protest, Paul denied the statement but left no doubt that she did not intend to raise the issue of racial disfranchisement, which in her opinion had already been settled by the Fifteenth Amendment. In its public releases the NWP continued to give unequivocal assurances that the woman suffrage amendment would "in no way complicate the race problem." The message was perfectly clear: Paul and the NWP did not care about protecting the voting rights of black women in the South.[65]

The NAACP was particularly worried that the suffragists, in order to make the amendment palatable to the South, might accept a diluted enforcement clause that would give the states the exclusive or concurrent power of legislation, as several senators had already proposed. For all practical purposes, this would have given the southern states a free hand to disfranchise African-American women and, perhaps even more dangerous, further eroded the power of the U.S. Congress to enforce the Fifteenth Amendment. In case the suffrage movement should cut such deal, the association vowed "to do all in our power" to defeat the amendment in Congress or to prevent its ratification by the states. Despite its long-standing commitment to the cause of woman suffrage, the NAACP deemed it "unjustifiable under any circumstances for white women to get the vote at the expense of their colored sisters." Both the NAWSA and the NWP denied, however, that they would settle for less than the original enforcement clause.[66] In the end, the Nineteenth Amendment passed undiluted, but the fears of the NAACP were hardly unwarranted. In the crucial phase of their struggle, the leaders of the woman suffrage movement had indeed embraced a states' rights rhetoric that was almost as hypocritical about racial disfranchisement as that of southern white supremacists.

Although little support could be expected from white suffragists, the passing of the Nineteenth Amendment nevertheless might give a boost to the struggle for black voting rights. The NAACP hoped that African-American women would be less easily intimidated than men and that "southern gentlemen" might be more reluctant to use physical force against them. Prior to the elections of 1920, the association urged its branches "to form classes for the training of newly enfranchised women in the duties and privileges of voting." It soon became painfully clear, however, that the guardians of white supremacy did not distinguish between black men and women. "We were somewhat surprised," wrote the president of the Mobile, Alabama, branch, which had been particularly active in organizing citizenship schools for black women, "to find that some of our women were treated so very rough—that is they were driven out of the office with threats that if they did not go they would be put in jail."[67]

The association did not fail to confront the woman suffrage movement with the blatant disfranchisement of black women. In December 1920, Mary Ovington approached the NWP to invite an African-American woman to speak at its national convention, scheduled for February 1921, and to appoint a committee to investigate the discrimination of black women. Alice Paul, however, continued her stonewalling. She refused to accept a representative of the NAACP because only organizations with a distinct feminist program could be invited. Since Ovington had nominated Mary B. Talbert, a member of the NAACP board of directors who was also a recent president of the National Association of Colored Women (NACW), Paul's objections were patently disingenuous. To Florence Kelley she freely admitted her fears that Talbert's presence might inflame the southern NWP members. Undaunted, the NAACP organized a deputation of black women to the NWP convention, but only after it had threatened to picket the event did Paul grudgingly receive the delegation three days before the convention met. As a representative of the NACW, Mary Church Terrell proposed a resolution to the NWP advisory board to appoint a special committee on the violation of the Nineteenth Amendment, but to no avail. When a white NWP delegate reintroduced the proposal from the floor, the motion was again defeated. The official program of the NWP convention, which listed about fifty different domestic and foreign women's organizations, gave no hint of the presence of black women at all.[68]

The League of Women Voters, the official successor to the NAWSA, was more forthcoming and granted NAACP field secretary Addie Hunton fifteen minutes to report to its national convention in April 1921. Although the southern delegates threatened a walkout, the League's board empowered the chairwoman to appoint a commission to study and possibly help remedy the violations of the Nineteenth Amendment with regard to black women. Hunton was "not altogether discouraged" by this gesture and praised the "splendid spirit" of the League's leadership, which favorably contrasted with Paul's hostility. Florence Kelley, however, came away thoroughly disillusioned with the foot dragging and tokenism of the white woman suffrage movement on the race issue. "I am certain," she advised James Weldon Johnson, "that we of the NAACP must take as our own, and as a new and enormously important part of our work, the active immediate defense of the 19th, 15th, and 14th amendments. The white women of this whole country are afraid of the trivial minority of active southern white women."[69]

The Garvey Challenge

The triumph of woman suffrage, rather than aiding the cause of black Americans, painfully exposed their political isolation. Even a movement that appealed to the same egalitarian and participatory ideals as the NAACP willingly complied with the color line, if this seemed imperative for advancing its own goals. While the NAACP leaders continued to castigate white feminists for their "cowardly capitulation to race prejudice,"[70] they could hardly ignore the underlying political realities. The ironclad segregation of the American political culture made the search for white allies a frustrating and humiliating experience. Nevertheless, the NAACP did not waver in its integrationist creed when it faced a challenge from the black nationalist Universal Negro Improvement Association (UNIA) and its charismatic leader, Marcus Garvey.

A native of Jamaica and a printer by trade, Garvey had become interested in black nationalism and pan-Africanism early in his adult life, and in 1914 he had launched the UNIA in Kingston, Jamaica. Inspired by Booker T. Washington, Garvey at first advocated a program of racial accommodation and hoped to establish an industrial training school modeled after the example of Tuskegee. In 1916, he came to the United States, claiming an invitation by Washington, even though the Wizard had died the year before. For almost an entire year, Garvey traveled throughout the country to acquaint himself with racial conditions and to lecture in front of black audiences. In 1918, he incorporated the first UNIA branch in New York. Most of his early followers were Harlem-based immigrants from the West Indies, but Garvey successfully employed his formidable oratorical skills to convey his message of race pride and a glorious future for black people in Africa to a wider audience.[71]

The founding of the Black Star Line in 1919, a shipping company financed by the sale of stock to ordinary blacks, lent a tangible credibility to his visions and gave the UNIA a tremendous boost. The organization's claim to spearhead a coming powerful African nation state was bolstered by lavish symbolism, including a flag, a national anthem, and the pseudo-military Universal African Legion. Garvey pronounced himself the provisional president-general of Africa and reveled in wearing colorful uniforms. In August of 1920, the UNIA staged the first International Convention of Negro Peoples of the World in New York City. It lasted an entire month and featured pageants and parades of tens of thousands of Garvey's followers. By the mid-1920s, the Garvey movement claimed more than 3 million members worldwide. Reliable figures on the UNIA membership are not available, however. In 1923, Du Bois estimated that it had no more than eighteen thousand active and dues-paying members.[72] Nevertheless, there is no question that Marcus Garvey accomplished the remarkable feat of building a considerable following among urban blacks in America within a very short time.

Garvey and the UNIA posed a serious ideological challenge to the NAACP's integrationist creed. Although *The Crisis* welcomed the West Indian immigrant as "a new ally in the fight for black democracy," a wide gap of race and class divided the NAACP from the UNIA. Garvey's message blended traditional concepts of self-help and solidarity with a romantic nationalism and a race consciousness that deliberately emulated the ideologies of white racism and nationalism. In particular, the dark-skinned Jamaican of working-class origins resented the social and cultural dominance of the mulatto elite. When he first visited the headquarters of the NAACP in the spring of 1916, Garvey later recalled, he was puzzled to find out that most of the staff were white people and African-Americans of a very light complexion. Although Garvey made repeated overtures to NAACP leaders, such as Du Bois and William Pickens, his racial convictions had little in common with the association's integrationist program.[73]

The relationship between Garvey and the NAACP, never cordial in the first place, began to deteriorate at the end of 1920 and would soon assume the character of "unconditional warfare," as David Lewis has put it. The NAACP's disenchantment with Garvey's pompous demeanor and his open endorsement of racial separation was heightened by growing apprehensions over his various business affairs, which appeared to be extremely risky to say the least. In December 1920 and January 1921, Du Bois featured a series of articles in *The Crisis* in which he acknowledged Garvey's skills as a leader, conceding that he was "a sincere, hard-working idealist," but chided his dictatorial temperament and exposed the inscrutable financial transactions in Garvey's empire.[74] The feud escalated in early 1922, when Garvey was indicted by the federal government for mail fraud in connection with the promotion and sale of the Black Star Line stock. The official UNIA organ, *The Negro World*, insinuated that the troubles that had occurred on the aged vessels of the Black Star Line had been caused by men paid by "organizations calling themselves Negro Advancement Associations"—a statement that was obviously directed against the NAACP and which James Weldon Johnson angrily rejected as "a malicious falsehood of the most contemptible sort."[75]

Driven by the imminent breakdown of his commercial enterprises,

Garvey hoped to find new strength for the UNIA in the South. To pave the way, he decided to court favors with white supremacists by approving segregation and disavowing "social equality" and "racial amalgamation." When the news of a secrete meeting with the imperial wizard of the Ku Klux Klan in Atlanta broke, however, it provoked a split in his own organization and a backlash from which the UNIA leader would never recover. Among other black leaders, A. Philip Randolph and Owen Chandler, the editors of the radical black magazine *The Messenger,* began organizing a "Garvey Must Go" campaign, demanding the deportation of the alien demagogue whose bankrupt dealings had cost many African-Americans their savings.[76]

While the NAACP never officially associated itself with the anti-Garvey activities, individual leaders hit hard at the Jamaican. Field secretary William Pickens, who had earlier flirted with joining the UNIA, told Garvey that he had no right "to concede America as 'a white man's country'" to the Klan. Pickens and the NAACP director of branches, Robert W. Bagnall, signed an open letter of January 1923 by eight prominent African-Americans that denounced Garvey's followers as "the most primitive and ignorant element of West Indian and American Negroes" and called upon the U.S. attorney general to "use his full influence completely to disband and extirpate this vicious movement." Du Bois did not sign the letter but attacked Garvey for both his opaque handling of finances and his flirtations with the Klan. Garvey and the Klan, he wrote, were "birds of a feather, believing in titles, flummery and mumbo-jumbo, and handling much gullible money." Garvey retaliated by scorning Du Bois as an "unfortunate mulatto who bewails everyday the drop of Negro blood in his veins." Defiantly, the UNIA leader defended his contacts with the Klan, whose honesty in racial matters he considered much preferable to the hypocrisy of the "National Association for the Advancement of Certain People."[77] The NAACP denounced Garvey's charges that it had pressed for his conviction as a "malicious lie," but it was certainly not unhappy when in June 1923 he was found guilty of fraud and sentenced to five years in prison. For Du Bois, Garvey remained "the most dangerous enemy of the Negro race in America and the world . . . either a lunatic or a traitor." Returning the compliment, the UNIA convention of 1924 declared Du Bois "an enemy of the black people of the world."[78]

Such blustering rhetoric may easily obscure the larger aspects of the rivalry between the NAACP and the UNIA. The Garvey movement embodied a radical and charismatic alternative to the NAACP's rationalism and legalism, which tended to neglect the emotional and affective needs of people living in a world of ubiquitous discrimination and humiliation. When Du Bois ridiculed Garvey's "Back to Africa" schemes and promised his readers: "Twenty-five years more of the intelligent fighting that the NAACP has led will make the black man in the United States free and equal," he perhaps offered the more realistic perspective, but hardly the more inspiring vision. In fact, his time frame turned out to be far too optimistic. The NAACP's "fight for right" did not have the "enemy on the run," as the editor claimed.[79] On the contrary, the backlash against black aspirations after World War I led to a period of stagnation with few tangible gains in the field of civil rights. It is indicative of the decline of civil rights activism during the 1920s that the association's membership fell from around one hundred thousand to a meager twenty thousand by the end of the decade.[80]

The surprising, if short-lived, success of Garvey and his vision of a glorious African future demonstrated that the goals of integration and equal rights within the framework of American society were not as self-evident for all African-Americans as the NAACP leaders assumed. The swift disintegration of the Garvey movement in the United States after his incarceration and subsequent deportation, however, exposed the crucial weakness of all charismatic movements, which, according to Max Weber, depend on the "devotion to the heroism or exemplary character of an individual person" and tend to fall apart if they are deprived of their leader or if the charismatic appeal of the leader founders in the face of reality. In contrast, the sober and sometimes bureaucratic approach of the NAACP had created the organizational stability that enabled the association to endure through hard times.[81]

By the early 1920s, the NAACP had established itself as an integrationist and interracial civil rights organization. The demand for the full participation and inclusion of African-Americans in the political process was a key tenet of its discursive strategy, but the pursuit of this goal still ran into formidable barriers. The southern system of white supremacy was firmly established and continued to enjoy wide acceptance in the rest of the nation. There was no denying that blacks were an isolated minority without political clout or powerful allies. What then could the association do to foster the integration of blacks into the mainstream of American politics?

Educating Black Voters and White Politicians

In 1909, the National Negro Conference demanded "that in accordance with the Fifteenth Amendment the right of the Negro to the ballot on the same terms as other citizens be recognized in every part of the country." Since almost 90 percent of all African-Americans lived below the Mason-Dixon line according to the 1910 census, it made perfect sense that the NAACP concentrated its protests on the de facto nullification of the Fifteenth Amendment in the southern states.[1] But the disfranchisement of southern blacks also had profound consequences for the political status of African-American voters in the North and the nation at large. In a pluralistic democracy, voters are mobilized and educated by parties and candidates promising to represent their interests and values. African-American citizens in the early twentieth century, however, found themselves in the peculiar situation of having no candidates or parties who were really interested in their votes.

After 1890, the Republican Party for all practical purposes had conceded the South to the Democrats because its expanding electoral base in the newly admitted western states insured its national predominance without the need for waging a losing battle in protecting the voting rights of its southern black constituency. Whatever attempts the GOP made to regain influence below the Mason-Dixon line had to be on a strictly "lily-white" basis. Meanwhile, black voters in the North were courted with memories of the "Great Emancipator," as the "Party of Lincoln" more and more succumbed to racism. Since the racial outlook of the Democratic Party was dominated by its southern white supremacist wing, it offered no meaningful alternative at all.[2] Prior to the presidential elections of 1924, NAACP executive secretary James Weldon Johnson aptly spoke of a "gentlemen's agreement" among the two parties: "The agreement provides that the Republican Party will hold the Negro and do as little for him as possible and that the Democrats will have none of it at all." Johnson had few illusions about the political clout of 12 million blacks in the United States. They were "the least influential and least effective political unit in the whole country . . . a political nonentity."[3]

Even after the Great Migration of the First World War, African-Americans made up no more than 2 to 4 percent of the voting-age population of such northern states as New York, New Jersey, Pennsylvania, Ohio, Illinois, and Michigan—a percentage too small to represent a serious statewide political force. Nevertheless, in the big cities that absorbed the lion's share of the Great Migration, the black population grew at a stunning pace of up to 600 percent between 1910 and 1920.[4] Thus the expectation that the constant northward migration of African-Americans would increase their voting strength was not completely unwarranted. In 1928, the black Republican Oscar DePriest was elected to the U.S. House of Representatives from a district in Chicago, the first African-American member of Congress in almost thirty years. But this process was slow and fraught with ambiguity. Southerners hoped that the black migration would win over white northerners to their viewpoint on race, and not entirely in vain: When black voters helped elect "Big Bill" Thompson, a scandal-ridden foe of prohibition, as mayor of Chicago in 1927, the *New York Evening Post,* which had once belonged to NAACP co-founder Oswald Garrison Villard, commented: "Chicago, like Indianapolis and other northern cities, is learning what Negro control means and why the South has kept these voters from the ballot box. May the day never come when Harlem runs New York." James Weldon Johnson protested that such race-baiting was "unworthy of the tradition" of the paper.[5]

Black support for corrupt party machines was a constant source of embarrassment and frustration for the NAACP activists. That blacks as a group were politically immature was no fault of their own, however. They were, as Du Bois argued, simply left out of the political education by the parties, which at best treated them as an ignorant "bloc vote" to be bought off with a few breadcrumbs: "They are given over to the lowest white politicians and ward heelers, and the only arguments used are money and honeyed words. . . . As a method of government, a way of securing decent schools, healthful conditions of living, the right of administration of the laws and the like, the colored voter is singularly in the dark. He needs systematic education."[6]

If the parties refused to do their job, the NAACP had to step in and enlighten African-Americans about candidates, issues, and the best interest of their people. By an "intelligent" use of the ballot, black voters could put themselves on the political map and force parties and candidates to respond to their growing strength. Political "intelligence" first and foremost meant voting as independents. Not tradition, habit, or petty gains, but an enlightened nonpartisan approach to politics should govern black voting. "Men and measures" had to be considered strictly in relation to black interests. "Friends" would be rewarded and "enemies" punished.[7] In short, the NAACP assumed the task of educating both black voters and white politicians about black interests and voting power.

In pursuit of these goals, the association committed itself to the principle of nonpartisanship. Whenever it became involved in a political campaign, the NAACP took pains to make it known that its action was not affiliated with any party but "wholly independent, planned, financed and carried to consummation solely by the organization itself." When a "friend" whom assistant secretary Walter White had supported in his 1920 election bid sent a $50 contribution, White immediately went on record that his support was predicated only on the candidate's "clean record on the Negro problem."[8] Obviously, there was a fine line between supporting "friends" on the basis of their stands on civil rights and the official endorsement of parties and candidates. The NAACP carefully collected information on the candidates' civil rights records and made it available to the public. "Let every black voter look up the record of his particular Congressman," *The Crisis* admonished its readers in 1922. "If he cannot find it, write us!" Officials of the association, however, were not permitted to use the NAACP's name in connection with their personal political activities, let alone to promote their own ambitions. As early as 1913, the board of directors temporarily suspended the charter of the Washington, D.C., branch because the local NAACP president had tried to secure a political office for himself. The goal of the black political struggle was not "the appointment of a few figure heads at $2,500 salaries," Du Bois wrote in 1921, but to improve the political and economic welfare of all African-Americans. Still, the political activities of NAACP officials remained a permanent source of potential conflicts of interest. Prior to all major elections, the board of directors issued resolutions that paid executives must not accept service on a committee of any party or candidate.[9]

Nonpartisanship was not only supposed to preserve the association's integrity and credibility, it also formed the cornerstone of an electoral balance-of-power strategy that the NAACP hoped would revive party competition for black votes. Given that African-Americans were a minority in the first place and that only the tiny fraction living in the North could vote freely, the association cultivated the idea that black voters could sway the balance of power in close races and then expect the gratitude of the victorious side. For this theory to work, it was necessary that no party or candidate could ever take black support for granted. African-Americans, NAACP cofounder William English Walling told the 1926 annual conference, had to follow the lead of the pro-

gressive, labor, women's, and prohibition movements, which all had practiced "organized nonpartisan voting" and gained considerable influence in
both parties.[10]

Of course, the balance-of-power theory is not exactly an original idea. In
fact, it has been employed by many interest groups and minorities throughout American political history. Unfortunately, the specific conditions on
which balance-of-power elections are based hardly applied to the African-
American electorate in the early twentieth century.[11] First, the strategy requires a homogeneous, disciplined, and well-informed voting bloc that can
be easily mobilized. Yet, as the NAACP constantly lamented, educating black
voters was a long haul. Second, to lend credibility to the claim of volatile
nonpartisanship, a voting bloc must continuously shift its electoral allegiance
in a clear and visible manner. To most African-American voters, however,
Frederick Douglass's famous statement remained an article of faith: "The
Republican Party is the deck, all else is the sea." Third, only if the white majority is divided into two camps of roughly the same strength will blacks be in
a position to tip the scales. In this situation, though, the specter of the "Negro
bloc vote" could easily be exploited to unify white voters in the name of white
supremacy. Where racial polarization shaped electoral campaigns, blacks
could hardly expect to be allowed to hold the balance of power.

Despite its obvious flaws, the balance-of-power theory remained the
NAACP's political mantra for many decades. To dramatize the alleged key
position of black voters, the association did its best to inflate their numbers
by blurring the difference between the potential electorate and actual turnout. Before the 1924 elections, for example, *The Crisis* estimated that about
2.25 million blacks could vote freely. Afterward it claimed that 2 million had
actually cast their ballots, assuming a fantastic turnout of almost 90 percent,
whereas the overall non-southern turnout varied from 40 to 70 percent.[12]
None of this impressed parties and politicians, who knew quite well that African-Americans, except in a few localities, could be safely ignored because
their numbers simply were not large enough. When the NAACP started out
to educate African-American voters and white candidates, it took tremendous
optimism to envision the black minority as a powerful force in American
politics.

Between the Democratic Devil and the Republican Deep Sea

During its early days, the association's political influence was limited to the
publications and speeches of its leaders, most importantly *The Crisis*, under
the editorship of Du Bois. Pondering the options of African-American voters

was no easy or pleasant task, however. Indeed, the very first presidential elections after the founding of the NAACP painfully highlighted the black political predicament. Although the three-way race of 1912 should have increased the relative weight of black ballots, none of the candidates made serious advances toward the black community. President William H. Taft, a leading proponent of "lily-white" Republicanism, had shown such cool indifference toward racial discrimination and violence during his term that a year before the elections *The Crisis* had declared him unfit for his high office. Former President Theodore Roosevelt had frittered away much of his credit with black people after the infamous 1906 Brownsville riot, when he had dishonorably discharged 167 black soldiers from the U.S. Army without trial or proof of guilt. Although Roosevelt's third-party bid for the presidency seemed to offer an alternative for black voters, he made it perfectly clear that the new Progressive Party, too, was "a white man's party." At its national convention, black delegates from the South were excluded in favor of lily-white delegations. An attempt by Jane Addams and Joel Spingarn to insert a moderately worded plank into the Progressive platform, which called for "the repeal of unfair discriminatory laws and the right to vote" was defeated, and the party took no official stand on the race question.[13]

While Addams believed that the Progressive program of "political democracy and industrial justice" nevertheless offered the best choice to blacks, Du Bois was ready "to take a leap in the dark" and call for the election of Democrat Woodrow Wilson, so his party could "prove once for all if [it] dares to be Democratic when it comes to black men."[14] When Wilson won the presidency by a safe plurality, the editor was fully aware that "we have helped call to power not simply a scholar and a gentleman, but with him and in his closest counsels all the Negro-hating, disfranchising and lynching South." Still, Du Bois trusted in Wilson's personal integrity and his assurances that with him as chief executive blacks could count on an "absolute fair dealing." In an open letter upon Wilson's inauguration, *The Crisis* called upon the new president to emancipate himself from the race prejudice of his "Southern friends" and to get "to know the real Negro." To aid in his racial education, the NAACP board of directors sent Oswald Garrison Villard to present Wilson with a plan for a national race commission dedicated to "a nonpartisan, scientific study of the status of the Negro in the life of the nation."[15]

That Wilson's "New Freedom" was for whites only became painfully clear, however, when several members of the new administration began segregating their department facilities, which Wilson defended as a necessary and benevolent measure to reduce racial friction. In August 1913, Du Bois, Villard, and Moorfield Storey published an open letter of protest to the president, but to no avail. Du Bois complained bitterly that since his election "not a single act and not a single word" of Wilson had indicated "the slightest interest in the colored people or desire to alleviate their intolerable position." As it turned out, this assessment would remain correct for the rest of his presidency.[16]

But why should Wilson have cared? In addition to his personal racial prejudice, the president had no political incentives to accommodate black hopes and demands. Before the election, Du Bois had reckoned that there were six hundred thousand eligible African-American voters outside the South and predicted that they would decide the outcome in the key states of Illinois, Indiana, New York, and Ohio. In fact, Wilson won all four states at a comfortable margin. According to Du Bois's generous estimate, the Democratic candidate received about one hundred thousand black votes—a negligible quantity with regard to his total of 6.3 million, as the editor himself conceded. That Wilson or his party would soon become dependent on the support of black voters, as The Crisis speculated, was simply a fantastic notion in 1913.[17]

In retrospect, there could be little doubt that the "step toward political independence," which Du Bois had urged in coming out for Wilson, had been a mistake that was not to be repeated. Unfortunately, four years later the choices for African-Americans were hardly any more attractive. The Republican candidate, Supreme Court Justice Charles Evans Hughes, made his obligatory showings before black audiences, pontificating about "equal and exact justice for all," but in Du Bois's view he knew "nothing about Negroes and [had] neither time nor inclination to learn." If elected, he would display the same neglect and indifference toward blacks as recent Republican presidents, yet he was "practically the only candidate for whom Negroes can vote," since ballots for the Socialists would be wasted. In a campaign that was largely dominated by the looming war, the grievances of African-Americans received even less attention than usual. Wilson's narrow reelection evoked only a brief comment from The Crisis, that for the next four years a "representative of the Southern Negro-hating oligarchy" would continue to occupy the White House.[18]

The association's growth in the wake of the First World War to more than three hundred branches nationwide created an important communication network for educating black voters and bolstered its assertiveness. Typically, letters and cables to white politicians would now begin: "The National Association for the Advancement of Colored People, representing 12,000,000 Negroes of the United States...."[19] There is little evidence, however, that this claim was taken very seriously as far as the electoral strategies of parties and candidates were concerned. In the summer of 1920, Walter White alerted the Republican National Committee that black Republicans in Oklahoma were denied registration, indicating that vigorous action would assure black voters "that the Republican Party is genuinely interested in the Negro." The white Republicans of Oklahoma confirmed White's charges but advised against any "agitation on the race question . . . that would hurt the party in the state." Even in counties where African-Americans could freely register, they were not actively encouraged to vote by the GOP. Obviously, black supporters were not welcome because they might taint the party's lily-white image. And indeed, Warren Harding was the first Republican presidential candidate to win Oklahoma since the state had joined the Union in 1907.[20]

To his credit, Harding was one of the two candidates who answered a questionnaire on black civil rights that the NAACP had sent out to seventeen contenders in the 1920 presidential primaries, albeit in the most evasive language. In fact, the only reference to the race issue in the Republican platform was a single, noncommittal phrase urging Congress "to consider the most effective means to end lynching in this country." In a postconvention meeting with James Weldon Johnson, Harding continued to decline any public statements on the NAACP touchstones. However, he showed a keen interest in Johnson's information on atrocities against Haitians committed by the U.S. occupation forces, which he used as a campaign issue against the Democratic administration. As little as Harding had to offer to black voters, he seemed much preferable over his Democratic opponent, James B. Cox, who denounced the Republican candidate for allegedly promoting "social equality" between the races.[21]

Before the general elections, the NAACP augured that African-Americans "will constitute the balance of power . . . in 8 pivotal states which have 165 votes in the electoral college." Blacks might not only decide who would be president but also greatly influence the make-up of the new Congress.[22] Neither prediction proved correct. The Republicans swept both the House and the Senate, and Harding won an unprecedented 60 percent of the popular vote, amounting to almost three-fourths of the electoral college. His landslide left no room for speculation about the critical impact of black votes, let alone for claiming that Harding owed the presidency to his black supporters. Moreover, a candidate who had promised to lead the nation "back to normalcy" could hardly be expected to make bold moves on behalf of blacks. Still, Du Bois wanted to impress on Harding that African-Americans would not be satisfied with the usual modicum of patronage, but demanded measures on lynching, disfranchisement, and segregation. In a conversation with the president-elect in January 1921, James Johnson found Harding "cordial" but absolutely noncommittal. The future president, the secretary reported, knew "absolutely nothing" about black people and needed to be "educated on the race question."[23]

On this occasion, Harding expressed his desire to establish a new Republican Party in the South and recommended "that the colored people in the South should willingly accept white leadership until such time as prejudice was worn down." Indeed, the inroads that the GOP had made in the southern states encouraged the Republican leadership to expand on their lily-white strategy. Vice President–elect Calvin Coolidge and the chairman of the Republican National Committee, William Hays, sang the praise of racial and sectional harmony that would allow for the reestablishment of the two-party system under the auspices of white supremacy. Former President Taft approvingly cited the proposals by southern Republicans to limit the appointment of black federal officers to the North. Taft conceded that the voting rights of southern blacks were unconstitutionally denied but argued that "the only hope the negro has . . . is in developing his intelligence and economic utility, so that individual negroes of character and intelligence may gradually have accorded to them what is theirs now by right." When Harding nominated the former president as chief justice of the U.S. Supreme Court a few months later, black political and civil rights leaders activists were understandably appalled. NAACP secretary James Johnson and Robert Church, a board member of the association and a prominent black Republican from Memphis, briefly considered a public campaign against Taft's nomination but realistically decided that the NAACP was too weak to take on a former U.S. president.[24]

The lily-white Republicans had their words followed by deeds. With Harding's tacit backing, they started a massive, if not entirely successful, campaign to purge African-Americans from their southern party organizations and delegations. Reflecting on the consequences of lily-white Republicanism for black voters, Du Bois came to the unwelcome conclusion that they might be forced to limit their votes to black candidates only: "Thoughtful Negroes do not want racial candidates and parties," he wrote, "they see the ultimate contradiction and futility of this. But what is one to do who has to choose between the Democratic devil and the Republican deep sea?" The only workable way out of this predicament was a strictly nonpartisan approach—voting solely on the basis of an individual candidate's record on race and civil rights. In local elections, African-Americans should continue to vote for "friends" and defeat "enemies" regardless of party labels, but in national elections no self-respecting black voter could support the two major parties "without writing himself down an ass."[25]

The NAACP's disenchantment with the GOP grew stronger in the face of the party's flirtations with a resurgent Ku Klux Klan that had won considerable influence on Republican organizations in several non-southern states, including Colorado, Ohio, and Indiana. As the association kept on pressuring Calvin Coolidge, who had moved into the White House after Harding's sudden death in August 1923, for an "unequivocal statement" against the Klan, the new president lived up to his reputation as "Silent Cal" and refused to take any public stand on the Klan in the 1924 campaign. His running mate, Charles Dawes, mildly reproached the Klan's methods of enforcing law and order, but acknowledged that the racist and nativist organization represented the popular sentiment in many localities. Even the Democratic presidential candidate used stronger words to distance himself from the Klan, while the Democratic convention narrowly defeated an anti-Klan plank. "You don't really care a rap who is president," Du Bois advised his readers, "Republican presidents are just about as bad as Democratic and Democratic presidents are little better than nothing."[26]

Since the American winner-takes-all electoral system makes it extremely difficult for third parties to succeed, the NAACP leaders had always advised against wasting ballots on parties and candidates without a serious chance of winning. In 1912 Du Bois had even resigned his membership in the Socialist Party so he could support Wilson, and four years later he had called the Socialists "an excellent party" but grudgingly endorsed Hughes, because a vote for a third party would be thrown away.[27] In 1924, however, the third-party bid by Wisconsin senator and social reformer Robert La Follette seemed to offer a meaningful political alternative for the first time in many years. In July, the NAACP annual convention eagerly welcomed the third party because it "may save us from . . . the necessity of voting for the same oppression under different party names." The NAACP delegates went even further and sent a message to the Progressive convention, which was simultaneously meeting in Cleveland, frankly addressing the major gap between black people and the pro-labor Progressives: the traditional racism of the American labor movement: "We appeal to the Cleveland Conference for Progressive Political Action to take such enlightened and far-sighted steps against race and color discrimination as will enable us to appeal to our people in behalf of the liberal and labor parties of the nation, without being faced by the present incontrovertible fact that these very persons are today greater enemies of our right to earn decent bread and butter than the captains of monopoly and privilege." In light of the otherwise good program of the Progressives, Du Bois editorialized, it was "disheartening" and "inexcusable" to find the party dodging the issue of racial discrimination.[28]

At least La Follette came out with a public statement denouncing the Klan, and his "Independent Colored Voters La Follette-for-President Club" actively sought the support of prominent NAACP leaders. The association declined any official endorsement, but individual leaders were less guarded. Field secretary William Pickens rather wanted to vote "for a third or fourth or fifth or sixth party than . . . for either of the old liars and double-crossers" and agreed to stand as an elector for La Follette in New York. Du Bois also declared his support for La Follette because of the candidate's personal honesty and his party's economic program.[29] James Johnson and Walter White, however, remained unconvinced and disappointed that La Follette had not responded to the "most generous gesture" of the NAACP's annual conference with a more forthright stand on the race issue. An economically liberal program, White reasoned, was all good and well, but unfortunately blacks had to "think Negro before we can think liberal." An "enlightened and progressive program" was not enough, Johnson told the La Follette campaign. If they wanted the black vote they had to make a "special appeal to colored people."[30]

Johnson's reservations vis-à-vis the Progressives were not fully plausible. The secretary himself denounced the anti-black "Gentlemen's Agreement" between the two major parties and called for voting independently. What did African-Americans have to lose casting their ballot for La Follette? When would they get the next opportunity to vote for a credible third party to demonstrate the very political independence that the NAACP kept on preaching to the black community?[31] After the elections, Du Bois rejoiced that "Negroes voted with greater intelligence and finer discrimination than ever before." According to his inflated numbers, 1 million African-Americans had voted Republican, while another million split evenly between the northern Democrats and the Progressives. The strong black support for La Follette was "a splendid and far-reaching gesture," because the "Third Party has come to stay and the Negro recognizes its fine platform and its finer leaders."[32] The editor was a little too enthusiastic, however. Robert La Follette's death in 1925 led to a swift disintegration of the Progressives and dashed all short-term hopes for a viable alternative to the "Gentlemen's Agreement." Still, in retrospect the growing inclination of black voters to desert the GOP foreshadowed their massive loyalty switch of the next decade.

For the time being, however, Calvin Coolidge and his party remained tall in the saddle and cherished their lily-white image. When Du Bois invited the influential GOP senator William Borah to contribute his views on black suffrage to *The Crisis,* Borah seriously claimed that the South was trying to solve the problem in good faith according to the Constitution.[33] In the same vein, the party's 1928 presidential candidate, Secretary of Commerce Herbert

Hoover, showed very little interest in the plight of African-Americans. Despite his reputation as a progressive reformer and a humanitarian, Hoover's attitude toward blacks was aloof and at best paternalistic. After the great Mississippi flood of 1927, the secretary of commerce, who was in charge of coordinating the relief efforts, and the NAACP clashed over the blatant racial discrimination against black flood victims, leading to a lasting mutual dislike. When Hoover announced his presidential candidacy the next year, Du Bois attacked him for allegedly considering African-Americans as "sub-men."[34]

The Democrats, in contrast, nominated New York governor Al Smith, a representative of the northern urban wing of the party that the NAACP had already credited with "great fairness" toward blacks prior to the 1924 elections.[35] In the spring of 1928, Al Smith confidentially approached Walter White to win him over to his campaign, assuring him "that the old Democratic Party . . . is on its way out and that we Northern Democrats have a totally different approach to the Negro." But Smith never made the public statement he had allegedly promised to the NAACP assistant secretary. Instead, the Democratic convention in Houston, Texas, was held without official black delegates, and black visitors were strictly segregated. The convention picked a southerner as Smith's running mate and passed a platform that made no references to black concerns.[36] As the son of Irish immigrants, a Catholic, and an opponent of prohibition, Al Smith obviously believed he already had more than enough liabilities and could not afford to offend the South with gestures of racial liberalism. That Smith was afraid of the South, Du Bois commented, was extremely short-sighted, for blacks were so disgusted with the GOP that the Democratic contender would only have "to raise a finger" to garner an unprecedented number of black votes. Smith's cowardice, however, proved that all hopes for the party to free itself from the control of the southern race-baiters were misplaced. The editor announced that this time around he would vote for the Socialists, who had taken a clear stand on lynching and disfranchisement. The Socialist candidate received less than 1 percent of the popular vote.[37]

In spite of his deference toward the South, Al Smith got more votes from northern blacks than any Democratic presidential candidate before him, coming close to 30 percent in the black districts of New York, Chicago, and Cleveland.[38] It did not help him, though, as he was trounced by Hoover in a landslide that added five states of the former Confederacy to the Republican column. Under Hoover's leadership, lily-white Republicanism continued to flourish. His southern strategy may have been inspired by a progressive vision for an enlightened New South, but he was completely unable and unwilling to communicate to African-Americans that he was not just "the man in the lily-White House," as Walter White began to call him.[39]

Defeating Enemies

Arguably, the NAACP's efforts to educate parties and candidates bore precious little fruit, but its attempts to reward "friends" and punish "enemies" at the ballot box were not altogether unsuccessful. In 1922 and in 1930, the association launched two major efforts to defeat lawmakers who had voted against black interests as defined by the association. The first campaign was directed against the opponents of the so-called Dyer bill, which proposed to make lynching a federal crime. The second targeted U.S. senators who had supported the nomination of Judge John J. Parker to the U.S. Supreme Court.

In April 1918, Republican congressman Leonidas Dyer of St. Louis, Missouri, a district with a large African-American constituency, had introduced a bill that proposed to make participation in a lynch mob a capital offense under federal law and threatened officials who failed to prosecute lynchers with up to five years in prison and fines of $5,000. The counties that allowed lynchings to happen would have to pay indemnities of up to $10,000 to the victim's family. Although the NAACP leaders had second thoughts about the constitutionality of punishing lynchers under federal law, they welcomed the bill since lynching mobilized African- Americans like no other civil rights issue. After several unsuccessful attempts, the bill came to the House floor in January 1922. The roll call on the Dyer bill, Du Bois admonished his readers, was "a splendid indication of how we ought to vote." Lawmakers who voted against it or abstained, he declared, "are our enemies."[40] The bill passed the House, but afterward was stalled in the Senate Judiciary Committee because several key senators, including the powerful Republican William Borah, considered it unconstitutional. Even after the measure was finally reported by the committee in late June, its opponents managed to prevent a vote on the Senate floor.[41]

In this situation the NAACP decided to demonstrate the power of the black electorate by defeating opponents of the Dyer bill who were up for reelection in November. The association intervened in six races in which African-American voters might make the difference. In Michigan, the NAACP mobilized its branches against a Republican congressman who had voted against the Dyer bill and now sought the nomination of his party for the U.S. Senate. The association supported the incumbent, who dutifully acknowledged "the valuable assistance of the colored voters" after winning the primary.[42] In New Jersey, the NAACP targeted a Republican representative and lent its support to his Democratic rival, after the latter had pledged himself to the Dyer bill. According to the association, this gesture assured him both the black vote and a seat in the House of Representatives.[43] The NAACP also claimed that in Milwaukee, Wisconsin, its local branch played a critical part in defeating a Republican anti-Dyer congressman and electing his Socialist opponent. When Leonidas Dyer himself approached the association for help because his antilynching fight was held against him by his adversaries, James Johnson immediately offered to send William Pickens to campaign for Dyer among the black community. The NAACP secretary soon learned, however, that Dyer's troubles were not due to his stand on civil rights but to an extramarital affair. Since the black voters of his district were backing him unanimously, Dyer informed Johnson that additional assistance would be unnecessary.[44]

The most interesting race took place in Delaware, where Caleb Layton, the state's only congressman and a professed enemy of the antilynching bill, had been renominated by his party over the vocal protests of black Republicans. The NAACP organized an "Anti-Layton League" and Johnson, White, Pickens, and other NAACP leaders gave speeches to rally black voters against the incumbent. Not only was Layton retired, his losses also roughly equaled the approximate number of black voters in the district. In addition, the Republican senator who had supported Layton's nomination lost by a narrow margin. Black voters, the NAACP gloated, had served a "fair warning" to the Republicans.[45]

Apparently, the warning was not strong enough. When the Dyer bill was debated in a special session of the Senate after the elections, the southerners staged a filibuster and the Republicans agreed to drop the bill, despite a desperate public appeal by the NAACP to President Harding that this would have an "incalculable effect civilly and politically on the colored people of the whole country."[46] Nevertheless, the association's efforts had not been in vain. Not only did the fight for the antilynching bill generate considerable publicity, but the NAACP for the first time had staged an orchestrated electoral campaign in which its local branches served as a reliable "transmission belt." Even if the association exaggerated both its own role and the weight of black ballots in these races, Du Bois's claim that "these splendid results mark a long step forward in the political emancipation of colored voters" was not entirely based on wishful thinking. In 1923, local elections in Chicago and Baltimore confirmed the trend among African-Americans toward voting independently, ignoring party labels.[47]

In the spring of 1930, President Hoover nominated John J. Parker, a federal judge and a Republican from North Carolina, to the U.S. Supreme Court. Since Parker had no particular distinction as a jurist, his nomination was widely regarded as a reward to the lily-white GOP of his home state, which Hoover had carried in 1928. The NAACP's investigation of Parker's political record unearthed a statement from his 1920 gubernatorial campaign in which he had condoned the disfranchisement of black voters and boasted the lily-white credentials of his party: "The Negro as a class does not desire to enter politics," Parker had declared. "The Republican Party of North Carolina does not desire him to do so. We recognize the fact that he has not yet reached that stage in his development when he can share the burdens and responsibilities of government. . . . The participation of the Negro in politics is a source of evil and danger to both races and is not desired by the wise men in either race." Obviously, a Supreme Court justice with such views posed an imminent danger to the association's legal strategies and to black civil rights at large. When Parker declined to answer an inquiry whether he still stood behind this statement, the national office immediately called upon its local branches to put pressure on their senators to vote against Parker's nomination.[48]

And indeed, Parker went down in the Senate by a very close margin of two votes. It would be misleading, however, to attribute his defeat to his racial views. Parker's rulings as a federal judge to uphold so-called yellow dog antiunion labor contracts were much more controversial and provoked vigorous opposition from the American Federation of Labor. The anti-Parker forces, moreover, did not stage a joint battle. On the contrary, AFL leader William Green pointedly distanced himself from the NAACP's acting secretary, Walter White, when both testified against Parker before the Senate Subcommittee of the Judiciary. The only anti-Parker senator who pejoratively mentioned Parker's stand on black rights in the final confirmation debate was Robert Wagner, a liberal Democrat from New York. While the pressure from the NAACP and their black constituents may have had an impact on several northern Republicans, the liberal opposition against Parker clearly rallied around the labor issue. Nevertheless, it was widely recognized that the vote against Parker amounted to a stinging defeat for Herbert Hoover's southern strategy, for which the association readily took credit.[49]

Emboldened by this victory, the NAACP leadership was eager to continue the fight and go after senators who had voted for Parker's nomination. On the day after the final Senate roll call, Walter White advised the local branches that black voters were now obliged to reward friends and punish enemies:

"Our slogan must be," the secretary decreed, "any Negro is a traitor to his race who votes for any senator who voted for Parker." *The Crisis* published a list of eighteen pro-Parker senators from states with a sizeable black community and admonished its readers to remember their names when they ran for re-election. Not everyone was convinced, however, that the Parker nomination was a fitting issue to sort out friends and enemies. After all, some of the most notorious race-baiting southern Democrats had voted against Parker to thwart Hoover's southern strategy, while several of his supporters had otherwise commendable records on black rights.[50]

The prospect of boosting the NAACP's membership and political visibility overruled all skepticism. In July, the board of directors officially decided to try to defeat the senators who had voted for Parker wherever this seemed possible.[51] All of the association's targets were Republicans from the North or from border states. After the 1934 congressional elections, when the pro-Parker senators had all stood for reelection, *The Crisis* proudly claimed that "all the senators who voted for Parker and who could be reached by the colored voters have been defeated." An NAACP press release counted seven "victims" of the Parker campaign in the 1934 elections alone. In his memoirs, Walter White attributed the defeat of ten Republicans to the "implacable and effective opposition of Negro voters."[52]

As the association's leaders themselves knew perfectly well, their head counts were somewhat spurious to say the least. Since the Republican congressional delegations were virtually massacred in the Democratic landslides of 1932 and 1934, it makes little sense to speculate about the possible impact of the Parker issue on the defeat of individual Republican senators. Only in the cases of Senators Henry J. Allen of Kansas and Roscoe McCulloch of Ohio, who both ran in 1930, can a plausible link between the NAACP's campaign and the outcome of the electoral races be established. Both won in the Republican primaries but were defeated in the general elections. In both races the NAACP made a major effort and sent prominent leaders to campaign against Allen and McCulloch among the African-American community. In Kansas, William Pickens vigorously disciplined local branch leaders who had not been immune to the advances of the Allen campaign. The former Kansas governor had previously enjoyed the support of the black electorate, but this time he only received one out of four black votes in the primary. In the general elections he was soundly defeated by his Democratic opponent, who later took an NAACP membership in recognition of the support he had received from black voters. On top of it, the second senator from Kansas, Republican Arthur Capper, who happened to be a member of the NAACP board of directors, was easily reelected. One year later the association targeted former New Jersey senator David Baird, who ran for governor. Baird also lost his bid.[53]

Whether the anti-Parker campaign was indeed "the most sensational and significant political movement by Negroes in the last generation," as *The Crisis* boasted, is debatable.[54] Even Allen and McCulloch were relatively easy targets who had a weak political home base and faced powerful opposition from labor unions. Nevertheless, the NAACP could not only savor the satisfaction of having punished "enemies," it also reaped considerable organizational benefits. The campaign strengthened the ability of the national secretariat to stage effective political action in coordination with the NAACP state conferences and local branches. Moreover, the Parker fight undeniably increased the association's prestige and political clout. As its records bear out, the NAACP headquarters began to receive numerous requests for endorsement and support from candidates for all kinds of offices. At the same time, local branches and individual blacks were eagerly seeking information on candidates and races. Although it retained its traditional posture of nonpartisanship, the Parker affair made the association into a much more political organization.[55]

The Parker fight, to be sure, did not radically change the political world of African-Americans. Before the presidential elections of 1932, the NAACP, as usual, appealed to blacks "to use the franchise with intelligence" and warned the parties of "the growing potency of the black vote."[56] As usual, the association pressured parties and candidates to take clear-cut positions on black rights and interests, but to no avail. The Democratic platform remained entirely silent on the race issue, while the GOP gratuitously declared itself "the friend of the American Negro." At least the Democratic contender, Franklin D. Roosevelt, denied rumors about the Klan backing his campaign.[57] The arguments that black Republicans and Democrats presented in *The Crisis* in favor of their respective parties were hardly inspiring. While the former relied on tradition and on Hoover's proven leadership, the latter attacked Republican hypocrisy but had very little to say about what the Democrats had to offer to blacks. In striking contrast, the Socialists and Communists, who were also invited to state their case, could point to their impeccable records on racial matters. For example, the Communists were the first party in American history to nominate an African-American for vice president. Needless to say, the radical left had no chance of winning.[58]

The "greatest political revolt among Negroes that has ever been known in a national election," which Walter White predicted for November 1932, did not materialize. On the contrary, while Hoover lost almost 20 percentage points of the popular vote nationwide, his share slightly increased in the predominantly black districts of several major cities, such as Chicago and Cleveland. After twelve years of lily-white Republicans in the White House, African-Americans still remained a loyal GOP constituency. There were some exceptions, however. In New York City, where liberal Democrats had wooed black voters for a long time, Hoover's losses among blacks equaled the national average, and more than 50 percent of the black vote went to Roosevelt.[59] Little in the election results, however, supported the NAACP's claim that African-American voters had ended their "blind allegiance" to the GOP and declared their "political emancipation." Still, African-American dissatisfaction with the GOP, Walter White reasoned, offered the Democratic Party the "great opportunity to wipe out the distrust with which it has justly been regarded by many colored people. The coming years will tell whether that opportunity has been taken or not. Meanwhile the NAACP will remain on watch and on guard."[60]

For the time being, Roosevelt gave no indication that he felt grateful to black voters. In January 1933, Walter White tried to secure an appointment with the president-elect, but it took the NAACP secretary until the spring of 1934 to meet FDR face to face. In the conversation, which had been arranged by First Lady Eleanor Roosevelt, the president displayed his characteristic charms, but on substantial issues, such as the resurrected antilynching bill, he "was frankly unwilling to challenge the southern leadership of his party."[61] In struggling with the worst economic crisis in a generation, black civil rights clearly were not a priority on his administration's agenda.

The Challenges of the Great Depression

The Great Depression fundamentally affected the conditions under which the NAACP had to work and led to far-reaching changes in its political outlook. In economic terms, the depression years were an unmitigated disaster for African-Americans, who suffered from unemployment rates of up to 50 percent and aggravated discrimination according to the "last hired, first fired" rule of America's segregated labor markets. In the rural South, millions of poor black farmers, sharecroppers, and laborers were cast below the subsistence level and literally faced starvation, since they were largely excluded from the meager relief that was available. As blacks struggled to survive, many of the NAACP members could no longer afford their dues of one dollar a year. Donations from wealthy white liberals also were drying up. Between 1931 and 1933, the annual income of the association plummeted from almost $60,000 to less than $35,000. In 1932, the salaries of the NAACP staff were slashed three times and several clerks had to be dismissed. At a time when the defense of black rights and interests was more urgent than ever, the association found itself in dire straits. But the deep crisis of American capitalism also triggered waves of radical social protest that did not leave race relations untouched. The rise of the left and the increasing appeal of class solidarity undermined the traditional racism of the American labor movement and were crucial factors in breaking the political isolation of the African-American minority.[62]

The black economic plight and the growing currency of radical social criticism presented the NAACP with new challenges to revise its agenda and inspired heated internal debates. Perhaps the most conspicuous controversy was sparked by W.E.B. Du Bois's demand for black self-help and autonomous economic and social institutions, which he raised in *The Crisis* in 1934 and which led to his resignation from both the magazine and the association. Building his argument on the distinction between discriminatory segregation and voluntary separation, the NAACP veteran hailed "the race-conscious black man cooperating together in his own institutions and movements who will eventually emancipate the colored race." While a fully integrated society remained the goal for a distant future, blacks had to face the reality of racism and had to demand their fair share of the social resources without being "stampeded by the word segregation." "The opposition to segregation is an opposition to discrimination," the editor proclaimed, "and there should never be an opposition to segregation pure and simple unless that segregation does involve discrimination."[63]

Few blacks would deny that segregation was a fact of life with which they had to deal, or that solidarity in the face of unrelenting racism was a positive good. But for Du Bois, the implacable antagonist of both Booker T. Washington's accommodationism and Garvey's separatism, to speak of voluntary segregation in terms that came suspiciously close to the separate-but-equal doctrine seemed mind-boggling and unbelievable to many of his readers. William Hastie, a prominent black lawyer who had recently been appointed as assistant solicitor in the federal government, assailed Du Bois for "making a puny defense of segregation and hair splitting about the difference between segregation and discrimination!" Such a statement coming from the most respected African-American intellectual, Hastie correctly predicted, would be "a powerful weapon in the hands of our enemies." To ignore the plain fact that segregation was built on the notion of black inferiority and always meant discrimination was "either dumb or mentally dishonest." Confronted with the public stir over the segregation editorial, NAACP secretary Walter White wanted Du Bois to publish a statement that maintained that the association had never "budged in its opposition to segregation." The editor, however, declined and announced that in the next issue of *The Crisis* he would first publish his own record on the NAACP's stand on segregation.[64]

In his account, Du Bois tried to demonstrate that the NAACP had only fought enforced and discriminatory segregation, but had never attempted "to lay down any general rule as to how far the advancement of the colored race in the United States was going to involve separate racial action and segregated organization of Negroes for certain ends." He also reminded his readers that the association had more than once compromised with enforced segregation, such as in the case of the separate training camp for black officers during the war, and that it regularly appealed to black voters as a class. "That race pride and race loyalty, Negro ideals and Negro unity, have a place and function today," the article concluded, "the NAACP never has denied and never can deny."[65]

All of this was incontrovertible, as both Joel Spingarn, the chairman of the board of directors, and Walter White conceded in their replies in the March 1934 issue of *The Crisis*. But the editor's critics were certainly correct that Du Bois's perspective did not accurately reflect the integrationist spirit that had animated the association's struggle since its founding. That the NAACP had always been opposed to the practice and principle of segregation, even if it had to compromise in concrete situations, "was so completely accepted by all of us," Joel Spingarn recalled, "that we never realized that the board had never made a clear and official pronouncement." At the same time, the NAACP officers had always expressed "unqualified opposition to segregation without the disapproval of the board." The distinction between discrimination and segregation, the chairman reminded Du Bois, had been invented by southern lawyers in defense of the separate-but-equal doctrine that the NAACP was fighting in the courts. Indeed, as Walter White added with unconcealed reproach, Du Bois's editorial had already been used to delay the admission of blacks to government-financed relief projects. Any acceptance of voluntary segregation would inevitably be exploited as an "opening wedge" to spread Jim Crow. It was a matter of self-respect to "continue the grim struggle for integration and against segregation."[66]

The controversy over segregation, it is easy to see, did not reflect any irreconcilable philosophical differences. Rather, it marked the culmination of a long-standing power struggle between Du Bois and Walter White, who had been appointed as the NAACP executive secretary in 1931 and who wanted to bring *The Crisis* under the control of the secretariat. Du Bois, for his part, had come to despise White and his assistant, Roy Wilkins, as second-rate schemers whom he wished to remove from the association's leadership. Unfortunately for the editor, *The Crisis* had fallen into heavy debts and become dependent on subsidies from the NAACP. In late 1932, the board of directors had already relieved Du Bois of the "unnecessary and onerous administrative duties" of the magazine's business management. According to his biographer David Lewis, Du Bois hoped for a permanent teaching position at Atlanta University and in early 1933 decided to leave the association in the near future. When he realized that his plans for radical changes in the NAACP's staff and program would not be acceptable to the board, the editor "decided to exit with a bang."[67]

In reckoning with his opponents, the distinguished intellectual was not above playing the race card, accusing the light-skinned Walter White of having long since "passed" into the white world: "Walter White is white. He has more white companions and friends than colored. He goes where he will . . . and meets no Color Line, for the simple and sufficient reason that he isn't 'colored.'" The dark-skinned champions of integration, although the products of separate black institutions, were trying to ingratiate themselves to the white society. Such opportunists, Du Bois insinuated, had forgotten what racial self-respect meant: "[W]hen white Americans refuse to treat me as a man, I will cut my intercourse with white Americans to the minimum demanded by decent living."[68] When the NAACP board of directors repudiated Du Bois's propositions on voluntary segregation, the editor defiantly reaffirmed his views and publicly asked his readers if the board was afraid to admit that it did not believe in the viability of black culture. In response to this deliberate provocation, the board resolved that no salaried officer could criticize the NAACP in *The Crisis,* which was after all "the organ of the association." Unwilling to be muzzled, Du Bois tendered his resignation. In July 1934, the board finally accepted it with the ceremonious regret due to a cofounder of the NAACP.[69]

In his letter of resignation, Du Bois insisted that the real reason for his departure was not the segregation issue but the association's inability for renewal. The NAACP was "without a program, without effective organization, without executive officers, who have either the ability or disposition to guide [it] in the right direction." Since the beginning of the Great Depression he had "tried to work inside the organization for its realignment and readjustment to new duties. I have been almost absolutely unsuccessful. My program for economic readjustment has been totally ignored. My demand for change in personnel has been considered as mere petty jealousy, and my protests against our mistakes and blunders has been looked upon as disloyalty." While the editor's bitterness may be understandable, his account was rather self-serving and inaccurate. In a resolution that was not to be published, the board of directors denied that Du Bois's demands had fallen on deaf ears and observed that the editor, while sending a few letters and memoranda, had not attended the board meetings since September 1933.[70]

More importantly, it was not true that the association had ignored the economic catastrophe that the Great Depression had visited upon African-Americans. In an "Address to the Country" passed by the 1932 NAACP annual conference, the delegates acknowledged that the civil rights struggle of the past two decades had not yet yielded a decisive breakthrough. "The American Negro is going to find freedom and adjustment mainly through an improvement in his economic status," the statement read. "We are becoming convinced that it is because we are poor and voiceless in industry that we are able to accomplish so little with what political power we have, and with what agitation and appeal we set in motion. We are going to continue to agitate. We are going to use our political power to the utmost. But we believe that what the Negro needs primarily is a definite economic program." The ensuing economic principles, which were devised by W.E.B. Du Bois among others, had a remarkably radical thrust. They recognized the "identical interests" of black and white workers, called for the "redistribution of present wealth by the systematic taxation of high incomes," and advocated the introduction of sickness, old age, and unemployment insurance. The delegates appealed to the American labor movement to renounce its traditional racism and to include the interests of black workers. This program of economic and racial reform, the NAACP conference asserted, was "the only alternative to the complete breakdown in the present social system." The struggle, however, remained essentially political. "Without the free and untrammeled right to vote Negroes have no chance to help economic reform and no hope of obtaining economic security."[71]

Many of the association's internal critics were not content with reformist rhetoric, however. To intensify the dialogue, Joel Spingarn invited a group of some forty, mostly young, black intellectuals and NAACP activists to his country seat in Amenia, New York, as he had done in 1916. In the free-floating discussions, Marxist rhetoric and criticism of the NAACP's legalism and middle-class orientation were running high, but except for "the leaning toward communism" Mary Ovington found nothing that contradicted the NAACP program. Du Bois, in contrast, was disappointed, because he had hoped that the emphasis on economic issues would lead to a focus on racial solidarity, while most of the young radicals gave priority to class as the determining factor of social life. In his search for a synthesis of socialism and ethno-cultural pluralism, Du Bois was appalled by the simplistic economic determinism that was espoused at the meeting. Yet if the young radicals were naive about interracial class unity, Du Bois's hopes that blacks could create "a haven of economic security" within a segregated society appeared no more realistic in the face of a devastating depression that had eradicated much of black economic wealth and independence. The overwhelmingly negative reactions among the black public to his ideas on voluntary separation a year later revealed that Du Bois had misread the prevailing mood of the times.[72]

Immediately after Du Bois's resignation, the NAACP board of directors appointed a Committee on Future Plan and Program, headed by Abram Harris, a thirty-five-year-old sociologist at Howard University and a leading spokesman for the younger radicals. Although the committee included protagonists of the traditional civil rights approach, such as James Weldon Johnson and Mary Ovington, the report that was presented in September 1934 clearly reflected the ideas of Harris and his fellow socialists. It criticized the fact that, in its struggle to secure civil rights and equal opportunity for African-Americans, the association was still wedded to the principles of eighteenth-century liberal individualism that were no longer appropriate for an industrial society. The economic plight and discrimination of black Americans, the report's key proposition read, was not primarily a matter of race but of class. Hence the NAACP needed to change its methods and objectives: "Instead of continuing to oppose racial discrimination on the job and in pay and various manifestations of anti-Negro feeling among white workers, the association would attempt to get Negroes to view their special grievances as a natural part of the larger issues of American labor as a whole." In other words, the report advocated that the NAACP should transform itself from a civil rights organization into an integral part of an interracial labor movement. In addition, it called for "decentralization and a more closely knit but democratic type of organization" in which the authority of the national office and the board of directors would be drastically curtailed.[73]

This medicine was too strong for the proponents of the civil rights approach, who denied that most blacks viewed themselves as part of an exploited working class rather than as an oppressed racial minority. Even Mary Ovington, herself a socialist, opposed Harris's program because the message of class struggle could only be successfully preached by the socialists or the communists but not by the NAACP, which would lose its identity, credibility, and following.[74] Nevertheless, the need for a new and more radical economic program was incontestable, and after Du Bois's departure the leadership wished to avoid new internal controversy. The board of directors added some modifications to the Harris report, especially with regard to the organizational demands, and submitted it to the 1935 annual conference of the NAACP in St. Louis, Missouri, which passed it without much discussion. In his opening speech, Joel Spingarn clarified that the association's new economic program would be implemented under "our present constitutional democracy" and that the NAACP remained committed to "fighting for full equality for colored Americans" in the first place.[75]

Although the association refused to merge into an interracial labor movement, it began forging alliances with labor unions, especially with the industrial unions that joined into the Congress of Industrial Organizations (CIO) in the mid-1930s. While the CIO embraced racial egalitarianism and civil rights issues, such as the NAACP's antilynching campaign, the NAACP supported the cause of labor, and its local branches, particularly in industrial cities such as Chicago, Detroit, and Baltimore, began to reach out to black workers. When Walter White openly encouraged black workers to join the United Automobile Workers (UAW) in its 1941 strike to unionize the River Rouge plant of the Ford Motor Company in Detroit, even though Henry Ford was traditionally considered a benefactor of the black community, this sealed the NAACP's inclusion into a political coalition that was both pro-labor and pro-civil rights. From the 1930s on, the NAACP consistently supported liberal social policies that would benefit not only blacks but all poor Americans.[76] It did so, however, without sacrificing its identity on the altar of working-class unity. The association broadened its agenda and won new allies, but retained its character as an integrationist African-American civil rights group.

In particular, the association's opening toward the labor movement and the left did not include the Communist Party of the United States of America (CPUSA), which had been founded in 1919. Although the party had quickly identified African-Americans as the most oppressed and exploited part of the American proletariat, its ideological twists and turns on the race question were extremely erratic. Early attempts to organize black workers in the American Negro Labor Congress came to no avail. After the Sixth World Congress of the Communist International in 1928, the CPUSA, following Stalin's writings on the issue of national minorities, adopted the position that blacks constituted a national minority within the United States and were entitled to a separate state in the Black Belt of the Deep South. To demonstrate its antiracism, the party waged campaigns against "white chauvinism" in its own ranks and nominated a black candidate for vice president in the 1932 elections. Throughout the Great Depression the Communist Party succeeded in winning some popularity among the black working class of the big industrial cities. Even in Birmingham, Alabama, a clandestine but active cell of black communists formed.[77]

The conflicts between the NAACP and the communists had little to do with fanciful ideological notions such as a separate black state but developed over the defense of the "Scottsboro Boys," the most spectacular case of southern-style racist criminal justice of the 1930s. In March 1931, nine black youth had been arrested in Scottsboro, Alabama, for allegedly raping two white girls. Only three weeks later, eight of them were sentenced to death. Although there was no evidence for rape in the first place, the defendants had no chance for a fair trial before an all-white jury imbued with the sexual obsessions of white supremacist ideology demanding that white women had to be protected against the "black beast" by all means, including lynching and the death penalty.[78]

In the struggle to save the "Scottsboro Boys," the NAACP clashed with the International Labor Defense (ILD), an affiliate of the CPUSA. While the NAACP, and especially its executive secretary, Walter White, at first underestimated the potential of the case and hesitated to become involved, the ILD managed to obtain the mandate to represent the youths in court and turned the case into a big propaganda campaign that evolved into an international cause célèbre of the left. According to the ILD, black proletarians could not expect justice from a court of the white ruling class but would only be freed by the revolutionary pressure of the masses. Pursuant to their ideological struggle against "social fascism" and "petty-bourgeois reformism," the communists hurled a barrage of attacks against the NAACP leadership, which was accused of "joining the lynching mob" and of betraying the "Negro masses and . . . the Negro liberation struggle." The CPUSA made no secret of its intention to drive a wedge between the "masses of the NAACP followers" and their reformist "misleaders." To its credit, the ILD's legal team was able to prevent the execution of the young men, and after the Communist Party had embraced the new "popular front" tactics in the mid-1930s, a coalition of civil rights groups, including the ILD and the NAACP, continued to pursue the case. In the third Scottsboro trial of 1937—the U.S. Supreme Court had twice overturned convictions for violating the due process guarantees of the Fourteenth Amendment—four of the defendants were acquitted, while the remaining five were eventually pardoned.[79] No love was lost, however, between the CPUSA and the NAACP, which continued to look upon the American communists with utter distrust.

Toward the New Deal Coalition

Given that the NAACP had always looked to the federal government for enforcing black civil rights, the activism of the Roosevelt administration in fighting the depression was seen as an encouraging signal. Echoing the sweeping economic interventionism of the New Deal's first hundred days, the NAACP annual conference of 1933 demanded "that President Roosevelt exercise broad, executive, virtually dictatorial powers against those sections of the country which engage in lynching, peonage, disfranchisement and all forms of vicious discrimination and persecution."[80] This was not to happen, of course. In fact, the New Deal programs, especially in the South, were administered in a blatantly unfair and discriminatory manner, as the NAACP pointed out in numerous protests to the president. The introduction of minimum wages, for example, resulted in the laying off of black workers, while the crop reductions under the Agricultural Adjustment Act led to the eviction of black sharecroppers and tenants from the plantations. The social security bill of 1935 omitted agricultural and domestic workers, occupational domains of African-Americans. In many southern states, black youths were all but excluded from the Civilian Conservation Corps. Formal rules of nondiscrimination notwithstanding, the Roosevelt administration had no intention of jeopardizing its political agenda by raising the race issue. Appropriately, the NAACP made "Oppression of the Negro under the New Deal" the theme of its 1935 annual conference.[81]

Nevertheless, Roosevelt and the New Deal became increasingly popular among African-Americans, and in 1936 black voters supported FDR and his party in record numbers. There were several reasons for this remarkable shift in political allegiance. To begin with, some of the prominent New Dealers, particularly Secretary of the Interior Harold Ickes, who happened to be a former president of the Chicago NAACP, were working hard to include African-Americans in the federal relief programs, despite the prevailing patterns of discrimination on the local level. Among other things, Ickes insisted that a fixed percentage of blacks were hired in the projects of the Public Works Administration. Moreover, in spite of its reluctance to address civil rights issues, the Roosevelt administration let it be known that blacks were welcome in the New Deal coalition. By the standards of the time, the number and ranks of FDR's black appointments counted for much more than tokenism, even if the famed Black Cabinet was merely an informal group of black officials with relatively little influence. Among others, NAACP lawyer William Hastie was appointed as the first African-American federal judge, William Houston as assistant attorney general, and Mary McLeod Bethune as a divisional head of the National Youth Administration. More than a hundred blacks served as administrators in governmental departments and New Deal agencies.[82]

Most importantly, for all its racial inequities the New Deal paid more attention to African-Americans than they were accustomed to from any previous administration. Despite widespread segregation and discrimination, the New Deal programs made an economic and a symbolic difference in the lives of millions of blacks, who began to view the federal government as a potential ally. In 1938, for example, the Works Progress Administration was flooded with letters from southern blacks after a circular letter from the agency had assured its 2.5 million workers that they had the right to vote for any party or candidate they chose. What was meant to counteract Republican charges that the WPA jobs were buying votes for the Democratic Party was understood by many blacks as a promise that the federal government would protect their suffrage. As one respondent wrote to WPA director Harry Hopkins: "I want to serve notic on you that I am in a Country where they don't alie colored folks to go to the pole and cast their battle an if they are alying colored people to vote in Mississippi this year please write me at once please so I will be ready when the time come."[83] To be sure, the time for voting would not come to black Mississippians for almost three decades, but the fact that barely literate black workers from the Deep South directly appealed to the head of a federal agency illustrates how the New Deal affected the political awareness of many ordinary African-Americans.

Those blacks who could vote in the 1930s were increasingly willing to cast their ballots for the New Deal Democrats and their popular presidential leader. And given that most observers expected a close race for the 1936 presidential elections, their votes might actually have a crucial impact. Citing opinion polls by the *Literary Digest,* Walter White claimed that black voters would hold the balance of power in seventeen pivotal states, with a total of 281 electoral votes.[84] As usual, the NAACP confronted the parties with its demands for a meaningful platform, including support for a federal antilynching bill, the protection of black voting rights, and an end to racial discrimination in the administration of federal relief. As usual, neither the Republicans nor the Democrats made any substantial commitment to black interests in their electoral programs. But the Democratic convention at least displayed signs of a new spirit by seating black delegates for the first time and by featuring a black pastor to say the opening prayer at one session, prompting an angry walkout of South Carolina senator "Cotton Ed" Smith. Black congressman Arthur Mitchell from Chicago, who had defeated Republican Oscar DePriest two years earlier, was the first black speaker from the Democratic convention floor in the party's history. Moreover, compared to Roosevelt's arresting personality, the Republican candidate, Kansas governor Alf Landon, appeared aloof and uninspiring. For the first time, the majority of the black press endorsed the Democratic contender.[85]

Nonpartisanship notwithstanding, the NAACP also sided with FDR short of a formal endorsement. While he attacked Landon for his vague statements on civil rights and his states' rights rhetoric, Walter White repudiated the use of NAACP signs by picketers of the Democratic National Headquarter who had protested against the party's silence on lynching.[86] In October 1936, NAACP president Joel Spingarn, a lifelong Republican, publicly endorsed FDR and went on a speaking tour before black audiences in several mid-western cities. Protests by Republican NAACP members were dismissed with the disingenuous rebuttal that Spingarn was speaking as an individual and not as the head of the NAACP. After all, Spingarn based his support for Roosevelt solely on the president's attitude toward black people and saluted him as a "sincere friend and well-wisher of the American Negro."[87] Since the vast majority of black voters was hardly familiar with the subtleties of the association's principles of nonpartisanship, they very likely understood Spingarn's words as an official endorsement by the NAACP.

In 1932, FDR's support among African-American voters had trailed be-hind his national average. Four years later, his showing in most predomi-nantly black electoral districts even exceeded his sensational popular vote of more than 60 percent; in Harlem the president received 81 percent! In all of American political history, no comparably significant and visible group of voters had ever changed its voting behavior so dramatically. The blind alle-giance to the GOP that the NAACP had castigated for so many years as a major reason for black political impotence had been impressively laid to rest. Walter White could not resist to bid farewell to a retired Republican congress-man with a triumphant "I told you so!"[88] Of course, Roosevelt's landslide left no room for claiming a crucial role of black ballots in his reelection, but their potential future importance for the Democratic electoral coalition could no longer be overlooked.

While the NAACP leadership celebrated FDR's victory, it also had second thoughts about whether the swing toward the Democrats had perhaps gone too far. In his post-election assessment, Walter White frankly admitted that "the NAACP would have been happier had the results been more close as the efforts for fair play of a minority group are always more effective when there is greater balance between political parties." The secretary warned the Demo-cratic Party not to consider blacks as their "chattel" and predicted that they would desert the party if it did not meet their expectations. Roosevelt's over-whelming triumph, White reasoned, had liberated the president from the control by the southern racist wing of his party and obliged him to pursue a determined civil rights policy.[89]

Yet the power of the Solid South was far from broken. Although the New Deal never directly challenged white supremacy and segregation, many southern conservatives became more and more suspicious of the federal government's design for liberal economic and social reform, which threatened the region's traditional power structure. When FDR tried to oust his leading southern opponents in the 1938 senatorial primaries, he suffered a stinging setback. The Solid South also held firm in filibustering against the federal antilynching bills, for which the NAACP unsuccessfully continued to lobby in the late 1930s. Still, the almost unanimous support for the antilynching bills from northern Democrats and labor leaders documented that the association was now firmly integrated into a liberal reform coalition based on civil rights and economic interventionism by the federal government.[90] Although FDR's second term did not bring any substantial progress on civil rights issues and the New Deal drew to a close in the face of mounting international tensions, black voters kept their faith with Roosevelt. According to a Gallup poll of February 1940, the president's approval rate among black voters was over 80 percent, as opposed to 63 percent among the general electorate. In his unprecedented bid for a third term, Roosevelt lost an overall 6 percentage points compared to 1936 but gained votes in many predominantly black districts. Even black Chicago, a longtime GOP stronghold, went for the Democrat. Obviously, FDR had replaced Abraham Lincoln as the political hero of black voters.[91]

It is difficult to gauge which part the NAACP played in the political sea change among the African-American electorate in the 1930s. If civil rights, as the association kept on preaching, was the key measure for black voters to distinguish between "friends" and "enemies," their enthusiastic embrace of Roosevelt and the New Deal remains a riddle, given that racial reform was never an official part of the federal government's agenda. Historian Nancy Weiss has argued, however, that black voters were primarily motivated by economic considerations, to which FDR's charisma gave the necessary emotional boost. The rhetoric of civil rights leaders did not accurately reflect the perception of ordinary African-Americans, who tended to accept racial discrimination as a fact of life but gratefully appreciated any relief that trickled down to them under the New Deal. In focusing on the bread and butter issues, blacks, according to Weiss, simply "behaved like most poor people in the United States."[92]

This discrepancy between civil rights rhetoric and the more immediate concerns of black Americans is also clearly discernible in the NAACP's efforts at political education. Although the association claimed to be the political mouthpiece of all African-Americans, its rational choice ideal of the "intelligent" black voter had an obvious elite bias. The advice to vote for "men and measures" rather than for party labels made good sense, but distinguishing between "friends" and "enemies" was never easy when few measures that addressed the special grievances of the black minority made it onto the political agenda at all. Apart from the fact that the association did not necessarily reach the so-called black masses of the large industrial cities, its recommendations were not always very clear. What should motivate ordinary black people to register and vote, if the educated NAACP leaders kept on telling them that the differences between the parties were marginal and that blacks only faced the unpleasant alternative between "the Democratic devil and the Republican deep sea"?[93] This lack of meaningful choices, and not so much their lack of political education, was the real predicament of black voters, or as political scientists Steven Rosenstone and John Hansen put it: "People participate not because of who they are but because of the choices and incentives they have."[94] When black voters perceived Franklin Roosevelt and the New Deal as a political alternative that promised to improve their economic situation, they responded with enthusiasm.

The NAACP, of course, did not have the power to change the structure of the American party system, nor could it really substitute for the parties in the task of mobilizing black voters. Nevertheless, as its campaigns against the opponents of the Dyer bill and the pro-Parker senators demonstrated, the association and its branches were able to play an important part in politicizing the black population, if the issues were clear-cut and spoke directly to black interests. Through its continuous lobbying and propaganda efforts, the NAACP acquired a reputation as the leading civil rights organization in the United States whose word carried weight among the black electorate. As long as the number of black voters remained relatively small, however, its political influence remained quite limited. The northern migration of southern blacks increased black political strength in the big industrial cities, but it did not lead to sweeping changes. In 1921, Du Bois had predicted that the states of Missouri, New York, Pennsylvania, and Illinois would elect black candidates to the U.S. Congress within the next four years.[95] As a matter of fact, Chicago sent the first black man to the House of Representatives in 1928, but no other African-American congressman was elected until 1945. Most importantly, on the eve of America's entry into the Second World War, more than three-fourths of all African-Americans continued to live in the South. Their reenfranchisement remained the most formidable task in the struggle for black political power. As southern blacks faced a multitude of legal barriers to political participation, the NAACP looked to the courts for redress.

Chasing the Rainbow?

Black Voting Rights in the Courts

Much of the prestige the NAACP enjoyed among African-American was predicated upon its legal battles against racial discrimination, most conspicuously those before the U.S. Supreme Court. While the association's lawsuits involved fundamental constitutional principles and created important precedents, they did not necessarily affect the lives of many black people. Nor did they, for that matter, seem to change the racial attitudes and prejudices of whites very much. Not surprisingly, the wisdom of making legal action a mainstay of the NAACP strategy never went unchallenged by its critics. Even W.E.B. Du Bois, who had long placed great hopes in this approach, finally concluded that the quarter-century campaign against segregation had yielded little more than "fictions of law and administration" when he made his plea for voluntary separation in 1934. In an article published in the *Journal of Negro Education* a year later, the young radical sociologist Ralph Bunche, soon to become a paragon of the liberal black establishment, chided the NAACP for its failure to realize that, occasional victories notwithstanding, the courts would always represent "the political and economic ideology of the dominant group."[1]

Such criticism was not confined to the field of public segregation, but also extended to the efforts of the association to enforce black voting rights in the courts. What exhausted the patience of many NAACP members and other political activists more than anything else was the frustrating experience that favorable court rulings did not actually clear the way to the ballot box, because the guardians of white supremacy simply devised new legal barriers. After the Texas legislature had passed a new election law in 1927 to nullify a recent U.S. Supreme Court decision against the state's white primary, an African-American lawyer from Galveston, Texas, raised a set of critical question: "How long will black men continue to be the sport of cunning legislatures and political committees? Are we chasing the rainbow? If favorable decisions be secured in such contests, are we not immediately confronted with some law or rule similar in effect and necessitating our return to a court process? Have you stopped to consider that such a course is apparently without end?"[2]

In his book *The Hollow Hope*, which is based on case studies on black civil rights, abortion, congressional representation, environmental politics, and criminal justice, political scientist Gerald Rosenberg has systematically investigated the role of the judiciary in bringing about social and political change in the United States. His conclusions are fairly sobering indeed. Rather than initiating broad-based social change, the courts merely reflect and ratify those changes that have already been wrought by social movements, according to Rosenberg. Given the high costs of legal action and the largely symbolic nature of court victories, devoting scarce resources to lawsuits may even be counterproductive. Favorable court rulings can easily create a false sense of complacency among the movement's rank and file, while the opponents of reform are often galvanized by legal defeats, as happened in the wake of the Supreme Court's 1954 *Brown* decision.[3] As far as the correlation between court rulings and black voting rights is concerned, Rosenberg finds little evidence for any positive impact. Although the Supreme Court almost consistently struck down discriminatory electoral rules, these decisions did not result in a significant increase in the number of registered black voters, whereas such a correlation is much more plausible for congressional and executive action during the 1960s.[4]

Was the NAACP thus chasing the rainbow when it tried to secure black suffrage in the courts? Would it have made more sense to attack the political system of white supremacy with a different strategy? For example, the lawyer from Galveston, quoted above, suggested that rather than spend large amounts of money on a futile legal contest with the Democratic Party over its primary rules, the NAACP should try to find and support "some ambitious and popular white man" willing to challenge the Democratic nominee in the general elections. Rosenberg, for his part, argues that nonviolent direct action, as practiced by the civil rights movement since the late 1950s, was much more effective than the NAACP's tedious and elusive legal strategies.[5]

Rosenberg's propositions have not gone unchallenged, however, particularly because they tend to neglect the indirect windfalls of litigation, regardless of its immediate results. In examining the Supreme Court's decisions on racial discrimination in criminal cases prior to 1950, legal historian Michael Klarman has concluded that these rulings, for all their self-serving rhetoric, "had virtually no impact" on the southern criminal justice system, which continued to exclude blacks from jury service, browbeat African-Americans defendants into confessions, and frame them in sham trials. Still, Klarman argues that, even if unsuccessful, litigation played an important role in educating blacks about their rights, in mobilizing local communities, and in creating publicity among northern audiences. Moreover, Klarman holds that criminal justice, very much like school desegregation, represented the hard core of white supremacist concerns. In these matters the enforcement of Supreme Court rulings was much harder than in voting rights cases. The latter, Klarman believes, had a more direct and far-reaching impact on the struggle for civil rights.[6] Indeed, the argument that going to court did not yield the results for which the plaintiffs or the black community had hoped does not prove that alternative strategies would have been more successful. The strategic options of reform movements are not a matter of deliberate choices but depend on a number of determinants, including their organizational resources, the political opportunity structure, and the strength of opposing forces. As the previous chapter has demonstrated, black voters had precious little clout with parties and candidates during the first half of the twentieth century, even in the North. In most of the South, where politics was imbued with racial demagoguery, it was virtually inconceivable that any "ambitious and popular white man" would openly appeal to black voters, if any were allowed to vote at all, let alone come out for black rights. On the contrary, even where two-party competition persisted, the Republicans also posed as a "white man's party."[7] As to the feasibility of nonviolent direct action, Rosenberg's argument may be convincing for the 1960s, but seems quite anachronistic for the 1920s and 1930s.

Since the road to political mass mobilization was closed in the South and open protest or revolt appeared suicidal, resorting to the legal system made perfect sense from the perspective of the NAACP. The existence of written constitutional rights and of a judiciary that, for all its racial bias, was bound by procedural rules and professional ethics opened up a much-needed stage for articulating grievances and obtaining at least a modicum of redress. Perhaps most importantly, the instrument of judicial review by the U.S. Supreme Court put limits on the arbitrariness of state legislation. After all, by casting the disfranchisement of African-Americans into the form of law, southern white supremacists had responded to the need to retain at least a semblance of legality. Legal action, to be sure, could not do away with the political, social, economic, and cultural underpinnings of racism, but it might help to strip racial discrimination of both legality and legitimacy. This was a formidable task all by itself.

The Burdens of Legal Action

At its third annual conference in March 1911, the NAACP committed itself "to secure proper legal aid to maintain and defend the colored man's rights."[8] A year earlier the association had taken up the case of Pink Franklin, a black farm laborer from South Carolina who had shot and killed a police officer in self-defense and had been sentenced to death. However, finding no flaw with the trial, the Supreme Court on appeal affirmed the decision of the state courts. The NAACP nevertheless was able to save Franklin's life because Oswald Garrison Villard used his personal channels to President Taft to persuade the governor of South Carolina to commute the sentence to life imprisonment. Several other criminal cases followed. To avoid spreading its limited resources thin, the association defined two criteria for entering a case: First, it had to be a clear-cut case of racial discrimination, and second, it had to involve a fundamental right of citizenship offering the potential of setting a precedent.[9]

Over the following years, the NAACP's aid to black defendants in criminal cases yielded both important legal decisions and publicity. In 1923, the U.S. Supreme Court in *Moore v. Dempsey* struck down the death sentences against six blacks from Arkansas, ruling that a trial that was dominated by a mob violated the due process clause of the Fourteenth Amendment. The men had been convicted for murder after an attempt to form a black sharecropper's union in 1919 had triggered a race riot that left up to two hundred blacks and five whites dead. The NAACP not only succeeded in saving the lives of all the defendants, but the decision also led to a closer scrutiny of state criminal trials by the Supreme Court.[10] Another highly publicized NAACP criminal case was the murder trial against Dr. Ossian Sweet and his brother, Henry, held in Detroit in 1925 and 1926. Dr. Sweet, a well-to-do black physician, had defended his newly bought home in a white neighborhood against a mob. One of the attackers was killed, though it was unclear who had fired the fatal shot. The NAACP persuaded Clarence Darrow, one of the country's most prominent trial lawyers, to represent the Sweet brothers. The first trial produced a hung jury and the second ended with a verdict of not guilty.[11]

In comparison to racial discrimination in murder cases in which nothing less than the defendant's life was at stake, disfranchisement constituted a much lesser personal evil. In voting rights cases, the NAACP's objective was not individual redress but decisions that promised to undermine the political system of white supremacy. Unfortunately, the U.S. Supreme Court, in a series of decisions handed down around the turn of the century, had given its blessings to the most important institutional pillars of racial disfranchisement. In 1897, the year after it had legally sanctioned racial segregation in *Plessy v. Ferguson*, the Court ruled in *Williams v. Mississippi* that the literacy test required by Mississippi registration laws did not violate either the Fourteenth or the Fifteenth Amendments to the federal Constitution because it did not explicitly discriminate by race. A few years later, the Supreme Court, in one of its most formalistic decisions ever, made clear that it had no intention of protecting the voting rights of blacks. An African-American plaintiff from Alabama who had sought an order to add his name to the registration rolls of his home state was confronted with a mind-boggling example of "Catch-22" logic: If the voter list of Alabama had been drawn up in violation of the Constitution, as alleged by the plaintiff, the Court could not become complicit in this unconstitutional action by adding another name![12]

In 1915, however, this legalistic stonewall was breached for the first time when the NAACP joined the suit of the U.S. government against the Oklahoma grandfather clause. This 1910 amendment to the state constitution exempted all persons who had been eligible voters on January 1, 1866, and their lineal male descendants from the newly introduced literacy test, thus making the clause into a loophole for illiterate whites. In *Guinn v. United States,* the Supreme Court unanimously rejected this rather crude instrument as unconstitutional on its face, since its only purpose was to nullify the Fifteenth Amendment. The Court's willingness to look behind the facade of ostensibly color-blind language has earned *Guinn* the reputation as "the first really modern voting rights decision," yet its practical impact was almost zero.[13]

To begin with, the decision did not enfranchise a single black voter, but only made it more difficult for illiterate whites to register. Moreover, the Court said nothing about the constitutionality of the Oklahoma literacy test, leaving the main obstacle to black registration firmly in place. In one respect, *Guinn* even dealt a blow to the enforcement of African-American voting rights. The decision explicitly stated that registrars who had applied the literacy test and the grandfather clause to the disadvantage of black registrants could only be prosecuted on proof of criminal intent. Because this was nearly impossible, the federal government, citing *Guinn* as a precedent, would decline to bring suits against state registrars under federal law for a long time to come.[14]

Guinn was not an original NAACP case, but instead had been brought by the Taft administration to show some token concern for black Republicans. The association's president, Moorfield Storey, filed a concise amicus curiae brief that called for scrutinizing the purpose and effect of the grandfather clause, but this brief was hardly decisive for the outcome. Perhaps Storey's prestige lent additional weight to a strong case against a preposterous law that was ridiculed even by its framers.[15] Understandably, the fledgling NAACP tried to make the most of its role in Supreme Court cases that yielded rulings considered favorable to black civil rights. At a closer look, however, it becomes clear that these "victories" were indeed hollow, as they were inconsequential both in practical and in legal terms.

Another such celebrated "victory" was the decision in *Buchanan v. Warley*, rendered by the Supreme Court in 1917 after the NAACP had brought a suit against a Louisville, Kentucky, ordinance mandating the racial segregation of the city's residential areas. The Court unanimously invalidated the ordinance as contrary to "the right of the individual to acquire, enjoy and dispose of his property" guaranteed under the Fourteenth Amendment, but the opinion was clearly driven by the concern for the rights of white property owners. Moreover, the purpose of residential segregation could also be achieved by so-called restrictive covenants, private agreements among developers or white neighborhood organizations not to sell or rent to African-Americans and other "undesirables." It was only in 1948 that the Supreme Court held such covenants unenforceable by law. The de facto racial segregation of urban residential areas in the United States, however, largely persists to date.[16]

To be sure, most of the association's cases never made it to the U.S. Supreme Court. The bulk of the legal work, as it is reflected in the NAACP records, was made up by numerous routine cases on the local level that did not produce much publicity or tangible results.[17] Typically, the victims of disfranchisement first approached the local NAACP branches, which then informed the national secretariat, where the association's legal staff gave a tentative evaluation. If litigation appeared promising, the national office would provide financial assistance and legal advice. Information and affidavits were collected, which then were sent to the U.S. Department of Justice with the demand for an official investigation. The NAACP also tried to exert pressure on local and state authorities, albeit with little response. For want of time, staff, and money, the national office could become involved in local suits only in exceptional cases, such as the campaign against the Texas white primary. In most cases, advice was given to contact a "capable local attorney."[18]

Three factors, in particular, determined the national secretariat's response to local calls for help: costs, risks, and the degree of local support. In 1919, for example, the NAACP branch president of Greenwood, South Carolina, reported on the serious beatings blacks had received upon their attempt to register, and pleaded with the national office to send a representative who would investigate the facts and initiate a lawsuit. The secretariat declined, however, because it had no funds to spare. The local branch was too intimidated to act on its own.[19] If the danger to the life and limb of would-be plaintiffs appeared too high, the NAACP counseled against legal action, as in the case of one Mississippi black who was told: "The experience of the association has shown that in some instances it has not only been futile but dangerous for individuals to enforce their right to vote in some southern communities. The temper of the community, the number of colored and white in the community, as well as the probability of vindictive action on the part of whites . . . should be considered before any legal step should be taken."[20]

For reasons of both safety and funding, lawsuits needed to have the support of the larger black community. Initiating legal action also provided the NAACP with an opportunity to expand its organizational base. In 1918, African-Americans from Waco, Texas, who had been prohibited from voting in the Democratic primary approached the national office with a plea for help. The New York headquarter informed them that the first step should be to form a local NAACP branch and to contact the five branches that already existed in the state. In addition, the other Texas branches were called upon to begin a joint statewide legal campaign against the white primary under the leadership of the Houston branch, which already had acquired some experience in this field. Incidentally, not only was an NAACP branch formed in Waco, but the lawsuit also succeeded in obtaining an injunction against the city's Democratic executive committee to allow black voters in the party's primary.[21] The struggle against the Texas white primary, however, had only just begun.

Elsewhere enthusiasm was more limited. The NAACP branch of Little Rock, Arkansas, also fought the white primary in the courts but had serious difficulties raising the necessary funds, although the local black community was relatively well-to-do. One reason for this lack of interest was that many blacks considered themselves to be Republicans and saw no point in voting in the Democratic primary. The national office did not conceal its disappointment with such a narrow view. The association had spent, with one exception, more money in Arkansas than in any other state, Walter White replied to the Little Rock branch's request for additional funds: "Yet the Negroes of Arkansas have given very little towards the work of the N.A.A.C.P. Our assistance in worthwhile cases is, of course, not conditioned upon contributions but . . . it is not fair to other states who have by their contributions enabled the association to continue in existence that we should give a disproportionate amount in cases in states where little has been done to help the association carry on its work." White sent a check for fifty dollars with an instruction for the branch to raise their own matching funds. Moreover, the NAACP felt that it should concentrate its resources on the campaign against the white primary in Texas, where the struggle had been most successful. Branches in other states could build on these precedents but had to bring and finance their own suits.[22]

In its tireless quest for money, the NAACP had established contacts with the American Fund for Public Service, financed by Charles Garland, a young, rich, and altruistic heir who had dedicated himself to advancing the rights of the working class and minorities. In early 1930, the association applied for a grant of $300,000 to finance large-scale litigation to secure "equal rights in the public schools, in the voting booths, on the railroads, and on juries." Although the proposal was couched in radical terms, claiming that such a campaign would be instrumental in raising the political consciousness of the black masses and in revolutionizing the economic order of the South, the representatives of the Garland Fund were highly critical of the NAACP's legalistic approach. Nevertheless, the Fund approved a grant of $100,000, of which only $20,000 was eventually paid, however, due to the financial problems it experienced in the Great Depression. The NAACP used the money to hire Nathan Margold, a young, white graduate of Harvard Law School, to devise a strategy for the planned litigation campaign. Margold's report, delivered in early 1931, focused on segregation in education and laid the groundwork for the ensuing campaign to desegregate universities and public schools but paid no attention to voting rights.[23] There is also no evidence that any of the Garland money was used to finance voting rights litigation.

The financial burden of going to court was somewhat eased by the fact that the NAACP leadership included prominent white lawyers, such as Moorfield Storey and Arthur Spingarn, who rendered their services pro bono or at a much reduced rate. Other famous lawyers, including Louis Marshall, Clarence Darrow, and Felix Frankfurter, sat on the association's legal committee or argued important cases that added to both the NAACP's efficacy and prestige. Black lawyers, in contrast, were few and far between. By 1910, less than 1 percent of all lawyers in America were black. In the Deep South, the handful of African-Americans with legal training faced great difficulties in getting admitted to the bar. As a result of racial discrimination in legal education, black lawyers were frequently lacking competence and experience, and in addition faced hostility from white juries and judges. The widespread belief among black people that they needed a white lawyer in order to stand a chance in court was all too often justified.[24]

Even the white lawyers working for the NAACP were not always first rate. A good example is Fred Knollenberg, the attorney who represented the NAACP branch of El Paso, Texas, in its litigation against the white primary. Knollenberg was a well-meaning man who enjoyed the confidence of his black clients but committed several serious professional blunders, prompting Arthur Spingarn to complain about the "unfortunate fact that in choosing a lawyer in a southern state to undertake causes as unpopular as ours, we have not the same freedom of selection that we should like." In all fairness, it must be added that it took a great deal of courage for white lawyers in the South to represent African-Americans in civil rights cases. A Florida lawyer who had advised blacks on their voting rights before the 1920 elections, for example, received a threat from the Ku Klux Klan that anybody who interfered with white supremacy "must face the consequences."[25]

Fighting the White Primary

The centerpiece of the NAACP's voting rights litigation was, of course, the fight against the white primary. All other disfranchising devices amounted to "nothing," Du Bois wrote in 1925, compared to the effect of the Democratic primary elections in the South.[26] Indeed, from the viewpoint of white supremacists, the white primary represented a panacea. It allowed for disfranchising all blacks and no whites at all, and without the legal complications or hypocrisy that were involved in literacy tests or grandfather clauses. Ironically, primary elections were introduced throughout the United States in the early twentieth century in order to democratize the electoral process by curtailing the power of bosses and party machines. But while most states regulated their primaries by law, the southern states left the conduct of primaries almost entirely to the party organizations.[27] Since parties were considered to be private associations not bound by the Fifteenth Amendment, they were presumed to be perfectly at liberty to limit participation in their primaries to eligible white voters. As long as this constitutional doctrine was generally accepted, the white primary was virtually unassailable.

Of course, the alleged "private" status of parties was a mere subterfuge to disguise the fact that the states, by giving party organizations a free hand, deliberately disregarded the Fifteenth Amendment. In reality, the Democratic Party had established a quasi-monopoly after the Republicans had abandoned the South. The only election that really mattered was the Democratic primary. The subsequent general elections, in which few voters cared to cast their ballots, merely served to ratify its results. For all practical purposes, the Democratic nomination was tantamount to election. Even though most blacks saw themselves as Republicans and were understandably disgusted with a party devoted to white supremacy, they had no choice but to seek a vote in the Democratic primary as the only meaningful channel of political participation. It fell upon the NAACP to persuade the U.S. Supreme Court that the southern Democratic primaries were not a private affair but an integral—in fact the crucial—part of the electoral process covered by the protections of the Constitution.

There were two major reasons why the legal campaign against the white primary unfolded in Texas. First, the state had a relatively prosperous and politically conscious black middle class that was concentrated in the cities of eastern and southern Texas. As early as 1918, there were five NAACP branches in Houston, Beaumont, El Paso, Fort Worth, and San Antonio, with a combined membership of more than twenty-five hundred.[28] Second, the race issue did not hold Texas politics in the same iron grip as the rest of the South. With 18 percent of the total population being African-American, the Lone Star State had the lowest percentage of blacks among all former Confederate states. In only eight of the state's 217 counties were African-Americans in the majority. Although the representatives of the white oligarchy of eastern Texas, where most blacks lived, had long since called for eliminating blacks from voting, the state did not introduce a poll tax before 1902. Three years later, the party committees of the Texan counties were authorized to set the qualifications for voting in their primaries, but in many counties blacks continued to cast their ballots in the Democratic primary.[29]

However, the wave of racism and nativism that swept America around the First World War also reached Texas and made the Ku Klux Klan a viable force in state politics. As a result, the Texas legislature passed a law in May 1923 that gave all eligible voters who took an oath as Democrats the right to vote in the Democratic primary, with one explicit exception: "[I]n no event shall a negro be eligible to participate in a Democratic Party primary election held in the State of Texas and should a negro vote in a Democratic primary election such ballot shall be void and election officials are herein directed to throw out such ballot and not count the same."[30] This made Texas the only state to mandate the white primary by law—a peculiarity that virtually invited a constitutional test case.

The lawsuit was brought by the NAACP national office in close coordination with the local branch in El Paso. The city, located in the western corner of the state, hosted a small black community that had not experienced any voting discrimination so far. In the Democratic primaries of 1924, however, black voters were refused, pursuant to the new law. In response, Dr. Lawrence A. Nixon, a black physician who was relatively immune to economic reprisals, volunteered to be the plaintiff in a legal challenge and sued the election officials for damages. In late 1924, Nixon's case was dismissed by the Federal District Court for the Western District of Texas; it was accepted for review by the U.S. Supreme Court a year later. Confident about the prospects of the case, the board of directors had decided that the NAACP's foremost legal experts, including Storey, Arthur Spingarn, and Louis Marshall, should take charge, while the secretariat announced "the opening of a general attack upon disfranchisement of colored people in the South." In *The Crisis*, Du Bois augured that "a favorable decision will mean the elimination of the white primary not only in Texas but throughout the South" and called for financial contributions. Other black editors joined in this optimism.[31]

Nixon v. Herndon was argued before the Supreme Court in January 1927. The NAACP brief contended that the Texas Democratic primary was a public election under the Constitution and the laws of the state and that the legal exclusion of African-Americans violated both the Fourteenth and Fifteenth Amendments. Predictably, the Texas authorities insisted on the "private" character of nominating primaries that were no election but a "purely political matter" over which the courts had no jurisdiction.[32] Thus the fundamental issues and conflicting arguments relating to the constitutional status of the white primary were plainly before the Court. However, in its decision, rendered in March 1927, the Supreme Court dodged the key issue of whether primaries were public elections protected by the Fifteenth Amendment. Instead, the ruling focused on the flagrant denial of equal protection of the laws by the state of Texas. As Justice Oliver Wendell Holmes declared for a unanimous Court: "We find it unnecessary to consider the Fifteenth Amendment, because it seems to us hard to imagine a more direct and obvious infringement of the Fourteenth. . . . States may do a good deal of classifying that is difficult to believe rational, but there are limits, and it is too clear for extended argument that color cannot be made the basis of a statutory classification affecting the right set up in this case."[33]

Such harsh language, however, could easily obscure the very limited scope of the *Herndon* ruling. In striking down the 1923 Texas primary law, the Supreme Court merely reprimanded the state for legally barring its black citizens from a political activity to which all white citizens were explicitly entitled. This was almost a textbook violation of the equal protection clause that could not possibly stand scrutiny, even if the Supreme Court had agreed with the state of Texas that primaries were a purely private matter. Incidentally, the state law belied the alleged autonomy of parties since the exclusion of blacks was clearly predicated upon state action. In short, *Nixon v. Herndon* did not nullify the white primary as such but only its legal enforcement by the state.

Even commentators in the white southern press conceded the inconsistencies of the Texan argument. A South Carolina newspaper opined that the decision had been an "invited slap" and wondered "how Texas got away with its foolish, faulty, unconstitutional election law so long as it did." Fortunately, the editorial assured the reader, the ruling had no impact on the rest of the

South, because the other states did not regulate their primary elections by law. Apparently, Texas governor Dan Moody had gotten the message, too, as he was quoted with the proposal that the legislature give "the party executive committee power to fix qualifications for primary voters." This procedure, he hoped, would not conflict with the Fourteenth Amendment.[34]

In contrast to the relatively calm reactions of the white South, the NAACP tried to make the most of its legal victory. Not only did the association declare the end of the white primary, Walter White even presaged the decline of corruption and plutocracy in American politics at large. Executive secretary James Weldon Johnson celebrated "the magnificent work" and idealism of the NAACP lawyers and of all members who had made this triumph possible. Fair enough, but Johnson, himself a trained lawyer, clearly overshot the mark when he claimed that in *Nixon v. Herndon* the Supreme Court had established "that the primaries are part of the general election system and, as such, subject to federal control." Although the NAACP experts knew better, this misinterpretation was repeated in the association's review of 1927.[35]

Despite its limited scope, *Nixon v. Herndon* encouraged black voters in other southern states to challenge the white primary, too. In Arkansas, Virginia, and Florida, NAACP branches participated in suits against state elections laws that left the parties free to set the qualifications for voting in their primaries. The results were mixed. In Arkansas, the state courts dismissed the case and the U.S. Supreme Court denied appeal. In Florida, the lower court upheld the state's primary laws, but the state supreme court, after four years of litigation, reversed the decision, citing *Nixon v. Herndon*. The Virginia case, which received considerable help from the NAACP's legal committee, was the most successful. Both the Federal District Court at Richmond and the U.S. Circuit Court of Appeals went beyond *Herndon* in their opinion and ruled that primaries were part of the electoral process. The Circuit Court even explicitly mentioned "a material right guaranteed under the Constitution . . . to participate in the selection of candidates to be voted for in the election." Much to the NAACP's disappointment, the Virginia Democrats did not appeal the decision to the Supreme Court. Blacks in the Old Dominion could now vote freely in the state's Democratic primary almost everywhere, but a cumulative poll tax of $1.50, payable six months prior to the general election and due for three preceding years, effectively depressed the black turnout.[36]

Texas, however, remained the crucial battleground in the legal fight against the white primary. Shortly after the defeat before the Supreme Court, the Texas legislature passed a new law to enable the executive committees of the parties to determine who could vote in their primaries. The Democratic executive committee immediately resolved that only "white Democrats" were entitled to participate. Before the primaries of 1928, several NAACP branches in Texas sued for court orders to restrain the Democratic Party from excluding black voters, but to no avail. After Dr. Nixon presented himself at the primary polls in El Paso and was refused a ballot, he again sued the Democratic election judges for damages, thus initiating the next Supreme Court decision to bear his name.[37]

Nixon's second case was dismissed by both the Federal District and Appeals Courts, and it took almost four years before it reached the U.S. Supreme Court. On the part of the NAACP, the litigation process was seriously impaired by the deaths of Moorfield Storey and Louis Marshall, who had been instrumental in the *Herndon* case. Other problems were caused by Fred Knollenberg, the white lawyer of the El Paso NAACP branch who was not always up to the job. As the association's legal experts were shocked to find out, Knollenberg's brief for the Supreme Court did not include a historical argument to demonstrate that primaries had been introduced to make politics more open and democratic and not to establish parties as private clubs. Nor had Knollenberg gathered the statistical evidence to show that nomination by the Texas Democratic Party was indeed tantamount to election.[38] After six years of litigation against the white primary, it was indeed mind-boggling that Knollenberg did not appreciate the importance of these issues.

Before the Supreme Court, the NAACP prudently argued closely along the lines of the *Herndon* decision. The new Texan primary law of 1927 had but one purpose, its lawyers maintained, namely "to evade and nullify" the Court's earlier ruling. According to the association's view, the new statute also violated the Fourteenth Amendment, because it authorized classification based on color and made the Democratic Party's executive committee an "agency of the state." In addition, the NAACP lawyers reiterated their opinion that primaries were also covered by the protections of the Fifteenth Amendment. Nevertheless, in *Nixon v. Condon* the Supreme Court again refused to rule on the latter claim and limited its opinion to the issue of state action. Speaking for a narrow majority of five to four, Justice Benjamin Cardozo reasoned that the power exercised by the executive committee in excluding blacks was not the power of the party as a voluntary association, but derived from a statute that made its action the action of state. In invalidating the Texas law, Cardozo reproached the Texas legislature for authorizing the wrong agency, since the power to speak for the party as a whole did not reside in the executive committee but only in the party's state convention. In his dissent, Justice James McReynolds refused to see the executive committee as a state agency. The law of 1927 had only attempted to restore the private status of the Texas Democratic Party that had existed before the 1923 law—a perfectly legitimate objective in his view.[39]

In its public pronouncements following the decision, the NAACP celebrated *Nixon v. Condon* as its "third decisive victory against the disfranchisement of colored Americans" after the rulings in *Guinn* and *Herndon*. Obviously, this was propaganda with little base in the decision itself. At a closer look, *Condon* amounted to a defeat in disguise. The Court not only distanced itself from all substantive arguments made by the NAACP on the constitutional status of primaries and based its opinion solely on a formal error by the Texas legislature, but by stressing the powers of the party conventions, the decision implicitly strengthened the concept of parties as voluntary associations and openly pointed to how the white primary could be secured in a constitutionally acceptable manner. Even this narrow ruling was only supported by the closest possible majority. Understandably, the NAACP congratulated itself that it had prevented the appointment of Judge John J. Parker to the Supreme Court two years earlier. The two justices who had joined the Court after the Parker fight had voted with the majority.[40]

In fact, the NAACP leaders knew well that *Condon* hardly represented a legal breakthrough. In his report on the reaction in Texas, Field Secretary William Pickens cautioned against the illusion that the fight was over. Texas authorities were already contemplating new ways to "rescue" the white primary. Pickens's assessment got straight to the heart of the matter: "[T]he colored voter will still be confronted with the problem of dealing with private individuals and party officials, who on their own initiative and unauthorized by any law, proceed to restrict the Negro's right to vote in parties and in primaries. . . . [T]echnically, this latest decision of the Supreme Court puts us back where we were before Texas legislated in the matter, but puts us back there with more light on the subject, and I trust more iron in our backbones."[41]

Pickens was perfectly right. The NAACP litigation had been a defensive action, in that it had tried to prevent a customary form of disfranchisement from receiving the sanction of the law. After nine years, this goal had been achieved. The state of Texas now knew that it was not permissible to legislate the white primary and gave up on its attempts, as Pickens correctly predicted. Instead the executive committee of the Texas Democratic Party immediately rescinded its resolution of 1928. A state convention was called, which resolved that "all white citizens" of Texas were eligible for membership in the party and participation in its primaries—a curious phrasing that did not even explicitly exclude African-Americans.[42]

All protests by black Democrats fell on deaf ears, and with a few exceptions the Texas Democratic primaries of 1932 remained for whites only. Especially in urban centers with sizeable black populations, such as Houston, Dallas, and San Antonio, African-American voters were uniformly rejected. In Houston, the home of a black newspaper editor who had been actively involved in fighting the white primary was torched. When Dr. Nixon tried to vote in the Democratic primary of El Paso, he was once again refused. As usual, his lawyer Fred Knollenberg filed suit.[43]

Setbacks and Stalemate

In the meantime, the continuation of the legal campaign against the white primary became more and more difficult, mainly because the Great Depression had plunged the NAACP into dire financial straits. Between 1931 and 1932 its income dropped from $59,000 to less than $46,000, with a deficit of almost $10,000. Although the costs of roughly $3,000 for each of the two white primary cases had not been excessive, the association was hardly able to raise the funds necessary to carry on. Citing three pay cuts for the NAACP staff in 1932, Walter White pledged a fee of $750 to Fred Knollenberg for the new Nixon case, half of what the attorney had asked for.[44] Surprisingly, Nixon won his case before the Federal District Court of Western Texas in early 1934 on the grounds that the party convention had not explicitly barred blacks from voting. When he presented himself at the next primary, he was permitted to vote, but his ballot was marked as "colored" so it could easily be thrown out.[45]

Although the NAACP had won two cases before the Supreme Court, the local voting activists in Texas had become increasingly disgruntled by what they saw as the elitist style of the association's legal experts. The core of the opposition was a group of black lawyers, journalists, and businessmen in Houston. While they did not question the wisdom of going to court, they resented the dominance of white jurists. When the oral argument before the Supreme Court was coming up in the *Condon* case, the group pressured the NAACP to include Jack Atkins, a black lawyer from Houston, as the representative of the local black community. The national office rejected the request in a rather condescending manner and made no secret of its displeasure with two amicus curiae briefs that the Houston group had filed without consultation. After *Condon*, the Houston group and the NAACP engaged in a petty and pointless controversy over who deserved credit for this "victory."[46]

The dissenters, for their part, were no longer willing to accept the leadership of the NAACP and began their own case to force a final decision on the constitutionality of the white primary. They got what they asked for, but the result was a disaster. In April 1935, the Supreme Court ruled in *Grovey v. Townsend* that the resolution of the Texas Democratic state convention restricting party membership to white citizens did not constitute state action and therefore violated neither the Fourteenth nor the Fifteenth Amendments. This time, the unanimous Court also gave a substantive opinion on the constitutional status of parties and primaries. The fact that Texas regulated its primary elections at all was a legitimate exercise of its police power and did not alter the character of parties as private associations. The factual political monopoly of the Democratic Party made no difference in any legal or constitutional respect. Equating the primaries with the general elections, the Court concluded, was "to confuse the privilege of membership in a party with the right to vote for one who is to hold a public office."[47]

Understandably, the decision came as shock to all civil rights activists. But much of this disappointment was due to the illusions over the "victories" in the *Herndon* and *Condon* cases. A careful reading of both decisions should have left no doubt about the high risks that were involved in pressuring the Supreme Court for a new ruling on the white primary. The NAACP was embittered that ten years of its own work had been voided by the hasty action of the Houston group. *Grovey*, Fred Knollenberg wrote in letter to Jack Atkins, who had finally had his day before the Supreme Court, "places us back to the point from which we started," but with the "additional handicap" of an adverse precedent. In the extremely unlikely case of a rehearing, Atkins should seek the cooperation of the NAACP attorneys who, Knollenberg added with a vengeance, "have a standing with the Court that we country lawyers do not have." In its public reaction, the NAACP insisted it had no responsibility for the defeat. To reverse the ruling, an entirely new case would have to be built under the leadership of the association.[48]

Clearly, this was not likely to happen anytime soon, since the principle of stare decisis would make the Supreme Court very reluctant to reconsider its *Grovey* opinion. It would be too simple, however, to blame the setback in the white primary fight exclusively on the impatience and professional deficiencies of the Houston group. It is true that some of their legal arguments were not very sophisticated. For example, the contention that the national Democratic convention had never decreed the exclusion of black voters from the party's primaries was entirely irrelevant to the question of whether or not Texas had violated the Constitution.[49] But the outcome of *Grovey* was not determined by the weakness of the written or oral arguments of the plaintiffs. Rather than being a digression from the two previous rulings, the decision followed the same logic, namely the distinction between state and private action. Neither in 1927 and 1932, respectively, when the NAACP had elaborately presented the argument, nor in 1935 was the Supreme Court prepared to accept the proposition that the southern Democratic primary was not a private affair, but an integral part of the electoral process.

Despite their defeat, the black NAACP critics from Texas maintained that the association had ignored the local black leadership for too long and bore a major responsibility for the division of forces in the primary fight. They also demanded that black lawyers be given a larger and more prominent role in the association's legal work.[50] In principle, the NAACP accepted the necessity to shift the responsibility to African-American jurists and accelerated its pertinent efforts, which had been under way for some time. By 1932, already half of the members of the legal committee were African-Americans. Two black Harvard graduates, William Hastie and Charles Houston, were diligently building a small, elite corps of black lawyers at the Howard University Law School. In 1935, Houston directed the first NAACP case before the Supreme Court that was handled exclusively by black lawyers—a successful challenge to a death sentence against a black man handed down by an all-white jury—and was subsequently appointed special counsel of the NAACP. Four years later, his famous disciple Thurgood Marshall, later to become the first black Supreme Court justice, succeeded Houston in this position, while William Hastie replaced Arthur Spingarn as chairman of the legal committee. Similar to the transition in the association's leadership at large, the transfer of responsibility from white to black lawyers happened without serious conflict or frictions.[51]

For the time being, however, the legal campaign against the white primary had come to a halt. Yet in 1939, the NAACP achieved another success in a voting rights case before the U.S. Supreme Court. The case went back to the old Oklahoma grandfather clause, which had exempted illiterate whites from the state's literacy test and which the association had hoped to have buried with *Guinn*. In response to *Guinn*, the Oklahoma legislature had passed a law in 1916 mandating that all eligible citizens had to register within a fixed twelve-day period or forever lose their suffrage. The law, however, exempted all voters who had voted in the general election of 1914, that is to say almost all whites, including those who had registered under the old grandfather clause struck down by the Supreme Court. The unmistakable purpose of this preposterous rule was to preserve the effects of the grandfather clause and to place a new burden on blacks by subjecting them to an extremely short period of registration that many of them, it was hoped, would miss, thus rendering them perpetually disfranchised.

Unfortunately, Robert Williams, the Oklahoma governor who had been the driving force behind the 1916 registration law, several years later became a federal district judge with jurisdiction in voting rights cases. Williams excelled at drawing out cases of racial disfranchisement without end by disallowing class action suits. In one instance, he ordered that each of about one thousand black petitioners who had been denied registration by the same county registrars all file separate suits and appear personally before the court. When in 1935 the NAACP entered a case against the 1916 law, it took a major effort to pressure Judge Williams to disqualify himself. His substitute, however, also ruled against the black plaintiff, as did the Federal Appeals Court.[52]

The case *Lane v. Wilson* was decided by the U.S. Supreme Court in May 1939, more than four years after the election for which the appellant had tried to register but had been rejected on the grounds that he had missed the twelve-day registration period of 1916. With a six-to-two majority, the Court reversed the lower courts, finding that the 1916 law stipulated different qualifications for black and white voters in much the same way as the old grandfather clause had done. There was no doubt that the law incorporated the grandfather clause, albeit in a slightly altered form. As Justice Felix Frankfurter emphatically proclaimed: "This Amendment [the Fifteenth] nullifies sophisticated as well as simple-minded modes of discrimination. It hits onerous procedural requirements which effectively handicap exercise of the franchise by the colored race although the abstract right to vote may remain unrestricted as to race."[53]

This sounded like a "modern" interpretation of the Constitution because the Court appeared to look at the practical effects of color-neutral language. But *Lane* was far from being consistent in this respect. While the Court rebuked the extremely short registration period of twelve days as a special burden on the black population, it did not discuss the even more questionable concept of disfranchising voters for life if they missed a one-time deadline or, for that matter, failed the literacy test once. After all, even adults may learn to read and write. In 1939, Frankfurter's much-quoted phrase was little more than a promise for the future. That this promise was made at all resulted from the appointment of four new Supreme Court justices in the wake of President's Roosevelt's notorious "court-packing" plan of 1937. In addition to Frankfurter, Justices Hugo Black, Stanley Reed, and William Douglas had joined the Court. All of the new members were much more favorably inclined toward black civil rights than their conservative predecessors. As a Harvard law professor, Felix Frankfurter had been a member of the NAACP legal committee and the mentor of Hastie and Houston. This did not mean, of course, that he always agreed with the constitutional views of the association's jurists.[54]

Like the *Guinn* decision of 1915, *Lane v. Wilson* did not represent a major breakthrough for African-American voting rights but merely voided an old and rather obscure state law. Nevertheless, the NAACP hailed the decision as a legal triumph and as the establishment of a "broader interpretation of the so-called Civil War amendments." *Lane,* the association proudly counted, was the twelfth victory the NAACP had won before the Supreme Court as opposed to one single defeat.[55] Four of these victories, namely *Guinn, Herndon, Condon,* and *Lane,* were related to racial disfranchisement. Yet what were the practical consequences of these rulings? Had it indeed become less difficult for African-Americans in the South to exercise their right to political participation? These were the questions the NAACP exultations conveniently avoided.

So far, with the exception of the grandfather clause, none of the legal instruments of racial disfranchisement had been eliminated. Poll taxes, literacy tests, and "understanding clauses," requiring registrants to give a "reasonable interpretation" of a section of the federal or state constitutions, were all firmly in place. In the early 1930s, a lawsuit of the New Orleans NAACP branch against the Louisiana understanding clause was dismissed by the state courts and denied a hearing by the Supreme Court. From the viewpoint of litigation strategy, the NAACP lawyers considered it extremely difficult to demonstrate both discriminatory intent and effect in the administration of literacy tests or understanding clauses.[56]

To be sure, there was some measure of success on the local level. After *Condon,* blacks were admitted to the Texas Democratic primary in some towns and counties. In Beaumont, they even helped to defeat a racist mayor. As mentioned above, the NAACP litigation finished the white primary in Virginia, although a stiff poll tax remained in effect. In 1936, the NAACP successfully pressured the U.S. Department of Justice to bring an indictment under federal law against a North Carolina registrar who had refused to register black voters for the general elections. Subsequently, the registrar was convicted and sentenced to a $300 fine, but the case was a rare exception. Sometimes taking legal action might also soften the resistance of southern electoral authorities. In Birmingham, Alabama, an unprecedented number of blacks were registered in 1939 after the local NAACP had filed suit in the state and federal courts.[57]

These were isolated achievements, however. As a general rule, the southern states were unimpressed by the threat of being sued. The state courts were solid pillars of white supremacy in the first place, and individual registrars did not have to worry about being convicted by all-white juries. Even if a case reached the Supreme Court and resulted in an adverse ruling for the state, there were ways and means to circumvent the decision, as the Oklahoma and Texas legislatures aptly demonstrated. After twenty-five years of litigation in voting rights cases by the NAACP, there was little hard evidence that the political system of white supremacy had been seriously shaken. By 1940, the number of registered black voters in the South did not exceed 5 percent of the black voting-age population, according to our best estimates—almost a negligible quantity.[58]

Smith v. Allwright

It took the NAACP awhile to recover from the blow *Grovey* had dealt to its litigation strategy against the white primary. For a new case to be built, the damaged relationship between the national office and the local black leadership of Texas needed to be mended and a new legal path had to be mapped out. For some time, the NAACP lawyers pondered the idea to exploit the fact that the Democratic primaries were paid for by tax money, but they found that the funding of primary elections was not uniformly regulated throughout the state. Moreover, in 1938 a new lawsuit by the Houston NAACP branch was dismissed by the Federal District Court with the judge explicitly citing *Grovey* as the governing precedent.[59]

There was no question, however, that the legal fight against the white primary would be carried on, with Texas as the main battleground. Branches in other states were advised to carefully watch the litigation in the Lone Star State. In 1941 the Houston branch, with the support of the national office, filed suit on behalf of a black man who had been refused a ballot at the recent Democratic primary. In their brief, the NAACP lawyers developed a substantive concept of the right to vote that included three steps, namely registration, the selection of candidates, and participation in the general elections. Exclusion from the primary elections therefore was a violation of the Constitution equal to the denial of registration or casting a ballot in the general elections.[60]

The crucial question was, of course, whether the Supreme Court would be more receptive to this theory than in the past. Surprisingly, in May 1941 the Court handed down a decision in a Louisiana case involving electoral fraud in a congressional primary that also had significant implications for the white primary. In *United States v. Classic,* the Court found that the U.S. Constitution in Article I, Sections 2 and 4, protected the right of eligible voters to cast their ballots and have them fairly counted in congressional elections, including the primaries, provided that state law had made the primary an "integral part of the election machinery" and that it was indeed tantamount to election. Although the opinion by Chief Justice Harlan Fisk Stone did not mention *Grovey* or the issue of racially exclusive primaries, *Classic* indicated that the Court was beginning to shift its position on the constitutional status of primaries at large. The three dissenters in the case only found fault with the criminal statute that authorized the federal government to prosecute electoral fraud. Even Justice Owen Roberts, the author of the *Grovey* decision, voted with the majority without voicing an opinion of his own. To Thurgood Marshall and his colleagues, the ruling appeared so important that they decided to drop their pending case in order to build a new one that resembled *Classic* as closely as possible. In particular, it had to involve primaries for federal office.[61]

The new case was filed on behalf of Dr. Lonnie Smith, a black dentist and NAACP member from Houston, and dismissed by the federal courts in 1942. Review was granted by the Supreme Court in the spring of 1943, and oral argument began at the end of that year. Smith was represented by Thurgood Marshall and William Hastie, while many sympathetic groups, including the American Civil Liberties Union, the National Lawyers' Guild, and the left-wing Workers Defense League, introduced amicus curiae briefs. The Justice Department, however, declined to support the case. Shortly before the decision was announced, the NAACP reminded the American people that the ruling would also affect the rights of hundreds of thousands of black soldiers who were currently defending democracy against totalitarianism.[62]

The hopes in the civil rights community were running high, and this time they would not be disappointed. On April 3, 1944, an eight-to-one majority of the Court in *Smith v. Allwright* declared the Texas white primary to be state action in violation of the Fifteenth Amendment and explicitly overruled *Grovey*. The lone dissent was registered by Justice Owen Roberts, who bitterly criticized his brethren for interpreting *Classic* as having been a sub silentio overrule of the opinion he had written only a few years earlier for a unanimous Court. This, he fumed, brought "adjudications of this tribunal into the same class as a restricted railroad ticket, good for this day and train only."[63]

Indeed, Roberts was perfectly right in observing that *Smith v. Allwright* was distinguished from *Grovey* only in the names of the parties. What had dramatically changed, however, was the composition of the Supreme Court and the historical context in which it had to make it decisions. Only two justices who had participated in *Grovey* were still sitting, namely Roberts himself and Chief Justice Harlan F. Stone, the author of *Classic*. All other seven members had been nominated after 1937 by President Roosevelt in an effort to break the conservative grip on the nation's highest court. And although it was not discussed in the deliberations of the Court nor explicitly mentioned in the decision, the fact that the United States was fighting a world war in the name of democracy certainly hovered in the background. Justice Felix Frankfurter had even wanted to state openly that *Allwright* was not predicated on new facts but on a different political viewpoint.[64]

Both in language and in substance, *Allwright* developed a realistic assessment of the function of the Democratic primary in the southern political system. But it went further and held the southern electoral practices to the evolving standards of national citizenship. "The United States is a constitutional democracy," Justice Stanley Reed affirmed. "Its organic law grants to all citizens a right to participate in the choice of elected officials without restriction of race. This grant to the people of the opportunity for choice is not to be nullified by a State through casting its electoral process in a form which permits a private organization to practice racial discrimination in the election. Constitutional rights would be of little value if they could be thus indirectly denied. . . . The privilege of membership in a party may be, as this Court said in *Grovey v. Townsend,* . . . no concern of a State. But when, as here, this privilege is also the essential qualification for voting in a primary to select nominees for a general election, the State makes the action of the party the action of the State."[65]

Basically, this was the constitutional theory the NAACP had advocated for more than twenty years. Everyone who had been involved in the white primary struggle felt joy and satisfaction. Thurgood Marshall, however, knew that the fight was far from over. The decision by the Supreme Court, he commented, restored the right of qualified blacks to vote in primary elections, but everything depended upon the willingness of state officials to follow in good faith. Since in the light of past experience this was not very likely, Marshall immediately called upon the Department of Justice to prosecute all state officials who continued to bar African-Americans from primary elections. But even though *Allwright* had clearly rendered such behavior illegal, the Justice Department persisted in its view that the requirement to prove criminal intent made convictions impossible to obtain. In fact, when black voters tried to vote in the Democratic primaries of Florida and Alabama in May 1944, they were rejected with the same contempt as before. The NAACP advised its branches to collect affidavits so that legal proceedings could be instigated.[66]

The reactions in the white South to *Smith v. Allwright* were mixed. The decision was criticized for its infringement on states' rights, but most critics did not anticipate dramatic changes. After all, the white primary had also survived *Herndon* and *Condon*. Some of the white "gradualists" even declared their support for the decision. Virginus Dabney, the editor of the *Richmond Times Dispatch,* reminded his readers that blacks had voted for some time in the Democratic primaries of Virginia and the "skies haven't fallen on the Old Dominion." The Supreme Court decision was "one more milestone on the way to fairness and justice for the Negro." The notorious race-baiters, on the other hand, indulged in their usual hyperbole. Admitting three hundred thousand blacks to vote in the Democratic primaries of South Carolina, the *Charleston News and Courier* warned, would make the state "uninhabitable to decent white people." It was much preferable to abolish primaries altogether and to restore the nomination of candidates to the party conventions.[67]

As was to be expected, the southern states devised various schemes to nullify the *Allwright* decision. While most of the Texas counties abided by the ruling, the so-called Jaybird Democratic Association of Fort Bend County, a party clique that held an unofficial primary that invariably determined who won the Democratic primary and the general elections, made a last stand and forced the Supreme Court to issue a final word on the white primary in *Terry v. Adams*. Although the Jaybird elections were further removed from state action than the regular Democratic primary, the Court did not accept that the Jaybirds were a private club and prohibited their all-white preselection of candidates for public office.[68]

In South Carolina, the state legislature tried to shield the white primary from judicial review by repealing all laws pertaining to primaries. Ruling on a case brought by the NAACP, U.S. District Judge Watis Waring held that this move did not alter the fact that the Democratic primary was "the only practical place where one can express a choice in selecting federal and other officials." It was time, Waring admonished his home state, "to rejoin the union . . . and adopt the American way of conducting elections." Ironically, Waring's opinion was affirmed in the Federal Appeals Court by Judge John J. Parker, whose nomination to the Supreme Court the NAACP had so bitterly opposed in 1930.[69] In Alabama, the Democratic Party abolished the white primary, but a plebiscite introduced a new understanding clause into the state constitution that required registrants "to understand and explain" the U.S. Constitution— a phrase that gave virtually unlimited discretion to the registrars. In 1949, the U.S. District Court struck down this amendment as exceedingly vague and clearly intended to disfranchise black voters but affirmed that a standardized and impartial understanding test would be permissible.[70]

Mississippi, living up to its reputation as the most violently racist state in the United States, had no taste for legal niceties and chose to rely on intimidation and repression. In the summer of 1946, the *Jackson Daily News* gave the following advice to black voters: "Don't attempt to vote in the Democratic primaries anywhere in Mississippi. . . . Staying away from the polls will be the best way to prevent unhealthy and unhappy results." U.S. senator Theodore

"The Man" Bilbo, one of the worst race-baiters of his time, told his followers: "You know and I know what's the best way to keep the nigger from voting. You do it the night before the election. . . . Red-blooded men know what I mean." White supremacists, indeed, understood, and Mississippi saw a wave of racist violence against black citizens trying to vote in the 1946 primary.[71] Even without the white primary, the remaining legal suffrage restrictions and the climate of terror and repression remained formidable barriers to black political participation in most southern localities.

Nevertheless, overcoming the white primary had been no small achievement and much of the credit must certainly go to the NAACP and its lawyers, perhaps most of all to Thurgood Marshall. However, this does not mean we have to accept the association's self-congratulatory account of the white primary fight. According to this narrative, which has been echoed by many historians, there is a continuous chain of progress leading from *Guinn* to *Herndon* to *Condon* to *Lane* to *Allwright* and its aftermath.[72] Only when inexperienced and impatient hotspurs interfered did the legal campaign for black voting rights suffer a setback in *Grovey*.

This success story made good public relations but hardly reflects the actual course of litigation and constitutional history. The real continuity goes from *Herndon* to *Condon* to *Grovey*, because in all three decisions the Supreme Court did not follow the key constitutional and material arguments of the NAACP. Only when the political climate began to shift in the mid-1930s and the composition of the Court changed did legal action by the association yield substantial results. It was no coincidence that the first breakthrough in the legal campaign against segregation also occurred in the late 1930s, when the Supreme Court ordered the University of Missouri to admit a black student to its all-white law school, because the state did not provide "separate but equal" training facilities to black law students. Although the decision did not repudiate segregation per se, it paved the way for the *Brown v. Board of Education* decision of 1954.[73] In the field of voting rights, the shift was first discernible in *Lane v. Wilson* and made considerable headway in *United States v. Classic*, perhaps not the least because the latter case did not directly involve the race issue.

From the late 1930s on, the Supreme Court decisions on racial discrimination reflected the gradual advancement of a more "realistic" constitutional thinking that was no longer content with relying on deductive reasoning and precedent but looked at the material consequences of laws and statutes.[74] Applied to *Smith v. Allwright*, this meant that the Supreme Court held the white primary, as it actually worked, to the standard of a modern constitutional democracy and no longer focused on the formal distinction between private and state action. This, of course, represented an overdue recognition of black participation rights, but the decision was more ambiguous than contemporary commentators and historians have acknowledged.

The ambiguity becomes clearer if race, for the sake of the argument, is excluded from the picture. In a pluralistic democracy based on multiparty competition, it does not seem unreasonable to define parties as voluntary associations of like-minded citizens that must be largely independent from governmental supervision. Nor is it impermissible that parties demand a minimum of loyalty from their members. In the American political system, this notion is reflected by the fact that a majority of the states require their citizens to register as Republicans, Democrats, or Independents before they can vote in primary elections.[75]

Yet the guardians of white supremacy had perverted the arguments in favor of parties as autonomous private associations to such an extreme that the Supreme Court ultimately felt compelled to acknowledge that there was no difference between the action of the southern Democratic Party and the action of the respective states. By doing so, the Court tacitly sanctioned a peculiarity that was clearly at odds with the American political system at large. The "historical dialectics" of *Smith v. Allwright* lay in the need to accept the realities of the political system of white supremacy, so that constitutional remedy could be found to bring about its demise.

4

Protest and Loyalty

The NAACP in the Second World War

When Gunnar Myrdal in October 1942 wrote the author's preface to his milestone study, *An American Dilemma: The Negro Problem and Modern Democracy*, the Swedish sociologist affirmed as the "one main conclusion" that "not since Reconstruction has there been more reason to anticipate fundamental changes in American race relations, changes which will involve a development toward the American ideals." The United States, the last chapter of the book emphatically argued, was fighting "a life-and-death struggle for liberty and equality" that would inevitably lead to "a redefinition of the Negro's status in America." The Second World War had once and for all ended American isolation and endowed the United States with an international leadership role which demanded that American racial practices be reconciled with the nation's egalitarian and democratic ideals: "America, for its international prestige, power, and future security," Myrdal wrote, "must demonstrate to the world that American Negroes can be satisfactorily integrated into its democracy."[1]

There were indeed various social and ideological forces at work that made the Second World War into a catalyst of racial change. Economically, the wartime boom ended the Great Depression, which had hit blacks harder and longer than any other group of Americans. Although they were still the last to be hired and confined to low-paying menial jobs, African-Americans benefited from the expanding industrial economy. During the war, the number of gainfully employed blacks increased by 1 million, while black unemployment fell from more than 900,000 to roughly 150,000.[2] In addition to improving the standard of living of millions of African-Americans, the soaring demand for labor triggered the mass migration of almost 1.6 million southern blacks to the industrial centers of the North and the West between 1940 and 1950. The overcrowding of metropolitan areas, such as Detroit and Los Angeles, led to severe racial tensions and violent outbursts, which highlighted the fact that the race issue was a not a sectional but a national problem.[3] The demographic changes also had obvious political implications. As the NAACP had hoped for a long time, black voters emerged as a serious political force at least outside of the South.

Another war-related development affecting African-American civil rights was the unprecedented economic interventionism of the federal government during the war. If the government could set wages and prices, civil rights leaders insisted, it also had the authority and obligation to proscribe racial discrimination in the war industries. In addition, ideas of "social citizenship," as they were reflected in President Roosevelt's 1944 "Economic Bill of Rights," bolstered demands for a more active role of the government in the protection of civil rights. In a 1947 address to the NAACP, President Harry S. Truman explicitly acknowledged the emergence of "a new concept of civil rights" based not on "the protection of the people *against* the Government, but protection of the people *by* the Government."[4]

Even more important was the ideological dimension of the war itself. While the blatant contradiction between democratic ideals and racial oppression had been conveniently ignored by the American public during the First World War, this was no longer possible in World War II. The United States could not fight Nazi Germany without confronting the striking affinities between the Nazi racial ideology and the southern doctrines of white supremacy. At the same time, the Japanese tried to sell off their war of conquest in Asia as an anticolonial struggle for the liberation of nonwhite peoples. The military and ideological battle against both regimes was bound to have repercussions on race relations at home.

Finally, the black military experience during the Second World War inspired a new assertiveness in demanding fairness and equality. As in World War I, African-American servicemen suffered from ubiquitous segregation, discrimination, and harassment, but they were no longer willing to accept such treatment quietly. Numerous bases and training camps saw violent clashes between black soldiers and the military police. Even fighting in a Jim Crow army, however, could be an uplifting experience. Defeating the self-proclaimed "master race" gave pride and self-confidence to black veterans in their fight against racism back home. "I'm hanged if I'm going to let the Alabama version of the Germans kick me around when I get home," a black corporal announced at the end of the war. "I went into the Army a nigger; I'm coming out a *man*."[5]

While the ongoing social and ideological changes were evident to attentive observers, Myrdal was nevertheless overly optimistic when he assumed an almost inexorable historical trend toward the "gradual realization of the

American Creed," which even the white South would eventually embrace.[6] Modernization is not a self-executing process, and deeply rooted ideologies and mentalities do not easily lose their power simply because external circumstances change. In fact, the guardians of white supremacy were not at all impressed by the much-proclaimed need to solve the "American Dilemma." In early 1944, Senator James Eastland of Mississippi gave American war aims his own twist when he explained that white southerners were fighting for the integrity of their social institutions: "Those boys are fighting to maintain the rights of the States. Those boys are fighting to maintain white supremacy and the control of our election machinery."[7] As far as the race issue was concerned, the Second World War did not revolutionize the white South. However, the war did strengthen both the resolve and the resources of African-Americans in their struggle to make the "American Creed" a reality for themselves.

Between Cynicism and Patriotism

Recent historical scholarship has increasingly recognized the international dimension of the African-American civil rights struggle.[8] That the United States played a crucial role in the momentous conflicts of the twentieth century between democracy and dictatorship provided black civil rights leaders with the opportunity to expose the hypocrisy of preaching democratic ideals abroad while practicing racism at home. When in 1912 the U.S. Congress passed a resolution against the persecution of Jews in Czarist Russia, *The Crisis* found it difficult to see "how our honorable legislative body preserved a straight face over the fervent declarations, especially impassionated from southern representatives, that discrimination because of race is un-American."[9] The NAACP also insisted that the United States respect the right to self-determination of nonwhite peoples. Not surprisingly, the association paid particular attention to the fate of Africa. In 1919, it helped finance the Second Pan-African Congress, which was organized by W.E.B. Du Bois in Paris, despite efforts from the U.S. government to prevent the meeting. Rather moderately, the congress did not call for an immediate decolonization but proposed that the former German colonies be placed under international supervision until its populations were capable of self-government. In subsequent years the rhetoric became more assertive. The NAACP's 1933 annual conference, for example, called the Republic of Haiti, which had been occupied by U.S. troops since 1915, "a tragic victim of American imperialism" and demanded the "immediate and permanent withdrawal" of all U.S. forces. The independent African state of Liberia was to be accorded the right to work out its own destiny without interference from American business corporations. Likewise, the Virgin Islanders were entitled to complete autonomy, since they suffered "intense economic and political oppression under American control."[10]

Although it predominantly focused on the domestic condition of black Americans, the NAACP commented on all major international affairs that bore a relation to issues of race and human rights. Thus the 1933 annual conference denounced "the vicious campaign of race prejudice against Jews and Negroes by the Hitler government in Germany" and called upon the Olympics Committee to transfer the 1936 games to a different country, unless the German government gave assurances that it would not tolerate racial discrimination during the Olympics. Two years later, the association urged against American participation in the Berlin games, since this would amount to a tacit approval of the racial and religious persecution under the Nazis. When the black U.S. athlete Jesse Owens, to Hitler's disgust, won four gold medals in track and field, *The Crisis* proudly featured the black hero on its cover and celebrated his defiance of the master race ideology.[11]

Throughout the 1930s the NAACP organ ran various articles that drew parallels between the Nazi ideology and racism in the United States and warned against the menace of fascism.[12] However, the persecution of Jews and other minorities in Germany was not a particularly salient topic of *The Crisis* or the black press at large. The international event that first and foremost captured the attention of the NAACP and the broader African-American public was the 1935 Italian aggression against Ethiopia, "the most shameless act of wholesale murder and robbery of modern times," according to the 1936 NAACP annual conference. The NAACP repeatedly appealed to the U.S. Department of State, the League of Nations, and the Soviet Union to take a stand against Italian imperialism, but the great powers had few qualms about sacrificing the sovereignty of an African nation for the sake of good relations with the Duce. Although African-Americans lacked the power to influence U.S. foreign policy on Ethiopia, the movement to support the African kingdom marked the first high point of foreign policy activism within the black community.[13]

As an interracial civil rights organization in which Jewish Americans played a traditionally strong role, the NAACP distanced itself from all anti-Semitic stereotypes that could also be found among the black community. Yet black NAACP leaders were not always able to conceal their chagrin over the obvious double standard of the American public in condemning the persecution of Jews in Nazi Germany while ignoring the discrimination of African-Americans at home. A few weeks before the infamous November pogrom of

1938 against German Jews, assistant secretary and *Crisis* editor Roy Wilkins assailed such hypocrisy in rather strong words. "Maybe some day we will see," he reasoned in an editorial, "that until a Negro can study medicine at, say, the University of Michigan, we cannot make a convincing argument why Jews should be permitted to study at Heidelberg. . . . [U]ntil we stamp out the rope and the faggot . . . we cannot make a good case against the cruelties of storm troopers." Of course, Wilkins did not seriously propose to stop criticizing the Nazis. But his editorial echoed the bitterness among black activists that the oppression of German Jews received more publicity in the United States than domestic racism, while some Jewish-American business people actually colluded in the discrimination against black customers and employees.[14]

Cynicism and skepticism also dominated African-American attitudes toward the looming American involvement in a new world war. Understandably, the bitter memories from the first one lingered on and were invoked in the commentary of *The Crisis*. "If war should come, why should the Negro fight?" the magazine asked in the spring of 1938, and added that "the answer to that question would make interesting reading." In early 1939, *The Crisis* ran a series on "Old Jim Crow in Uniform," reminding its readers of the shameful discrimination against black servicemen during the last war. When the war in Europe began, the NAACP journal wryly observed that since everyone was now talking about defending democracy, blacks were hoping that democracy, for a change, might begin at home.[15] The widespread sentiment among black opinion leaders against British colonialism also found its way into the pages of *The Crisis*, which printed several articles that denounced the war as a plot to save the French and British colonial empires. One essay, published in July 1940, went so far as to condemn the Churchill government as a dictatorship and to demand that the United States stay out of the war in order to preserve democracy at home. The article provoked an angry rejoinder from Alfred Baker Lewis, a white member of the NAACP board of directors, who emphatically implored the magazine's readers that England was the last bulwark in the defense of democracy and had to be supported at all costs.[16]

Yet although the NAACP kept on demanding democracy at home, it did not take an isolationist stand on the worldwide struggle between democracy and fascism. The association never endorsed the argument that the war between the Western powers and Hitler Germany was just another imperialist showdown in which black people had no stake. Nor did it embrace the isolationist creed that freedom and democracy could survive in the western hemisphere and would be served best by American neutrality. In fact, the resolutions of the NAACP annual conference held in June 1940 left no doubt that the association expected U.S. participation in the war against Hitler and that it would loyally support this war. At the same time, it also made perfectly clear that the impending war for democracy would also be waged on the home front:

> Democracy has been virtually wiped out in other parts of the world since we last met. It is gravely threatened in America. . . . Adequate defense to repel invasion from without is necessary. But equally important is the strengthening of the democratic process within our borders so that all who reside here may feel that they have a vital stake in democracy because of the benefits of that form of government are given to all Americans without discrimination on account of race, creed or color. . . . In arming ourselves psychologically and materially against Hitlerism and other forms of totalitarianism we must not allow the spirit of Hitlerism to make gains at home. . . . We will do our part and more to defend our country and its principles. We are equally determined to make our country and its practices worth defending.[17]

Roughly eighteen months before the United States actually became a belligerent nation, the NAACP publicly devised its political and discursive strategy for the upcoming struggle. The association kept on telling the American people that racism was the ideology of the enemy and that fighting its domestic manifestations was a patriotic act strengthening American credibility and war morale. Black Americans would fight and die for their country, but they demanded the same first-class citizenship that was accorded to their white compatriots. Over the next five years, the NAACP concentrated their efforts to a large extent on the struggle for equal treatment and opportunity in the military and the defense industries. Its 1941 annual conference was held under the motto "The Negro in National Defense."[18]

The situation of black soldiers in the armed forces had hardly improved since the First World War. They continued to serve on a strictly segregated basis and were excluded from all prestigious ranks and units, including the Marine Corps and the Air Force. As late as July 1941, the U.S. Army counted only six African-Americans among its 14,700 commissioned officers, and the Navy had no black officers at all. In the defense industries blacks were confined to unskilled and janitorial jobs, while white workers jealously protected their privileges. Even during the war, with its patriotic fervor and growing labor shortages, whites launched numerous hate strikes in opposition to the hiring and promotion of black workers. The egalitarian CIO unions had great difficulties in curbing such action.[19]

This time around, however, blacks were going to challenge discrimination and exclusion head-on. After President Roosevelt had signed the Selective Service Act in September 1940, NAACP secretary Walter White requested that FDR meet with representatives of the black community to discuss the issue of racial discrimination in the armed services and the defense industries. The president agreed to consult with White, Arnold Hill of the National Urban League, and A. Philip Randolph of the all-black Brotherhood of Sleeping Car Porters, black America's most prominent labor leader. Much to their shock, however, the guidelines on racial policy in the military that were released by the White House a few weeks later bluntly declared that segregation would be continued in order to preserve morale and discipline. The black leaders felt betrayed and began to prepare for open protest. In January 1941, Randolph called for a protest march of ten thousand blacks in Washington, D.C., under the motto "We Loyal Negro Americans Demand the Right To Work and To Fight For Our Country!" The appeal met with enthusiastic responses from the black community and led to the formation of an organizational committee made up of prominent civil rights leaders, including the NAACP's Walter White. The date was set for July 1, and the number of expected marchers was optimistically raised to fifty thousand. In all phases of the project, the NAACP worked closely with Randolph and gave full support to the march.[20]

But while the NAACP leadership did not shy away from nonviolent mass protests, it did not pursue it as an end in itself. Nor did A. Philip Randolph. The plan of a mass rally in Washington had been launched to put pressure on Roosevelt, and, indeed, the president became more and more disquieted over the prospect of a mass demonstration in the nation's capital. Two weeks before the march was scheduled, he summoned White and Randolph to the White House. Once there, they firmly demanded an executive order to prohibit all discrimination in the armed services and defense industries and boldly told Roosevelt that they expected no less than one hundred thousand protesters to show up on July 1. Finally, Roosevelt relented, and on June 25, 1941, he issued executive order 8802, which banned discrimination on account of race, creed, color, or national origin in defense industries or governmental agencies. To enforce the order, a temporary Fair Employment Practices Committee (FEPC) was established. Although the order did not mention segregation and discrimination in the military, the organizers called off their March on Washington.[21]

Not surprisingly, this compromise did not meet with the undivided support of black civil rights activists. In retrospect, it is tempting to speculate whether a powerful demonstration of black discontent and determination might not have had a greater effect on the American public than settling for a half-way measure. Not only was the FEPC designated as a wartime agency, it also lacked coercive authority and largely relied on the power of persuasion and the negative publicity that emanated from its investigations and public hearings. Southern companies and unions, however, tended to ignore the FEPC's orders to end discriminatory practices. Hopelessly underfunded and understaffed, the committee workers nevertheless did their best and even achieved some modicum of success, but there is little doubt that the employment gains of blacks after 1942 resulted from the wartime boom and not from governmental pressure. In 1946, the agency was killed by a filibuster of southern senators, despite Randolph's persistent lobbying for a permanent FEPC.[22]

From the perspective of 1941, however, executive order 8802 appeared to be a crucial breakthrough. After all, the decree represented the first direct presidential intervention on behalf of African-Americans since Reconstruction. Although the order was officially justified as a national defense measure, it created a valuable precedent for expanding the jurisdiction of the federal government in the area of civil rights. Obviously, had the presidential order been issued after a successful March on Washington, this would have been a consummate triumph of black assertiveness. But no one knew for sure whether fifty thousand or one hundred thousand protesters would actually show up; after the grandiose announcements that White and Randolph made to the president, anything less would have been a serious embarrassment. Moreover, the danger of violent clashes with white mobs or the police could not be ruled out. Under these circumstances White and Randolph considered it prudent to be content with Roosevelt's concessions. Publicly, the black union leader insisted that the march had only been "postponed."[23] With a delay of twenty-two years, Randolph would actually deliver on this promise.

The fact that a concerted effort of civil rights groups had successfully brought pressure on the president of the United States was a tremendous encouragement for the future. It was even more remarkable that the new militancy of the black community and the NAACP in particular was not subdued by an acquiescent patriotism after Pearl Harbor. On the contrary, in its January 1942 issue The Crisis emphatically proclaimed: "Now is the Time not to be silent." Certainly, the magazine would not print another "Close Ranks" editorial, as it had done in 1918! And the NAACP annual conference of July 1942 stated unequivocally: "We will not abandon our fight for racial justice during the war." The association did not limit its criticism to the U.S. government, but also attacked America's allies. In several speeches early in the war Walter White blamed the Japanese sweep through Southeast Asia on British colonialism, which made the Japanese appear as liberators in the eyes of the indigenous populations. Without an end to racial oppression and colonial exploitation worldwide there would be no enduring peace for the white nations.[24]

Obviously, black America was in no mood to declare its unconditional loyalty. The *Pittsburgh Courier,* the leading African-American newspaper, launched a "Double V" campaign for victory at home and abroad that immediately became widely popular among the black community.[25] In February 1942, the NAACP and numerous other black organizations, many with a moderate or even conservative reputation, sent a sharp protest to FDR because the president had not appointed a single black member to the newly created War Labor Board and because he did nothing against the "brutalities and insults" to which African-American soldiers were subjected in the army. "What, Mr. President, in the light of these facts, is there for the Negro to hope and fight for?," the letter, signed by the leaders of the NAACP, the National Council of Negro Women, the National Urban League, the African Methodist Episcopal Church, and many others, asked. "It is not enough to say that under Hitler conditions for the Negro would be worse. Every intelligent Negro knows that already. A negative approach of this type can only create passive loyalty. . . . Give us something to hope for Mr. President, and give us some proof that there is a greater margin between the racial ideology and practices of the totalitarian governments and the democracies than is apparent to Negroes today."[26]

By today's standards, such words sound deferential, but in the context of 1942 they were nothing less than radical. Suggesting that the loyalty of African-Americans was predicated upon concessions from the government might easily be construed as sedition. In wartime, the mere suspicion of disloyalty could have severe consequences for vulnerable ethnic groups, as German-Americans had learned in the First World War and Japanese Americans were just about to experience. It is noteworthy, that the presidential order of February 1942 authorizing the relocation of almost 120,000 persons of Japanese descent, most of them U.S. citizens, from the West Coast to internment camps in isolated areas in the hinterland, could have been extended to other groups as well. Initially, the NAACP did not muster the courage to protest publicly against the summary internment of nonwhite Americans but merely called for their humane treatment. Only in 1944, when criticism of the measure became more vocal, did the association openly denounce its racist character.[27]

African-Americans also came under close scrutiny. In June 1942, FBI director J. Edgar Hoover commissioned an investigation of "Foreign-Inspired Agitation among American Negroes," which was completed in August 1943 and filed as a *Survey of Racial Conditions in the United States,* coded as RA-CON. According to historian Robert A. Hill, who has edited the voluminous report, the FBI's RACON operation foreshadowed the Bureau's infamous 1960s "counterintelligence programs" against black civil rights groups and radicals. But, unintentionally, it also documented the remarkable scope of black protest during the war.[28] In terms of actual subversion and disloyalty, however, the findings were quite meager. Except for a few sectarian groups, including the remnants of Marcus Garvey's UNIA, no substantial evidence of pro-Japanese propaganda, let alone pro-German sentiment, could be found among African-Americans. Blacks, the report conceded, were "fundamentally loyal," but the FBI was nevertheless concerned about their growing "aggressiveness or militancy." In line with Hoover's fanatical anticommunism, the Communist Party was named as the most outstanding among "the subversive forces" that were trying to cause "unrest and dissatisfaction." Anticipating the red-baiting of later years, the NAACP was viewed as a target for communist infiltration. A "confidential source" informed the FBI that "one Leroy Willkins [*sic*], Editor of the official organ of the National Association for the Advancement of Colored People, is strongly suspected of being a member of the Communist Party and is known to write material which could be construed as Communist."[29] The misspelling of Roy Wilkins, the NAACP's assistant secretary, editor of *The Crisis,* and incidently one of the most ardent anticommunists within the association's leadership, tells a lot about the quality of such "confidential sources."

The mounting racial tensions during the war were hardly due to agitation and subversion, but rather to the fact that the rapid urbanization brought blacks and whites into closer contact than ever before and led to numerous clashes over contested space. As a local newspaper wrote, Detroit resembled "a keg of powder with a short fuse." When it exploded in a two-day riot in June 1943, the city counted thirty-four dead and more than seven hundred people injured. Most of the victims were black, as was the vast majority of those who were arrested during the violence. According to Walter White's eyewitness account, the police committed innumerable brutalities and civil rights violations against black suspects or bystanders. The Detroit riot, however, was only the most spectacular of several hundred racial confrontations in more than fifty American cities during 1943.[30] Black violence and lawlessness, NAACP leaders claimed, were boiling up in "a caldron of misery and frustration," but they also knew perfectly well that violence threatened to discredit the black cause. When Harlem erupted in August 1943 after rumors that a black soldier had been killed by a white policeman, Walter White and Roy Wilkins personally took to the streets to help calm the situation. In fact, order was restored much faster than in Detroit a month earlier and the number of casualties was much lower.[31]

The Campaign against the Poll Tax

The wartime spirit of national unity opened up new political opportunities for interracial alliances that could build on the foundations laid during the New Deal. One of the most conspicuous campaigns emanating from these efforts was the fight against the poll tax. Unlike literacy tests, the payment of the poll tax as a prerequisite for voting had few defenders outside of the South. A form of direct per capita taxation, it had replaced more restrictive property qualifications for the suffrage at the end of the eighteenth century. In the twentieth century, however, only the South tied the tax to the ballot. Because the states made no effort to collect the poll tax as a source of revenue, it had developed into a de facto fee for exercising the right to vote. Although the yearly amount of one or two dollars may seem small, it imposed a considerable burden on the poor and mostly cash-strapped rural population of the South. Some states even required cumulative payment with interest if a voter had failed to pay the poll tax for several years. Critics viewed the poll tax as the key instrument of the propertied elites to preserve their political domination and to keep poor blacks and whites down. The poll tax was probably the single most important reason for the extremely low turnout in southern elections compared to the rest of the United States. In addition, it invited political corruption, as candidates offered to pay the poll taxes of voters in return for their support.[32]

Since the poll tax also disfranchised white voters, it could be persuasively attacked as a flagrant violation of America's democratic creed and might create a common ground for interracial cooperation. There were encouraging signs that even in the South the defenders of the tax were in retreat. Florida, North Carolina, and Louisiana had already abolished it in the late 1930s. The opponents of the poll tax, however, did not want to wait until the state legislatures, dominated by the beneficiaries of disfranchisement, took action but instead pressed for a federal law to prohibit the poll tax as a prerequisite for voting in national elections. Between 1942 and 1945, the U.S. House of Representatives passed such bills no less than five times by wide margins, only to be defeated by southern obstruction in the Senate. It was small consolation to the anti–poll taxers that Georgia, under the leadership of reform governor Ellis Arnall, repealed the tax shortly before the end of the war.[33]

The campaign for a federal law against the poll tax went back to an initiative by the Southern Conference for Human Welfare (SCHW), an interracial group of liberal New Dealers that had been founded in Birmingham, Alabama, in 1938. Although blacks and whites worked together in the SCHW, the organization proceeded with much caution on racial matters due to the region's etiquette.[34] In the campaign against the poll tax, the emphasis was on class rather than race. Liberals and union activists fought the poll tax as a device to disfranchise the lower classes in general and expected that its repeal would lead to the ousting of the reactionary oligarchy that ruled the South and represented it in Congress. Although they knew that its abolition would be most beneficial to poor whites, blacks also hoped that the common struggle against the tax might lay the foundations of interracial class solidarity. "The Negro is no longer afraid of . . . whites in the lower economic brackets," the African-American *Dallas Express* confidently predicted in 1938, "they will certainly be our allies in the years to come."[35]

The SCHW persuaded Representative Lee Geyer, a California Democrat, and Senator Claude Pepper, an ardent New Dealer from Florida, to sponsor the anti–poll tax bill in Congress. In order to back their efforts by a broad coalition of lobbying groups, the National Committee to Abolish the Poll Tax (NCAPT) was founded in May 1941. The NCAPT included fifty different organizations, mostly labor unions and civil rights groups, among them the AFL, the CIO, and the American Civil Liberties Union (ACLU), which pledged to support the campaign financially and politically. There was no question that the NAACP, as the largest and best-known African-American civil rights group, would play a prominent role in this coalition.[36]

The NCAPT based its propaganda on three key messages. First, the poll tax was undemocratic because it disfranchised large numbers of ordinary citizens and cemented the power of corrupt party machines and "permanent politicians," who got reelected time and again by a ridiculously tiny electorate and who governed "almost totally independent of the people of their states." In the congressional elections of 1942, an NCAPT brochure estimated that only 3 percent of the total population of the seven poll tax states had cast their ballots, compared to 25 percent in the rest of the nation. Thus the tax was a major reason for the notorious "overrepresentation" of the South in the U.S. Congress. More votes were cast in Rhode Island, the smallest state in the Union with roughly seven hundred thousand residents and two representatives, than for all of the thirty-seven representatives of Alabama, Mississippi, Georgia, Virginia, and South Carolina, with a total population of more than 11 million. Second, the struggle to repeal the poll tax was not a race issue. In fact, according to the NCAPT's estimate, it disfranchised three whites for every two black voters. Finally, the abolition of the poll tax was advertised as a war necessity, since it discredited American democracy abroad and undercut national unity at home.[37]

The NAACP, of course, did its best to support the lobbying efforts for the anti–poll tax law. Whenever votes on the poll tax bills were coming up in Congress, the NAACP mobilized its branches and members to begin letter-writing campaigns and to bring pressure on their congressmen and senators. The association's leaders tirelessly worked Capitol Hill. On a single day in November 1942, Walter White contacted forty-seven senators to win their support for a swift vote on the impending Geyer-Pepper bill.[38] Rhetorically, the big guns were brought up. The poll tax, the NAACP secretary declared, was "part and parcel of a Fascist system in no wise different in concept from that of Hitler and Hirohito." The southerners who were blocking the passage of the repeal law played "directly into the hand of the enemies of democracy—Tokyo, Rome and Berlin." Likewise, the NAACP strictly adhered to the NCAPT's rallying cry that the struggle against the poll tax was waged on behalf of all underprivileged Americans.[39]

The arguments of the anti–poll taxers were not entirely lost on the U.S. Congress. In September 1942, it passed the so-called Soldier Vote Act, which allowed members of the armed forces to vote by absentee ballot and exempted them from all poll tax requirements by their respective home states. Lawmakers from the poll tax states did not dare to stand openly against the untrammeled right to vote of those who risked their lives for democracy.[40] When it came to the issue of a general abolition of the tax by federal statute, however, southerners drew the line. If the federal government could ban the poll tax, it might also try to abolish literacy tests and understanding clauses. Such intolerable interference with state prerogatives raised the specter of the mass reenfranchisement of southern blacks and had to be averted at all costs. As in the congressional fights over the federal antilynching bills, southern obstructionists either successfully prevented the anti–poll tax bills from reaching the Senate floor or simply filibustered them to death. They always found enough allies among conservative Democrats and Republicans who refused to vote for cloture. When the leadership of the Democratic Party tried to liberalize the Senate cloture rules in 1949, the motion backfired badly. In fact, the new rule, which was pushed through by a coalition of conservative Democrats and Republicans, introduced the quorum of a two-thirds majority of all Senate members (instead of two-thirds of those present), thus making it even harder to stop a filibuster.[41]

Opposition against a federal anti–poll tax law was not limited to white supremacists, however. As one Democratic senator from Iowa explained to

Walter White, he was strongly opposed to both filibusters and the poll tax, but he had not "the slightest doubt that it is unconstitutional to allow the Federal Congress by statute to prescribe qualifications for voting in the individual states." Hence the only clear-cut remedy to do away with the poll tax was a constitutional amendment.[42] Indeed, the proponents of a federal ban on the poll tax were treading on uncertain constitutional ground. As late as 1937, the U.S. Supreme Court had unanimously ruled in *Breedlove v. Suttles,* a case brought by a white citizen of Georgia, that the poll tax did not violate the equal protection clause of the Fourteenth Amendment and that the states had considerable discretion in administering the tax.[43] How then could the poll tax be abolished at all?

In March 1940, NAACP legal counsel Thurgood Marshall wrote a memorandum in which he pondered the various strategic options for the anti–poll tax campaign. Basically, there were three potential ways of eliminating the tax, according to Marshall. First, the state legislatures themselves might repeal it, which Marshall deemed extremely unlikely, as these bodies were built upon the system of disfranchisement. The second option was to bring legal action, so the Supreme Court might reverse its *Breedlove* ruling. This did not appear entirely impossible, but it was also not likely to happen anytime soon due to the principle of stare decisis. Finally, the poll tax could be abolished by federal legislation, either by a constitutional amendment or by federal statute. Marshall was rather skeptical about the Geyer-Pepper bill, though, because it had been drawn up as an amendment to the so-called Hatch Acts of 1939 and 1940, which were directed at political corruption. Even if the poll tax was considered conducive to corrupt practices, Marshall explained, the Hatch Acts were clearly aimed at individuals and not at the states. Hence the bill was "not properly drawn and based on the wrong theory." Nonetheless, the NAACP legal expert called for its political support: "My reason for this opinion is that we certainly should do all we possibly can to remove the poll tax requirements and, further, that although the constitutionality of such a law may be questioned, it is certainly not *clearly* unconstitutional"—not exactly an enthusiastic endorsement. Marshall himself wanted to build the legal case against the poll tax on the theory that it was an unreasonable classification in violation of the equal protection clause of the Fourteenth Amendment, because there was no relation between the ability to pay taxes and the right to participate in the electoral process.[44]

Interestingly enough, Marshall did not discuss the option of seeking a constitutional amendment in his memorandum. This was no coincidence. The demand for constitutional amendments did not play a role in the NAACP's legal and political strategies. According to the association's view, the federal Constitution already guaranteed full equality of rights to African-Americans. Segregation, disfranchisement, and all other forms of racial discrimination violated the Constitution, which needed to be enforced, not amended. Moreover, constitutional amendments were a perilous and cumbersome route to take. If the civil rights activists were unable to pass a federal statute, how could they hope to pass a constitutional amendment with its requirements of a two-thirds majority in Congress and a three-fourths quorum for ratification by the states? Hence, the NAACP strictly insisted on the congressional authority to outlaw the poll tax in federal elections and attacked all proposals for a constitutional amendment as a "fraud on the American people." Appeals to leave the problem to the states met with equally harsh rebuttals. When President Truman made a statement to this effect in 1946, the NAACP castigated him for playing into the hands of the very reactionary cabal that blocked the president's liberal legislative program in Congress.[45]

Viewed from the perspective of the 1940s, the NAACP's position made perfect sense. To admit that a constitutional amendment was necessary to abolish the poll tax would have meant a far-reaching concession to the states' rights ideology of the South and would have created a dangerous precedent for all future civil rights legislation. The association's legal experts therefore stuck to their uncompromising advocacy of a federal law well into the early 1960s.[46] From hindsight, however, the NAACP's position on the poll tax appears a little dogmatic. While the efforts to pass a federal statute came to no avail, the end of the poll tax was achieved along the very routes that the association had always opposed as impractical and illusionary. By the mid-1950s, two more states, South Carolina and Tennessee, had repealed the tax. In 1964, the Twenty-fourth Amendment to the U.S. Constitution was ratified, stipulating that the right to vote in federal elections must not be denied or abridged by "reason of failure to pay any poll tax or other tax." Two years later the Supreme Court, in *Harper v. Virginia State Board of Elections*, struck down the poll tax as a condition for voting in local and state elections, thereby closing the book on this ignominious burden on democratic citizenship for good. Interestingly, the reasoning of the Court was very similar to the arguments Thurgood Marshall had suggested twenty-six years earlier, namely that the poll tax violated the equal protection clause because the right to vote had no reasonable connection to the economic status of the voter.[47]

There is no question that the NAACP wholeheartedly supported the anti–poll tax campaign. Still, it cannot be overlooked that the leadership of the association kept its distance from the NCAPT. No prominent members of the NAACP's national secretariat or its board of directors served as official sponsors of the NCAPT, a group that included such luminaries as Eleanor Roosevelt, Mary McLeod Bethune, and A. Philip Randolph. The financial contributions from the NAACP also seem to have been rather moderate. The association viewed the NCAPT as a useful clearing house, but it avoided all binding political and organizational commitments. One reason for this was the conspicuous role of notable leftists, such as Vito Marcantonio, a congressman from New York City who was affiliated with the American Labor Party and entertained open relations with the Communists.[48] When in late 1942 the radical Workers Defense League proposed to create a new organization that would unify the campaigns against both the poll tax and the white primary, Walter White in no uncertain terms insisted on the association's claim to leadership in the struggle for black voting rights:

> The NAACP has been fighting disfranchisement in its various manifestations for three decades . . . with a fair measure of success. . . . Had it not been for this basic work . . . the fight would not have moved forward to the point it has reached today. We are perfectly willing to cooperate with any and all reputable and sincere organizations. But having fought . . . as long as we have, we cannot be expected to turn over control of that fight or to commit ourselves to any program until we have decided what, in the light of our experience, is the most effective procedure for us to follow. We have spent a good many thousands of dollars and many years of work which we do not care to run the risk of negating by any new procedure until we have had an opportunity to determine whether that procedure is more effective than that which we have followed in the past.[49]

These words not only mirrored the NAACP's distrust of the radical left but also the self-confidence of an expanding organization that felt strong enough to pursue its own goals and projects and to claim a leadership role whenever cooperation with other groups was deemed expedient.

Toward a Mass Organization

The NAACP benefited from the politicization of the African-American community during the Second World War in a very direct way. As in World War I, the association experienced spectacular organizational growth. After a first peak of roughly 100,000 members in 1919, the membership of the NAACP had been in decline throughout the 1920s. According to an internal estimate, only 21,402 members had paid their dues in 1929; a decade later the figures stood around 50,000. Right after the war, however, the NAACP had at least 400,000 dues-paying members. Publicly, the association's representative even claimed up to 600,000; the Detroit NAACP branch, the largest in the country, alone boasted no less than 20,000 members. Lucille Black, the NAACP's longtime membership secretary, estimated in retrospect that the association's numerical strength reached its peak in 1946 at approximately 540,000. Even by the most conservative estimates, the NAACP membership increased by a factor of eight during World War II. The rush was so great that, due to the rationing of paper, many branches did not have enough envelopes to conduct their membership drives. As Myrdal had predicted at the beginning of the war, the NAACP was breaking out of its traditional middle-class constituency and building a mass following. Not surprisingly, this organizational expansion gave a tremendous boost to the self-confidence of its leaders. In 1947, the national secretariat set 1 million members as the goal for the upcoming membership drive.[50]

Clearly, the NAACP was gaining ground among the urban black working class. Even more important, however, was the headway it made in the South. By 1948, the South and the border states, according to the NAACP director of branches, Gloster Current, accounted for 734 out of a total of 1,123 branches, with about 175,000 members.[51] There are no exact data on the growth of the southern NAACP, but several local and state studies have provided some hints. In Georgia, the number of branches skyrocketed from six in 1943 to a stunning fifty-one (with a total of 14,000 members) only three years later. In New Orleans, where the NAACP had only a few hundred members prior to the war, the local branch claimed 6,000 members at its end, and even cities such as Baton Rouge and Shreveport, Louisiana, where a vicious racism was deeply entrenched, counted 1,000 each. In North Carolina, the number of NAACP branches increased from about twenty in 1942 to more than fifty. Even in Mississippi, still the most oppressive and racist state in America, the number of branches went up from six to sixteen. Although the strongholds of the association's growth were to be found in the expanding urban areas, it did not entirely bypass the rural South. The local leaders continued to be male and middle-class. A typical example was Kelly Alexander, the owner of a funeral home in Charlotte, who was elected the first president of the North Carolina NAACP state conference in 1943. To be sure, fear and intimidation continued to deter many southern blacks from openly affiliating with the NAACP. But in many black communities the association was now widely recognized as the undisputed leader in the civil rights struggle. Paying dues to the NAACP, Ralph Bunche found in his field research for *An American*

Dilemma, was "considered a minimum duty of a 'race man' and a sign of community spirit and social respectability."[52]

In the same pattern that had occurred after World War I, the numerical strength of the NAACP reached its peak in the first postwar year and began to crumble thereafter. The decline to roughly 350,000 members in 1948 could still be considered as a return to normalcy. But when a $50,000 budget deficit forced the association to double its annual fee from one dollar to two in 1948, membership plummeted dramatically. The leadership had expected to lose up to one-third of its dues-paying members, but in fact the numbers were cut in half by 1949 and hit the bottom a year later at 150,000.[53] This direct correlation between dues and membership, a clear indication of the shaky economic basis of the black civil rights struggle, would not change for a long time to come. In 1969–70, the association experienced the same effect, when its membership dropped from 462,000 to 362,000, after it had doubled its dues from two to four dollars. In both cases, however, the NAACP recovered within a few years. By 1953, its membership had again increased to 240,000, before it reached new heights of more than a half million in the early 1960s. Likewise, the losses of 1970 were almost made good by the mid-1970s.[54]

Even before its membership reached the levels of a mass organization, the NAACP had begun a process of professionalization. In 1940, the NAACP Legal Defense and Educational Fund (LDF) was created to secure tax exemption for contributions to the association's legal work. The new organization, with Thurgood Marshall as its chief counsel, was supposed to make the legal activities of the association more efficient and to put it on a sound financial basis. Indeed, the LDF's budget grew from roughly $14,000 in 1941 to almost $145,000 a decade later. Although the NAACP leadership initially kept the new subdivision under tight control, the LDF began to develop into a separate unit as more and more rivalries with the association's staff and leadership ensued. In the late 1950s, the Internal Revenue Service insisted on a complete separation of the two groups, and subsequently relations began to sour when controversies over tactics and competition for financial contributions led the association to demand that the LDF drop the NAACP initials from its name and even tried to enforce this claim in court—ultimately without success.[55]

To improve the NAACP's presence in the nation's capital, it created the Washington Bureau in 1942. Officially, Walter White headed the bureau, but most of its day-to-day business was conducted by a permanent assistant. After the war, the staff of the bureau was expanded by secretaries for veterans' and labor affairs, respectively. In 1946, Clarence Mitchell, a black journalist from Baltimore who had previously worked for the FEPC, was first appointed labor secretary, and in 1950 he became the director of the NAACP's Washington Bureau. Mitchell was responsible for promoting the association's legislative program and for negotiating with government agencies and officials. A highly visible and effective lobbyist, Mitchell would soon earn the reputation among his admirers of being "the 101st Senator."[56]

In the late 1940s, the national board of directors had forty-seven members from twenty-five different cities throughout the entire United States, even though the Northeast remained heavily overrepresented. The national secretariat had grown considerably. Apart from the executive secretary and the assistant secretary, it comprised a legal department, a department of public relations, a research department, and a department of branches responsible for coordinating and supervising the activities of the association's local chapters. The department of branches represented the bureaucratic center of the national secretariat, as it was directly in charge of the membership, youth, and field secretaries. The executive secretary and his assistant, in particular, were burdened with a workload of administrative and representative duties not second to the chief executive officers of large business corporations. For example, in the first nine months of 1951, Walter White had fifty-eight engagements outside of New York, traveling over twenty-two thousand miles.[57]

The national staff of the NAACP showed an astonishing loyalty to the association. Clarence Mitchell remained the head of the Washington Bureau until 1978. Henry Lee Moon held the post of the director of public relations from 1948 to 1974. Gloster Current, who had been the executive secretary of the Detroit NAACP during the war, served as the director of branches from 1946 to 1976. Lucille Black joined the NAACP staff in 1928 and worked as a field and membership secretary until 1971.[58] The same pattern can be found among the more prominent leaders. From 1937 to 1961, Thurgood Marshall served as legal counsel to both the NAACP and the LDF, before he became a federal judge, the U.S. Solicitor General, and finally, in 1967, the first black justice on the U.S. Supreme Court. When Walter White died in 1955, he had held the positions of assistant secretary and executive secretary for thirty-seven years. His deputy and successor, Roy Wilkins, could look back at forty-six years in the association's service when he finally retired in 1977.[59]

Under the leadership of White and Wilkins, the NAACP national office was definitely a place where hierarchy mattered. The two secretaries were highly sensitive to challenges to their authority and sought a tight control over all political and organizational matters. And, not surprisingly, both men had difficulties with assertive women within the association and treated them with condescension. Ella Baker, the energetic advocate of grassroots activism who served as the NAACP director of branches from 1943 to 1946, soon became highly critical of the top-down decision-making in the association and of White's vanity and egotism in particular. Exasperated by the secretaries' repeated personal attacks, she left the national office to begin her long search for an organizational framework that defined leadership as empowering people. As the director of branches, she had developed a training program under the motto "Give people light and they will find the way!" However, her subsequent work with Martin Luther King's Southern Christian Leadership Conference and then with the Student Nonviolent Coordinating Committee also did not spare her a good deal of disappointment as far as patriarchal attitudes of male leaders were concerned.[60]

Walter White cherished social and intellectual ambitions beyond his work for the NAACP and wrote several books, including works of fiction. He repeatedly toyed with the idea of a political career and actively sought out friends in high places, which earned him the reputation of being a self-promoting opportunist. As his biographer Kenneth Janken has observed, White always remained somewhat of an outsider to the black community. This was partly because of his fair complexion and his close social rapport with white elites. Despite his impeccable credentials as a courageous fighter for civil rights, the light-skinned White had always been suspected of trying to "pass" into white society. In the controversy over the association's opposition to segregation, Du Bois, it will be recalled, tried to discredit his antagonist by casually reminding his readers that "Walter White is white. He has more white companions and friends than colored." The executive secretary used to shrug off such invectives, insisting that he could have "stopped living as a Negro and passed as white" a long time ago. But he also refused to let his personal life be governed by racial etiquette. In 1949, Walter White secretly divorced his wife to marry journalist Poppy Cannon, a white woman with a record of three previous husbands, causing a major scandal among the NAACP membership. Right after the wedding, he took a year's leave of absence and, suffering from chronic heart disease, never fully resumed his old position.[61]

Roy Wilkins was appointed acting secretary when White left for his extended vacation, and he subsequently became the dominating figure in the NAACP leadership. In contrast to White, Wilkins was an organization man, if not to say a bureaucrat, who had dedicated his professional and most of his private life to the association. After he had worked as a journalist for the *Kansas City Call* for eight years, Wilkins joined the NAACP as its assistant secretary in 1931, and three years later he became the editor of *The Crisis* after Du

Bois's resignation. As the NAACP records bear out, he was a first-class work-horse. Few things went on in the NAACP in which Roy Wilkins was not involved. His superior administrative knowledge and his excellent personal relations with most members of the board of directors made his position in the NAACP leadership almost unassailable. Wilkins jealously guarded his authority and reputation and was extremely sensitive to criticism, up to outright vindictiveness. After one of his critics left the association following a rancorous power struggle, he ordered the name of his antagonist removed from all official NAACP documents and records.[62]

Wilkins was the most prominent among a whole generation of NAACP leaders who dominated the association's operations and agenda from the early 1940s to the early 1970s. Such continuity, partly reflecting the limited employment opportunities for black professionals in the age of segregation, was an asset when it came to professionalism and organizational stability. At the same time, however, it was also conducive to the bureaucratic top-down leadership style for which the NAACP became notorious. The association's national officers tended to view branches and members primarily as instruments for implementing the political agenda of the leadership. Not surprisingly, this attitude often came across as overbearing and arrogant. In 1949, Judge Hubert Delany, the chairman of the Committee on Branches of the board of directors, attacked Wilkins and the national secretariat for treating the branches in an "I am the law" fashion and for trying "to browbeat them into submission." This attitude, Delany maintained, was a major reason for the recent precipitous drop in membership.[63]

Since the judge knew that raising the membership dues, enacted after a vote by the board of directors, accounted for most of the losses, his criticism was somewhat disingenuous. Even so, Delany's characterization of the mind-set of the national office was hardly unwarranted. In his outraged reply, Wilkins inadvertently addressed a key problem when he wrote: "I want only that this association shall continue to grow and become a more effective instrument for achieving its purpose of full citizenship for American Negroes. I have given eighteen of my best years . . . not for glory or, God knows, for monetary reward, but for the cause."[64] True enough, but their long service for the NAACP had nurtured a self-perception in Wilkins and other NAACP officials that they themselves knew best what was good for both the association and the African-American civil rights struggle at large.

Bureaucratization and the establishment of hierarchical leadership structures perhaps are the inevitable price of organizational growth and stabilization. On balance, however, the development of the NAACP during the Second World War and its immediate aftermath is incontrovertibly impressive. As Myrdal observed in the early 1940s, the effectiveness of the national office gave the association "an influence out of proportion to its small membership."[65] Its two-pronged strategy of patriotism and protest during the war years paved the way toward a broad-based civil rights organization that was firmly rooted and highly respected among the black community—no small achievement indeed.

Civil Rights and Liberal Anticommunism

Like the rest of the nation, African-Americans greeted peace in an exuberant mood. When Walter White returned from his travels throughout Europe in 1945, he emphatically proclaimed: "A wind is rising—a wind of determination by the have-nots of the world to share in the benefits of freedom and prosperity which the haves of the earth have tried to keep exclusively for themselves. That wind blows all over the world."[1] African-American civil rights activists harbored ambitious goals for the future. Not only were they determined to put an end to segregation and discrimination at home, but they also insisted that colonialism had no place in the new world order and that the right of nonwhite peoples to self-determination could no longer be denied. Tragically, however, the struggle for racial equality got caught up in the emerging Cold War.

The impact of the Cold War on the African-American civil rights movement is hotly debated among historians, and the NAACP has played a key role in these debates. Approaching these issues, one must begin with an obvious paradox. On the one hand, the anticommunist hysteria of the early Cold War—customarily, if inappropriately, labeled McCarthyism after its most salient protagonist, Senator Joseph McCarthy of Wisconsin—infested all corners of public life in America and grotesquely blurred the distinction between dissent and treason. Southern racists were among the most ardent anticommunists and did their best to denounce the civil rights struggle as a communist conspiracy. During the heyday of the Red Scare, black leaders had to maneuver under serious political constraints.[2]

On the other hand, the global ideological confrontation between communism and democracy and America's claim to the leadership of the "Free World" made sure that domestic racial discrimination would remain an international issue, providing the civil rights movement with a potent discursive weapon. Indeed, since the late 1940s the federal government had supported the NAACP's lawsuits against educational segregation with amicus curiae briefs that pointed to the immense damage racism did to America's international prestige, particularly in the emerging Third World.[3]

Instrumentalizing the Cold War for civil rights, however, also implied embracing its anticommunist rationale. The split of the New Deal coalition early in the Cold War profoundly affected the struggle for black civil rights. On the left, the progressives who rallied behind former vice president Henry Wallace in the 1948 presidential elections refused to accept the imperatives of the Cold War, continued their cooperation with American communists, and demanded that the United States maintain its wartime alliance with the Soviet Union. In sharp contrast, the so-called Cold War liberals of the Truman administration insisted on a clear-cut break with the radical left as the domestic equivalent to their foreign policy of containing Soviet expansionism. In his influential book *The Vital Center*, published in 1949, historian Arthur Schlesinger Jr. called for an "unconditional rejection of totalitarianism" and attacked the progressive left as gullible "doughfaces" who shut their eyes to Soviet aggression and the designs of Moscow's domestic followers.[4]

Facing the alternative of either joining the camp of Cold War liberalism or casting one's lot with the progressive forces, unity among the civil rights movement was destroyed and its left wing fell victim to the witch hunts of the Red Scare. In this situation the NAACP followed a pattern of gradual and defensive accommodation to the anticommunist zeitgeist that was typical for the American public at large. It fervently denied all charges that it was dominated or infiltrated by communists and distanced itself from all groups and individuals suspected of communist affiliations. At the same time, it defended the necessity and justice of racial reform as an integral part of the liberal agenda. In a nutshell, the controversy over the attitude of the NAACP in the early Cold War mirrors the larger debate over the historical legitimacy of liberal anticommunism and its consequences for American society at large.

The leaders of the NAACP and authors with close ties to the association justified their anticommunism by emphasizing the sharp ideological antagonism between civil rights liberalism and the American Communist Party (CPUSA) and by the latter's alleged attempts to infiltrate the NAACP.[5] Recent historiography has been predominantly critical of the association's embrace of anticommunism, however. Marxist historians, in particular, have castigated the alleged opportunism of its leadership, which, in their view, tragically squandered a unique opportunity for a progressive civil rights alliance. "In refusing to work with Marxists," Manning Marable has argued, "the NAACP lost the most principled anti-racist organizers and activists. . . . By serving as the 'left wing of McCarthyism' [the leaders of the NAACP] retarded the black movement for a decade or more." Gerald Horne has spoken of a "fateful historical decision" that burdened the association with indirect responsibility for the deterioration of the living conditions of African-Americans in later years.[6]

Other historians also tend to view the NAACP's anticommunism critically but concede that it succeeded in preserving its organization and program throughout the McCarthy years. The price for survival, though, had been the detachment of black civil rights from a more comprehensive concept of social reform and a self-imposed limitation to the narrow goals of desegregation and voting rights. The anticommunist hysteria of the Cold War, historian Carol Anderson argues, "compelled the NAACP leadership to retreat to the haven of civil rights, wrap itself in the flag, and distance the association from the now-tainted struggle for human rights."[7] Moreover, several authors have claimed that the NAACP conducted large-scale "purges" of leftists from its ranks that weakened the organization and left it "rudderless and disoriented," to quote Gerald Horne again. Curiously enough, they do not offer any empirical evidence for these "purges" beyond citing anticommunist rhetoric and resolutions.[8]

The critics of the NAACP and liberal anticommunism built their argument on the proposition that the American labor movement and the left had emerged from the Second World War stronger than ever and that the prospects for a far-reaching transformation of American capitalism had never been better. "For a few short years in the late 1940s," Ellen Schrecker writes, "the American people had more political options than they would ever have again. McCarthyism destroyed those options. . . . From race relations to the mass media, almost every area of American life felt the chill."[9] In this perspective, it is largely the fault of short-sighted and opportunistic liberals that the grand opportunities of the postwar era were missed and the forces of reaction prevailed.

Whatever the merits of the counterfactual propositions implied in the concept of historical opportunity, the following chapter will demonstrate that much of the criticism of the NAACP's liberal anticommunism is misleading and inconsistent. For one thing, the critics grossly exaggerate the extent to which the association actually joined the anticommunist crusade, particularly its alleged "purges," while at the same time they play down the ideological cleavages between the NAACP and the communists. Rather than becoming "the left wing of McCarthyism," the NAACP desperately struggled to keep the cause of black civil rights on the historical agenda, operating under constraints that defy all political and moral certainties.

Petitioning the United Nations

At the end of the Second World War, the NAACP had not only gained hundreds of thousands of new members, but it also reunited with its cofounder and towering black intellectual W.E.B. Du Bois, who was appointed as the "Director of Special Research" in September 1944 after the seventy-five year-old-scholar had been forced into retirement by Atlanta University, depriving him of a decent livelihood. However, the association did not simply provide "a great man" with the means to pursue his research, as Roy Wilkins later claimed. Du Bois still enjoyed enormous prestige both in the African-American community and in international circles, from which the NAACP hoped to benefit. Vice versa, Du Bois joined an association that was much stronger than the one he had left a decade earlier and that might give his ideas and projects a solid organizational backing. As the next four years would bear out, however, the animosity between Du Bois and his old adversaries, Walter White and Roy Wilkins, had not subsided. More importantly, in political terms Du Bois and the NAACP were heading in radically different directions.[10]

Du Bois's foremost task was to devise the NAACP's position toward the emerging postwar order in general and the colonial question in particular. In the fall of 1944, the board of directors urged President Roosevelt "to make clear now that the United States government will not be a party to the perpetuation of colonial exploitation of any nation" and to appoint "qualified Negroes" as representatives in the upcoming peace conferences. Du Bois sharply criticized the proposals of the Dumbarton Oaks conference of October 1944, because they did not give rights and voice to colonialized peoples in the future United Nations. Still, in May 1945 Du Bois, Walter White, and Mary McLeod Bethune were appointed by the Department of State as official consultants at the UN conference in San Francisco. To their disappointment, the civil rights leaders soon realized that the U.S. government had no intention to quarrel with its European allies over colonial issues. The American delegation, to be sure, proposed an amendment to the UN charter that prohibited discrimination "on account of race, language, religion, or sex," but decisively weakened that clause by adding that it did not authorize intervention in matters "within the domestic jurisdiction of the state concerned." On the colonial question, the United States did not call for independence but merely supported a UN trusteeship for all colonies that were already under international mandate or seized from the enemy or surrendered voluntarily by the colonial powers. In response, black spokespersons of all political persuasions castigated American hypocrisy, while the anticolonial pronouncements of the Soviets were widely applauded.[11]

Nevertheless, the founding of the United Nations and the declaratory ban on racial discrimination offered political opportunities to expose American racism on the international stage that the civil rights movement was determined to exploit. In June 1946, the National Negro Congress (NNC), an umbrella group that had been founded in 1936 with Philip Randolph as its first president but which subsequently came under communist influence, presented the United Nations with a brief petition that called upon the world organization to address the oppression of black people in America. Not surprisingly, UN officials balked.[12] Undaunted, Du Bois, who believed that the NNC petition was "too short and not sufficiently documented," pursued his own project, which he had already launched a few months earlier and which boldly claimed a mandate for the NAACP to speak not only for black Americans but "to represent the peoples of Africa before the UNO." The director of special research proposed a detailed document of up to two hundred pages that would be distributed to all members of the UN assembly and distinguished world leaders. Thus the NAACP would go on record as part of a worldwide movement of oppressed populations. "The necessity of a document of this sort," Du Bois wrote, "is emphasized by the fact that other groups of people, notably the Indians of South Africa, the Jews of Palestine, the Indonesians and others are making similar petitions."[13]

In September 1946, the board of directors approved of Du Bois's proposal for a UN petition, but much to his chagrin they limited its authorization to the condition of blacks in the United States. By the end of the year, Du Bois and several coauthors had put together a preliminary draft that was approved by the board of directors and revised during the spring of 1947. It was by no means certain, however, whether the UN would actually receive the petition. Nongovernmental groups did not have formal standing in the world organization, and the fact that the petition pilloried the UN's most powerful member state made it a highly delicate matter anyway. After several weeks of stonewalling from the UN bureaucracy, Du Bois leaked the petition to the press, after which John Humphrey, the director of the UN's human rights division, agreed to receive the document officially.[14]

On October 23, 1947, Walter White and W.E.B. Du Bois presented the NAACP petition to the UN Commission on Human Rights. Titled *An Appeal to the World: A Statement on the Denial of Human Rights to Minorities in the Case of Citizens of Negro Descent in the United States of America and an Appeal to the United Nations for Redress*, it had more than 150 pages and provided a detailed account of racial discrimination in the United States. Yet the appeal itself remained somewhat vague, due to the obvious limits that both the UN's charter and international law placed on the body's ability to interfere with the domestic affairs of its member states. Hence, the NAACP urged the United Nations "to step to the very edge of its authority" in protecting African-Americans who found no protection from their own government, which claimed limited jurisdiction under the doctrine of states' rights. "Perhaps," the petition reasoned, "it would not be too much to ask the United Nations through the world court to take the protection of such deliberately unprotected citizens under international jurisdiction and control. . . . Peoples of the World, we American Negroes appeal to you; our treatment in America is not merely an internal question of the United States. It is a basic problem of humanity." Yet for all its moral grandeur, the notion that the UN could assume jurisdiction over American race relations was patently fantastical. As the UN representative immediately cautioned, the world organization had no power to take any action and considered the petition to be confidential.[15]

The NAACP, of course, made every effort to see that *An Appeal to the World* received as much publicity as possible. The document was immediately released in a mimeographed version and in early 1948 published as a booklet. According to Walter White, his office was flooded with requests for copies. All major U.S. newspapers and magazines reported on the petition, and most of the commentary conceded that it addressed a painful weakness of America's international credibility. Inevitably, there were also numerous charges, particularly from southern commentators, that the NAACP had embarrassed the United States and furnished "Soviet Russia with new ammunition to use against us." The NAACP, Du Bois countered, was not going to be intimidated by red-baiting. "We are not spineless appeasers. When we see wrong . . . we protest. We have done this for forty years and we shall continue this program."[16]

An Appeal to the World also claimed that "it is not Russia that threatens the United States but Mississippi, not Stalin and Molotov but [the racist senators from Mississippi] Bilbo and Rankin."[17] Nevertheless, there was little chance that the NAACP petition would escape getting caught up in the ideological battles of the Cold War. It was the Soviet delegate to a subcommittee of the UN Commission on Human Right who officially proposed to put the NNC and NAACP petitions on the Commission's agenda in December 1947. Arguing that the UN's job was to "guarantee human rights for all minorities everywhere" and not to single out one particular group, his American counterpart insured that the move was soundly defeated. Another attempt failed in the summer of 1948, leading to a controversy between Du Bois and Eleanor Roosevelt, who happened to be a member of both the U.S. delegation to the

UN and of the NAACP board of directors. The former first lady stubbornly refused to introduce the NAACP petition into the UN general assembly, stating that the Soviets would seize upon the issue as an excuse for attacking the United States. Politely, but firmly, Du Bois replied that since its founding the association had never shied away from speaking the truth regardless of the quandary this might cause to America's international prestige.[18]

At this point, the NAACP leadership had already decided that the UN petition had served its propaganda purpose. In fact, Walter White fully agreed with Eleanor Roosevelt's "sound position" that it was not in the association's best interest to team up with the Soviets in embarrassing the U.S. government before world opinion.[19] Du Bois, of course, sharply disagreed. His relationship with the NAACP leadership had been full of tension virtually from the first day he was appointed as the director of special research. There was much petty bickering over office space and furniture, but the core of the conflict was political. Du Bois had never been willing to surrender his political independence to his obligations as an NAACP official, and his political leanings were increasingly toward the radical left. Since 1945, he had repeatedly angered White and Wilkins with his enthusiastic praise for the Soviet Union, calling Soviet foreign minister Molotov "the one statesman at San Francisco who stood up for human rights and the emancipation of colonies" and labeling the Soviet Union as "the most hopeful country on earth."[20] For his part, Du Bois became more and more disgruntled that his ideas about the right "foreign policy" of the association, especially with regard to the Pan-African movement and decolonization, did not meet with a favorable response from the NAACP's national office and board of directors.

The final stir came in September 1948, after Walter White had asked the director of special research to prepare a memorandum for the imminent meeting of the United Nations in Paris, in which White was going to participate as an official consultant to the U.S. delegation. Du Bois was furious. Instead of complying with the secretary's request, he sent a long memorandum to the board of directors that amounted to a scathing indictment of what he saw as the disastrous opportunism of the NAACP leadership:

> The United States Delegation to the United Nations has expressed clearly its attitude towards matters in which the NAACP is interested; it has refused to bring the curtailment of our civil rights to the attention of the General Assembly of the United Nations; it has refused willingly to allow any other nation to bring this matter up. . . . If we accept a consultantship in this delegation without a clear, open, public declaration by the Board of our position on the Truman foreign policy, our very

acceptance ties us in with the reactionary, warmongering colonial imperialism of the present administration. It is certain that no influence
applied in Paris is going to have the slightest influence on our delegation. . . . If, on the contrary, we are to be loaded on the Truman bandwagon, with no chance for opinion or consultation, we are headed for a
tragic mistake.[21]

Walter White indignantly denied that his acceptance of the consultantship
committed the association to support the Truman administration's foreign
policy and insinuated that Du Bois was simply jealous that he had not been
selected to represent the NAACP at the Paris meeting. A few days later, the
NAACP board of directors met and sharply reproached the director of special
research for his "written refusal to cooperate with the NAACP executive
staff" and for leaking his memorandum to the press, a charge that Du Bois
vehemently denied. Nonetheless, the board terminated his employment effective the end of 1948.[22]

Du Bois was perfectly right in his assessment that the NAACP leadership
was not willing to confront Truman in the field of foreign policy, even if this
meant turning a blind eye on the administration's less than principled stand
on decolonization. In contrast to Du Bois's grand, if not to say grandiose,
internationalist outlook, the NAACP leadership did not really expect any effective help from the United Nations or world opinion but continued to look
at the federal government of the United States as the institution with both the
authority and the power to enforce the rights of black Americans. One important reason why the NAACP did not wish to alienate the Truman administration was that the president's civil rights policy had begun to show encouraging signs of progress.

Onto the Truman Bandwagon

While implementing its strategies of containment at home and abroad, the
Truman administration had come to realize that racism was a major blot on
America's international reputation and required a more active role for the
federal government. Conveniently, the national interest dovetailed with
Truman's electoral strategy for 1948, in which northern blacks played a key
part. Determined to reach out to African-Americans, Harry Truman agreed to
address the NAACP annual conference of June 1947—the first president to
do so. In addition to an audience of ten thousand, his speech at the Lincoln
Memorial in Washington, D.C., was broadcast nationwide by all major radio
networks. In remarkably clear-cut words, the president acknowledged that

the United States could not prevail in the ideological contest with communism unless it came to terms with its racial problems. "Freedom," Truman explained, "is not an easy lesson to teach, nor an easy cause to sell, to peoples beset by every kind of privation. They may surrender to the false security offered so temptingly by totalitarian regimes unless we can prove the superiority of democracy. Our case for democracy should be as strong as we can make it. It should rest on practical evidence that we have been able to put our own house in order. . . . But we cannot, any longer, await the growth of a will to action in the slowest state or the most backward community. Our National Government must show the way."[23]

The way to put the American house in order was shown several months later by the report of the President's Committee on Civil Rights. Truman had created this expert body in December 1946 in response to mounting protests by the NAACP and other groups against the wave of racist violence that swept the South after the end of the war and claimed the lives of dozens of blacks, including several veterans. The association had made every effort to influence the work of the committee by continuously submitting demands and information. NAACP board member Channing Tobias was appointed as a member of the commission, and Walter White and Thurgood Marshall appeared as witnesses, making favorable and effective presentations according to one staff member of the committee.[24]

The committee report, entitled *To Secure These Rights,* was released in late October 1947, shortly after the NAACP presented its petition to the United Nations. It proposed a comprehensive set of institutional and legal measures to strengthen the protection of civil rights, including the elevation of the Civil Rights Section of the Justice Department to a full division and the establishment of a permanent Commission on Civil Rights under the auspices of the White House. Among other things, the committee supported the old NAACP project of a federal antilynching law and the repeal of the poll tax either by state or by federal action. Perhaps most importantly, it called for the elimination of racial segregation, which was declared as "inconsistent with the fundamental equalitarianism of the American way of life." Segregation in the armed forces was to be abolished right away, and federal assistance should only be granted to those public and private agencies that did not practice segregation and discrimination. A permanent Fair Employment Practice Act would secure fairness in private businesses. Similar safeguards were to be established in the educational, housing, and health care sectors. Finally, the experts proposed "a long term campaign of public education to inform the people of the civil rights to which they are entitled and which they owe to one another."[25]

Obviously, the image of an active federal government envisioned in *To Secure These Rights* corresponded closely to the NAACP's own ideas. In his message to the president, Walter White praised the report as "the most forthright governmental pronouncement of a practical program for assurance of civil rights not only to minorities but to all Americans which has yet been drafted." Although the report for the time being only represented the recommendations of a blue-ribbon commission, Truman himself hailed it as "an American charter of human freedom." Yet the president made no specific commitment as to how and when his administration would attempt to implement this charter. Nevertheless, the release of *To Secure These Rights* and Truman's favorable reaction put civil rights squarely on the American political agenda. According to his biographer David Lewis, Du Bois was "heartsick" that the committee's report had stolen the thunder from his own *An Appeal to the World.*[26]

Compared to the lofty appeal of the UN petition, *To Secure These Rights* not only featured a host of relatively precise proposals but also offered the prospect that it might actually become government policy. Indeed, in February 1948, Truman delivered a special message to Congress in which he recommended a ten-point legislative program that took up major items of the committee report, including a federal antilynching law, the repeal of the poll tax, and a new FEPC. In July, the president signed two executive orders against racial discrimination in federal agencies and the military. It is true that Truman's ten-point program cautiously sidestepped the committee's call for ending Jim Crow and that the executive order on the military only came in response to massive threats by A. Philip Randolph to launch a campaign of civil disobedience against the new draft laws.[27] But there is also no denying that Truman was the first president who had the courage to make such far-reaching proposals on the civil rights front. With Truman explicitly acknowledging that American national interest required an end to racial discrimination, it is easy to understand why the NAACP had no intention of confronting the administration over foreign policy issues. The question, much-debated among historians, of whether Truman acted out of moral outrage and commitment to common decency or whether he was primarily catering to black voters in the urban North—evidently both motives played a role—was of minor importance to the NAACP. After all, educating politicians to the electoral clout of black voters had always been a key feature of the association's political strategy.[28]

As a matter of fact, the alliance between the NAACP and Truman was anything but love at first sight. When Vice President Henry Wallace, a New Dealer with strong antiracist credentials, was dropped from FDR's Democratic ticket in 1944 and James Byrnes, a segregationist from South Carolina, was brought up as his possible replacement, Walter White was up in arms. Since many political observers expected FDR to step down once peace was secured, the new vice president would very likely be the next president. The nomination of a southerner, White bluntly told Eleanor Roosevelt, "would virtually drive the Negro vote into the Republican camp." During the closing session of the 1944 NAACP annual convention, the secretary thundered against the "conspiracy" to replace Wallace. As a token of his support, White sent the vice president a copy of his speech and asked him for an autographed picture.[29]

When Senator Harry S. Truman emerged as the compromise candidate for the vice presidency, the first lady hastened to assure White that he was a "good man." The NAACP leader, however, remained unconvinced. Truman, a machine politician from Missouri, was known for a family background of Confederate nostalgia and had a reputation of entertaining relations with the Ku Klux Klan. Before the elections, White took him to task on both issues. Truman, however, responded in a remarkably matter-of-fact tone, denying any affiliation with the Klan and pointing to his pro–civil rights voting record as a senator. Roy Wilkins, who as a journalist had watched Truman's early career in Kansas City, counseled not to put him in the same box with the southern race-baiters. By the standards of his time and upbringing, Wilkins judged, his racial views were moderate. To be sure, Truman did not believe in social equality, but he stood for fair play. More importantly, throughout his Missouri years "he had learned to count the black voters."[30]

As president, however, Truman soon alienated the left wing of the New Deal coalition. Prior to the mid-term elections of 1946, discontent with his leadership had grown into outright rebellion. In September, the CIO's political action committee and other groups issued a "Call to Progressives" to meet for an emergency conference in order to mobilize the old Roosevelt coalition. Walter White was asked to sign the "Call" and to serve as one of the keynote speakers. Since this was clearly a political event, the secretary first sought the approval of the NAACP's Committee on Administration, a clearing house made up of members of the national office and the board of directors. Although White's participation could easily be viewed as committing the association to the progressive left, the secretary was encouraged to attend as long as the conference was formally nonpartisan.[31]

However, when the news broke that Truman had fired Henry Wallace, who had remained in the fourth Roosevelt administration as the secretary of commerce, for publicly criticizing the president's policy toward the Soviet Union, the meeting turned into a pro-Wallace rally. A unanimous resolution urged

Wallace to carry on his "hard fight for peace and freedom and security"—a thinly veiled call to run for the presidency. In his speech, Walter White expressed his shock that the most principled antiracist of the administration was ousted but also cautioned against establishing a third party that would only weaken the progressive forces. Nonetheless, the NAACP board of directors had to defend the secretary against attacks in the black press that he had committed the association to the third-party cause.[32]

The disastrous defeat of the Democrats in the 1946 congressional elections sealed the split of the New Deal coalition. Its left wing blamed the debacle on Truman's alleged betrayal of FDR's domestic and foreign policy legacy and set up the Progressive Citizens of America, thus creating the platform for Henry Wallace's presidential bid. Ironically, many of the Cold War liberals also did not believe that Truman had the strength to lead the Democratic Party to victory in 1948.[33] The president, however, had no intention of giving up and began building his own coalition, with the black vote of the urban North as a cornerstone. Whatever his moral convictions, the establishment of the President's Committee on Civil Rights and his subsequent endorsement of the committee's report, his speech before the NAACP convention, and his message to Congress all neatly reflected Truman's evolving electoral strategy. In late 1947, the president's advisers concluded that the "urban minorities" held the balance of power in the big northern industrial states. To stem a possible defection of black voters to Wallace, Truman had to come out strongly for civil rights. This would surely offend the South, but the Truman campaign calculated that southern disaffection could be "safely ignored."[34]

Early in the election year, the NAACP reaffirmed its traditional policy of nonpartisanship.[35] In reality, however, the NAACP leadership was neither neutral nor nonpartisan. After Henry Wallace had declared his candidacy in late 1947, White, Wilkins, and the director of branches, Gloster Current, made every effort to silence whatever support Wallace might enjoy among the NAACP staff and membership. To discredit the candidate's antiracist credentials, White actively solicited information that Wallace had tolerated racial discrimination during his tenure in the federal government. In February 1948, an editorial in *The Crisis* reminded its readers that Wallace had not always been the "shining knight doing battle against prejudice and inequality." At the association's annual convention in June, the secretary attacked Wallace for not having done enough against segregation, whereas Truman received praise for his civil rights policy. White also shunned the Progressive convention and merely sent his assistant, who declared that so far the party had not yet demonstrated "the sincerity of its pronouncements."[36]

While the NAACP secretary worked against Wallace, the director of special research made no secret of his support for the Progressive cause. In a January 1948 column for the *Chicago Defender*, Du Bois had called Wallace "the one man alone, who is worthy of leadership and of support." Although he had no chance of winning, blacks should vote for him to express their protest, "even if our protests put a reactionary Republican in the White House or a Southern-supported Democrat." Du Bois's endorsement of Wallace was no different from the editorials he had written for *The Crisis* in earlier years,[37] but White was determined to use Du Bois's political activities as the leverage to settle their old rivalry for good. Triumphantly, he informed the director of special research of a vote by the board of directors that "no exception" would be allowed to the NAACP principles that prohibited employed officers from endorsing candidates or party programs and from speaking at party meetings. Understandably, Du Bois was "bewildered" by what he saw as an attempt to silence him. He had tried his best to draw a clear line between his personal views and his position as an NAACP official, but if the decision of the board was interpreted narrowly, how could he continue to comment on any current political issues? If he had known that his "usual freedom of expression was to be curtailed," Du Bois complained to Arthur Spingarn, he would not have returned to the NAACP. Unmoved, the board insisted that "paid Executives did not and should not have the right to independent action, in areas in which the association works."[38]

Since the association covered a broad range of areas, most of them distinctly political, this decree practically amounted to a muzzle, which Du Bois could not possibly suffer. He ignored the board's reproach and continued to support the Progressives, although he earnestly tried to make it clear that in doing so he spoke as a private individual and not as an officer of the NAACP. The press, of course, did not pay attention and never failed to mention his organizational affiliation. But, as Du Bois correctly pointed out, Walter White also expressed his political views almost on a daily basis, and even the secretary's personal assistant could not find fault with Du Bois's conduct. Nevertheless, White prevailed and the NAACP Committee on Administration again voted to reprimand the director of special research for violating the ban on partisan politics.[39] The clash over the preparations for the United Nations meeting in September 1948 was merely the final straw. By refusing to cooperate with the secretary—and by his defiant demeanor in front of the board of directors, where he still enjoyed considerable support—Du Bois certainly did his part to make the break inevitable. Conveniently, the association's official pronouncements focused exclusively on the UN controversy and did not mention the quarrels over Du Bois's support for the

Progressives. But it was also patently clear that an unbridgeable political cleavage had led to Du Bois's dismissal, despite lame denials "that no political questions whatsoever entered into the action of the Board on Dr. Du Bois."[40] Given Du Bois's great prestige, nobody could be surprised that his dismissal evoked sharp protests from both the association's membership and the public at large. The left, in particular, reacted with angry protests. In dramatic hyperbole, Henry Wallace called the firing of Du Bois "a tragic example of how American fascism is creeping into all facets of our life."[41]

Interestingly, there was also harsh criticism from the right. In the *Pittsburgh Courier,* black journalist George Schuyler, a convert from socialism to conservatism and a former member of the NAACP public relations department, wrote a caustic comment on Walter White's subservience to the Truman administration. NAACP members with Republican affiliations protested against the continued support by the secretary and other staff members for Truman and demanded an investigation by the board of directors. In response, the NAACP Committee on Administration came up with a rather weak defense for White, arguing that his recent pro-Truman articles "were his own evaluations and did not represent the views of the association"— exactly the same position Du Bois had claimed for himself.[42]

Undeniably, the NAACP leadership applied a double standard that could hardly conceal that it had entered into an alliance with the Truman administration. Basically, this was realpolitik pure and simple. Wallace was certainly the most antiracist candidate, but as the NAACP director of public relations Henry Lee Moon wrote in his book *Balance of Power: The Negro Vote,* published in early 1948, voting for Wallace "would only be a gesture of protest and despair" the black minority could not afford. As early as January 1948, the NAACP had boasted that "the Negro vote may be decisive" in the presidential race and Walter White had sent the president a copy of Moon's book with a note that he would "enjoy and profit from it." Since Truman was apparently willing to heed this advice by making bold civil rights proposals, the NAACP leaders believed they had little choice but to support him. It was true, Clarence Mitchell of the NAACP's Washington Bureau reasoned in May 1948, that Truman so far had done very little to implement his proposals, but if blacks did not back the president and he lost, this would send the fateful message that civil rights was a losing position.[43]

For better or worse, the NAACP boarded the Truman bandwagon, even if the incumbent's prospects of reelection looked rather dim. When several liberal Democrats joined forces with prominent southerners before the party's nominating convention in order to jettison Truman and to draft the popular war hero General Eisenhower as the Democratic nominee, Walter White furiously attacked them for collaborating with the "avowed enemies of liberalism." At the same time, the secretary implored Truman not to appease the southern Democrats, who were threatening a walk-out from the convention if a strong civil rights plank were adopted. During the convention held in Philadelphia, the NAACP and other black groups ran a large advertisement in the *Philadelphia Bulletin* declaring: "Let 'Em Walk!" At the end of the day, the civil rights advocates prevailed and passed a plank that included most of the proposals Truman had made in his congressional message of February. Bombastically, the NAACP spoke of "the greatest turning point for the South and for America which has occurred since the Civil War," while the delegations from the Deep South walked out in protest and organized the "Dixiecrat" revolt, with South Carolina governor Strom Thurmond as their presidential candidate. The president himself would have preferred a weaker civil rights program, but northern Democrats, convinced that Truman would be defeated anyway, were eager to secure the black vote for their local and state tickets.[44]

The November elections demonstrated that both Truman and the NAACP had made the right bets. The incumbent defeated his complacent Republican opponent, Thomas Dewey, with a 4 percent lead in the popular vote. Neither the Dixiecrats nor the Progressives, which each received about 1.1 million votes, had been able to weaken the Democratic camp decisively. Most importantly from the NAACP's point of view, black voters had voted overwhelmingly for Truman and provided him with crucial support in several key industrial states. According to Moon's estimates, about 70 percent of all black voters had voted for Truman, while Wallace had not received more than 10 percent of the black vote nationwide. In California, Illinois, and Ohio, with a total of seventy-eight votes in the electoral college, the estimated number of black ballots cast for Truman far exceeded his slim winning margins and allowed him to carry these states. Without the solid backing from black voters, he very likely would have lost the election.[45]

Cheerfully, Walter White congratulated the president on his "triumph . . . over both the extreme right and the extreme left," which the secretary greeted as a "mandate" to carry out his civil rights program now that the Democrats were also in control of Congress again. In the aftermath of the elections, Truman reaffirmed his proposals several times, but did not take the "unequivocal stand," as the NAACP secretary publicly suggested he had done. To be sure, the president's legislative program of 1949 included antilynching, anti–poll tax, and FEPC bills, but they were all soundly defeated by the usual bipartisan coalition of conservatives. With the onset of the Korean War in 1950, civil rights took a back seat on the administration's agenda.[46]

The Anticommunist Hysteria

The poor showing of the Progressive's in the 1948 presidential elections reflected the traditional weakness of the American left, but it is also true that red-baiting played a part in the party's swift decline. Wallace's favorable views of Soviet foreign policy and his willingness to accept the support of the communists made him vulnerable to charges that a vote for him was a vote for Stalin.[47] In the political climate of the early Cold War, charges of communist sympathies were not confined to the progressive left, however. Before long, liberals also became the targets of the antisubversive hysteria that threatened to wreck both civil liberties and civil rights in America.

Accusations that the NAACP was pursuing communist goals had long preceded the Cold War but had never been taken very seriously. For example, when in 1944 the ultraconservative Republican senator Robert Taft spoke of "the NAACP communists," Walter White defiantly responded that the association was "proud" to have earned the enmity of a die-hard reactionary like Taft.[48] From 1946 on, however, allegations of communist infiltration became more frequent within the liberal camp itself. In a lengthy article on the Communist Party of the United States published by *Life Magazine,* historian Arthur Schlesinger Jr. spoke of attempts by the CPUSA to "sink its tentacles into the NAACP." Walter White immediately demanded a clarification from Schlesinger, who explained that he had only tried to pinpoint impending dangers and did not question the association's opposition to communism. Still, the NAACP leaders became increasingly nervous. In a letter of April 1947 to the chairman of the American Newspaper Guild, Roy Wilkins freely admitted: "Like many another organization on the liberal front we are being sniped at in the current hysteria over the Communists. . . . Perhaps we are more jittery than we ought to be, but it is natural that we would become alarmed lest many projects we have underway should be endangered by the old cry of 'Communism.'"[49]

Wilkins's worries were hardly unfounded. Government publications had also begun to suspect the NAACP of communist infiltration, and the question of membership in the association was raised by "loyalty boards" scrutinizing civilian and military personnel.[50] The NAACP sharply protested the equation of civil rights with communism, but during the heyday of the Red Scare in the late 1940s and early 1950s it felt compelled to constantly show off its anticommunist credentials. Even NAACP activists who had been murdered by racists were eulogized as fighters against communism. The national office carefully watched over all contacts that members might entertain with communists. In one case, Walter White personally intervened with the U.S.

attorney general to clarify that a branch president who had signed the 1951 Stockholm Peace Appeal for nuclear disarmament had not known of the petition's communist background.[51]

At the same time, the association insisted that the communist peril, to the extent that it was real, was first and foremost the result of the wrongs and grievances in American society. Conservatives who blocked the necessary reforms did more damage to American democracy than "all communists and their fellow-travellers in the world." The NAACP demanded that racist groups such as the Ku Klux Klan should also be classified as subversive and subjected to loyalty hearings. Its most important goal, however, was to prevent the struggle for black civil rights from becoming publicly identified with communism. During the infamous Hollywood hearings of the House Un-American Activities Committee (HUAC) in 1947, the NAACP warned against the red-baiting of film artists who had portrayed black characters with fairness and empathy. In 1950, Clarence Mitchell firmly declared before the HUAC: "We cannot overcome a real or imagined threat of foreign ideologies by the enactment of harsh legislation which will silence the voice of reform in our own country." When the HUAC in 1954 published its report on "The American Negro and the Communist Party," which attested to the loyalty and anticommunism of African-Americans in general and the NAACP in particular, Channing Tobias, the chairman of the association's board of directors, was relieved that at last "the facts" had been acknowledged.[52]

In June 1950, the NAACP annual convention held at Boston resolved that the board of directors appoint a committee to investigate the extent to which the local branches had become infiltrated by communists and, if necessary, to suspend the charter of branches that had come under communist control. However, this resolution, passed by an overwhelming majority, did not give the go-ahead for a witch hunt. On the contrary, in a detailed memorandum Walter White admonished the association's local chapters:

> The resolution adopted at Boston does not give branches the right to call anybody and everybody a Communist. The resolution does not give branches the right to eliminate members just because those members disagree with the branch or its officers. . . . Because a man or a woman is a critic of the National Office or of the NAACP is not in itself reason under the Boston resolution for elimination. That criticism must be in line with Communist party philosophy, and must be consistent. It must be emphasized that under the Boston resolution, the branches themselves do not have the power to eliminate anyone. . . . DO NOT BE-

COME HYSTERICAL AND MAKE WILD ACCUSATIONS. We do not want a witch hunt in the NAACP, but we want to be sure that we, and not the communists are running it.[53]

Pursuant to the Boston resolutions, the local branches were obliged to report all attempts at communist infiltration to the national office. These reports had to be referred to a newly formed Committee on Political Domination. In addition, the board of directors established a formal procedure for the exclusion or rejection of members. Charges could only be brought by NAACP members or officers, and all cases had to be heard by the executive committee of the branch—with the "accused parties" having the right to present any testimony they desired. Expulsions or rejections had to be ratified by the branch as a whole, and all persons who were denied membership could appeal to the board of directors. As of late 1952, however, the Committee on Political Domination had considered only a single case, while several denials of membership were still pending.[54]

Indeed, the NAACP records do not produce evidence of either massive communist infiltration or anticommunist "purges." Although the national office had complained about attempts by the communists "to capture control of NAACP branches and youth councils" since 1946 and insisted that the branches seek the advice of the New York office before cooperating with any other national or local group, the NAACP leadership considered the communist influence among its membership as a minor problem. Out of a total of roughly fifteen hundred local units nationwide, there were no more than ten to twelve cases that the national secretariat considered to be serious. All of these cases were related to branches and student groups in the North or on the West Coast, while the South remained completely unaffected.[55]

Not surprisingly, there was considerable confusion among both NAACP leaders and the membership over what constituted infiltration. In late 1947, board member Alfred Baker Lewis noted that it made little sense to crack down on branches for adopting resolutions along the Communist Party line, often critical of U.S. foreign policy, unless the national office and the board of directors first launched an educational campaign. The most important objective was to avoid political embarrassment by independent action of the association's local units. No branch was permitted to take a position on national or foreign affairs unless the matter had been decided by the NAACP's annual conference. No branch could send money or delegates to any organization or meeting without the approval of the national office.[56] Nonetheless, the association's leadership did not establish a regime of tight supervision and control over its local units. Even branches that were suspected of being infiltrated by communists were treated with remarkable indulgence and regard for due process, as the archival record bears out.

The Richmond, California, NAACP had been under communist influence since 1945, according to the association's regional secretary for the West Coast. After the promulgation of the Truman Doctrine in March 1947, the branch passed a fiery resolution against U.S. support for the British intervention in Greece. At the end of the same year the group was shaken by clashes over alleged attempts of the communists to manipulate the election of the branch officers. The national office, however, did not see any violation of the association's standard electoral procedures and dismissed the protests by the defeated anticommunists. When in early 1949 local black businessmen and church representatives complained about the communist domination of the group and demanded the suspension of its charter, the national office refused to follow up on the charges. "Individual political beliefs," Roy Wilkins stated, were no reason for exclusion.[57]

The San Francisco branch was also considered a communist stronghold. In 1946, it endorsed the Communist candidate for governor of California in clear violation of the NAACP policy of nonpartisanship, but the national office merely insisted that the endorsement be withdrawn immediately. Although the group kept on ignoring the association's guidelines on political pronouncements and serious financial irregularities transpired, no action was taken. Even the distribution of a communist newspaper at a branch meeting was grudgingly tolerated, because no formal ban existed. However, with complaints from branch members mounting and a precipitous decline in membership from three thousand in 1947 to four hundred in 1949, the national office finally felt compelled to act. In the branch elections of late 1949, the regional secretary successfully mobilized the membership to elect a new anticommunist branch leadership. Charges of fraud from the defeated faction were dismissed by the board of directors. When an active member of the CPUSA was elected to a leadership position a year later, the board, citing the Boston resolutions, simply nullified the vote and ordered a new one. At last, the San Francisco group had been brought in line with the NAACP's anticommunist stand.[58]

In the Great Neck, Long Island, NAACP branch a new leadership was voted into office in late 1949, after the group had been allegedly dominated by communists for the past two years. Charges of manipulation were raised by the ousted president and his followers, but rejected after a careful examination by the board. This did not end factional strife in the branch, but it was impossible to distinguish political from personal motives. The national secretariat tried to mediate between the rival groups and even persuaded the new president to withdraw a lawsuit she had brought against her antagonists for allegedly threatening her life. When two years later she again tried to have her opponents excluded for repeatedly disrupting the branch meetings, the board invalidated her action, even though the dissidents belonged to the procommunist American Labor Party.[59]

In Philadelphia, Pennsylvania, rumors surfaced in early 1949 that the local NAACP branch had been placed on the official list of "subversive" organizations due to its communist leanings. However, Walter White refused to inquire with the Department of Justice, lest he alert the government's suspicion. Apparently, the rumors were not entirely unfounded, for the following year a special committee appointed by the branch president conceded that the local labor unions refused to cooperate with the branch because of its reputation for being dominated by the Communist Party. Moreover, the committee complained about a lack of "organizational democracy" and gave a long list of administrative shortcomings and financial troubles in the branch. The national office eagerly seized the opportunity for a reorganization of the group and proposed to appoint an administrator who would run the branch affairs for up to six months. Eventually, the executive committee of the Philadelphia branch itself agreed to this drastic step. The action taken by the national office was prompted, however, by the group's bleak financial situation rather than communist infiltration.[60]

There were also several student chapters where the issue of communist leanings led to strife and disruption. The national office had considerable reservations granting a charter to the chapter that formed at the University of California, Berkeley, in 1949, and the group indeed split into rival factions shortly after its founding. Typically enough, ideological differences and personal animosity were difficult to separate from each other. Since the faction identified with the radical left was soon voted out of office, the national secretariat was never forced to take action.[61] At Cornell University, the NAACP student chapter was also divided into a leftist wing and a group that supported the anticommunist line of the national office. Because the latter usually prevailed, there was no need for any disciplinary measures against the chapter.[62] The NAACP chapter at the University of Wisconsin, Madison, was torn by the same factionalism for several years until it came to the verge of disintegration. When an attempt at revival was made in late 1953, a member of the Labor Youth League, which was officially classified as a communist front organization, was elected as chairman of the group's program committee, prompting the national secretariat to press for his resignation.[63]

There is no question that the NAACP leadership kept a close eye on the activities of communists and alleged communists in the local branches and tried to check them with as little publicity as possible. This action, however, did not even come close to a "purge." Rather, the national officers tried to inject themselves as a moderating force into the internal quarrels of the local units, which often were in dismal shape due to disorganization, financial troubles, and personal feuds. First and foremost, the national secretariat was concerned that the branches abided by the NAACP resolutions, guidelines, and procedural rules. This included ensuring that members who were accused of communist affiliations received a fair hearing, and in several cases the board of directors decided in their favor. Apart from trying to avoid unwelcome public attention, the fact that many of the alleged communists in the NAACP were white also explains why the association's leadership proceeded rather cautiously. After a significant number of white delegates had opposed the anticommunist resolutions at the 1950 Boston annual conference, white NAACP members came under a general suspicion of being communists. Eager not to play up racial conflicts among its own membership, the NAACP conspicuously avoided the topic of race in connection with the issue of communist infiltration.[64]

While the NAACP treated the issue of communists in its own ranks with discretion, it pointedly distanced itself from all civil rights groups in which communists participated either overtly or covertly. In particular, this policy applied to the Civil Rights Congress (CRC), a successor organization of the National Negro Congress and the International Labor Defense. The Justice Department and HUAC had branded the two groups as communist fronts.[65] To be sure, during the heyday of McCarthyism there were few organizations to the left of the American Legion and the Daughters of the American Revolution that were not denounced as communist fronts at one time or another, but it cannot be overlooked that black and white communists played a leading role in the CRC. The association refused to send any official representatives to the CRC's founding conference held in Detroit in April 1946, although several NAACP branches sent delegates of their own. The unofficial observer of the national office came away with the impression that the CRC was "dominated by the extreme left." Subsequently, the NAACP leadership concluded that the new group posed a political and organizational threat to the association and rejected all advances by the CRC. When in late 1949 the NAACP issued a call for a "Civil Rights Mobilization" in Washington in support of a new FEPC bill, Roy Wilkins bluntly turned down the CRC's offer for "support" and "cooperation." In an open letter to William L. Patterson, the CRC's black executive secretary, Wilkins recalled the acrimonious attacks by the ILD on the association during the Scottsboro campaign and proclaimed that the NAACP had "no desire for that kind of cooperation, or that kind of 'unity.'" Likewise, the Legal Defense and Education Fund categorically refused to work with the CRC.[66]

Whether an alliance between the NAACP and the CRC would have been a viable political option is more than questionable. Historian Gerald Horne has retrospectively advocated the idea of a "center-left unity" between the "two civil rights giants," but has little to show for this proposition. For one thing, the CRC, by Horne's own account, had a peak membership of merely ten thousand, which made it a rather little giant compared to the NAACP's several hundred thousand members. While Marxist historians may believe that the CRC nevertheless represented the true interests of the "black masses," there is no reason why the NAACP should have subscribed to this point of view.[67] The same applies to the CPUSA itself, which was torn by ideological strife and shaken by governmental repression, both of which sent the party into rapid decline after the end of the Second World War. According to FBI director J. Edgar Hoover, hardly prone to belittle the dangers of communism, party membership dropped from about fifty-five thousand to roughly forty-three thousand in the year 1950–51 alone.[68] The CPUSA was certainly not a grave threat to American national security, but also not exactly an attractive ally.

In refusing to cooperate with communists, the NAACP insisted that the party did not honestly care about the plight of African-Americans but merely sought to exploit the race issue. The party was denounced as being completely dependent on the political and ideological directives from Moscow and of sacrificing without hesitation the interests of black people to the foreign policy concerns of the Soviet Union. The prime example for this charge was the CPUSA's erratic course during the Second World War. After the infamous Nazi-Soviet pact of August 1939, the party had immediately dropped its "popular front" tactics and argued that American workers and blacks in particular had no stake in the "imperialist war" in Europe. As soon as the Nazis attacked the Soviet Union, however, the American communists declared that victory over fascism had to take absolute precedence over all other objectives, including the civil rights struggle. Protests against racial discrimination in the military or the defense industries now became anathema, even though the party's rank and file did not terminate them completely.[69]

To dismiss the antiracism of the CPUSA as mere tactics was less than fair, however. The members and activists of the Communist Party practiced racial egalitarianism to an extent unmatched by any majority-white group in American society. Yet there was a somber side to this as well. The campaigns against the "white chauvinism" that the Communist Party leadership waged in the late 1920s and again in the late 1940s showed all of the unpleasant traits of sectarian rituals of self-purification and indeed aggravated race relations within the party. Moreover, the focus on black rights and the party's deliberate violation of interracial sexual taboos seems to have contributed to its alienation from its base among white ethnic workers. Even where communists enjoyed some influence, interracial class solidarity clearly had its limits. Vice versa, the dogma that the class interests of black proletarians must enjoy precedence over their identity as members of an oppressed racial minority put narrow limits on the Communist Party's attractiveness for African-Americans. According to a former activist, there were no more than two thousand black party members left after the Second World War.[70]

While some historians have played down the Communist Party's subservience to the Soviet Union and tried to reconstruct it as a progressive grassroots movement for social justice, the fact that the American communists loyally followed the Kremlin's directives had crucial political consequences and cannot be dismissed as a figment of Cold War ideology. As labor historian Robert Zieger has aptly put it: "Being a Communist in the 1930s and 1940s was not just being a liberal in a hurry. . . . To be a Communist or even to be a consistent ally or defender of Communists, was to link yourself to Stalinism."[71] Even if the postwar anticommunist hysteria had never occurred, there would have been sufficient reason for the NAACP to think twice before entering into political alliances with the Communist Party. After all, the association had grown into the largest and strongest black civil rights organization with a solid base among the black working class. Why then should it align itself with a political force with which it had often clashed in the past, whose key ideological commitments it did not share, and that was widely viewed with suspicion? Finally, there is no evidence that the NAACP membership ever pressed for an alliance with the radical left or even seriously questioned the leadership's liberal anticommunism.

Still, the early Cold War hardly represents a glorious chapter in the association's history. There is no question that the NAACP showed a good deal of opportunism in steering its course through the Red Scare. Its rhetoric was replete with devout declarations of loyalty and patriotism.[72] Moreover, the association kept a roaring silence on the violations of the civil rights and liberties of communists. When the leaders of the CPUSA, including two African-Americans, were sent to jail solely because of their adherence to the communist ideology, Roy Wilkins barred all NAACP units from actions of solidarity, even though the association's legal experts considered the sentence unconstitutional.[73] As long as the anticommunist crusade did not specifically target black civil rights, the NAACP preferred not to go on record. In 1952, it declined to join the Americans for Democratic Action, a spearhead of liberal anticommunism, in a public condemnation of Joe McCarthy, because the senator's attitude toward blacks was not openly negative. Only after McCarthy's influence had begun to dwindle did the NAACP speak out against McCarthyism, while anticommunist proclamations remained standard tenets of its rhetoric long after the demagogue's fall.[74]

Nonetheless, the association never became "the left wing of McCarthyism." It did not conduct witch-hunts or purges within its own ranks, nor did it deliberately fan the anticommunist hysteria. Although the confrontation between the United States and the Soviet Union offered some opportunity to take the U.S. government to task on protecting democracy at home, the NAACP considered the Cold War and its domestic repercussions a calamity that potentially threatened its very existence. As historian Adam Fairclough has succinctly put it, "During the McCarthy years survival became the name of the game; the NAACP survived."[75] Among other things, survival required that the association unequivocally distance itself from America's global antagonist, which implied a partial retreat from its anticolonial internationalism, a position that had become closely associated with support for the Soviet Union. But this was not such a great sacrifice after all, because civil rights at home had always enjoyed priority over international issues on the NAACP's agenda.

In joining the camp of liberal anticommunism, the association did not have to betray its history and long-standing ideological commitments. In retrospect, its choices were good politics in the basic sense that they helped prevent the cause of civil rights from being discredited along with communism. In exploiting the discourse of national interest, the NAACP saved its political legitimacy and laid the foundations for the achievements of later years. This is not to deny that the anticommunist hysteria retarded the struggle for racial justice and narrowed the political options of the civil rights movement.[76] It is highly doubtful, however, whether any viable alternative existed. The counterfactual proposition of a broad-based progressive center-left alliance both tends to inflate the strength of the American left and to identify the fate of the left with the fate of the civil rights movement at large. Contrary to the gloomy picture painted by some historians, the most important social movement of twentieth-century America did not become a casualty of the Cold War and its concomitant anticommunist hysteria. For all its detrimental impact on American society, McCarthyism could not destroy the desire for first-class citizenship among African-Americans. To nourish this spirit remained a key objective of the NAACP.

6

"Aren't You an American Citizen?"

The NAACP Voter Registration Campaigns in the South, 1940–1962

From its early days on, the NAACP had pursued the goal of getting a maximum number of blacks to register and vote in order to make the political system more responsive to their needs and interests. What looked like an ostensibly simple strategy was actually a daunting task, particularly in the South. Even where political participation was relatively free, voting rights activists continued to complain about the apathy they encountered among black citizens who still abided by the old rule that "politics is white folks' business."[1] Under these circumstances, the association faced a dual challenge. In addition to waging its legal and legislative battles against disfranchisement and discrimination, it had to educate blacks about the benefits of the ballot and convince them to take the often considerable personal risks that were attached to asserting the claim to first-class citizenship in the land of white supremacy.

The political mobilization of southern blacks had to start almost from scratch. In 1940, no more than 5 percent of the black voting-age population of the eleven former Confederate states, or roughly 150,000 persons, were registered voters. With a pitiful 2,000 each, Alabama, Louisiana, and Mississippi, where African-Americans made up between 35 and 49 percent of the total population, were at the bottom. In many rural counties not a single black person was listed in the registration books. Even cities such as Shreveport and Alexandria, Louisiana, with a total of more than 50,000 black residents, practically disfranchised their entire nonwhite citizenry.[2]

Two points must be emphasized: First, the number of southern blacks who actually cast a ballot on election day was of course still lower than the registration figures. Second, the exact data on black registration are unavailable. The southern states did not keep centralized registration records and obviously had no interest in compiling and publishing the numbers on black

Table 2. Black Registration in the South, 1940–1952

State	1940	1946	1947	1948	1952
Alabama	2,000	8,000	6,000	8,000	50,000
Arkansas	4,000	16,000	47,000	35,000	60,000
Florida	18,000	50,000	49,000	80,000	150,000
Georgia	20,000	150,000	125,000	145,000	125,000
Louisiana	2,000	7,000	10,000	43,000	130,000
Mississippi	2,000	5,000	5,000	3,000	40,000
N. Carolina	35,000	75,000	75,000	50,000	97,500
S. Carolina	3,000	5,000	50,000	35,000	130,000
Tennessee	20,000	55,000	80,000	50,000	155,000
Texas	30,000	200,000	100,000	300,000	200,000
Virginia	15,000	50,000	48,000	65,000	70,000
Total	151,000	621,000	595,000	814,000	1,207,500

Sources: Luther P. Jackson, "Race and Suffrage in the South Since 1940," New South 3 (June–July 1948): 3–4, copy in: NAACP Records II A 452; NAACP Division of Research and Information: "Negro Vote in Southern States: 1946," NAACP Records II A 478; memorandum by Palmer Weber to Roy Wilkins et al., 8 November 1948, NAACP Records II A 452; memorandum by Henry Lee Moon to Walter White, 20 August 1952: "Report on NAACP Registration and Voting Campaign in South," NAACP Records II A 452.

voters. Thus all estimates were based on local surveys by voting rights activists, which at best convey a general trend but may vary considerably. For example, in 1952 the NAACP state conference of South Carolina had boasted 175,000 registered blacks in the state, while an *Associated Press* survey estimated the number at 130,000. When the NAACP director of public relations, Henry Lee Moon, inquired about the discrepancy, the South Carolina NAACP president meekly admitted that the lower figures were much more realistic. Still, in his own estimates of southern black registration for the same year, Moon himself used numbers that varied from 1.2 million to 1.35 million.[3]

Despite this lack of accuracy, the figures that were compiled by NAACP field-workers and other researchers all indicate the same, unambiguous overall trend of a rapidly rising black registration rate throughout the South during the 1940s and early 1950s. Between 1940 and 1952, the absolute numbers of registered black voters increased by a factor of eight, and the percentage came close to 25 percent of the black voting-age population.[4] This development mirrors the first expansion phase of the southern black electorate in the twentieth century, which, unlike the famous registration campaigns of the 1960s, so far has received little attention from historians.

The NAACP Approach to Voter Registration

For many years the NAACP leadership considered voter registration basically a local task. As late as 1949, Roy Wilkins declared that "what is needed is persistent and skilled work in registration, but obviously that must be done by the people in the locality. We hope to stimulate our branches to special effort[s] on registration, and perhaps will get a man into principal centers, but in the end the job must be done locally."[5]

This approach was based on the model of the relatively strong NAACP branches in the large cities of the North and the Midwest, where black voters faced few obstacles and were even increasingly courted by white politicians. Below the Mason-Dixon line, however, similar conditions could only be found in the border states and in the peripheral South. In the early 1940s, the NAACP branch of Baltimore, Maryland, and the Virginia Voters League, which worked closely with the local NAACP branches, made considerable headway in their registration activities. According to the League's president, historian Luther P. Jackson, only a handful of the four to five hundred registrars in Virginia were still trying to block African-Americans from enrolling. The low participation rate among blacks was due to the stiff poll tax and to widespread "lethargy," according to Jackson, who mused that "ninety percent of our people have not awakened to the value of the ballot."[6]

Nevertheless, throughout the 1940s the conditions for more effective and successful registration work began to improve for several reasons. First, the 1944 *Smith v. Allwright* decision of the Supreme Court against the white primary gave a tremendous boost to black political awareness. As long as they were barred from the Democratic primary as the only meaningful election, blacks had little incentive to register for the general elections, particularly if they also had to pay a poll tax and pass a discriminatory literacy test. Although most southern states did not intend to obey the ruling in good faith and hastily devised alternative modes of disfranchisement, black activists were undaunted. As NAACP leader and attorney A. P. Tureaud reported from Louisiana, the local branches had raised ample funds and were "bursting over with anxiety" to knock out the remaining legal obstacles to voting.[7]

Second, the advance of New Deal liberalism had opened a widening rift in the southern Democratic Party. The rise of New Dealers such as Ellis Arnall of Georgia, James Folsom of Alabama, Claude Pepper of Florida, and Lyndon Johnson of Texas, to name some of the more prominent men who were progressive on economic issues and racial moderates by the standards of their time and place, provided black voters with a meaningful choice and an incentive to register. That southern liberals also had to pay tribute to the mantras of white supremacy was taken for granted. Accustomed to ignoring this kind of rhetoric, Henry Moon explained, "the southern Negro generally supports the candidate with the most progressive record on economic and social issues such as public housing, minimum wages, social security and the like."[8]

Finally, the growth of the NAACP during the Second World War created a solid organizational base for conducting systematic voter registration campaigns. At the end of the decade, the association had more than seven hundred branches and about 175,000 members in the South. Eight out of ten newly chartered NAACP branches were located below the Mason-Dixon line, which made the association into "one of the strongest institutions in the southern black community" next to the black church, according to political scientist Doug McAdam.[9] The parallel growth of the NAACP and black registration was hardly a coincidence. Voter registration was an almost perfect field for the many new NAACP members who were eager to engage in practical work but had limited time and resources. Registration drives lasted only for a few weeks and created peaks of excitement and solidarity in the entire black community. As one veteran of NAACP voter registration campaigns observed, he never had any difficulties in recruiting volunteers, at least as long as the risk of violent repression was relatively low.[10]

Although it considered voter registration drives primarily a local affair, the NAACP leadership came to realize the need for a more coordinated effort. As early as 1942, an internal report to the board of directors had complained that too few branches were able to plan and conduct effective campaigns.[11] However, the association's impressive expansion rendered any direct control and coordination of local activities by the national headquarters increasingly difficult. As a consequence, the intermediate organizational level was strengthened. In many states the largely defunct NAACP state conferences, charged with directing statewide action, were revived. Moreover, regional offices headed by paid secretaries were established to coordinate the NAACP work in larger geographic areas. The first regional office was opened on the West Coast in San Francisco in 1944, followed by the offices for the Southwest in Dallas, Texas, and the Southeast in Birmingham, Alabama.[12]

After the Second World War, the NAACP annual conferences routinely resolved to call upon "all branches to conduct an intelligent and continuing campaign designed to induce all people to register and vote."[13] Within the national office, all tasks that were related to registration work fell to the department for public relations. Its director, journalist Henry Lee Moon, had earned a reputation as an expert on voting issues through his 1948 book *Balance of Power: The Negro Vote*, in which he had analyzed the history and political significance of the black vote in American elections.[14] Moon believed that the first and foremost purpose of voter registration was to provide the necessary political muscle for the association's legislative program. In a paper titled "What NAACP Political Action Can Accomplish," presented to the 1948 annual conference, Moon explained the rationale behind the NAACP voter registration efforts in terms that deserve to be quoted at length. The legal victory over the white primary, he reminded his audience, was no more than a start:

> The Association has engaged in this long and costly legal battle not merely to establish the Negro's constitutional right to the ballot but, more importantly, to get him to use the ballot as an instrument in attaining the NAACP goal—the eradication of Jim Crow from all phases of American life. . . . As a national organization with nearly half-a-million members, we should, with a realistic and aggressive program, be able to develop and organize an army of 50,000 men and women to mobilize our political resources in communities throughout the nation and make the power of this vote recognized in Washington. We need such an army to back up our Secretary and the Washington Bureau when they are making demands for our legislative program. . . . Once we have really mobilized our full political potential, we will get the kind of government action we need, on the local and state levels as well as in national affairs. . . . Unfortunately, the effective job of mobilizing the Negro vote is not now being done by any organization on a national scale. The field is wide open for the NAACP to step in and take the leadership.[15]

Moon clearly spelled out three key ideas that continued to govern the approach of the NAACP leadership to voter registration and mobilization over the next decades: First, the firm if somewhat simplistic conviction that the untrammeled and "intelligent" use of the ballot offered the key to the solution of virtually all problems of the black minority in America. Second, the insistence on the priority of the goals and objectives set by the national leadership. Third, the claim to a leadership role for the NAACP in defining and articulating the interests of the African-American community at large. In short, the conceptual approach of the NAACP to voter registration was top-down and instrumentalist inasmuch as it tended to look at the local units mostly as the foot soldiers whose duty was to implement the strategic plans of the leadership. However, in practice the notion of a quasi-military chain of command was little more than wishful thinking due to the vast regional and local differences and the still very limited resources the association could muster for voter registration. Although the national board of directors and the secretariat set the political goals and guidelines, the success and failure of registration campaigns largely depended on local conditions.

With few exceptions, most southern politicians either deliberately shunned black voters or at best tried to buy their votes for petty hand-outs. This political culture of apathy and corruption put the NAACP mobilization effort at an additional disadvantage since the association obviously had no direct material benefits to offer. When W. C. Patton, a leading registration activist, went into bars and pool halls to beat the drum, he could not throw around dollar bills or buy drinks. On the contrary, he called upon his audiences to pay the poll tax and appealed to their civic pride by asking, "Aren't you an American citizen?" Sometimes the NAACP rhetoric of civic duty sounded rather dull and uninspiring, as in a flyer by the Birmingham, Alabama, branch that admonished the reader: "Voting is the responsibility of every first-class citizen. To prove that Negro people intend to shoulder their responsibility of citizenship, Negro citizens must share the burden of the ballot."[16]

According to Henry Moon, the political mobilization effort included several key responsibilities for the local branches. First, they had to organize registration drives and provide the local population with the practical information and assistance necessary to overcome the considerable obstacles to signing up as a voter. In addition, the branches had to educate voters about the issues of the campaign and about the candidates' records on civil rights and other items of interest to the association. Finally, the branch had to make every effort to insure that all qualified voters actually went to the polls on election day. If possible, transportation should be provided and phone calls made to remind voters of their duties.[17]

In 1947, the national office put together a manual that gave the branches detailed advice on how to handle both the political questions and the practical details of voter registration campaigns. The branches were reminded that they could not endorse candidates or parties, but that their task was to scrutinize all local and state legislative proposals and referenda as to whether they might contain open or hidden racial discrimination. Each NAACP chapter was expected to appoint a registration and voting committee to coordinate all of the pertinent activities. Publicity was the most important factor. The message to register and vote needed to be brought home to the local population through leaflets, public rallies with music and entertainment, the black press, and radio programs. The NAACP even produced three-minute trailer films to be shown in movie theaters catering to black audiences. The manual also gave detailed advice on how to make door-to-door canvassing, the heart and soul of registration campaigns, most efficient. In order to reduce the number of invalid ballots, voter schools were to be held, if possible in cooperation with black churches, schools, and fraternal orders.[18]

It is easy to see that these guidelines assumed organizational resources that only the large branches of the urban centers commanded. As a matter of fact, the Baltimore branch was explicitly cited as a model. In the rural and small-town South, however, there were few African-Americans who had a telephone or a car they could use in registration drives, let alone blacks who controlled radio stations or movie theaters. But the community networks in these areas were usually tightly knit and conducive to mouth-to-mouth propaganda. A typical registration drive might begin with a mass meeting in a church. Activists gave speeches, an organization committee was formed, and assignments were made to volunteers. According to W. C. Patton, volunteers came from all walks of life, but most of them were "ordinary folks," with middle-aged and elderly persons making up the majority—basically the same women and men who were also active in church work and benevolent associations.[19]

The cooperation with local churches was a cornerstone of the NAACP's political mobilization effort, but by no means an exclusively harmonious relationship. Churches were often the only place where hundreds of blacks could gather undisturbed without immediately arousing the suspicion of the white authorities. The support of ministers who were preaching to their congregations about the rights and duties of citizenship was invaluable for the success of a campaign. However, the prominent role that black clergymen such as Martin Luther King Jr., Ralph Abernathy, Fred Shuttlesworth, and others played in the history of the civil rights movement should not obscure the general conservatism prevailing among this group. Many ministers were dependent on white benefactors and did not wish to be associated with the "radicals" of the NAACP. Others feared for their influence and status in the black community. As Gunnar Myrdal had already observed in the early 1940s, ministers were losing their leadership role to a "new upper class of Negro businessmen and professionals"—incidently the same class from which most of the local NAACP leaders were recruited. It is therefore not surprising that ministers were very diverse in their attitudes toward the NAACP registration work. Some allowed meetings in their churches and the distribution of information after the service, while others were intimidated or indifferent.[20]

Still, from the association's point of view the churches were indispensable as allies and community centers. NAACP activists were strongly encouraged to approach ministers and convince them of "the importance of the ballot in securing for people the very things for which the church stands," as Maynard

Jackson, himself a minister and the father of the future mayor of Atlanta, put it. If the pastor remained impervious, members of the church should press—"in acceptable ways"—for his cooperation. At the same time, preachers had to be educated not to mistake political mobilization as an opportunity to sell the votes of their congregation or to pursue personal ambitions for public office.[21] On the whole, however, the relationship between the association and the southern black ministers did not involve serious frictions or problems. Only when Martin Luther King Jr. and his Southern Christian Leadership Conference appeared on the scene did the NAACP perceive a serious threat to its leadership position from the clergy.

A second important group of potential multipliers whom the association tried to enlist in its registration work were black teachers. Obviously, teachers could render invaluable services in the political education of both black children and adults. Unfortunately, though, the black teachers in the segregated school system of the South were more vulnerable to economic reprisals than any other black middle-class group. Some of the civil rights activists were even highly suspicious of teachers, who were not only hesitant to register themselves but might report political activities to their white superiors. In addition, the relationship between the NAACP and black teachers was complicated by the issue of school desegregation. Teachers had certainly benefited from the association's struggle against racial discrimination in education, especially from the litigation to equalize the salaries of black and white teachers. However, when the NAACP began to attack the very principle of segregated schools, black teachers began to fear for their jobs, correctly anticipating that southern whites would fiercely object to black teachers for their children. After the Supreme Court's 1954 school desegregation ruling in *Brown v. Board of Education,* many black teachers in the South gave in to pressure from the school authorities and quit the association. Those who continued to cooperate did so at considerable risk to their careers.[22]

Whereas the NAACP had serious misgivings about collaboration with other civil rights groups when it came to legal action, it was eager to cooperate in the field of voter registration. Apart from pooling scarce organizational and financial resources, joint action with labor unions, churches, fraternal orders, and other groups provided the association with an opportunity to extend its influence beyond its own membership. Often these alliances took the shape of so-called civic associations or voter leagues, such as the Virginia Voters League mentioned above, which was "in reality a mere auxiliary of the National Association," according to its president. NAACP leaders such as A. T. Walden of Atlanta, Arthur Shores of Birmingham, or Harry Moore, the president of the NAACP Florida state conference, were also heading independent voter leagues. This formal separation conveniently allowed the leagues to bypass the association's policy of nonpartisanship and to endorse individual candidates, but it carried other advantages as well. Blacks who were hesitant to associate with the "radical" NAACP found it easier to join groups with a less notorious name. When in the mid-1950s several southern states began to enjoin all NAACP activities through court orders, its work was partly continued by civic groups such as the Alabama State Coordinating Committee for Registration and Voting.[23]

Of course the NAACP was not the only organization active in voter registration, nor did it everywhere attain the leadership position it sought. When NAACP field officer Frederic Morrow returned from his trip through Florida in the spring of 1950, he painted a rather bleak picture of the registration work done by the local branches. The state was in the midst of a mud-slinging primary campaign in which liberal senator Claude Pepper, assailed by his archconservative opponents as "Red Pepper" and "nigger lover," was desperately fighting for his reelection. Nevertheless, Morrow found that "[o]ur branches are pitifully weak on the matter of cooperating with other agencies interested in the same program. Few of them have any sense of organizational methods, nor experience in working with, or introducing themselves to the persons or forces that run their local communities." In contrast, the NAACP officer expressed his unreserved admiration for the activists of the Congress of Industrial Organization: "Any cold objective analysis of this project in Florida must indicate and admit that the CIO and its efficient representatives did the best and most effective job in the matter of organization and increasing the registration of Negroes. Armed with adequate funds, capable workers, and trained in the fundamentals of organization, the CIO group did a job incredible in scope and results."[24]

Unfortunately, despite an unprecedented black turnout, of which nine-tenths went to Pepper according to Morrow's estimate, the incumbent lost his reelection bid. Among other factors, the massive effort at mobilizing black voters had apparently backfired and drawn support to Pepper's opponent from "the backwoods and among the poor whites of Florida, whose sole comfort in life is the white-supremacy doctrine." This was hardly a new experience. A few years earlier, the CIO had launched a massive membership drive called "Operation Dixie" in which it hoped to unionize 1 million new workers in the South. Despite an enormous investment of money and staff, however, the campaign yielded a meager 280,000 new union members at the most, as the CIO had to admit. The iron-clad resistance of the ruling oligarchies against unionization and the racial divide between black and white workers proved too strong even for the giant labor union.[25] In comparison, the NAACP commanded much fewer resources than the CIO, while the opposition it encountered was even more vicious, violent, and sometimes deadly.

The Hazards of Citizenship

With the doctrines of white supremacy still firmly entrenched in most of the South, it was no surprise that the campaigns for mobilizing black voters met with fierce resistance. Even after the constitutional ban on the white primary, the southern states continued to administer the process of registration and voting in a blatantly discriminatory manner, while in many places threats of economic reprisals and physical violence remained only too real. Still, despite numerous protests by the NAACP and the voter leagues and a flood of affidavits from the victims of disfranchisement, the U.S. Department of Justice made no effort to protect black voters.[26] Needless to say, state authorities were even less interested in safeguarding black rights. Where violence was a routine method of political repression, registration workers could easily wind up dead. On Christmas Eve 1951, a bomb killed Harry Moore, president of both the Florida NAACP state conference and the Florida Progressive Voters League, and his wife in their home. No one was ever charged with the crime.[27] Even in the most oppressive environment, however, there were African-Americans who risked their livelihoods and their lives for the elusive rewards of first-class citizenship. Two examples may be given, to pay them their due.

In September 1948, twenty-eight-year-old veteran Isaac B. Nixon of Montgomery County in southwestern Georgia was shot on the steps of his home in front of his wife and children. Before he died, Nixon was able to identify the killers to his neighbor Dover Carter, the president of the local NAACP branch. According to Carter's account, the murder was committed by Jim and Johnnie Johnson, two brothers who enjoyed a nasty reputation as brutal and trigger-happy racists. Nixon was killed because he had ignored warnings to stay away from the Democratic primary. Prior to the murder, Dover Carter himself had been assaulted and severely beaten by Johnnie Johnson and his brother-in-law Thomas Wilson while he was hauling black voters to the polling station on election day. The two Johnson brothers were arrested and indicted for murder but acquitted of all charges by an all-white jury in early November 1948. The NAACP demanded that the U.S. Department of Justice take steps to bring the perpetrators to justice under federal statute. After an investigation into the Carter beating, however, the Department dropped the case since it could not be proven that the NAACP president had been beaten because of his political activities. The two white men had testified that he had threatened them with a gun, and several witnesses had confirmed that Carter had indeed carried a gun when he was driving voters to the polls[28]—quite obviously he had good reason to do so!

Forty-one-year-old Dover Carter, married and a father of ten children, had lived for eighteen years in Alston, Georgia, where he worked the farm of his father-in-law. Although a simple farmer, Carter apparently was a vigorous community leader. In 1946, he had founded the local NAACP branch and taken up registration work in a county where blacks made up about one-third of the population, but virtually none of them voted. Despite constant threats from the Ku Klux Klan, Carter succeeded in enlisting roughly one hundred members in the NAACP and in registering approximately six hundred blacks for the 1948 Democratic primary, including Isaac Nixon and his wife. After the Nixon murder, however, Carter had no choice but to leave his home, as the acquittal of the Johnson brothers made it perfectly clear that the life of a black man did not count for anything in Montgomery County. In early 1949, Carter turned to the NAACP for help after he had relocated his family to Philadelphia, Pennsylvania. Without a job or a claim to public assistance, the large Carter family lived in the slums of Philadelphia with the family of Carter's brother, who had five children himself.[29]

The NAACP leaders felt morally obliged to support the Nixon and Carter families. Not only were they victims of the association's struggle for the right to vote, but both the state conference and the national office had seized upon the case for propaganda purposes and sent out fund-raising letters with the stories and pictures of the two families. A member of the legal department, rather insensitively, had even extolled the "terrific publicity value" of the two incidents. Following an advance of fifty dollars, the board of directors resolved to support Carter financially and to assist him in finding employment and housing.[30] By the summer of 1949, the Carter family had received about $900 in cash. In the meantime, however, the NAACP officer in charge of the case had become increasingly annoyed with Carter, who had turned down a job offer and instead visited friends in Georgia. He recommended terminating the payments because of Carter's "non-cooperative attitude." Carter not only accepted the cut-off without complaint but wrote a moving letter of gratitude to the NAACP, vowing "to do all I can to help the cause." Unfortunately, the NAACP records hold no information of what became of Dover Carter and his family in later years.[31]

A similar case happened in Belzoni, Humphreys County, Mississippi, in 1955. Defying relentless intimidation, two local NAACP leaders, the Reverend George Lee and a grocer named Gus Courts, had tenaciously tried to get blacks to register. The racial climate in Humphreys County, a majority-black county in the Delta region, was so oppressive that even after the vigorous registration campaign led by Lee and Courts only four hundred out of roughly sixteen thousand adult blacks had dared to register. On May 7, 1955, George Lee was killed in a drive-by shooting, but the local white press spoke of an "accident" and the sheriff declared the shotgun pellets in Lee's face to be "fillings from his teeth." No investigation was launched and no one was ever charged with the murder. In November 1955, sixty-year-old Gus Courts, by then the only registered black voter of Humphreys County, was also shot and severely injured, but luckily he survived the attempt.[32]

Staying in Mississippi was no longer an option for Gus Courts. After brief interludes in Dallas and Los Angeles, he ended up in Chicago in the fall of 1956. Evidently, the NAACP supported the civil rights hero generously. The association paid his medical bills, several debts on his store in Belzoni, and the cost of his trips to relatives in Texas and California. In return, Courts appeared at numerous NAACP events as a living witness to the brutality of racism in Mississippi. But while Courts at first had much praise for the NAACP's generosity, he soon began to complain that it had forgotten him.[33] Actually, the association continued to assist Gus Courts with small amounts of money, and when he approached the NAACP for a loan of $2,000 to start a new business in Chicago, he received $1,500 without a fixed schedule of repayment. At the end of the 1960s, Courts still resided in Chicago, but due to health problems he had given up his business and lived on public assistance, contemplating a return to Mississippi. Although no longer a member of the NAACP, he nevertheless declared that he did not regret anything he had done in the fight for the ballot.[34]

Isaac Nixon and George Lee payed with their lives for their unwavering commitment to equal citizenship. Dover Carter and Gus Courts lost their livelihoods and, perhaps even worse, their homes. For all the racist oppression they faced in the South, both men had been well-respected community leaders. Following their expulsion, they went through a brief period of ephemeral public attention organized by the NAACP, after which they and their families found themselves on the margins of urban life in the North. That Dover Carter in this situation temporarily returned to his home state instead of looking for a job perhaps reflected less his "non-cooperative attitude" than plain homesickness and disorientation. Certainly, the instant termination of support does not betray a particular awareness of these problems on the part of the NAACP office.

It would be unfair, however, to accuse the NAACP of indifference toward the fate of the women and men who fell into need and deprivation as a consequence of their civil rights work. Carter's and Courts's requests for assistance were promptly answered, and the association subsequently tried to help them in rebuilding their lives. Yet the NAACP's financial means were very limited and would never suffice to cover the high personal risks that voting rights activists faced in the South. As far as the records bear out, the national secretariat and the board of directors earnestly tried to aid NAACP members and workers who had become the targets of economic pressures. W. C. Patton has mentioned a special fund in a black-owned bank in Memphis to provide relief and loans to victims of economic reprisals in Mississippi. However, each case needed to be reviewed individually, and no assurances of material help could be given in advance.[35] Whatever precious little aid was available, this could never change the basic fact that the voter registration work of the NAACP had to be carried out by ordinary people who had much to lose without being able to hope for personal security, let alone gain.

The 1952 Registration Drive

Support for destitute activists was not the only financial burden of voter registration that the association found difficult to shoulder. Even though NAACP members and other volunteers usually worked without compensation, the purchase of technical equipment, the rent for office space, the printing of leaflets and brochures, and other items of that kind caused considerable expense. Basically, the costs of registration drives had to be paid for by the local branches. The budget of the national organization covered mostly the expenditures of running the operations of the New York headquarters and left little room for subsidizing local projects. On the contrary, in addition to the membership fees, the branches had to make so-called annual apportionments of between $50 and $300, depending on their numerical strength. The NAACP budget was almost completely financed by its members, while external funding, which would play an important role in the 1960s, was almost negligible. In its five-year consolidated budget covering the period from 1948 to 1952, the NAACP listed a total income of slightly more than $1.5 million. Only about $46,000 came from external sources, compared to $1,338,000 derived from membership fees, branch contributions, and subscriptions to *The Crisis*. The lion's share of the $1,653,000 expenditures, namely $927,000, went to paying the salaries of the NAACP staff. Throughout this period the association was running an average annual deficit of almost $37,000 that was covered by reserve funds accumulated during the Second World War, when the membership figures had skyrocketed. In short, its financial situation did not allow the national NAACP to plan and implement a large-scale, coordinated voter registration effort.[36]

In early 1952, however, the NAACP received an unexpected contribution of $25,000 that was specifically earmarked for a political action program in the South. The money came from Loula Davis Lasker, a wealthy Jewish social worker and philanthropist who wished to remain anonymous.[37] Understandably, the NAACP was thrilled by this extraordinarily generous donation and immediately began to plan a concerted registration campaign aimed at a substantial increase of the southern black electorate in the upcoming national elections in the fall. Secretary Walter White proposed to target eight southern states and to hire "four top-flight persons," each of whom would be in charge of coordinating the drive in two states. White estimated an allocation of $6,000 per person for salary, travel, and maintenance, thus leaving merely $1,000 for other expenses, such as printing and other administrative expenditures. In addition, the secretary hoped to win black celebrities from sports, entertainment, and the media for short radio recordings to be produced at minimum cost.[38]

White's proposal to spend the entire grant on the employment of four relatively well-paid activists and to tackle practically the entire region did not meet with the approval of the NAACP staff, however. Henry Lee Moon, who was much more knowledgeable about voter registration issues than the secretary, considered it too ambitious and warned against the danger of spreading the money thin. He would have preferred to concentrate upon a single state or selected congressional districts, but since the donor had requested a larger project, Moon pleaded to target three states with a good chance of close and competitive races, namely Alabama, Florida, and North Carolina. Moreover, the NAACP drive should seek the cooperation of other organizations, particularly the CIO. Moon also suggested holding a coaching session as soon as the field staff for the campaign had been selected.[39]

In March a staff conference of the national secretariat agreed to launch the registration drive in the six states of Alabama, Florida, Georgia, the two Carolinas, and Virginia. For each state a coordinator would be hired at the rather modest compensation of a $25 per diem plus travel and living expenses. The secretariat calculated a total of roughly $8,000 for personnel and $5,000 for printing costs. Another $1,000 were set aside for a preparatory meeting. In addition, each state conference would receive $1,000 to defray miscellaneous expenses, provided that it was able to raise matching funds. This budget left at least $5,000 of the Lasker grant for later projects, and indeed, money from the fund continued to flow until 1955.[40]

Two weeks later, the NAACP publicly announced a "non-partisan drive to double the present number of Negro voters in the South before the November election." Since the present number was estimated at 1 million, this announcement amounted to the ambitious goal of 2 million registered black voters, more than ten times the figure of a decade earlier. Apart from the proclamation that the North Carolina NAACP would take the lead, no details were given. Understandably, Henry Moon did not want "to forewarn the hostile elements and, possibly, to endanger the life and limbs of our workers."[41] Although the pay was not exactly generous, capable and experienced state coordinators were soon found. In April a coaching session, called the NAACP Political Action Institute, was held at Clark College in Atlanta where fieldworkers were instructed in the organizational techniques and legal aspects of voter registration. Confidently, the meeting passed a statement that reaffirmed the goal of 2 million registered black voters before November.[42]

Although the campaign funded by the Lasker grant was launched with impressive speed, it started too late to come even close to its self-imposed threshold. In Alabama, the deadline to pay the poll tax had already expired, so special attention was payed to veterans, who were exempt from the poll tax requirement. In Florida and Georgia, the registration dates for the crucial Democratic primary had also passed.[43] In a preliminary appraisal in August, Henry Moon estimated the number of registered black voters in the eleven states of the former Confederacy at approximately 1.2 million, but hoped for further gains in the remaining two months. Half a year after the 1952 elections, the NAACP director of public relations gave a total of 1.35 million but admitted that this was not absolutely reliable. Still, it seems reasonable to assume that around 1.2 million southern blacks had registered to vote prior to the 1952 elections, which represented an increase of four hundred thousand compared to four years earlier.[44]

Obviously, the goal of 2 million had been missed by a wide margin; nor could it be pretended that the increase had exclusively resulted from the activities of the NAACP. Given the fragmentary and vague registration data, it is not even clear whether the NAACP was more successful in the states that had been specifically targeted than in the rest of the South, where the local branches acted—or did not act—on their own. Nevertheless, to see the 1952 registration drive as a failure would be totally off the mark. If the NAACP figures are roughly accurate, they indicate that the number of registered black voters in the South went up by at least two hundred thousand within a few months. Without any doubt, the association could legitimately claim a large part in bringing about this increase. Despite the failure to achieve the symbolic 2 million target, never realistic in the first place, the NAACP leaders were rightly satisfied. The coordinated effort had worked and ought to be put on a regular basis, Henry Moon concluded, because "an effective program of political action requires year 'round work." He suggested hiring full-time registration workers for each of the southern states and putting a member of the national office in charge of coordinating and supervising their activities. Also, he argued that more attention should be paid to local and state elections, which generated growing interest among southern blacks.[45]

For all its shortcomings, the 1952 drive had obviously sparked a fire among the southern NAACP branches and state conferences. A report of November 1953 by Lucille Black, the membership secretary of the national office, painted a picture full of optimism and activism. Virtually all state organizations had held meetings on registration and voting. The fact that representatives of the association's headquarters, including Walter White, Roy Wilkins, and Henry Moon, were present at all of these meetings underscored how important the leadership considered this work. Even the Arkansas NAACP state conference, so far not exactly a hotbed of political action, featured a large meeting in Little Rock, with Walter White as the principal speaker. On this occasion, the NAACP secretary was presented with the "key to the city" by the mayor—an indication that the growing political presence of southern blacks had not escaped the attention of white office holders.[46]

Much groundwork remained, however, especially in the Black Belt counties of the Deep South. A report from Alabama of early 1953 showed that in eleven counties where the black population equaled or exceeded that of whites, only a minuscule average of 1.3 percent of all eligible African-Americans were registered. Two counties had no black voters at all.[47] Undaunted, W. C. Patton, the NAACP's tireless registration worker in the state, promised Walter White "to stay in the fight until we have 200,000 qualified Negro voters in the State of Alabama." Indeed, in the three-month registration drive prior to the 1954 primaries, Patton and his coworkers of the Alabama State Coordinating Committee for Registration and Voting, an umbrella group largely identical with the NAACP, toured the state in a marathon of countless mass meetings, speeches, voter "clinics," and door-to-door canvassing. The registration effort neatly dovetailed with organizing for the NAACP. At a meeting in Selma, fifty new memberships were sold and $300 taken in for the association. In several smaller towns the nuclei for new branches were set up. As a consequence, black registration in Alabama increased considerably, even in areas where blacks had been almost entirely disfranchised. In Russell County, for example, the number of registered black voters grew from fifty-four to more than four hundred, according to Patton. In the cities of Birmingham, Mobile, and Tuscaloosa it soared by several thousand each. In his report to Loula Lasker, whose grant had paid for the Alabama drive, Walter White boasted that about sixty thousand blacks out of a total registration of eighty thousand had voted in the primary and helped to reelect Senator John Sparkman, a racial moderate by Alabama standards.[48]

White was not the only NAACP leader in an upbeat mood. When in the spring of 1954 the popular African-American magazine *Jet* asked Henry Moon for figures on the potential black vote in the South and the future goals of the NAACP registration work, the director of public relations could not resist a little grandstanding. For the 1956 elections, he projected 2.7 million registered black voters for the eleven former Confederate states plus Kentucky and Oklahoma. Except for Mississippi and Alabama, the margin for each state was set at slightly more than 50 percent of the black voting-age population. Even for the Magnolia state, where perhaps forty thousand blacks out of a half million adults had been registered in 1952, Moon envisioned the aspiring goal of one hundred thousand.[49]

Such high-flying optimism soon foundered on the harsh realities of southern racism, which again intensified in the wake of the Supreme Court's momentous *Brown* ruling of May 1954. Race-baiting politicians, the White Citizens' Councils, the Klan, and all others who rallied to defend white supremacy were fully aware that segregation could only last if blacks were kept politically powerless. As a consequence of the "massive resistance" movement against school desegregation, racial demagoguery reached new heights and hostility against black voters grew. Prior to the gubernatorial primaries of August 1955, state authorities and the Democratic Party of Mississippi conspired to purge the registration books of black voters, declaring "all attempted registrations since January 26, 1955, not valid and of no effect whatever." With few exceptions, all voters had to register again, furnishing registrars with the opportunity to reject as many black applicants as possible. According to the NAACP, black registration in the state dropped to eight thousand. At the same time, a wave of racial violence swept Mississippi. In addition to the attempts on George Lee and Gus Courts mentioned above, voting rights activist Lamar Smith was shot to death in front of the courthouse in Brookhaven, Mississippi, on August 13, 1955. As usual, no one was held accountable for the murder.[50]

Instead of rising to one hundred thousand, the number of registered black voters in Mississippi stood at about twenty thousand in the election year of 1956. Southern black registration at large hovered around 1.2 million no more than four years earlier, and a far cry from the NAACP's goal of 2.7 million.[51] Moreover, the association felt the supremacist backlash directly and painfully. On the pretext that the NAACP was running business operations in the state, Alabama required the association to register as a private corporation liable to taxation and to disclose its financial records and membership lists. Since the NAACP for obvious reasons declined to give the names of its members to the state authorities, a state judge issued an injunction that barred the association from all activities and set a fine of $100,000 for contempt. Other southern states followed suit with similar legal attacks. The association, of course, challenged these injunctions in court and won several major victories, including a series of favorable rulings by the U.S. Supreme Court, but it took until 1964 to enforce the NAACP's constitutional right to free association in the state of Alabama. Although its work was carried on by civic associations—incidently the Alabama State Coordinating Committee for Registration and Voting changed its name to the Alabama State Coordinating Association for Registration and Voting, with W. C. Patton as its president—these attacks did serious damage to the NAACP's organizational strength in the South. In the second half of the 1950s, it lost 250 branches and almost fifty thousand members in the region.[52]

This setback, of course, did not leave the registration effort unaffected. While the white backlash could not wipe out the groundwork that had been done since the 1940s, the optimistic expectations that the black electorate in the South would smoothly continue to expand clearly did not materialize. In 1956, the NAACP field-workers constantly complained that the injunctions and the arbitrary purges of the voter lists made their election year job exceedingly difficult. In June, the Communist *Daily Worker,* much to Roy Wilkins's dismay, quoted the NAACP regional secretary for the Southeast, Ruby Hurley, as saying that due to its preoccupation with the school desegregation issue the NAACP had neglected the struggle for the vote and was "a long way off from the two million Negro voters in the South in 1956 of which Walter White spoke."[53] Evidently, even the NAACP activists felt that their registration efforts had entered a stalemate.

The NAACP Voter Registration Committee

In her 1956 annual report, Ruby Hurley had argued that "until Congress and the Federal Government take positive action to insure for Negroes the unhampered right to register and vote, our goal in this area will be difficult to reach." The following year, Congress indeed passed the first civil rights bill since Reconstruction. Among other stipulations, it authorized the Department of Justice to seek court injunctions against interferences with the right to vote. Although the practical impact of the law was almost negligible, its mere existence inspired the optimism of civil rights workers. Medgar Evers, the NAACP field secretary for Mississippi, enthusiastically called it "a solid foundation upon which we can build a better Mississippi for the Negro as well as the whites."[54]

Even before the law was signed by President Dwight D. Eisenhower, Gloster Current, the NAACP director of branches, assembled a conference on registration and voting for November 1957 in order to discuss the opportunities emanating from the new legislation. Current wrote a working paper for the meeting in which he anticipated the key features of the association's registration campaign in the coming years. He proposed to concentrate on the "centers of Negro urban populations" where resistance was relatively weak and considerable numerical gains could be expected. The director of branches accepted that other areas would be temporarily neglected, although he wanted to tackle some of the "hard spots," too, not so much to increase the number of black voters as to provoke test cases of voting discrimination to be pursued by the federal government. Current also suggested appointing a new director for voting and registration in the national office who would operate directly under the supervision of the executive secretary and coordinate the grassroots registration campaigns in the South. The money should come from the national budget and from special fund-raising efforts. Voter registration, Current concluded, should be "the number one program item in southern branches for at least the next three or four years."[55]

For the most part, the Atlanta conference of NAACP activists followed these proposals. In its final declaration, the conference pledged itself to the goal of bringing the registration of southern blacks to the same level as that of white voters. This was to be achieved in cooperation with the churches, organized labor, and civic associations. For the 1960 election year, the margin was set at 60 percent of the potential black electorate, or approximately 3 million registered voters. In January 1958, Roy Wilkins reported that a budget of $60,000 had already been allocated for the southern registration campaigns. All paid personnel would be recruited from the association's southern state organizations and employment would depend "entirely on the production of new voters." Even fixed quotas were briefly considered.[56]

A new Voter Registration Committee was created by the national office, with Kelly Alexander, president of the North Carolina state conference, as its chairman. At the February 1958 meeting of the board of directors, Wilkins proposed to hire John M. Brooks, an employee of the Virginia NAACP, as the Southwide registration director. W. C. Patton, who had been without permanent employment since the NAACP had been banned in Alabama, was made the field secretary. While Alexander represented the committee on the board of directors, Brooks and Patton did the job on the ground operating from their offices in Richmond, Virginia, and Memphis, Tennessee, respectively. The two men remained in charge of the NAACP voter registration in the South until the early 1970s, when Brooks declined to relocate his office to Birmingham and Patton succeeded him as the director.[57]

John Brooks began his work in March 1958, bursting with energy. He immediately went on a trip to Mississippi to get the local registration drives going and then continued to Orlando, Memphis, and several other southern cities. In May, he cautiously asked Wilkins if perhaps he was stretching his travel budget too far. When Brooks requested $1,000 for bureau machinery a few months later, Wilkins told him to "slow down." But in general the secretary was highly satisfied with Brooks's hands-on approach and with his frankness that brought "a fresh viewpoint" uninhibited by internal politics to the association's fieldwork.[58]

With the registration efforts largely focusing on the urban areas of the South, the NAACP activists saw apathy among potential black voters as the major obstacle to be overcome. Even where little discrimination existed, as in Virginia, blacks neglected to pay the poll tax, and many of those who did pay subsequently failed to register and vote—with the firm grip of the political machine of Senator Harry Byrd on state politics, there was in fact little to vote on for black Virginians. In Tulsa and Oklahoma City, blacks could register freely, but less than 25 percent of those eligible actually cast a ballot.[59] Moreover, on his travels throughout the South, Brooks realized that the registration work of many branches left much to be desired. Local leaders ignored the association's policy of nonpartisanship and got heavily involved in partisan politics, blurring the line between their own political ambitions and their work for the NAACP. Others were simply inept. Brooks described the Texas state conference he attended in the fall of 1958 as "chaos." Obviously, the grassroots level seemed to need some guidance from above. In early 1959, Patton exhorted all southern branches to immediately appoint voter registration committees and to double their efforts in the upcoming drives.[60]

In order to overcome the lamentable state of apathy among potential black voters, the NAACP activists tried to make clear that political powerlessness and economic and social discrimination were two sides of the same coin. John Brooks designed a variety of voter registration posters that dramatized the vast gaps in job opportunities, wages, and community services between whites and blacks, captioned with rhetorical questions and answers, such as, "We Do the Heavy Work . . . Why? Because We Don't Use the Ballot." When some racist madman fired at six black children in Richmond, wounding two,

Brooks had leaflets printed that read: "Voting Can Stop This!" And, of course, the NAACP registration director sought the cooperation of preachers and teachers as the two most important multipliers in the black community. Brooks found, however, that ministers were wary that the NAACP voter registration propaganda might divert contributions away from their church funds, while teachers were afraid of reprisals. In March 1959, the black Mississippi Teacher Association cancelled an invitation to John Brooks to speak before its annual convention.[61]

Nevertheless, the NAACP voter registration drives made good progress. At the end of 1958, Medgar Evers reported from Mississippi that the campaign Brooks had helped to start in April had pushed the numbers of registered blacks up to 1,500 in Meridian and 5,000 in Jackson. Even in several of the hard-core rural counties the first inroads were made. When Brooks presented his estimates of southern black registration for the same year, he found five states with an increase and six states with a decrease, adding up to a total net gain of 28,450 new black voters. According to Brooks, there was a simple explanation for the state-by-state differences: "Where state and local branch officials gave active support to the NAACP voter registration program, we had an increase in the number of Negro voters."[62]

This conclusion may have been a little self-serving, but it was hardly unwarranted. Tennessee provides a good illustration of how the interplay between local activism, support from the NAACP's voter registration committee, and a favorable environment could yield impressive results. In Tennessee the number of registered black voters more than doubled between 1956 and 1958, soaring from 90,000 to 185,000. Even if Brooks's estimate is taken with a grain of salt, it gives a generally correct picture of a state that appeared to have waited for a vigorous mobilization campaign. Of all the states of the former Confederacy, Tennessee had retained the strongest remnants of a two-party system with competitive elections. The poll tax had been abolished and, except for a few Black Belt counties in the southwestern corner of the state, resistance to black voting was relatively mild. Moreover, with Memphis, Nashville, Chattanooga, and Knoxville, Tennessee had four large urban centers with a significant black electorate. Next to New Orleans, Memphis had a larger African-American population than any other southern city. When W. C. Patton had to leave Birmingham because of the ban on NAACP operations, he moved his office to Memphis.

In March 1958, the Memphis NAACP branch asked the national office for support to organize a large-scale registration drive. In May, Patton launched the Shelby County Non-Partisan Registration Campaign, whose network of one thousand volunteers added several hundred new black voters to the rolls every day. When the drive ended in July, black registration had been increased from 43,000 to 56,500, according to Patton's count. In the first three months of 1959, a new campaign was started in Shelby County in which another nine thousand blacks were registered. At the same time, however, pursuant to Tennessee laws, all registered persons who had not voted within the last four years were struck from the books, which Patton believed affected about seven thousand African-Americans. Despite this purge, the NAACP-led drive managed to achieve a net gain of two thousand black voters.[63]

One important stimulation for this campaign was that for the first time several black candidates were running for public office in Memphis who seemed to have a reasonable chance of beating their white opponents. Eventually, none of them was elected, but all came in second place. Out of fifty-eight thousand registered black voters, approximately forty thousand went to the polls. Yet the city elections of 1959 also saw the largest overall turnout in the history of Memphis, a good example that the mobilization of black voters often triggered a "countermobilization" among whites. Still, the political enthusiasm of Memphis's black citizenry was unbroken and continued into the presidential elections of 1960, when the NAACP campaign pushed the number of black voters to a record seventy-six thousand. Since the first drive in 1958, the figures had almost doubled.[64]

The growth of the black electorate yielded some political results as well. Patton argued that black voters in Tennessee had tipped the scale in favor of U.S. senator Estes Kefauver, a moderate, in the Democratic primary of August 1960 and secured the state for the Kennedy-Johnson ticket in the presidential race. Perhaps more importantly, the change was also felt at the local level. In the city and county administrations of Memphis, new job opportunities for blacks opened up, including the hiring of several deputy sheriffs and twenty policemen, and the public library and the city auditorium were officially desegregated.[65]

Not all of Tennessee showed such encouraging signs of racial change, however. In Fayette County, a rural Black Belt county adjacent to the Mississippi border, where only 450 out of 30,000 blacks were listed on the rolls, the registration effort met with massive economic reprisals by the local planter and merchant oligarchy. Public employees were fired, and sharecroppers were denied credit and evicted from the plantations. Merchants and wholesalers refused to sell their goods to customers who had tried to register. For more than half a year, the NAACP organized the distribution of food and clothing to families who had become the targets of economic pressures. Perhaps Patton had these events in mind when in late 1960 he evaluated his achievements in remarkably sober terms: "I believe that the whole matter can be summed up by saying the intensified political action program in the south during the past two and a half years has more than paid off and justified its existence. We must remember, however, that we barely scar[r]ed the surface. This should be a day by day, month by month and year by year program."[66]

Although they could not expect a quick breakthrough, John Brooks and W. C. Patton had good reason to be proud of their work. In addition to their achievements in Memphis, sizable numbers of black voters were registered in other southern cities. In Tampa, Florida, the Non-Partisan Registration Committee launched by Patton added four thousand new names to the list between January and April 1960. In Atlanta, thirty-five hundred were registered during the same period, pushing the total to forty thousand. In his 1959 annual report, Brooks had already noted that "due to our activities in many sections of the south, more and more Negroes are taking an active part in the politics of their communities." Although he dutifully acknowledged that many groups and individuals had a part in this effort, the NAACP voter registration director left no doubt that the credit was due to the association: "In the south, you will find 95% of the voter registration programs, regardless of the name, initiated and led by staunch NAACP leaders and members."[67]

This statement of course cannot be verified, but there is no question that Brooks and Patton did their job with admirable skill and dedication. Between 1958 and 1960, the NAACP's southern political action program touched more than four hundred cities and counties. The tangible increases in the southern black electorate that these activities helped to produce even caught the attention of the national press. In October 1960, *Newsweek* ran a state-by-state estimate of the black vote in the South, concluding that it might decide the outcome of the presidential race in no less than seven states. After the election, pollster George Gallup confirmed that black voters had saved several southern states for Kennedy. Emphatically, the NAACP voter registration committee proclaimed that "the cloudy skies of political apathy among Negroes are becoming clear." More manpower and money were needed to expand on the successful work of the past two years.[68]

However, except for a single clerk in each of their offices, Brooks and Patton basically had to do the job all by themselves. In 1961, they helped organize seventy-eight registration drives and fifteen regional workshops. By his own account, W. C. Patton traveled eighty-six thousand miles, gave twenty-one speeches, sent out ten thousand letters, and had more than thirty-seven thousand pieces of literature distributed.[69] Still, the national office did not come up with any substantial increase in staff or funds. On the contrary, the registration activists were constantly prodded to participate in the general NAACP fund- raising and membership drives and to exercise strict financial discipline in all of their activities. When he established his office in Memphis, Patton had to lease used furniture, and only after five years did he dare to request the purchase of an air conditioner to alleviate the oppressive summer heat in the Mississippi Delta. In response to the permanent bickering over the high costs of their work, John Brooks correctly observed that voter registration made an important contribution to the overall program and success of the NAACP and deserved to be funded more liberally.[70]

For 1962, the voter registration director proposed an unprecedented budget of $100,000 to underscore the key importance of his work. It was hard to tell, though, from where the money should come. Since 1958, the annual budgets of the association had nominally allocated yearly amounts of $60,000 to $70,000 for voter registration, but apparently these sums never fully materialized. In the fall of 1962, Assistant Secretary John Morsell estimated that the NAACP had spent a total of $150,000 on registration over the past five years, which makes an annual average of just $30,000. These funds mostly covered the operations of Brooks and Patton. All other expenses had to be defrayed by local fund-raising, which usually yielded around $4,000 in the larger urban black communities of the South.[71]

Against this backdrop, the numerical results of the NAACP voter registration drives were truly impressive. The association itself claimed to have registered up to a half million southern blacks between 1958 and 1962.[72] This figure may be exaggerated, but it does not seem to be entirely fictitious, given the fact that the NAACP was indeed the only civil rights organization conducting registration campaigns throughout the entire region. To be sure, there were also several weak spots. In Alabama, the NAACP was formally banned, although Patton actively participated in the work of the Alabama State Coordinating Association for Registration and Voting. Arkansas did not play a major role in the NAACP drives and was rarely mentioned in the reports by Brooks and Patton. In Louisiana, the NAACP made a considerable registration effort but ran into stiff and often violent resistance. If anything, the situation was even worse in Mississippi, despite the tireless efforts by Medgar Evers and W. C. Patton.[73]

Nevertheless, in other states, especially of the upper South, black registration continued to grow and began to make an impact. As Patton put it in his annual report of 1961, "Demagogues are replaced by liberals or moderates and in many instances, demagogues made every effort to become moderates or liberals." However, conciliatory rhetoric by white politicians and a few public jobs for blacks did not yet represent fundamental changes in the power structure and the political culture of the South. Moreover, John Brooks continued to lament the immaturity and opportunism of local black leaders, who were used to ingratiating themselves to the white elites. "Most of our politicians," he described the average type, "are hungry, insecure and easily bought for a quarter." As a remedy Brooks suggested that the NAACP pursue a "program of practical politics" to educate African-American leaders about the long-term interests of the black community.[74]

The national office, however, did not wish to see its registration activists become too directly involved in local politics, but instead wanted them to influence the political balance "by simply rolling up respectable increases in registration." Of course, voter registration and practical politics could never be neatly separated, since controversial political issues and attractive candidates usually provided crucial incentives to register and vote. As mentioned above, the success of the 1959 NAACP registration drive in Memphis and the ensuing record turnout of black voters had only been possible because black candidates had a real chance of winning. Registration and politics went hand in glove, as the NAACP voter registration committee freely admitted: "We are certain the techniques learned by Memphis leaders in our voter registration program were used to a good advantage by the Volunteer Committee for the Sugarman [the black candidate for Public Works Commissioner] campaign."[75] In this basic sense, registration was always "practical politics," even if the NAACP stuck to the principle of nonpartisanship.

In view of the progress that the association's registration drives yielded in the South, the shortcomings in the North were all the more striking. As early as 1959, Roy Wilkins, shocked by the low registration rates of many northern black communities, straightforwardly asked Brooks: "How do we light a fire under the Northern branches of the NAACP?" The voter registration director had no doubt that he could launch an effective program in the North as well, but warned against spreading the association's resources thin. Brooks nevertheless embarked on an information tour through Pennsylvania, Ohio, Michigan, and Illinois. His impressions were not exactly favorable. The majority of the branches he visited did not even have a voter registration committee and left the job largely to labor and party organizations. While the NAACP work in the South was hampered by "Uncle Toms," the northern black communities were plagued by professional politicians who specialized in manipulating the black vote with the use of a few dollars. The first tasks, Brooks emphasized, were to impress on the local NAACP leaders that the association was no place for "political shenanigans" and to prove to the black community that "we are non-partisan and strictly interested in Negroes voting in large numbers and voting intelligently."[76]

As in the past, the NAACP's concept for the political mobilization of the black community continued to be inspired by the ideal of enlightened self-interest that would sooner or later produce first-class citizenship and equality of opportunity for African-Americans. By the late 1950s, however, the belief in the power of the ballot was increasingly challenged by the dynamics of nonviolent direct action, which opened up a new and crucial phase of the civil rights struggle.

7

Voter Registration or Nonviolent Direct Action?

While the NAACP voter registration workers were chipping away at the political pillars of white supremacy, the association's lawyers had scored a long-desired breakthrough in the legal battle against racial segregation. In its 1954 decision *Brown v. Board of Education of Topeka, Kansas,* the U.S. Supreme Court at long last repudiated the "separate but equal" doctrine in the field of public education. Although *Brown* sparked a furious backlash among the white South and did not bring about the fast desegregation of southern schools, the leaders of the NAACP nevertheless felt that their faith in legal action had finally been vindicated.[1] On the eve of the NAACP's fiftieth anniversary, executive secretary Roy Wilkins wrote a letter to Whitney Young, the dean of Atlanta University and future director of the National Urban League, predicting that the association's historical mission was close to being accomplished: "We have won our propaganda battle. It is no longer a tenable or fashionable policy to discriminate racially. Those who do so are on the defensive. We have nailed down the propaganda victory with legal decisions. All is by no means won . . . but as the NAACP looks back as it enters its fiftieth year, it can say truthfully that it hewed to the goals laid down in 1909."[2]

Wilkins knew quite well, however, that there was little reason for complacency. In particular, he worried that the association was in danger of losing touch with the aspiring younger generation of blacks. "I want to bring about changes," he wrote to the NAACP voter registration director, John Brooks, "not just because I want to do so, but because the times have changed and we have got to have a different organization if we are to lead our people in these new times. If we don't change our ways, some other organization will come along and take our place."[3] Thus, while boasting the association's historical achievements, the NAACP leader did not overlook that the struggle for civil rights was developing into a broad social movement, threatening to leave the NAACP behind.

The challenge was both strategic and organizational. With the Montgomery, Alabama, bus boycott of 1955–56, southern blacks revived the concept of nonviolent direct action and successfully challenged racial segregation head-on rather than in the courtrooms. Moreover, the Montgomery boycott propelled Martin Luther King Jr., a young Baptist minister from Atlanta with a charismatic personality and a gift for mesmerizing oratory, to national prominence. In early 1957, King and his followers formed the Southern Christian Leadership Conference (SCLC) in order to coordinate nonviolent protest in the South.[4] And the SCLC did not remain the only new civil rights group. Following the spontaneous sit-in movement of early 1960, southern black students, with the help of former NAACP director of branches Ella Baker, organized the Student Nonviolent Coordinating Committee (SNCC), pronounced "SNICK." A year later, the Congress of Racial Equality (CORE), a pacifist civil rights group that had been founded in Chicago during the Second World War but become largely defunct in the 1950s, launched its campaign of "freedom rides" throughout the South in order to test a recent Supreme Court ruling banning racial segregation in interstate travel.[5]

Hence, by the early 1960s the NAACP faced a paradoxical situation: black civil rights activism was soaring, but the association seemed to be falling into the rearguard of the movement and its methods began looking outdated. Even if the SCLC, CORE, and SNCC took pains to emphasize that they had no desire to replace the NAACP, they nevertheless posed an unmistakable challenge to the association.[6] Like all established organizations, the NAACP did not exactly welcome external competition and viewed the newcomers with deep suspicion. Open conflict, however, had to be avoided since this would hurt both the cause of civil rights and the association's reputation. Also, the NAACP leaders did not ignore the need to readjust their goals and methods to the new times. In March 1962, a joint committee of board members and executive staff that had been formed to develop a response to the expanded activities of the direct action groups concluded: "We should not engage in attacks upon them but rather accept the challenge, strengthen our weaknesses and accelerate our program in employment, housing, education, political action and other fields to make certain of the continuance of the NAACP as the number one civil rights organization in America."[7]

However, the NAACP did not simply embrace nonviolent direct action; nor did it renounce its claim to a leadership role in the civil rights movement. Instead it responded by stepping up its already considerable efforts in the field of voter registration. From the association's perspective this approach held two distinct advantages: First, voter registration offered an alternative to direct action by channeling mass participation into the political process. Second, it provided the association with an excellent opportunity to reassert its organizational strength and superiority over its rivals.

Between Rivalry and Cooperation

It should not be surprising that the NAACP leaders did not eagerly welcome new players on the civil rights field. They had given many years of service to the association and were deeply convinced that their own goals and methods represented the best interest of the black community at large. This claim to leadership created tensions even with those groups that largely shared the NAACP's outlook. After the Internal Revenue Service had enforced the complete separation of the Legal Defense and Education Fund (LDF) from the NAACP in 1957, an increasingly unpleasant bickering over fund-raising activities and legal strategy developed between the two groups.[8] There were also occasional quarrels with the National Urban League, which got more directly involved in the civil rights struggle after Whitney Young became its leader in 1961. Interestingly, in these clashes the NAACP often posed as the "militant" part and ungraciously chided the Urban League for compromising with racial discrimination.[9]

The attitude of the NAACP leadership toward the SCLC, SNCC, and CORE, however, was shaped by a combination of paternalism and suspicion that sometimes bordered on outright hostility. Although the SCLC had decided not to form a large organizational structure and saw itself as an umbrella group for various local initiatives, the NAACP feared that the ministers planned to fill the void that had been opened up by the ban against the association in several southern states following the *Brown* ruling. As a fund-raising letter by SCLC cofounder Reverend Ralph Abernathy stated, the group did not wish to replace the NAACP but "to supplement it and work in areas where it is prevented legally or psychologically from functioning."[10] NAACP activists, for their part, had no use for unsolicited help and were determined to protect their turf. John Brooks, the tireless registration worker, looked with utter disdain at the fledgling SCLC: "They hold emotional mass and prayer meetings, take up money and do nothing on the civil rights front," he wrote in one of his reports. According to Brooks, the NAACP continued to enjoy strong support among southern blacks and was in no danger of being superseded by a bunch of preachers.[11] Roy Wilkins also did not conceal his mistrust. Martin Luther King Jr. himself might not harbor the idea of replacing the association, he wrote to Dr. Benjamin Mays of Moorehouse College, one of King's closest advisers, "yet the very items that he announces are traditional NAACP items and it is natural that many of his followers would assume not that he is attempting to help the NAACP or supplement its efforts, but that he is supplanting the organization."[12]

Shortly after the SCLC had been founded, the national secretariat informed the NAACP field staff that they were not allowed to participate in any activities of the King group until the association had decided upon its future relations with the new organization. To set the tone, Gloster Current, the director of branches, included an editorial by the Pittsburgh Courier that questioned the need "for having two organizations with the same goal when one has been doing such an effective job."[13] Unfortunately, Medgar Evers, the NAACP field secretary in Mississippi, had already attended an SCLC conference and agreed to serve as its assistant secretary. Wilkins told him to resign quietly at a convenient time and without jeopardizing any future cooperation with King's organization. Evers got the message. He stepped down from his SCLC post and subsequently saw to it that attempts by the SCLC to establish a foothold on his home turf in Jackson, Mississippi, were "tactfully" discouraged. While the national secretariat did not prohibit its branches from cooperating in SCLC projects, it insisted on retaining control over all such activities.[14]

In addition to the inevitable organizational competition, the personal rivalry between Martin Luther King Jr. and Roy Wilkins, although never openly admitted, complicated matters between the NAACP and the SCLC. In public, the two leaders went out of their way to demonstrate an amicable relationship. As early as 1957, Martin Luther King, by then not even thirty years of age, was given the NAACP's Spingarn Medal, an annual award established by Joel Spingarn in 1913 to honor an African-American for outstanding achievements in the service of the race. Earlier recipients of the prestigious award included such black luminaries as W.E.B. Du Bois, Mary McLeod Bethune, and A. Philip Randolph. When the Pittsburgh Courier in early 1958 reported on an alleged "rift" between King and the NAACP, the SCLC leader immediately bought a $1,000 life membership in the association. In his speech at the fiftieth annual NAACP convention held in New York in July 1959, King pointedly called Roy Wilkins his "good friend" and celebrated the work of the NAACP as "one of the glowing epics of our time."[15]

In fact, the relationship between King and Wilkins was far from friendly and deteriorated in subsequent years. The NAACP leader, despite his sober demeanor, was no stranger to personal vanity, and he watched with growing disenchantment as the upstart preacher almost thirty years his junior outshone him as America's most prominent spokesman for civil rights. Wilkins's dislike of King did not escape the attention of the FBI, which, under the direction of J. Edgar Hoover, waged a vicious clandestine campaign against Martin Luther King in the 1960s aimed at destroying the civil rights leader's reputation and mental sanity. In the summer and fall of 1964, Wilkins had two confidential meetings with Hoover's assistant, Cartha DeLoach, in which he allegedly denounced King as a "liar," a "sexual degenerate," and a fellow traveler of the communists. According to DeLoach, Wilkins nevertheless begged the FBI not to expose King. Personally, he did not mind seeing King ruined, but his downfall must not harm the civil rights movement at large. The best solution would be if King could be persuaded to retire from public life and accept a college presidency or the pastorship of a large church. It is important, however, to read the FBI reports on these meetings with extreme caution, since there is no independent corroboration of Wilkins's words, while DeLoach was known for telling Hoover exactly what the "Boss" wanted to hear. The NAACP leader, for his part, approached the FBI because he was alarmed by the Bureau's growing hostility toward King and the civil rights movement.[16]

But even if Roy Wilkins did not make common cause with the FBI's campaign to discredit Martin Luther King, there is no doubt that the NAACP secretary saw his rival's personal lifestyle—King reportedly had numerous extramarital affairs—as a risk for the civil rights struggle and tried to cast himself in the role of the "responsible Negro leader." After King turned against President Johnson's Vietnam policy, their personal relationship reached a low point. Wilkins's April 1968 obituary for the martyred civil rights hero is remarkable only for its cool and detached tone.[17]

While Roy Wilkins saw his seniority challenged by King, the generational conflict within the civil rights movement was even more pronounced in the relations between the NAACP leadership and the young activists of SNCC, many of whom were barely past their twentieth birthday. When the SNCC founders publicly criticized the association for its alleged legalism at their kick-off conference in April 1960, Wilkins fumed at the "doctrinaires" and "upstarts" who were still "little boys" when "the NAACP was battling tooth and toenail . . . to knock out Jim Crow." Subsequently, the NAACP patriarch, born in 1901, kept on complaining about the "ignorance" and "arrogance of youth" who had "absolutely no knowledge of anything prior to February 1, 1960"—the day the sit-in movement began in Greensboro, North Carolina.[18]

Its youthful zeal notwithstanding, SNCC was eager to establish a cooperative relationship with the NAACP. SNCC leaders Marion Barry and Jane Stembridge politely asked the association to send a regular representative to their meetings, because [the] "NAACP is playing such a vital role in the lives of students today that we could profit greatly by its presence at our sessions."[19] Obviously, the association's leadership would have preferred the young activists to work in the NAACP's student chapters but accepted the invitation to keep in touch with SNCC's activities. From an organizational point of view, SNCC appeared to be a nuisance more than a threat. After a meeting with SNCC representatives in late 1961, Assistant Secretary John Morsell assured Wilkins that "SNCC does not constitute competition in the true sense. They are too much at odds internally, they are lacking in resources, and there is a good chance, either that they split or that they wither on the vine if they do not get substantial financial aid."[20] As with the SCLC, the NAACP officials did not see any good reason for creating a new organization. Its moderate and constructive element might as well join the association, while the rest were dismissed as noisy troublemakers.

The NAACP's attitude toward CORE was similar, though somewhat mellowed by the fact that CORE leader James Farmer, born in 1920, was a seasoned veteran of the civil rights struggle who could not be easily ridiculed as a youthful braggart. Farmer had been a founding member of CORE in 1942 and had participated in the group's nonviolent direct action during the 1940s. Prior to his return to CORE in 1961, Farmer had worked as a program director for the NAACP. Surprisingly, Roy Wilkins did not consider Farmer as a traitor, but apparently even encouraged his departure. "You're going to be riding a mustang pony, while I'm riding a dinosaur," he broodingly bid Farmer farewell. The personal relationship between the two men remained loyal and respectful, which did not, however, prevent Wilkins from lashing out against CORE when he felt that the group tried to steal publicity or donations from the association.[21]

In terms of membership and organizational strength, none of the three new civil rights groups posed a serious threat to the association. There are no reliable membership data available for SNCC, CORE, and the SCLC, none of which tried to build a large, formal structure in the first place. August Meier and Elliott Rudwick have estimated that CORE reached the peak of its numerical strength in 1964 at about five thousand activists. In contrast, by the end of 1963 the NAACP claimed more than a half million dues-paying members in over seventeen hundred local branches. Even if the association lacked a charismatic leader like Martin Luther King, its officials viewed the SCLC as no match for themselves. "Dr. King is movement in himself," Roy Wilkins proudly told the Alabama NAACP when it finally resumed its operations in 1964, "but ours is an organization of structure."[22]

The crucial reason, however, why the NAACP never ceased to regard the smaller groups as rivals rather than allies was their reliance on nonviolent direct action. This strategy did not require many organizational resources but could be implemented by a small band of dedicated activists. Shrewdly staged confrontations between peaceful protesters and brutal racists involved spectacular drama and threatened to steal the public eye away from the legal and political action preferred by the association. When CORE launched its "freedom rides" in the spring of 1961, the NAACP staff at first dismissed the action as a publicity stunt to boost the group's fund-raising efforts.[23]

Direct Action and Boycotts

This derision was patently unfair because the interracial freedom riders acted out of a deep moral commitment and stoically suffered brutal abuse by white mobs in the Deep South. The practitioners of nonviolent direct action were inspired by the Sermon on the Mount and by the role model of Mohandas Gandhi, whose nonviolent struggle against British colonial rule had helped bring about independence for India. The imperative to love one's enemies perhaps was proclaimed most emphatically at SNCC's founding conference in April 1960: "Love is the central motif of nonviolence. . . . Such love goes to the extreme; it remains loving and forgiving even in the midst of hostility. It matches the capacity of evil to inflict suffering with an even more enduring capacity to absorb evil, all the while persisting in love." The central message was that in the end nonviolent action would lead to the liberation of both the oppressed and the oppressors. As Martin Luther King eloquently explained to a national television audience on NBC's *Meet the Press*: "I do believe that if the non-violent resistors continue to follow the way of non-violence they eventually get over to the hearts and souls of the former oppressors, and I think it eventually brings about the redemption that we dream of."[24]

The ethical convictions of its protagonists notwithstanding, nonviolence was also a shrewd strategy to claim legitimacy for the civil rights movement. Incidents of black counterviolence against racist assaults, as it flared up during the SCLC's 1963 desegregation campaign in Birmingham, Alabama, jeopardized the movement's moral aura and had to be contained at all costs.[25] Moreover, if conservative critics charged the civil rights movement with provoking violence, they were not entirely mistaken. Violent reactions to nonviolent protests were an integral part of the protesters' strategy to put pressure on the federal government and the American public at large. As James Farmer once put it, nonviolent direct action was "a sort of moral and tactical judo . . . using the opponent's violence . . . to aid in his own defeat."[26]

It has often been pointed out that nonviolent direct action was no invention of the 1960s but had a long history reaching back into the antebellum period. However, according to August Meier and Elliott Rudwick, there was no continuous tradition or ideology of nonviolent protest among African-Americans, which led every new generation of activists to believe that they had discovered an entirely new strategy.[27] Once again the historical context of black protest had changed dramatically when the struggle entered into a new phase during the 1960s. Most importantly, the United States claimed to be the champion of international democracy, while at the same time American society was undergoing a process of rapid modernization. Perhaps no other single factor was more important for the civil rights movement than the sweeping advance of television. In 1950, less than two hundred thousand households in the United States had a television set, but ten years later the new medium had been introduced into 90 percent of all American homes.[28] While it remains difficult to gauge the impact of television on diverse audiences, the fact that images of hateful racist mobs and frenzied police descending on peaceful black demonstrators were broadcast nationwide and internationally can hardly be overestimated. President John F. Kennedy had a point when he told civil rights leaders not to "be too hard on Bull Connor," Birmingham's irascible police commissioner, since he had "probably done more for civil rights than any one else." Where local authorities refrained from excessive violence against civil rights protesters, as in the 1962 desegregation campaign by SNCC and the SCLC in Albany, Georgia, the media coverage remained low profile and the movement scored few tangible results.[29]

To its devoted adherents, nonviolent direct action essentially meant two things: first, an absolute commitment to suffer abuse and injustice without resorting to force, not even in self-defense, and second, a direct, often dramatic face-to-face confrontation with "an opponent who is in a position to make a change," as one CORE document put it. In trying to desegregate the lunch counters of southern department stores, black students simply refused to leave until they were served.[30] In a broader sense, however, nonviolent direct action was not confined to immediate attacks on Jim Crow rules but included mass demonstrations and boycotts as well. Also, the term did not necessarily imply defying the law. The interracial freedom riders of 1961, for example, did not break any laws but simply rode a bus to see whether the southern states abided by a new ruling of the Supreme Court outlawing segregation in interstate travel.[31] The real lawbreakers were the police who arrested them anyway or refused to protect them against violent assailants. As Martin Luther King explained before a national television audience, the protagonists of nonviolent action had the highest respect for the law, so much so that "they are willing to suffer and sacrifice in order to square local customs and local laws with the moral law of the universe . . . with the Federal constitution and with what is the just law of the land."[32]

Nonviolent direct action was largely defined by the level of repression and violence black protesters could expect when launching their campaigns. Hence the line between direct action and voter registration often became blurred because it did not matter much to violent racists whether African-Americans challenged white supremacy at a "whites only" lunch counter or by trying to register and vote. Its adherents also did not advocate nonviolent direct action as an alternative to voter registration. At least until the mid-1960s, the voting rights rhetoric espoused by the SCLC, SNCC, and CORE was not different from the NAACP's. For Martin Luther King the suffrage was the "Civil Right No. 1," and the SCLC placed voter registration, not direct action, at the core of its fund-raising efforts. SNCC even chose the catchy slogan "One Man—One Vote" for its letterhead. Prior to the 1960 party conventions, the SNCC "kids" politely asked Roy Wilkins's support for their wish to present their case to the platform committees of the parties. A little condescendingly, the NAACP leader commended the new group for its eagerness to work through the political process.[33]

However, a closer look reveals significant conceptual differences between the NAACP and its new allies with regard to the vote. The advocates of direct action viewed the ballot not primarily in instrumental terms but focused on voting as a way to build a collective identity. "We register both to secure better community services and to assert our own essential dignity," James Farmer said, describing the goals of CORE's voter education program. Moreover, they were not willing to accept that voter registration should enjoy precedence over direct action, as the NAACP argued. In the 1964 presidential campaign, CORE joined in an all-out registration effort to mobilize black voters in order to defeat Senator Barry Goldwater, the ultra-conservative Republican presidential candidate, but refused to obey a temporary halt of demonstrations demanded by the association's leadership.[34]

Finally, even if the adherents of nonviolent action vowed that they did not wish to jettison the NAACP's time-honored ways altogether, they did not conceal their dissatisfaction with the association's legalism and incrementalism. After all, nonviolent direct action had to be defended on two fronts. While conservatives blamed peaceful protesters for inciting violence, militants often dismissed nonviolence as cowardice. Therefore, Martin Luther King, arguably the most articulate spokesman for nonviolent direct action vis-à-vis white audiences, deliberately paid tribute to the "radical" impetus behind the protest movement. In a television interview of late 1960, King praised the impatience and courage of the sit-in demonstrators in clear-cut words that were unmistakably addressed to the NAACP: "They require action, and they do not merely wait and deal with a century of litigation, and they do not involve themselves in endless debates, but we see here real action, working to bring about the realization of the ideals and principles of democracy."[35]

Such criticism did not sit well with NAACP officials, who pointed out that the association had never confined its activities to the courtroom and political lobbying. Indeed, only a few years after its founding the NAACP had led the movement to boycott the racist movie *The Birth of a Nation* and staged a mass demonstration on New York City's Fifth Avenue to protest the bloody 1917 race riots of East St. Louis. Roy Wilkins himself claimed to be a pioneer of direct action, having been arrested for picketing the Department of Justice as early as 1935.[36] And the Montgomery Bus Boycott of 1955–56, which made Martin Luther King famous, developed out of an initiative planned by the local NAACP branch. Rosa Parks's legendary refusal to give up her seat to a white passenger was part of plan masterminded by NAACP activist Edgar Daniel Nixon, who was also one of the main organizers of the boycott.[37]

In 1958, NAACP youth groups launched sit-ins at segregated lunch counters in Wichita, Kansas, and in Oklahoma City. The Wichita youngsters informed the national office in advance of their plans, but were told by the NAACP youth secretary that this was not "NAACP tactics." Both Gloster Current and Roy Wilkins also withheld approval. The group went ahead anyway, supported by the majority of the branch, and eventually scored an inspiring victory by desegregating the largest drugstore chain in Kansas. Following their lead, the NAACP youth of Oklahoma also staged several successful sit-ins. Because nothing succeeds like success, Gloster Current, in late 1960, proudly claimed the credit for having started the sit-in movement for the NAACP.[38] Still, the national leadership was never too enthusiastic about such free-wheeling activities and did not make them part of the association's program. The NAACP annual conventions remained conspicuously vague on the issue. In 1956, the association's highest decision-making body welcomed the "effectiveness of the non-violent resistance in Montgomery and Tallahassee, Florida," where blacks had also waged a boycott against the local bus company, but added that it was "not yet ready to take a position on this as a national project." Not before 1960 did the annual convention, after claiming historical precedence of the sit-ins for the NAACP, "go on record as approving the intent and method of operation of these movements." The following year, it declared its unqualified support for the freedom rides, pointing out that the right to nonsegregated facilities in interstate travel had been won in the courts by the NAACP.[39]

The 1961 resolution also stressed that NAACP members who participated in nonviolent direct action were not required to reject bail and go to jail if they were arrested. For many followers of the nonviolent protest movement, the battle cry "jail, no bail" represented the epitome of their unconditional commitment to the cause. As James Farmer emphatically told the delegates of the NAACP convention: "As long as they have the cells in their jails, we will have the people to fill them—living witnesses to the injustice of segregation."[40] Such a principled stand did not make good sense in the eyes of the association's officials, who feared that thousands of promising young black women and men might incur criminal records that could preclude them from advancing to leading positions in government and society. Moreover, as Thurgood Marshall lectured SNCC activists, "jail, no bail" violated the ethics of the legal profession because a lawyer's first duty was to get his clients out of prison.[41]

Paradoxically, the inability of the nonviolent protesters to sustain the principle of "jail, no bail" led to serious frictions between the NAACP and other groups. Southern judges often set excessive bond in order to squeeze the civil rights movement financially. For example, CORE had to post no less than $12,500 to get its Louisiana chairman out of jail when he was charged with "criminal anarchy" and faced a maximum sentence of ten years at hard labor. In 1960, the NAACP annual convention had pledged its continuing moral, financial, and legal support for the participants of the nonviolent struggle. This pledge was indeed honored to a remarkable extent. There are no precise figures available, but apparently the NAACP put up substantial amounts of money. By its own account, it raised more than $250,000 to bail out demonstrators and activists during just the 1963–64 Mississippi campaigns.[42] Even the NAACP could barely afford to have so much cash tied up and eventually lose some of it if defendants did not show up in court.

Against this backdrop, NAACP officials understandably resented being criticized for their legalism. John Brooks at one point suggested that the association might simply hit its critics in their "weakest spot . . . legal defense." This never happened, but the NAACP refused to commit itself "to free-wheeling activity planned and launched by another organization," as Wilkins informed a SNCC leader. "If we are expected to pay the bills, we must be in on the planning and launching, otherwise the bills will have to be paid by those who plan and launch." In particular, the NAACP chafed at combining voter registration with direct action campaigns, since the tensions created by the latter seriously impaired the success of the former. For example, in the fall of 1961 a SNCC registration campaign in McComb, Mississippi, yielded a total of eighteen new black voters to the list, while $15,000 had to be paid in fines, bail, and legal fees. "That is a pretty high cost per name on a voter registration list," Roy Wilkins wryly observed. "Uncle NAACP is picking up most of the tab." Medgar Evers fed Wilkins's anger when he reported that the SNCC activists had deliberately tried to keep the local NAACP out of the picture and only adopted a cooperative posture when they needed money and legal aid.[43]

Nevertheless, spending time in a southern jail had become a badge of honor that the NAACP leadership would not do without. In June 1963, Roy Wilkins went to Jackson, Mississippi, to picket the city's Woolworth department store. Together with local NAACP activists Medgar Evers and Helen Wilcher, the executive secretary was promptly arrested and charged with "conspiring to prohibit free trade and commerce," but soon released on a $1,000 cash bond. With Martin Luther King's Birmingham campaign going on at the same time, one is tempted to dismiss this action as a publicity stunt. This would not be fair, however, as the Jackson NAACP youth chapter had been waging a boycott against the city's downtown merchants since late 1962, combined with picketing and demonstrations to desegregate the public accommodations in the state capital. By May, the campaign was stepped up, resulting in violent assaults by white mobs, mass arrests of black protesters, and a firebomb thrown at Medgar Evers's home. The racist violence reached its horrifying peak on June 11, 1963, when the NAACP field secretary was murdered in his front yard by a sniper.[44] In the heat of the Jackson campaign, Roy Wilkins had employed stark rhetoric to put Mississippi authorities on the spot. The oppression of blacks in the Magnolia state, he asserted, was "an American phase of Hitlerism" leaving only "the establishment of the ovens to complete the picture of Nazi terror." At the same time, however, the NAACP leadership worked to de-escalate the situation by toning down demonstrations and direct action. The campaign had already cost $50,000 in bond money and legal fees. As a committee of NAACP officials had decided the year before, the association sought "success, by negotiation if possible, but demonstrations, if necessary."[45]

The NAACP clearly preferred boycotts over sit-ins and demonstrations. Boycotts and picketing, the 1961 annual convention stressed, had proven their effectiveness in numerous actions launched by the local branches throughout the entire South. This preference reflected the association's traditional pragmatism, which expected concessions not from moral persuasion but from tangible self-interest. Just as the NAACP believed that voter registration would make politicians responsive to blacks interests, it expected boycotts to educate white merchants about their financial stake in desegregation. The businessmen of Jackson were told in early 1963 that it was their decision either to negotiate the abolition of Jim Crow practices immediately or see the boycott continued "in the most militant fashion" until the demands of the boycott movement were met. Eighteen months later a defense group of white merchants conceded that the boycott had made itself felt on many stores that had lost all of their black customers, but they still refused to give in to "intimidation" by "agitating organizations."[46]

Not before the fall of 1965 did a concerted campaign of boycotting and demonstrations yield meaningful results in the Magnolia state. The campaign in Natchez was launched after George Metcalf, the local NAACP president, had almost been killed by a heinous bomb attack in late August. As usual, the city authorities reacted with extreme harshness to the protests, including curfews and mass arrests. The black community solidly backed the boycott, but behind the scenes there was a good deal of quarreling between the NAACP on the one hand and SNCC and the SCLC on the other. By early October, the NAACP leadership was no longer willing and able to come up with large amounts of bail money and decided that further direct confrontations would only be self-defeating.[47]

Under the leadership of Charles Evers, Medgar's older brother, the NAACP pressed for a negotiated settlement with the city fathers that was finally reached in early December. In this agreement the mayor and representatives of the Natchez business community agreed to the desegregation of public facilities, the hiring of black police officers, substantial investment to improve black neighborhoods, the co-optation of an African-American by the school board, and a plan for the integration of public schools within two years. Henry Lee Moon, the association's public relations director, hailed the deal as "far more meaningful than any settlement ever achieved as the result of a direct action program by the Negro community in any southern city." Critics, however, dismissed the bargain as tokenism and tried to continue the boycott, but Evers made sure that it was called off.[48]

By 1965, the civil rights movement was already on the verge of splitting up. In light of the recent federal civil rights legislation, the NAACP's skepticism toward direct action campaigns became even more pronounced. At the height of the Natchez campaign, Assistant Secretary John Morsell wrote to Aaron Henry, president of the Mississippi NAACP state conference: "It is a fact that the changes achieved locally by the demonstrations have been slight or non-existent. Wherever appreciable progress has been made it has come about either through persistent negotiation, or from federal action, or by the pressure of the ballot. . . . Expanded voter registration activity, well-planned selective buying campaigns, and the proper legal action are likely to be more effective. . . . It is the NAACP's overriding obligation as the custodian of the civil rights movement to supply constructive thought and meaningful action where they are called for."[49]

After initial hesitation, the NAACP leadership had accepted nonviolent direct action as "an idea whose time had come," but it never ceased to view the approach with reservations and misgivings, fearing that it might get out of control and provoke a backlash among the national public opinion.[50] Inasmuch as the civil rights struggle depended on grassroots action and bottom-up pressure, voter registration remained the association's weapon of choice.

The Voter Education Project

To be sure, there was no disagreement among civil rights activists over the necessity of mobilizing black voters. During the early 1960s, all major civil rights groups were active in organizing registration drives in the South. Not surprisingly, registration and political education turned into an important field of both cooperation and competition between the NAACP and its smaller rivals. Vying for donations and recognition, all groups were eager to boast their achievements in the political mobilization of African-Americans. In a joint statement of February 1965, for example, the SCLC, CORE, and SNCC claimed to be "the organizations most actively working on voter registration in the South." Martin Luther King even called the SCLC the "pioneer" of voter registration. Predictably, these claims did not sit well with the NAACP leaders, who saw voter registration as the association's turf. Roy Wilkins, for example, was furious that SNCC activists touted their dangerous work in Mississippi but failed to mention the NAACP martyr Medgar Evers.[51]

It is remarkable, however, that the material left by the SCLC, SNCC, and CORE on their registration work does not bear out the intense feeling of rivalry that speaks from the NAACP records. While a good number of complaints can be found that the NAACP allegedly lied about the results of its registration work, the overall attitude appears to have been one of cooperation, based on the pragmatic insight that constant squabbling would only be counterproductive. As Robert Moses, the legendary SNCC activist from Harlem, instructed his coworkers in Mississippi: "[W]e cannot do our job effectively, if we have to spend half our time fighting the NAACP, so those of you who are having trouble on this score should try to bend over backwards to help the NAACP and work out a cooperative program."[52]

In contrast, John Brooks and W. C. Patton of the NAACP Voter Registration Committee looked at the other groups with both distrust and disdain and rarely had anything positive to say about their work. Instead their reports reflect a bureaucratic "instinct" against what they considered "intruders" on their turf. The newcomers, they believed, had only "seized upon the voter registration issue as a means to build their organizational and financial strength." For Brooks, the way his rivals tried to capitalize on the groundwork done by the association amounted to nothing less than a "crime." The

NAACP, he thought, was much "too nice." Time and again, the association's leading registration officers made it clear that they preferred to run their own show.[53]

Unfortunately, from their perspective, the call for cooperation could not be ignored, since it came from the White House in Washington, D.C. After the freedom rides in the spring of 1961, the Kennedy administration was eager to minimize politically disruptive direct action and developed a plan for a large Southwide registration effort to be sustained for several years and funded by private public interest foundations. The project should include all major civil rights organizations and be coordinated by the Southern Regional Council (SRC), a moderate interracial organization founded in 1944 to improve race relations. U.S. Attorney General Robert F. Kennedy personally made sure that the funds disbursed by the Voter Education Project (VEP), as it was called, would be tax-exempt. The president's brother also promised FBI protection for the registration activists—a promise that would never be honored, however. The political interest of the Kennedy administration was easy to see. It wished to funnel the energies of the civil rights struggle into safe channels and hoped that the increasing numbers of black voters would strengthen liberal and moderate Democrats in the South. Officially, the VEP had to be strictly bipartisan.[54]

Eventually, all major civil rights organizations agreed to participate in the project. The proponents of nonviolent direct action, however, refused to renounce their favored approach. After heated internal discussions, SNCC insisted that registration and nonviolent action were twin pillars of their struggle and subsequently embraced the VEP as an effort that was "revolutionary as well as reformist in its potential."[55] Needless to say, the NAACP leadership preferred voter registration to direct action. But this did not mean that it jumped on the VEP bandwagon.

In late August 1961, the Taconic Foundation, a New York City–based contributor to liberal causes and the principal financial supporter of the VEP, invited representatives of the civil rights movement, the federal government, the Southern Regional Council, and other potential donors to discuss the organizational makeup of the project. According to the scheme devised by SRC director Leslie Dunbar, the VEP would be coordinated and supervised by the Council, which would also select a director. Although Dunbar emphasized the autonomy of the participants, the SRC claimed "undivided responsibility and authority" to allocate and terminate the funds for registration drives. In addition to the five national organizations—the Urban League had also come aboard—support would also go to independent local groups.[56] Obviously enough, the money offered by the VEP was highly attractive.

Whether the NAACP would agree to submit to the control of an umbrella organization, however, was a different matter.

When Wilkins asked leading NAACP officers for their opinions, he met with much skepticism. The critics argued that the association was strong enough to manage its own operations successfully and had nothing to gain from sharing funds, resources, and credit with other groups. Clarence Mitchell, head of the Washington Bureau, even considered it "an insult" that the Taconic Foundation had not offered the money directly to the NAACP. Those who recommended participation insisted that the NAACP preserve its "identity" and "maximize" its part in the project. The most favorable response came from Kelly Alexander, a member of the national board of directors and president of the North Carolina state conference, who pointed out that many NAACP branches did not have an effective registration program and could use some external incentive. Moreover, Kelly believed that the project was constructive and would "contribute much toward the increase in voter registration in the South." Interestingly, none of the other respondents had even discussed this point.[57]

Before he committed the association, however, Roy Wilkins presented the SRC with a set of stiff conditions. Among other items, the registration drives were not to be accompanied by mass demonstrations. The NAACP would be free to select its target areas, and its branches would continue to conduct their own drives independently from the VEP. Perhaps most importantly, the executive secretary insisted that the funds were not to be allocated directly to local groups but to the national agencies, which supposedly had a better grasp of the strengths and weaknesses of their local affiliates. Clearly, the association's leaders wished to remain in the driver's seat. Basically, Leslie Dunbar concurred that the NAACP would retain control of its own affairs, but he shrewdly placed the ball into Wilkins's court by telling him that the SRC made its "participation in the registration effort conditional upon yours." Wilkins knew only too well that the NAACP could never bear the responsibility for the failure of a joint voter registration effort supported by liberal northern donors and the federal government. In late November 1961, he grudgingly notified Dunbar of the NAACP's participation, albeit not without reiterating his reservations against "so-called cooperative activity."[58]

In April 1962, the VEP, headed by Wiley Branton, a black lawyer from Arkansas, was kicked off with the blessings of numerous public interest groups, churches, and both major parties. According to the SRC, the project disbursed a total budget of $870,000 until it expired in November 1964. Seventy-five percent of the money went directly to the registration drives conducted by the national civil rights organizations and by a host of local groups.

In the end, the VEP claimed to have registered almost seven hundred thousand new black voters throughout the South. Mostly, Branton and his small staff were busy evaluating incoming proposals and supervising the appropriate use of the funds, but he also tried to make sure that the different participating groups would not step on each others toes.[59]

The VEP notwithstanding, the NAACP had no intention of giving up its own registration efforts. Its local branches were specifically instructed that they did not have to wait for VEP funds nor refrain from independent activities. Not surprisingly, the NAACP registration officers were less than enthusiastic about working within the new framework. Brooks even suspected Wiley Branton of pursuing his own political ambitions and kept on disparaging the VEP in his reports. But when he prodded the national secretariat in late 1963 to "wean away" from the project, he was rebuffed. Obviously, the NAACP could not ask publicly for money and at the same time pull out of a relatively well-funded program simply because it did not like to cooperate with other groups.[60]

There are no precise figures on how much money the NAACP received from the Voter Education Project. According to the reports for the first three months, NAACP projects were allotted $17,250 out of a total of $64,240. If this is a rough indicator for the ratio of the ensuing two years, the association's share probably amounted to more than a quarter of all VEP grants. The national secretariat was particularly eager to make sure that all checks passed through its own hands and were distributed according to "the judgements of our field people to whether a given locality is 'ripe' enough to justify a given expenditure." By and large, Wiley Branton went along with the NAACP's procedures. If the VEP approved of a local NAACP drive, the funds were first transferred to an NAACP account and then paid out by Brooks and Patton to the local branch.[61]

In general, the cooperation between Branton and the NAACP went smoothly, although the VEP director sent numerous complaints about inaccurate reports. The only serious frictions occurred when it came to distinguishing between VEP drives and NAACP campaigns. Branton showed much flexibility in financing NAACP activities as long as they had been approved by his office, and he even grudgingly accepted that the NAACP was sometimes running parallel campaigns. However, if he suspected that VEP money was diverted to independent projects, the director took the association to task. Of course, there was no clear line of demarcation as to whether a registration drive "belonged" to the VEP or to the NAACP. Branton claimed all campaigns for himself that were co-financed by his office, while Brooks and Patton took credit for any drive in which members and branches of the association were involved. At one point, Branton curtly told Patton that since he had enough legitimate achievements to boast, "there is simply no need for you to pirate the success of non-NAACP projects."[62]

Despite such occasional clashes, the VEP director acknowledged the NAACP's superior organizational capabilities. He repeatedly approved of NAACP drives in areas where other groups had been active but apparently had not produced enough new voters. The greater quantitative success, however, not only mirrored the experience and greater organizational resources of the association. It was also due to a markedly different approach deliberately taken by the smaller groups. The activists of SNCC and CORE, in particular, were firmly convinced that the gospel of the ballot had to be brought to the most isolated and oppressed rural blacks, regardless of how many new voters could be added to the list. Accordingly, CORE and SNCC had insisted that the rural areas of Mississippi would be included under the scope of the Voter Education Project. Because the repressive climate in Mississippi required maximum unity, all civil groups active in the Magnolia state had joined into the Council of Federated Organizations (COFO) by February 1962. The alliance was headed by NAACP state president Aaron Henry, SNCC's Robert Moses, and David Dennis of CORE.[63]

Public declarations of unity notwithstanding, the association's national leadership looked with growing suspicion at COFO and the prominent role played by SNCC. The NAACP branches in Mississippi were repeatedly advised to keep at a distance from this "temporary organization." W. C. Patton kept on complaining about COFO's organizational weakness. In October 1963, he openly criticized Wiley Branton for having "conceded" the entire state of Mississippi to COFO and notified the VEP director of his noncompliance with this arrangement. And indeed, Branton reluctantly agreed that the high expenditures for the Mississippi projects could no longer be justified. In November 1963, he informed Moses and Henry that for the time being the VEP had to suspend its financial contributions. Already more money had been spent in Mississippi than in any other state.[64]

When the dedicated COFO workers realized that they simply could not crack the impervious wall of racial disfranchisement in Mississippi, they decided to hold "freedom registrations" and "freedom elections" as an unofficial alternative to the gubernatorial elections scheduled for the fall of 1963. Their purpose was to demonstrate that the black citizens of the state were keenly interested in political participation, if only they were able to register and vote. COFO nominated Aaron Henry and Ed King, a white chaplain and a native of Mississippi, for governor and lieutenant governor, respectively. Eventually, a total of eighty-three thousand votes were cast for the ticket. Similar efforts were made during the Freedom Summer of 1964, when COFO urged local blacks to register as members of the Mississippi Freedom Democratic Party (MFDP), which presented itself as a challenger to the state's segregationist Democratic Party. Although the NAACP officially endorsed these activities, its registration activists were not at all happy. Mock registrations and elections, John Brooks believed, would only cause confusion and disappointment among black Mississippians, many of whom were led to believe that they were actually duly registered voters.[65]

Neither the end of the VEP in late 1964 nor the disintegration of COFO, from which the NAACP withdrew in early 1965, caused any regret among the association's leaders. At long last, they could go on with their own registration work without having to share the credit with all the "Tom, Dick, and Harry groups," as John Brooks rejoiced. For the summer of 1965, Roy Wilkins announced a large registration campaign in Mississippi, Alabama, and South Carolina, "with the NAACP family in charge" and without "strangers . . . moving alone into strange communities"—a not so subtle allusion to the white volunteers brought to the 1964 Mississippi Freedom Summer under the auspices of COFO. The association invited fifteen national groups, including the Anti-Defamation League, the United Auto Workers, and the National Council of Negro Women, to support the drive but conspicuously left out the SCLC, SNCC and CORE.[66]

Nevertheless, when the Southern Regional Council proposed a second Voter Education Project in the fall of 1965, the NAACP agreed to participate. Again, the White House had indicated a strong interest in the program. After he had secured the passing of the Voting Rights Act—a sweeping piece of legislation that will be discussed in the next chapter—President Lyndon B. Johnson could well expect that the NAACP would help register grateful black voters in the South to build a new base for the national Democratic Party. Again, the VEP money was too attractive for the association to ignore, while the potential of organizational bickering seemed much reduced, after SNCC had declined to participate. Still, when the new VEP director, Vernon Jordan, suggested that this time the funds should go directly to the local campaigns, the NAACP leadership again insisted on retaining control over the activities of its branches. All proposals first had to be approved by Brooks and Patton.[67]

During the second Voter Education Project, the NAACP, according to its own calculations, was able to increase its share of VEP grants to about 30 percent and claimed no less than 35 percent of the increase in black voters as a result of its work. Whereas the other groups needed an average of $2.24 per newly registered voter, the association made due with $1.45. The cooperation with Vernon Jordan, a former NAACP field-worker, was even easier than it had been with Wiley Branton. At the same time that SNCC and CORE were developing into radical splinter groups who repudiated the ideals of integration and nonviolence and called for a "Black Revolution," the association presented itself as the paragon of pragmatism and efficiency. When the VEP drew to a close in the fall of 1967, W. C. Patton triumphed: "Thanks, however, that the oldest, most revered and responsible of all civil rights organizations—the NAACP—has continued to plug away day in and day out. . . . The NAACP [branches] are striving day by day to help the Negro win a place in the sun, not with fire bombs, bricks and bottles, but by ever increasing our political strength."[68]

The "Unglamorous Work" Continues

The Voter Education Project was not the only factor that led to fundamental changes in the southern registration work of the civil rights movement. The Voting Rights Act of August 1965 put the voting laws and procedures of Alabama, Georgia, Louisiana, Mississippi, South Carolina, Virginia, and half of North Carolina under federal supervision. In addition to suspending literacy and understanding tests, the law authorized the U.S. Justice Department to assign federal registrars to enroll voters in the most repressive areas of the South. In early 1966, the U.S. Civil Service Commission announced that the federal registrars had already signed up more than ninety thousand black voters during their first six months. Still, federal registrars were assigned to only a minority of the areas covered by the new law. Nor could they completely overcome the continuing resistance of white supremacists or, for that matter, dispel the remaining fears and apathy on the part of many black citizens. In April 1968, the Civil Service Commission estimated that federal registrars had enrolled roughly 160,000 new voters since August 1965. Apparently, the momentum of the first six months had receded quickly.[69]

Not surprisingly, black registration increased at the fastest pace where the presence of federal registrars coincided with mobilization campaigns by civil rights groups. Needless to say, the NAACP pressed the Justice Department to send as many officers as possible. Yet the association never expected that it could leave the registration job to the federal government. Federal registrars were a welcome assistance, but the groundwork of getting eligible blacks to the registration offices continued to fall on the civil rights organizations.[70]

The NAACP had planned a large registration drive in Alabama, Mississippi, and South Carolina for the summer of 1965, even before the voting rights bill was introduced into Congress. The center of the action was to be Mississippi, where the association needed to boost its prestige after it had left COFO. Gloster Current, the director of branches, estimated the costs at $20,000 and suggested recruiting 260 volunteers who would canvass the state during July and August. Unlike the campaign during the previous summer, these volunteers would "consist largely of NAACP members and officers who have knowledge of the NAACP's program and are mature enough to understand and accept discipline." While intimidation and harassment were to be expected, the NAACP summer campaign wished "to avoid arrests or any violent conflicts and will do nothing to invite such reactions."[71]

The NAACP summer project of 1965 was unmistakably intended to set a clear counterpoint to the 1964 Freedom Summer dominated by SNCC and COFO. It was carefully planned and coordinated by the national secretariat, which lent its full support. Roy Wilkins himself flew to Jackson for a large kick-off rally. During the campaign, Gloster Current and Althea Simmons, the national secretary for training who had been appointed as the director of the summer project, established an office in Jackson. More experienced organizers were brought in from other states. Even a local newspaper acknowledged the difference: "The sometimes scruffy-looking college students, dubbed COFO workers, who roamed the city last summer rounding up voter applicants are gone. They have been replaced by a small staff of imported NAACP workers and volunteers." One of the NAACP activists was quoted with the statement: "We are here to register voters, not to demonstrate." Although some intimidation occurred, no serious violence was reported.[72]

When the NAACP took stock of its campaign, it claimed to have registered about fifty thousand new voters in all three states. Although this figure fell short of the stated goal of one hundred thousand, is was certainly a respectable achievement. In Alabama and South Carolina, where fewer resources had been spent, roughly fifteen thousand blacks were added to the lists of each state. The increase of twenty thousand in Mississippi, however, almost equaled the total black registration prior to 1965 and dwarfed the results of all previous registration drives there. This stunning success, the NAACP report stressed, had been achieved before any federal registrars were dispatched to the Deep South. Still, with the new law pending, many local registrars became increasingly cooperative, albeit reluctantly.[73]

For 1966, the NAACP pondered even more ambitious plans. In the fall of 1965, the association developed a program for a one-year registration campaign in all eleven southern states at a budget of almost $400,000. Major foundations were asked to fund the project, but the response remained weak.

In March 1966, Assistant Executive Director John Morsell admitted that the plan could not be carried out. Moreover, grants from the VEP also were not flowing as expected. And money was not the only problem. Although the NAACP leadership never ceased to call upon its members and activists to continue the "steady, hard, unspectacular voter registration job," signs of a slowing down were undeniable. Althea Simmons, for example, complained about a veteran registration activist in Mississippi who had changed remarkably after having been given the pompous title of the association's Mississippi Voter Education Program Director, suddenly showing "a reluctance to leave the desk, playing the part of an armchair executive."[74]

Even more important than the waning spirit of some activists, however, was the old problem of political apathy among African-Americans that had plagued the NAACP for decades. Monotonous appeals like "If you don't vote—don't squawk!" were surely not enough to reach the most alienated groups of the black population. When the NAACP youth chapter of New Orleans conducted a registration drive in the summer of 1967, they found that the registration level of roughly 60 percent among eligible blacks that had been reached during the previous years could not be increased any further. As the director of the campaign realized, many residents of "the hard-core Negro ghetto" simply refused to hear the message: "These are people who have suffered many years of deprivation, neglect and misery. . . . Therefore, they look upon everyone with an eye of suspicion and mistrust because of their plight. Poverty and fear has caused them to become indifferent and they live a life of despair. . . . We must prove to them that the ballot is their salvation." Certainly, this assessment applied to many localities throughout the United States.[75]

Nevertheless, the NAACP did not waver in its conviction that the vote was the key to improving the economic and social condition of all African-Americans. In 1967, the association's voter registration committee organized drives in eight southern states and extended its activities beyond the Mason-Dixon line to New Jersey, New York, Ohio, and even Minnesota, claiming to have registered at least 570,000 new voters during that year. Throughout the election year of 1968, Patton counted 220 campaigns in twenty-nine states, yielding an increase of more than 1 million black voters. "This achievement did not come about by wishful thinking," Patton prided himself, "it was the result of hard and skillful work on the part of our local branches, with funds being provided by our National Office."[76]

Unfortunately, though, the national office was running out of money, since the fund-raising could no longer keep pace with the expanding voter

Table 3. Black Registration in Eleven Southern States, 1960 to 1970

State	1956	1958	1960	1964	1966	1968	1970
Alabama	53,000	60,000	66,000	110,000	250,000	273,000	315,000
Arkansas	70,000	64,000	73,000	95,000	115,000	130,000	153,000
Florida	149,000	145,000	183,000	300,000	303,000	292,000	302,000
Georgia	163,000	158,000	180,000	270,000	300,000	344,000	395,000
Louisiana	161,000	130,000	159,000	165,000	243,000	350,000	319,000
Mississippi	20,000	35,000	22,000	29,000	175,000	251,000	286,000
N. Carolina	135,000	150,000	210,000	258,000	282,000	305,000	305,000
S. Carolina	100,000	58,000	58,000	144,000	191,000	189,000	221,000
Tennessee	90,000	185,000	185,000	218,000	225,000	228,000	242,000
Texas	214,000	150,000	227,000	375,000	400,000	540,000	550,000
Virginia	83,000	132,000	100,000	200,000	205,000	255,000	269,000
Total	1,238,000	1,267,000	1,463,000	2,164,000	2,689,000	3,157,000	3,357,000

Note: The rounded figures for 1956, 1958, and 1960 are based on the 1961 annual report of the NAACP Voter Registration Committee, NAACP Records III A 266; for the following years, see Smith and Horton, *Historic Statistics of Black America*, 2:12–13, based on VEP sources.

registration programs. In the spring of 1969, the situation became so difficult that John Morsell had to put on the brakes and for the time being terminate all plans for new campaigns. Although this temporary crisis was soon resolved, it clearly signaled that the association's registration effort, which had absorbed a large measure of its resources and energies for the past decade, was beginning to reach its limits.[77]

While the political mobilization of African-Americans had always been one of the NAACP's key activities, there is no doubt that the advent of nonviolent direct action was a major incentive for the association's leaders to step up their already considerable effort in this field. Voter registration, Roy Wilkins wrote after the passage of the Voting Rights Act, was the "unglamorous work," less spectacular than sit-ins, freedom rides, and mass demonstrations but more effective in the long run.[78] And indeed, a look at tables 3 and 4 shows the stunning upsurge of black registration between the mid-1950s and 1970. During this period the total number of registered black voters grew by more than 2 million and the percentage of eligible African-Americans who were enrolled soared from less than 30 percent to almost 60 percent. In 1960, the registration rate of white southerners had been twice the rate of blacks; eleven years later the racial gap had almost been closed, with whites leading by just 6 percent.

Understandably, the association's activists were eager to claim the lion's share of these impressive figures. W. C. Patton, for example, insisted that the

Table 4. Percentage of Eligible Blacks Registered, 1960 to 1971

State	1960	1971
Alabama	13.7	54.7
Arkansas	38.0	80.9
Florida	39.4	53.2
Georgia	29.3	64.2
Louisiana	31.1	58.9
Mississippi	5.2	59.4
N. Carolina	39.1	49.8
S. Carolina	13.7	49.2
Tennessee	59.1	65.6
Texas	35.5	68.2
Virginia	23.1	52.0
Total	¹29.1	58.6

Note: Smith and Horton, *Historical Statistics of Black America*, 2:1312–1313, based on VEP sources.

NAACP must be "credited with the major role in the registration of the 1,569,455 [new black voters] between 1956 and 1967." The NAACP was the only organization with "a full-time staff promoting not just spurt campaigns, but day by day grinding away." Patton himself believed that no less than 1 million blacks were registered during the drives he personally directed throughout his long years as the NAACP's leading registration officer. It is indeed surprising that the work of W. C. Patton and John Brooks has received so little attention from historians of the civil rights movement. Even if both often showed a rather petty outlook in dealing with other groups, their enormous achievements in the pursuit of the "unglamorous work" certainly deserves recognition.[79]

It is, of course, impossible and pointless to try to quantify the impact of each of the different civil rights groups on the growth of the southern black electorate. For one thing, the politicization of black citizens reflected a general trend toward social modernization based on rapid industrialization and urbanization. After the Second World War, the New South finally began to materialize, a process that could not leave race relations untouched. But modernization was not self-executing. It needed to be implemented on the ground against the resistance of the majority of white southerners who stuck to their traditional notions of paternalism and white supremacy. This formidable task fell to the civil rights movement as a whole. In the field of voter registration, each group contributed according to its resources and priorities.

As Pat Watters and Reese Cleghorn aptly summarized it for the first Voter Education Project: "SNCC's work was almost entirely in areas of bad resistance. CORE was in bad territory mostly, but in some easier areas too, as was SCLC, whose voter work was less. The NAACP was across all the South, good, bad, and in between."[80]

In its focus on increasing the black electorate, however, the association's leaders failed to see that numbers did not necessarily translate into power and influence. White "countermobilization" combined with racial polarization would continue to frustrate hopes for sweeping political change. In the 1966 Alabama gubernatorial elections, for example, the 235,000 registered blacks now represented an unprecedented 25 percent of the total electorate. Still, Lurleen Wallace, the stand-in candidate for her husband, former governor and champion of segregation George Wallace, easily defeated her moderate opponent in the Democratic primary, who had openly sought black support. Roy Wilkins took consolation with the thought that at least a start had been made and that the political clout of black voters would continue to grow along with their numbers.[81]

The proponents of nonviolent direct action, in contrast, had lost this unwavering faith in the concept of incremental political change. Their strategy was based on staging dramatic confrontations and on creating crises in order to force the federal government to intervene on behalf of civil rights. And indeed, the sweeping legislative achievements of the civil rights movement did not result from electoral politics in the first place, but primarily from the interplay of nonviolent protest and violent backlash. It was only against this backdrop that the lobbying efforts by the NAACP could finally succeed.

8

The Politics of Civil Rights

Persistent voter registration efforts and nonviolent direct action campaigns, as described in the previous two chapters, significantly altered the terrain of the civil rights struggle in the South in the years between the end of the Second World War and the mid-1960s. However, the NAACP leaders continued to believe that, whatever progress might be secured at the local and state levels, in order eliminate racial segregation, discrimination, and disfranchisement for good, tough and effective national legislation and law enforcement would be essential. Without a sympathetic Congress and administration, there would be no ultimate victory for civil rights. Moral appeals, however, obviously were not enough to make parties and candidates more responsive to black interests. Rather, they had to be educated about the political power of black voters, as the association had attempted to do since its early days.

As its numbers grew, the NAACP became more and more self-confident in claiming the role of being the black community's leading political mouthpiece. In 1948, it will be recalled, the NAACP leadership had entered into an alliance with the Truman administration, hoping that black electoral support would be rewarded with protective civil rights legislation. These hopes were dashed, however, by a reluctant Congress, the heightening of the Cold War, and the war in Korea.[1] Prior to the 1952 presidential elections, the political fortunes of the administration reached a low point and Truman declined to run for another term. When the GOP nominated the popular war hero General Dwight D. Eisenhower for president, a Republican victory seemed almost a foregone conclusion. Indeed, not only did Eisenhower win in a landslide, but his coattails were long enough to allow the Republicans to carry both houses of Congress.

The NAACP approached the presidential elections of 1952 with the familiar balance-of-power rhetoric that had become its political mantra. That June, the association eagerly cited a recent survey by pollster Elmo Roper that predicted black ballots would again provide the swing vote in key northern states. Moreover, Roper reported that 45 percent of African-American respondents named the NAACP when asked which organization they considered as their most important source of political advice—by far the most frequent answer. Civil rights, the association cheered on its activists, would be "one of the hottest political issues" in the upcoming campaign. In presenting the parties and candidates with its political demands, the NAACP leaders pointed to the ambitious registration drive the association had launched in the South to boost the number of black registered voters to up to 2 million. Only candidates who took a "forthright position on civil rights" could count on the support of the vastly increased black electorate.[2]

The NAACP leadership left little doubt that it continued to favor the Democratic Party. Walter White called on black activists to defend the "very substantial gains made by Negro citizens in recent years." When the Democratic convention adopted a civil rights plank that reaffirmed Truman's program of 1948, the secretary hailed this as a "signal victory for the forces of liberalism in the party." This time the southerners had no taste for staging a revolt. The Democratic nominee, Illinois governor Adlai Stevenson, assured Roy Wilkins that he stood behind the Party's civil rights program but might be willing to accept compromises "to get something done" on the issue.[3]

However, Stevenson's credibility was seriously impaired by his choice of Senator John Sparkman from Alabama as his running mate. While Sparkman enjoyed a reputation as a New Dealer and, by southern standards, as a liberal, a southerner who regularly voted against all civil rights bills was hard to stomach as a candidate for the vice presidency. In a confidential talk with NAACP lobbyist Clarence Mitchell, Sparkman professed his support for the party's civil rights plank but asked for indulgence, as he had to weigh his words carefully. After Sparkman had repeatedly distanced himself from the Democratic civil rights program during the campaign, Walter White informed Stevenson's advisors that the Alabamian was "the most difficult stumbling block" for the Democrats among black voters.[4]

But even with Sparkman, the Democratic ticket appeared as the lesser evil when compared to the stand the GOP and its nominee took on civil rights. Walter White had met Eisenhower during the war and remembered him as "charming and affable" but fairly ignorant on the race question. More importantly, in 1948 he had testified before the Senate Armed Services Committee that he did not favor a swift desegregation of the military. When Roy Wilkins interviewed candidate Eisenhower in August, he thought that "Ike" was "honest and sincere in his declared opposition to discrimination." But when the conversation turned to concrete measures, Eisenhower declared himself against a "compulsory" Fair Employment Practices Committee, foreshadowing his approach to civil rights as president. The Republican Party and Eisenhower, Walter White complained before the election, were obviously planning on making inroads into the Democratic South by catering to white supremacists. This misguided strategy, the secretary warned, would cost the general crucial black support in the North and most likely the presidency.[5]

According to the NAACP's estimates, the Democratic ticket received an average of 73 percent among African-American voters, more than Harry Truman had garnered four years earlier. Yet, instead of holding the balance of power, this time they unmistakably ended up on the losing side. Stevenson did not carry a single state north of the Mason-Dixon line, while Eisenhower won the electoral votes of four southern states.[6] Nobody could miss the point that the new president owed no political debts to black voters, which is exactly why not everybody had been happy with the NAACP's support for the Democrats. Shortly before the election, Daisy Lampkin, vice president of the *Pittsburgh Courier* and a registered Democrat who had worked for many years as an NAACP field secretary, had implored White: "Walter, I think it very wise that some of us are supporting the G.O.P. ticket. It would be tragic if the G.O.P. wins with no Negro support. We would be in a very bad bargaining position." Lampkin surely had a point. When the president-elect met the association's leadership a few weeks after the elections, he appeared friendly but noncommittal. That he called civil rights a "basic moral issue" was hardly encouraging, since the conservative creed held that moral issues could not be solved by legislation.[7]

Although the change in the White House came as no surprise, the NAACP had made no plans on how to deal with the new administration. A few days before the inauguration, Roy Wilkins sketched out two basic options: the association could either "sit tight" and continue to insist on its legislative program, or it could take the Republican campaign promises, vague as they were, at face value and try to work with the administration and GOP congressional leaders. A refusal to cooperate, the assistant secretary concluded, would shut the NAACP out from any decision-making and leave it in "the frustrating role of mere opposition." Still, it was not until the end of 1953 that the association invited a group of other African-American organizations to discuss the topic of "civil rights under the GOP." Eventually, very little came out of this conference. As usual, the black leaders castigated the Republicans for not living up to their campaign promises and warned conservatives about the future power of the expanding black electorate.[8]

With Eisenhower moving into the White House, the politics of civil rights entered a stalemate. The president, while not a racist by the standards of his time, did his best to dodge the race issue. He refused to publicly endorse the

Supreme Court's *Brown* ruling and privately expressed his understanding of white southerners who wished to preserve segregation. When Vice President Richard Nixon defended Eisenhower's civil rights policy before the 1955 NAACP annual convention, without a trace of irony he first of all mentioned the fact that the chief executive had "refused to make promises he couldn't keep." Ike himself showed an infallible sense for the wrong tone when he sanctimoniously urged "patience and forbearance" in his written address to the 1956 NAACP convention, provoking Roy Wilkins, by then the association's executive secretary, to an unprecedented personal rebuff of the president. Blacks, Wilkins thundered before the delegates, were "tired of crawling and having some people try to tell us we are 'going too fast.'" Years later in his memoirs, he acidly quipped that Eisenhower was "a fine general and a good, decent man, but if he had fought World War II the way he fought for civil rights, we would all be speaking German today." Surely, Wilkins was not mistaken in his impression that Eisenhower opposed an active role for the federal government in enforcing civil rights and desegregation. Only when his personal authority was challenged, as in the 1957 school desegregation crisis in Little Rock, Arkansas, was he willing to intervene.[9]

The 1957 Civil Rights Act

During his first three years in office, Eisenhower consistently refused to back civil rights legislation that he believed had no chance of being passed. Indeed, the notorious Senate Rule XXII, which required two-thirds of all members of the Senate to vote for cloture in order to break a filibuster, gave the southern segregationists a de facto veto position. Voting as a solid bloc to thwart civil rights measures, the southern Democrats always found enough conservative Republican allies to repel moves for cloture. Thus the Senate, as *New York Times* journalist Arthur Krock aptly put it, became the "graveyard of civil rights legislation and Rule XXII is the gravedigger."[10]

In the aftermath of *Brown*, the prospects of conquering this bulwark did not get any better. In March 1956, nearly all southern senators and congressmen signed the infamous "Southern Manifesto" endorsing resistance to "forced integration by any lawful means." Bills to enforce *Brown* would inevitably spark the kind of fierce opposition and controversy that the administration wanted to avoid. On the other hand, pressures were mounting for the federal government to stand up to the brazen defiance of southern white supremacists who were not content with rabble-rousing rhetoric but committed numerous acts of violence against black citizens. In this situation, strengthening the right to vote of southern blacks seemed to be a politically shrewd

strategy. Unlike the highly emotional issue of school desegregation, the protection of black voting rights enjoyed broad support among white Americans,
at least outside of Dixie. Moreover, the suffrage might offer a panacea for
solving the thorny civil rights problem gradually and by democratic means. A
resolution by the Republican Party of California to the 1956 GOP convention
succinctly captured this logic: "When the Negroes in the south are guaranteed free access to the ballot box they will themselves take care of school integration and other civil rights without the need for further federal intervention."[11]

As Eisenhower prepared his bid for a second term, support for a "moderate" civil rights bill was growing within the administration. Although he did
not have the president's unequivocal backing, Attorney General Herbert
Brownell, a liberal Republican from New York, drafted a bill in early 1956 that
included four titles: (I) the creation of a federal Civil Rights Commission with
a two-year mandate to investigate racial discrimination and to propose remedial measures, (II) the establishment of a Civil Rights Division within the
Department of Justice, (III) the authorization of the Department of Justice to
seek court injunctions against interferences with civil rights in general, and
(IV) the right to vote in particular. Since Titles I and II clearly fell under the
prerogative of the federal government, they aroused only mild opposition.
Titles III and IV, however, although they did not give the attorney general any
direct power over either state officials or private individuals, sparked angry
protests among southern legislators, who predicted that federal troops would
soon enforce the desegregation of southern schools.[12]

The bill was passed by the House of Representatives in April 1956 by a
large majority but remained stalled in the Senate Judiciary Committee,
headed by Mississippi senator James Eastland, for the rest of the year. Even
after his triumphant reelection, Eisenhower continued to drag his feet on
civil rights. In his 1957 State of the Union address, he endorsed his attorney
general's bill with a distinct lack of enthusiasm. Angered by the president's
apparent indifference, Martin Luther King Jr. and the NAACP called upon
Eisenhower to travel to the South and give a public speech on behalf of civil
rights and on the need to respect law and order, but to no avail. When the
congressional hearings on the bill began in February, the association mustered numerous witnesses for the reign of terror black activists faced in the
South, including Gus Courts, the NAACP chapter president for Belzoni, Mississippi, who had been severely injured in an attempt on his life in late 1955.
The anti–civil rights forces remained unmoved, however. In a cynical exercise of obstruction, Senator Sam Ervin of North Carolina questioned the in-
firm Courts for several hours about his income taxes.[13]

The most important objection that the southerners raised against the bill was the lack of a jury trial in cases of contempt of court arising under Titles III and IV. If state officials disobeyed a court injunction, the court was authorized to set a fine or jail sentence without a jury verdict. Conjuring up the specter of federal tyranny, the bill's critics posed as the defenders of constitutional rights and sacred legal traditions. In its response, the Department of Justice insisted that the absence of a jury trial was a long-established practice in cases in which the government sought injunctive relief and the orders of the court were subsequently ignored or defied. The court needed to be able to enforce its orders, while defendants were still entitled to all procedural safeguards, including the right to appeal. The political purpose of the demand for a jury trial, Attorney General Brownell told members of Congress in an open letter, was easy to see: "The effect of adopting current proposals for jury trial would be to weaken and undermine the authority of the federal courts by making their every order, even after due hearing and affirmed on appeal, reviewable by a local jury. . . . The innocuous slogan of 'jury trial' would permit practical nullification of the proposed civil rights legislation." Brownell put in writing what everyone remotely familiar with the southern justice system knew all along: no state official who defied a federal court order to enforce black civil rights had to fear conviction by an all-white jury of his peers.[14]

From the standpoint of the NAACP, the battle cry of "jury trial" rang especially perfidious, since the southern states liberally employed the instrument of court injunctions in their campaigns to force the association to disclose its membership records. NAACP officials were routinely held in contempt of court without ever being granted a jury trial. Nevertheless, the NAACP's legal analysts took pains to explain to its members that the association did not favor abridging the constitutional rights of defendants, which were duly secured by the attorney general's bill. In contrast, a bill with a jury trial amendment would be nothing but "an empty gesture." After the House had passed the civil rights bill without such an amendment in June 1957, the NAACP annual convention threw the gauntlet to all senators who would not vote for an undiluted version of the bill.[15]

The key question was what political price was the Eisenhower administration willing to pay for the acquiescence of southern lawmakers in the first national civil rights legislation since Reconstruction. Senator Richard Russell of Georgia, the southerners' unofficial leader, informed the president that the South worried primarily about enforced desegregation and had far fewer problems with a law to strengthen voting rights. This was fine with Ike, who publicly distanced himself from Title III's implied authorization for the Department of Justice to seek desegregation orders in federal court. Emboldened by this concession, the southerners also made their acceptance conditional on a jury trial clause. Although the attorney general continued to reject the amendment, Senate majority leader Lyndon B. Johnson, a Texan who harbored ambitions for the White House, engineered a compromise that met the core demands of the South but allowed the majority of "moderates" a face-saving way out. The final version of the 1957 Civil Rights Act, which both the House and the Senate passed by wide margins in late August, no longer included the original Title III and granted defendants in contempt cases a jury trial provided that the expected penalty exceeded $300 or forty-five days in prison. Most lawmakers had acted on the assumption that a weak law was better than no law at all. The southerners voted against the bill but did not stage a filibuster. Only South Carolina senator Strom Thurmond, the hero of the Dixiecrat revolt, could not resist the temptation of grandstanding and delivered a speech of no less than twenty-four hours—an unmatched record to date.[16]

The NAACP had harbored no illusions that the best it could get was "a mild bill designed primarily to insure the right to vote," but it remained steadfast in its public opposition to a jury trial, encouraged by leading Republican senator Everett Dirksen of Illinois, who had promised Wilkins to "vigorously oppose any jury trial amendment." Thus the sudden change of mind of the association's leaders in early August, after the Senate had passed the diluted bill, came as a complete surprise to most of its members and allies. In a stormy session of the Leadership Conference on Civil Rights, Roy Wilkins and Clarence Mitchell argued in favor of supporting the bill even with the invidious amendment. Justifying their position to the members of the national secretariat, Wilkins gave three key reasons: First, the bill might still be useful in improving the climate to register black voters in the South. Second, a stronger bill could not be passed during the ongoing session of Congress. Third, the 1960 presidential elections would offer a new chance to improve the law. Basically, the secretary admitted that after so many abortive attempts to pass civil rights legislation, some law needed to get off the ground: "We believe that if the bill is passed it will break the stalemate of eighty-seven years and will get us off of the very discouraging 'dead center' on which we have been operating because we could not secure the passage of a perfect bill. We believe this bill will constitute a start toward our goal, and a start is better than standing still."[17]

Sure enough, this was realpolitik, but predictably Wilkins drew plenty of fire from irate NAACP members who demanded his resignation and accused him of "betrayal" and of making a "tragic mistake." The NAACP's action, one letter read, appeared as a "precipitate rush" at a time when others were still fighting for an undiluted bill. Even those who agreed with Wilkins and Mitchell wondered if the two should not have consulted with the board of directors before committing the association on such an important issue. Senate liberals also were divided over the association's course. Senator Wayne Morse of Oregon rejected the compromise, declaring that no bill was better than this one, while Paul Douglas of Illinois praised Wilkins and Mitchell for their "wise counsel." The NAACP board of directors agreed and voted with only one dissent for a "full approval" of their actions.[18]

Whether maintaining a hard line, as the critics believed, would have been the better option remains debatable even from hindsight. It is certainly true that the political benefits of the 1957 Civil Rights Act did not go to the liberal camp: southerners viewed it as a toothless voting rights law that, they hoped, would relieve some of the pressure on the desegregation front; without having spent much of his prestige, Eisenhower had a civil rights law to his administration's record; majority leader Lyndon Johnson had reaffirmed his reputation as a crafty deal maker and bolstered his presidential ambitions; and many moderates could conveniently take cover behind the NAACP's support for the final compromise. Then again, Wilkins's argument that a stronger law simply had not been attainable can hardly be contested. And how would the national media and the American public at large have reacted if the NAACP had opposed the first civil rights legislation of the twentieth century? Accepting the watered-down bill was a considerable risk and a tough choice for the association, but, as liberal champion Hubert Humphrey told Wilkins during the legislative battle, the civil rights forces could not afford to turn their backs on a crumb.[19]

The potential value of the new law in protecting the right to vote hinged on the determination of the Department of Justice to take advantage of its strengthened authority. Roy Wilkins told the new attorney general, William Rogers, that blacks would not accept the department's limiting itself to the role of a "spectator." The association's Washington Bureau showered the attorney general and the new Civil Rights Commission with reports about the discrimination and harassment black voters faced in the Deep South. Still, in January 1959 Clarence Mitchell found that "there has been a constant failure of both of these agencies to give any effective remedies." Indeed, in the two years following the passage of the 1957 Civil Rights Act the Department of Justice brought a mere four lawsuits against local registrars, hardly enough to discourage southern voting officials from discriminating against black registrants.[20]

In contrast, the Civil Rights Commission, although maintaining a careful bipartisan and sectional balance, assumed an important role in educating the

American people about civil rights and the need for political action. Its printed reports and its public hearings, some of which were broadcast on national television, helped to expose the ugly face of southern racism before a national audience and lend authority to the demand for reform. In 1958, the commission, against the stubborn resistance of state officials, held hearings in Montgomery, Alabama, which minutely inquired into the manifold ways of racial disfranchisement. Its first report, published in 1959, proposed that the president be authorized to appoint federal registrars in those electoral districts where the Civil Rights Commission had found a pattern of voting discrimination.[21]

The Eisenhower administration agreed that the enforcement of black voting rights ought to be strengthened, but it did not wish to take direct responsibility. Instead, a bill drafted by the Department of Justice's Civil Rights Division proposed giving additional power to the courts. If a court passed an injunction against a local registrar, it would also decide whether the actions of the official were part of a "pattern of discrimination." In that case the court could appoint "referees" who would review the registration papers of rejected applicants and report back to the judges. Eventually, the court might add those voters to the list of applicants whom the referees had found qualified. Understandably, the NAACP was not very impressed with this cumbersome plan. Roy Wilkins called it "a useful tool," but insisted that it had "serious defects," especially in relying on drawn-out court proceedings that would only benefit individuals. Yet Robert Carter, the association's legal counsel, argued it was time that the NAACP appreciated for once the efforts of the Republicans: "We profess a non-partisan political bias as an organization. In the past, however, we have found ourselves allied to the Democratic Party. Under these circumstances, let me suggest that we can ill-afford to refuse to support a Republican sponsored civil rights measure where our objectives are strained or mere cavil."[22]

In the election year of 1960, both the GOP and the Democrats wanted another civil rights law, but it was also clear that the chances for passing a meaningful measure were very scant. In April, Congress adopted a bill that, apart from introducing some new and purely fictitious federal offenses, contained a version of the referee plan that was further diluted and inconceivably tedious. For example, even if a federal court had already found a pattern of discrimination, black voters still had to present themselves to the local registrars before the court could appoint referees. Southern lawmakers openly called the 1960 Act a "southern victory," and liberals bitterly decried this "so-called civil rights bill." The mountain had labored, Senator Paul Douglas scoffed, "and brought forth a mouse." Roy Wilkins quipped that in order to register under the new law, a black voter had to pass more checkpoints and examinations "than he would if he tried to get to the U.S. gold reserves in Fort Knox." In a realistic assessment of the 1960 bill's practical irrelevance, the NAACP had not made any serious lobbying efforts. Unlike three years earlier, it avoided any political association with legislation that amounted to little more than window dressing.[23]

The New Frontier and Civil Rights

The two largely symbolic civil rights laws of 1957 and 1960 fell far short of the high hopes and expectations that the NAACP had nurtured throughout the postwar years. Understandably, its leaders eagerly awaited the end of the Eisenhower presidency. Since none of the presidential contenders emerged as the clear front runner, the 1960 presidential race would probably be decided in a very close finish, and the black vote might hold the balance of power for the first time in twelve years. The Non-Partisan Crusade to Mobilize Negro Voters, sponsored by the NAACP and the SCLC, predicted that black voters would decide the elections in twelve key states, with a total of 267 electoral votes, including the southern states of Texas and Tennessee.[24]

The GOP nominated Vice President Richard Nixon, who had earned himself the reputation of a red-baiter early in his career but leaned toward the liberal wing of the party on the issue of civil rights. In the 1956 presidential campaign he had even boasted to be an "honorary member" of the NAACP in front of a black audience. In fact, he had paid membership fees to a California branch in 1946 and repeatedly made financial contributions to NAACP fundraising campaigns. Moreover, in the legislative battle over the 1957 Civil Rights Act the vice president had opposed the jury trial amendment. Although Nixon could hardly be seen as a staunch civil rights advocate, his record was decent enough to make him agreeable to black voters. Sometime before the elections, Roy Wilkins challenged him to make every effort to narrow the 24-point lead Adlai Stevenson had enjoyed over Eisenhower among the black electorate in 1956.[25]

The Democratic convention chose Senator John F. Kennedy of Massachusetts. While he promised in his acceptance speech to lead the nation to a "new frontier," he failed to mention the race issue. Since his election to the U.S. House of Representatives in 1946 and to the U.S. Senate in 1952, Kennedy had not exactly acquired the reputation of a steadfast supporter of black civil rights. Rather, the young and ambitious politician from a rich and well-connected Irish-American family represented the type of lukewarm moderate who could not be relied on in crucial roll calls. In an obvious attempt to curry favor with southern Democrats, Senator Kennedy had voted for the jury trial amendment in 1957.[26]

Although JFK had a generally liberal voting record, Roy Wilkins had decided that the presidential hopeful needed a little lesson about the limited tolerance of black voters. When the senator began to prepare his reelection campaign that year, the NAACP secretary publicly denounced him for his "fraternization" with the southerners. Kennedy denied having entered into an alliance with the segregationist South and implored Wilkins not to erect "an 'iron curtain' of misunderstanding . . . between our two offices." Having waved the stick, the NAACP leader now held out the carrot and attested to Kennedy "one of the best voting records on civil rights and related issues of any Senator in Congress." During the fall campaign, Wilkins's de facto endorsement was spread among the black voters of Massachusetts and contributed to the glowing victory JFK had sought to underscore his bid for the White House. Kennedy certainly appreciated the NAACP's support and sent a contribution the next year, but politely declined to become a life member of the association.[27]

In order to insure party unity, Kennedy named Lyndon Johnson, whom he had defeated in the vote for the Democratic nomination, as his running mate. To his credit, the Texan had been a loyal New Dealer throughout his entire political life and never indulged in race-baiting. During Johnson's early career the NAACP had supported him, but they had watched him with mixed feelings since his election to the Senate. Paying his dues to southern unity, he had voted against all civil rights proposals, but, knowing that a segregationist could never become president, had declined to sign the 1956 "Southern Manifesto"—one of only three southern senators to do so. In 1957, he had vigorously pushed for a compromise on the jury trial amendment to strengthen his credentials as a moderate. When Kennedy picked Johnson as the candidate for the vice presidency instead of Hubert Humphrey, the liberal stalwart whom the NAACP favored, the reactions among the association's leaders oscillated from outright dismay to a cautious wait-and-see attitude. Nobody could have anticipated that within a few years LBJ, as the folksy and vain Texan liked to called, would become the NAACP's knight in shining armor.[28]

Throughout the campaign, the civil rights issue did not play a salient role. Both candidates dodged the NAACP's proposal to include a black journalist on the panel for the televised presidential debates. The Kennedy campaign, however, skillfully publicized JFK's October 1960 phone call to Coretta King, whose husband had been jailed in Georgia on trumped-up charges and appeared to be in serious personal danger. Robert Kennedy, the candidate's brother, went even further and prodded the judge who had sentenced King to four months of hard labor to reconsider the case. The next day, Martin Luther King Jr. was released. In contrast, Richard Nixon declined to comment in the affair. The Reverend Martin Luther King Sr., both a Republican and opposed to Kennedy's Catholicism, publicly urged blacks to vote for JFK. The NAACP leadership, although insisting on its nonpartisanship, also indicated to members and supporters seeking political advice that it preferred Kennedy over Nixon.[29]

Apparently the African-American electorate listened carefully. Kennedy's nationwide share among black voters increased to 70 percent, a 10 percent hike compared to Adlai Stevenson's performance in 1956. More importantly, since JFK's lead in the popular vote amounted to little more than one hundred thousand votes, or a razor-thin 0.2 percent, it was clear that a majority of white voters had cast their ballots for Nixon. Only the massive support from African-Americans tipped the scales in favor of the Democratic candidate, especially in the key states of Michigan, Illinois, New Jersey, and Texas, which Eisenhower had easily carried four years earlier. If Nixon had managed to just hold on to Ike's share of the black vote in these states, he would have become president.[30]

Hence John F. Kennedy had every reason to be grateful to his black supporters. Shortly after the election, Roy Wilkins met with the president-elect to press for a far-reaching program of both legislation and executive action on civil rights. Suspicious that the new president would try to reward his black constituents with token concessions, he warned against "warmed-over, slightly revised, or piecemeal civil rights proposals which might have been daring in 1948 or 1953, but are mild as milk toast today." Other civil rights organizations with a reputation for moderation, such as the National Urban League and the Southern Regional Council, also demanded "thorough, decisive action now."[31]

Given the absence of a clear electoral mandate and the need to win the cooperation of the powerful southern lawmakers in Congress for his economic program, the new president had little leeway for showing his gratitude, even if he had wanted to. A seasoned lobbyist like Wilkins harbored few illusions that Kennedy would go out on a limb early in his presidency with bold civil rights initiatives. The NAACP leader correctly grasped JFK's intentions when he explained to a disappointed black Kennedy supporter that the president was simply trying to sidetrack "troublesome civil rights legislation" in order "to jam through his economic, health, and pressing foreign relations matters." Indeed, when the NAACP convention sent a high-ranking delegation to the White House in July 1961 to demand legislative action, the president politely, but firmly replied: "We remain convinced that legislation is not the way. At least, it is not advisable at this time."[32]

Apparently, Roy Wilkins was not unhappy with the sobering effect of the president's words on the NAACP delegates, as he confided to presidential aide Harris Wofford. Among Kennedy's advisers, the secretary was considered as "a friend of the administration" whose pragmatism favorably compared to Martin Luther King Jr.'s "philosophical and moralistic" attitude. The president much preferred meeting the NAACP leader over King or representatives from SNCC or CORE. Wilkins could be expected to show more patience with the gradualist approach that the administration planned to adopt in the field of civil rights, mostly relying on strengthening the right to vote and on executive action to promote integration and equal opportunity in all federal programs and services.[33]

To their credit, the administration and the president himself demonstrated a serious commitment to the integration of federal agencies and institutions, including appointments to high-profile positions. Among the most salient black appointments was the nomination of Thurgood Marshall, the NAACP's legendary legal counsel, to a federal judgeship in New York. In order to placate the predictable resistance from James Eastland's Senate Judiciary Committee, Kennedy also named Eastland's college buddy William H. Cox, a rabid racist whose nomination Roy Wilkins protested as putting "another cross over the weary shoulders" of Mississippi blacks. Eastland, however, was unimpressed and delayed Thurgood Marshall's confirmation for an entire year.[34]

During the campaign, Kennedy had promised executive orders to end segregation in federally assisted programs. After his ascent to power, civil rights advocates proposed that he make good on his pledge by issuing one big "monumental executive order to cover everything—a second Emancipation Proclamation," but their demand was consistently rejected. A weak housing order was issued only belatedly after the civil rights lobby had waged an "Ink for Jack Campaign," reminding the president that he had promised to end racial discrimination in federally assisted housing "with a stroke of a pen" as soon as he was in power.[35]

The Kennedy administration also adopted a more vigorous approach in enforcing the voting rights provisions of the 1957 Civil Rights Act. While the Eisenhower Department of Justice had brought a mere ten suits against local registrars in three years, Robert Kennedy's attorneys took legal action in twenty-three cases within two years. But litigation was extremely cumbersome to say the least. In one Alabama case, 36,000 pages of voter applications had to be inspected and 185 witnesses were subpoenaed. Moreover, the

Kennedy Justice Department continued to seek the "voluntary, peaceful compliance" of local authorities. Voting rights activists were angered by the FBI's refusal to protect registration workers involved in the Voter Education Project, as Robert Kennedy had promised. FBI director J. Edgar Hoover, who suspected the civil rights movement of being a communist conspiracy, took cover behind the constitutional restrictions imposed by the federal system of criminal justice. Administration officials later insisted that FBI protection would have emboldened the registration activists and provoked even more violence.[36]

While the Kennedy administration was more responsive to the demands of the civil rights movement than its predecessor, it continued to favor a gradualist and consensual approach that would possibly include the "moderate" white South. This incremental strategy did not materialize, because the nonviolent direct action wing of the civil rights movement refused to play along and, beginning with the freedom rides in the spring of 1961, continued "to put on pressure and create a crisis and they [the federal government] react," as CORE director James Farmer explained, describing the political thrust of nonviolent direct action. Eventually, the momentum created by the disruptive grassroots protests of the civil rights movement and by violent responses from white supremacists forced the Kennedy administration to initiate sweeping racial reforms.[37]

The 1964 Civil Rights Act

The turning point of Kennedy's civil rights policy came with Martin Luther King Jr.'s desegregation campaign in Birmingham, Alabama, in the spring of 1963. The televised images of the police attacking peaceful demonstrators, including teenagers and school children, with nightsticks, dogs, and high-pressure fire hoses shocked the president, the American public, and world opinion. On 11 June 1963, the day Alabama governor George Wallace made his pathetic "stand in the schoolhouse door" to prevent the integration of the University of Alabama, Kennedy went on national television to deliver his most important speech on civil rights. Calling the race problem a moral issue "as old as the Scriptures and . . . as clear as the American Constitution," the president urged his white compatriots to face both the reality of racial discrimination and the need for fast and thoroughgoing redress. The presidential appeal was tragically validated when NAACP field secretary Medgar Evers was murdered in front of his Jackson, Mississippi, home only a few hours later. At his funeral at Arlington Cemetery, Roy Wilkins solemnly proclaimed that the slain civil rights hero had believed in his country—it now remained to be seen if his country believed in him.[38]

On 19 June 1963, the president went to Congress and proposed a civil rights bill that would ban segregation in all public facilities, including those that were privately owned, give broader authority to the Justice Department in enforcing school integration, and deny federal funding for segregated programs. Kennedy frankly acknowledged that the mass protests of the civil rights movement had forced this legislation and that the protests had been legitimate, "because these racial injustices are real and no other remedy was in sight." Now that the civil rights bill was on its way, he quickly added, mass protests were no longer necessary and even dangerous. Although the bill did not meet all the demands of the civil rights movement, especially with regard to the right to vote and equal employment, the proposed abolition of racial segregation in the public sphere amounted to nothing less than a frontal assault on the hard core of white supremacy. In contrast to the mild laws of 1957 and 1960, the white South could hardly be expected to watch the Kennedy bill pass without a major fight.[39]

Of course the civil rights leadership eagerly wanted the bill, but it was deeply divided over the appropriate tactics. Martin Luther King Jr., emboldened by the success of his Birmingham campaign, supported mass demonstrations in the nation's capital, while Roy Wilkins urged "the quiet, patient lobbying tactics that worked best on Congress." Wilkins fully appreciated the considerable political risk that the administration took by introducing a sweeping civil rights bill only a year before the next presidential election. Like the Kennedy brothers, the NAACP leader feared that possible riots in Washington would play into the hands of the bill's opponents. But he also saw the need to keep up the pressure, lest the president's proposals might again be watered down in Congress. When the civil rights leaders eventually agreed to organize a "March on Washington for Jobs and Freedom," a compromise based on a long-standing project by A. Philip Randolph, the executive secretary did his best to insure that the demonstrations would be orderly and respectable. He opposed a visible role by civil rights veteran Bayard Rustin because of Rustin's radical past, and SNCC leader John Lewis was prodded to tone down the sharp criticism of the administration he had planned to voice in his speech at the march rally. The NAACP branches were called upon to send "the biggest possible group" to the capital and were given strict organizational guidelines. All vacations of the association's paid officers were cancelled not only for the march itself but "for the duration of the civil rights battle in the Congress."[40]

The interracial March on Washington of 250,000 Americans on August 28, 1963, not only remained peaceful but went down as a truly great day in the history of the civil rights movement, with Martin Luther King Jr.'s magnificent vision of a brotherly and color-blind America as the unforgettable climax. The country and the world, an ABC commentator enthused, had witnessed "a dramatic, authentic example of responsible citizenship." Demanding civil rights and decent jobs for all Americans, the organizers were able to unite a broad coalition of racial liberals, including all major civil rights groups, the United Auto Workers, the American Jewish Congress, and major representatives of the Catholic and Protestant churches. As soon as the March had ended, the president, relieved of his misgivings about potential violence, met with the civil rights leaders and urged them to concentrate on working for his civil rights bill. Securing a majority in Congress would be a tough, uphill battle.[41]

Kennedy did not need to tell the NAACP. Preparing for the great political fight, the association's board of directors immediately announced "active work for the defeat at the polls of any Congressman or Senator of either party who fails to vote for key provisions of a strong civil rights bill." The message was directed especially at the moderate lawmakers who opposed the bill's interference with the autonomy of private businesses and at the administration, should it be willing to settle for a diluted law. In that case black Americans would be compelled to take to the streets again to seek justice and equality, Bishop Stephen Spottswood, the chairman of the NAACP board of directors, warned Robert Kennedy. The NAACP branches were told to send delegations to their congressmen and senators and to hold demonstrations at their offices when they returned home for the Thanksgiving recess. On Thanksgiving of 1963, however, Americans did not discuss civil rights but mourned the violent and shocking death of their president.[42]

John F. Kennedy, to be sure, had been a reluctant warrior for civil rights, but eventually he had decisively moved the federal government toward ending legal segregation and discrimination. This had incurred him the hatred of white supremacists in the South, many of whom openly cheered the news of his assassination. In Mississippi, signs reading "K.O. the Kennedys!" could be seen at the roadsides, and businessmen frivolously talked about establishing an "Oswald Appreciation Fund," named after JFK's suspected murderer. For the NAACP and the civil rights movement, the president's death raised anxious questions about the future of the pending civil rights bill and the federal government's civil rights policy at large. Racial reform required strong presidential leadership. Would Kennedy's successor, Lyndon B. Johnson, be willing and able to provide it?[43]

Although Johnson had never been a race-baiter and had taken a constructive approach to black rights as head of Kennedy's Equal Employment Opportunity Committee, no one anticipated that the Texan would come out as a determined and uncompromising advocate of civil rights from the very first days of his presidency. From the viewpoint of veteran NAACP leaders, such as Roy Wilkins and Clarence Mitchell, who had lived through decades of presidential tokenism, finally there was a chief executive whose words were followed by deeds. LBJ's liberal vision of a Great Society in which the federal government secured the rights of and created opportunities for all Americans, lifting up the poor and disadvantaged, seemed to be exactly what African-Americans needed.[44] Johnson and the NAACP leaders developed not only a close and effective political alliance but also bonds of personal loyalty that endured after the inglorious end of LBJ's presidency. When Johnson died in January 1973, Roy Wilkins called him the "best [U.S. president] from the standpoint of poor white Americans and of non-white minorities." Clarence Mitchell did not hesitate to put him on a higher historical rank than even Lincoln and FDR.[45]

Only a few days after LBJ had been sworn in, Roy Wilkins was called to the White House for a meeting with the new president. Johnson assured the NAACP leader of his determination to get a strong civil rights bill passed. Obviously, the executive secretary was impressed by the famous eye-to-eye "Johnson treatment." Blacks were naturally skeptical of a man with a southern background, he told the press, but they had faith in the president's sincere convictions on civil rights. Still, as long as there was the danger of "politics as usual" in Congress, Wilkins refused to call for an end to civil rights demonstrations. After Johnson had declared himself repeatedly and unequivocally in favor of the pending bill, Wilkins informed him that the black community throughout the nation was slowly beginning to believe in changes for the better: "I must add in all candor," he wrote, "that Negro citizens are not all convinced, signed and ready for the cheering section, but they are far from the state of widespread hostility which might have been expected in the circumstances."[46]

In February 1964, the House of Representatives passed the Kennedy-Johnson civil rights bill by a large majority, but the real legislative battle would be fought in the Senate. Was the president willing to stick out the filibuster that threatened to paralyze his entire legislative agenda? "I don't care if it [the civil rights bill] stays for four, six or eight months," Johnson reassured Clarence Mitchell, "the President of the United States doesn't care if that bill is there forever. We are not going to have the Senate do anything else until that bill is passed. And it is going to pass." LBJ also made sure that his old friend Georgia senator Richard Russell, the unofficial leader of the South in the Senate, knew that he would not settle for a watered-down compromise. Russell publicly announced to fight "to the last ditch" but indicated that this did not necessarily mean obstructing the president's entire legislative program.[47]

The southerners staged the longest filibuster in the history of the U.S. Senate. It lasted eighty-two days and eventually filled about sixty-three thousand pages in the Congressional Record. The key figure in the fight for cloture was minority leader Everett Dirksen, a conservative Republican from Illinois, who opposed the bill's authorization of the Department of Justice to enforce desegregation in private businesses. In order to win the necessary Republican votes for cloture, liberals went out of their way to court the GOP leader. If it had been necessary, Hubert Humphrey later bluntly confessed, "I would have kissed Dirksen's ass on the Capitol steps." On the substance of the bill, the supporters did not waver but only made a few token concessions that allowed Dirksen to fall in line. On 10 June 1964, the Senate for the first time in its history voted for cloture to end a filibuster staged to obstruct a civil rights bill. Nine days later it passed the bill by a margin of almost three to one. As soon as the House had adopted the Senate bill, President Johnson signed it into law on July 2, 1964, paving the way to end legal racial segregation in the United States.[48]

During the lobbying campaign for the 1964 Civil Rights Act, the association concentrated on putting pressure on reluctant lawmakers, waging letter writing campaigns, and sending delegations to Washington prior to the crucial votes. Above all, the NAACP trusted in the power of the ballot. Supporters of the bill, the branches were instructed, had "a right" to expect gratitude at the polls, while foes would be punished, of course on a strictly nonpartisan basis. In Dayton, Ohio, Roy Wilkins threatened a Republican congressman who refused to support the bill with registering twenty-five thousand black voters who would remember in November, while praising another Republican for his "distinguished service to the cause of civil rights." Eventually, most of the Republican members of Congress believed it was politically prudent to come down on the side of civil rights.[49]

The association's annual convention of 1964, held in Washington only a few days after the crucial vote in the Senate, celebrated the passage of the Civil Rights Act as "a high point in the NAACP's long battle for national civil rights legislation." Although the delegates dutifully acknowledged that many groups and individuals had contributed to this victory, the NAACP eagerly credited the triumph to its own "unparalleled demonstration of organizational power [and] of intelligent militancy." Clarence Mitchell, the head of the

Washington Bureau, was honored as "one of the greatest authorities on the legislative procedure on the scene" and as the "leading lobbyist of his age." The association's self-aggrandizement was a little overblown but could perhaps be forgiven at a moment of truly historic significance. Indeed, the NAACP's political clout with the White House and with Congress had never been greater than in the crucial months preceding the adoption of the Civil Rights Act. The president of the United States made a point of being available for Wilkins and Mitchell as the national representatives of the largest civil rights organization with a membership of about a half million. Johnson surely hoped that the NAACP's influence among the black community would win him votes in his reelection bid, but, more importantly, LBJ could also rely on the association to communicate the imperatives of a "responsible" civil rights strategy.[50]

All the Way with LBJ

The paramount political interest that united Johnson and the NAACP in 1964 was fending off the emerging "white backlash," a term describing the growing resentment among the white working and lower middle classes against black "radicalism" and the favoritism liberals allegedly extended to African-Americans at the expense of whites. The appeal of the white backlash in the North became alarmingly evident in the spring, when George Wallace, Alabama's fervently segregationist governor, entered the Democratic primaries and garnered more than 30 percent of the vote in Wisconsin and Indiana. In the border state of Maryland, the NAACP waged a frantic registration drive to defeat Wallace, who nevertheless received almost 43 percent, grumbling that "if it hadn't been for the nigger bloc vote we'd have won it all."[51]

Wallace could not seriously hope to wrest the Democratic nomination from Lyndon Johnson, but he might run as an independent and weaken the Democratic columns in the South. His showing among Democratic core constituencies in the North was a clear warning signal that the president was vulnerable on the race issue. In this situation the NAACP felt obliged to cover LBJ's back. First, a maximum number of black voters needed to be registered and brought to the polls, and second, all "provocative" action by the civil rights movement that might fuel the backlash had to be avoided.

Mobilizing black voters turned out to be easier than expected. The Republicans, driven by a right wing revolt against the party's East Coast establishment, nominated Senator Barry Goldwater of Arizona, a states' rights champion who had voted against the Civil Rights Act. Goldwater's "antebellum oratory" might provoke racial violence, Roy Wilkins had warned him prior to the crucial roll call in the Senate, and the NAACP annual convention emphatically pleaded with the GOP to repudiate Goldwater and to nominate a candidate "in the tradition of Lincoln." Yet the Republicans apparently did not care about black votes and gambled instead on a major breakthrough among disgruntled white Democrats in the North and the South. After George Wallace withdrew from the presidential race, there seemed to be a good chance that many Wallace supporters in traditional Democratic strongholds might vote for Goldwater because of the race issue.[52]

In order to counteract the white backlash, the NAACP launched an unprecedented nationwide registration drive among the black electorate. The association took pains to emphasize that the campaign was not directed against all Republican candidates, many of whom had voted for the Civil Rights Act, but had the sole goal of defeating Barry Goldwater. To underscore its bipartisanship, the NAACP made a point of supporting several Republicans who had "stood by our issue" in the decisive moments of the legislative battle over the Civil Rights Act. As far as the GOP presidential candidate was concerned, however, the NAACP branches were mobilized for an all-out anti-Goldwater drive. The burden of this effort fell on the branches in the large metropolitan areas. No energy would be wasted on achieving token results in the Deep South. "In Mississippi," Roy Wilkins explained, "Negroes cannot register and speak on election day through their vote. Up here Negro citizens *can* register and *can* vote, without interference. Let us speak on election day for ourselves and for the suffering voiceless ones in Mississippi."[53]

The anti-Goldwater campaign met with a stunning response among the NAACP branches and black voters throughout the country. "The name 'Goldwater' has become a bad word in many, many areas, " registration activist W. C. Patton explained, describing the mood in Alabama, "say 'Goldwater' and the people would make efforts to register; say 'Goldwater' and they start working to get voters to the polls." The reports from major American cities painted an equally enthusiastic picture. In Baltimore, for example, black registration reached its historic peak at more than 70 percent. Based on the calculations of the NAACP registration workers, the 1964 anti-Goldwater drive yielded approximately 590,000 additional black voters outside of the South.[54]

Despite these encouraging reports, the NAACP leadership continued to worry about a potential Goldwater victory. Following the signing ceremony of the Civil Rights Act, the president had admonished the civil rights leaders that mass demonstrations were now unnecessary, even counterproductive. With race riots exploding in Harlem in mid-July, NAACP secretary Roy Wilkins fully agreed. "There is no safety in assumptions that Goldwater cannot win the elections," he implored the leaders of the other civil rights organizations, "he can win it and he can be helped to win it, if enough wrong moves are made." In late July, Wilkins, A. Philip Randolph, and Martin Luther King Jr. called for a voluntary moratorium of all "mass marches, mass picketing and mass demonstrations" until after the elections. CORE and SNCC, however, refused to heed the call, arguing that demonstrations were necessary to "channel in a militant fashion the justifiable frustrations and anger of the Negro community" and that a moratorium would not mollify the white backlash in the first place.[55]

Despite these tactical differences, the overwhelming majority of the civil rights movement supported LBJ and the national Democratic Party. At the same time, the die-hard segregationists of the Deep South also continued to claim the Democratic label, although they fiercely opposed the president and his civil rights policy. In response to this absurd situation, the civil rights movement in Mississippi, united in the Council of Federated Organizations, decided to create a new Democratic Party organization called the Mississippi Freedom Democratic Party (MFDP) that was based on the "freedom registrations" and "freedom elections" COFO had held in the fall of 1963 and the summer of 1964. The MFDP resolved to send their own delegation to the Democratic National Convention in Atlantic City in August 1964 to challenge the legitimacy of the regular Mississippi delegation and to seek recognition as the Magnolia state's official Democrats. The sixty-eight delegates who came to New Jersey could make an excellent legal and moral case. The all-white regular party delegation was based on the systematic and illegal disfranchisement of half of the state's population and had openly declared their oppositions to the national party's platform and ticket. In fact, the only reason the regulars went to Atlantic City at all was to stage a walkout. Nevertheless, Lyndon Johnson was not exactly delighted to welcome his black supporters from Mississippi at the convention. Above all, he wanted a show of unity and sought to avert other southern delegations from joining the Mississippi regulars in a new Dixiecrat movement.[56]

The Mississippi challenge put the NAACP into an obvious predicament. As mentioned in the previous chapter, the association's leaders watched the activities of COFO with suspicion and disapproval, and they certainly did not wish to see any damage done to the Johnson campaign. On the other hand, there was no question that the MFDP's claim had to be supported. After the NAACP annual convention had called for seating the "freedom" delegates, Roy Wilkins directed all of the association's branches to prevail upon the Democratic delegates in support of the MFDP. Reminding the members of the recent murder of three civil rights workers in the Magnolia state, the secretary emphatically demanded that "the representatives of this government-by-murder" must not be seated at Atlantic City. A preconvention rally was held jointly with other civil rights groups, but in observance of the moratorium on demonstrations, picketing and marches at the convention were explicitly banned.[57]

The fight of the "freedom" delegates from Mississippi to gain recognition from the Democratic Party was a textbook case of the perennial conflict between morality and politics. Much to the president's chagrin, the MFDP made an effective presentation before the convention and the national media, with Fanny Lou Hamer, a simple sharecropper, telling movingly about the violent abuse she had suffered after trying to register as a voter. Eventually, Johnson offered to appoint the MFDP mission as nonvoting "honorary delegates," except for two at large seats with voting privileges, while the Mississippi regulars would have to swear a loyalty oath to the party platform before being seated. Moreover, the convention rules would be changed to preclude lily-white delegations in the future. The MFDP, however, rejected the compromise almost unanimously, although prominent civil rights leaders, including Bayard Rustin and Martin Luther King Jr., pleaded with them for acceptance. "We didn't come here for no two seats when all of us is tired," Fannie Lou Hamer famously declared. Perhaps the MFDP delegates would have taken the deal if LBJ, in an overbearing display of paternalism, had not insisted on handpicking the two at large delegates and had not specifically excluded "that illiterate woman" Mrs. Hamer.[58]

NAACP secretary Roy Wilkins had also come to Atlantic City and eloquently supported the seating of the "freedom" delegates before the platform committee. However, Wilkins, aware that his close affiliation with the administration was well known, refrained from openly intervening in the negotiations that took place behind the scenes. Notably, the NAACP leader did not appear before the "freedom" delegates to advocate acceptance of the Johnson proposals. According to his memoirs, Wilkins merely offered cautious advice to SNCC activist Robert Moses. Fannie Lou Hamer, however, recalled later that after she had spoken for the rejection of the compromise, the NAACP secretary had angrily confronted her: "You people have put your point across, now why don't you pack up and go home?"[59]

While the MFDP delegation staged a symbolic sit-in, occupying the seats that had been vacated by the regulars, most of whom had refused to take the loyalty pledge, the events at Atlantic City did not lead to an immediate split within the civil rights movement. In fact, shortly after the convention a representative of the MFDP wrote a letter to Roy Wilkins cordially thanking him for his "dedicated support" at the Atlantic City convention. Although the ultimate goal had not been achieved, the delegation had scored "a great victory" by capturing the attention of the nation. The MFDP pledged itself to campaign for Johnson's reelection and announced its intention to run its own slate of candidates for Congress in another "freedom vote." Based on this election, the Freedom Democrats would then challenge the congressional seats of the regular Mississippi Democrats. Obviously, the MFDP had not given up on the political process and on gaining the support of the liberal party establishment.[60]

On election day, the fears that LBJ might be harmed by black "radicalism" turned out to have been much exaggerated. Civil rights had not even been a salient campaign issue and Barry Goldwater refrained from trying to boost his faltering popularity by stirring up racial animosity. Although Johnson's reelection had never really been in doubt, few had expected a landslide of 61 percent of the popular vote and a stunning 486 votes in the electoral college. LBJ had won the mandate for his Great Society that he had sought so eagerly. Moreover, the Democrats gained two additional seats in the Senate and thirty-seven in the House, giving them comfortable control of Congress and opening up excellent prospects for the president's legislative agenda. No other group of voters had supported Johnson as unanimously as African-Americans. According to the estimates by the NAACP registration experts, an all-time high of more than 6 million black voters had cast their ballots in the 1964 elections, an increase of approximately 1.5 million over 1960. The association proudly claimed to have registered 750,000 new voters itself during its 1964 drives. Based on the election results from predominantly black precincts, Henry Lee Moon, the NAACP director of public relations, figured that between 88 and 98 percent of the black electorate had marked their ballots for LBJ. An enthusiastic Roy Wilkins cabled to the president: "The people have not spoken, they have shouted. Congratulations!"[61]

While the national elections of 1964 looked like a great triumph for liberalism, careful observers could already see the harbingers of a strong conservative resurgence, with the white South as its power base. In marked contrast to his nationwide defeat, Barry Goldwater had easily carried the five states of the Deep South—in Mississippi he garnered 87 percent of the popular vote. In the remaining six states of the former Confederacy Johnson only won because black voters pushed him over the top. There was no doubt that these results were a direct response to the president's civil rights policy. LBJ himself had expected this to happen. When he signed the Civil Rights Act, he confided to one of his advisers that they had just delivered the South to the Republicans "for your lifetime and mine." With white southerners deserting the Democratic Party in droves, the full reenfranchisement of southern blacks became a matter of vital urgency.[62]

Toward the Voting Rights Act

The 1964 Civil Rights Act had focused on desegregation and largely left out protections of the right to vote. The NAACP accepted this flaw because it feared that the southerners would again try to buy time for segregation by agreeing to some weak voting provisions, as they had done in 1957 and 1960. However, the brutal resistance by the white supremacists of the Deep South against black voters, including the murder of three registration workers in the 1964 Mississippi Freedom Summer, made it painfully clear that a stronger law was needed to break the iron-clad grip of disfranchisement.[63]

Shortly after his reelection, President Johnson instructed his attorney general, Nicholas Katzenbach, to devise a legal strategy. At the end of the year, the Department of Justice's Civil Rights Division offered three alternatives: First, a constitutional amendment prohibiting all qualifications for voting other than age, residency, conviction for a felony, and confinement to an asylum for the mentally ill. Second, the authorization of a federal commission to supervise all registrations for federal elections. And third, a federal law that allowed the Department of Justice to take over the registration process, if specific conditions, as they prevailed throughout much of the South, were fulfilled. Each of these proposals had certain drawbacks, however. A constitutional amendment that in effect would have introduced universal suffrage to the U.S. Constitution seemed most desirable but would also be the most difficult to obtain. Limiting registration authority to federal elections would create a mess that nobody wanted. And placing the South under a selective law appeared radical and constitutionally suspect.[64]

LBJ hoped that introducing a new voting bill could be delayed for some time, but the campaign of mass demonstrations that Martin Luther King Jr. began in Selma, Alabama, in early January 1965 forced his hand. Like Birmingham two years earlier, Selma was a perfect place to expose the disfranchisement of southern blacks. Among an African-American voting-age population of roughly 15,000, a minuscule 335 were registered voters and all attempts to increase their number were flatly rebuffed. Like "Bull" Connor of Birmingham, Sheriff Jim Clark of Selma enjoyed a well-deserved reputation as a mean and irascible racist who would probably meet peaceful protests with brutal violence. Predictably, the confrontations at Selma between January and March 1965 led to a series of mass arrests and assaults against nonviolent demonstrators. On March 7, Selma's "bloody Sunday," mounted state troopers in front of television cameras cracked down on 600 marchers who were on their way to Montgomery to present a petition to Governor Wallace. Two days later, a white civil rights activist from Boston was beaten by a mob and subsequently died. Disgust and outrage were near universal and triggered historical analogies to the terror of the Nazis. The NAACP board of directors, usually quite restrained in its public promulgations, declared: "[C]ontinued assaults upon peaceably assembled Negroes might well force them, like the people in Nazi-occupied Europe, underground to protect themselves from oppression." Roy Wilkins compared the Alabama state troopers to Nazi storm troopers.[65]

Eventually, the danger of more violence at Selma compelled the federal government to intervene. When a federal court lifted the ban on demonstrations and the protesters prepared for another attempt to march to Montgomery, LBJ had the marchers protected by the federalized Alabama National Guard and a detachment of federal marshals. Finally, on March 25, the protesters completed their march by holding a large, peaceful rally at the state capitol in Montgomery. Tragically, a white female civil rights worker from Detroit was murdered by Klansmen while driving back to Selma in the company of a black fellow activist. But Johnson was not content with ensuring the safety of the marchers. Even before "bloody Sunday," the president had told Katzenbach to write "the goddamnest toughest voting rights act that you can devise."[66]

The bill that was drafted in early March thus followed the third and most drastic of the alternatives that the Department of Justice had sketched out in late 1964. The bill authorized the DoJ to send federal examiners to all jurisdictions where the overall registration or voter turnout in the 1964 presidential elections had been below 50 percent of those eligible to vote. The examiners would supervise both the registration and the elections. All literacy and understanding tests were to be suspended for five years. To insure that the states covered by the "trigger formula" of the bill did not try to legislate new discriminatory rules, they would have to submit all changes in their suffrage and elections laws for "preclearance" either by the Department of Justice or the Federal District Court in Washington, D.C.[67]

The bill was a radical measure indeed. In neutral language it proposed to place large parts of the South—Alabama, Georgia, Louisiana, Mississippi, South Carolina, Virginia, and half of North Carolina—under federal surveillance and suspended the traditional prerogatives of the states to determine their own suffrage laws. That the federal government resorted to such drastic steps was a clear indication that at long last Selma had exhausted the nation's indulgence of southern defiance. Appalled by the television pictures from Alabama, Republican Senator Dirksen told the attorney general that he would support even a "revolutionary law." On March 15, the president went to Congress and presented his voting rights bill in moving words. When he cited the civil rights anthem "We Shall Overcome," many members of Congress and the spectators in the gallery broke out in thundering applause. Many had tears in their eyes, Roy Wilkins observed, and the NAACP leader later confessed: "[A]t that moment, I loved LBJ."[68]

Perhaps Wilkins also thought of the association's long years of struggle for the ballot. It must be noted, however, that the NAACP, like two years earlier in the Birmingham campaign, had not been directly involved in the events at Selma. To be sure, it had called its members to hold rallies and vigils to express their solidarity, but the credit for the final breakthrough undoubtedly belonged to the protesters at Selma. Roy Wilkins himself acknowledged this when he politely declined to march among the first civil rights activists to enter Montgomery, where he had traveled to participate in the concluding rally. Given his well-known skepticism toward nonviolent mass protests, the NAACP secretary would have looked like a Johnny-come-lately trying to steal the attention from the real heroes. Only a few weeks later the association's headquarters warned against "Selma-type demonstrations" that Martin Luther King Jr. had announced to dramatize racial discrimination in northern cities.[69]

The civil rights movement supported the administration's voting rights bill, but nevertheless tried to strengthen it further during the legislative process. In a joint declaration, the SCLC, CORE, SNCC, and the MFDP called for vigilance against "another fraudulently ineffectual piece of legislation." In particular, they objected to a trigger formula based on "arbitrary permissible percentages for disfranchisement" and instead demanded federal registration *"where the people who are not free to register* request it, and where there is a *prima facie* evidence of voter intimidation, obstruction and subversion of the right to vote." Sure enough, this proposal had the charms of simple justice, but the administration's critics missed a crucial point. Complaints from the local population would be subject to court reviews, which had been a major stumbling block for efficient remedy in the past. With its quantifiable trigger formula, however, the DoJ hoped to sidestep the tedious path of litigation.[70]

The NAACP also was not entirely happy with the bill's trigger formula and supported an amendment that would have substituted an African-American registration of less than 25 percent for the 50 percent margin in overall registration favored by the administration. The race-specific criterion would have broadened the law's geographical scope considerably. Even more important from the association's point of view, however, was another amendment outlawing the poll tax as a prerequisite for voting in state and local elections. Since a constitutional amendment of 1964 had already abolished the poll tax as a suffrage qualification in federal elections, the NAACP's insistence on including an anti–poll tax provision in the voting rights bill looked somewhat pointless, if not to say dogmatic. The federal anti–poll tax law for which the NAACP had fought for decades had obviously become an end in itself. As late as July 1965, Clarence Mitchell told Vice President Hubert Humphrey that the NAACP preferred to delay the passage of the voting rights bill until a majority for the poll tax provision was assured.[71]

The administration considered a federal law banning the poll tax in state and local elections constitutionally suspect and did not want to jeopardize its voting rights bill by this minor issue. To appease the anti–poll taxers, a declaratory statement was added that authorized the attorney general to challenge all remaining poll tax qualifications in court. In 1966, the Supreme Court eventually struck down the poll tax as a prerequisite for voting in all elections. The reasoning of the Court's majority was very similar to the arguments that NAACP legal counsel Thurgood Marshall had developed twenty-six years earlier, namely that the right to vote had no reasonable connection to the economic status of the voter.[72]

Although it took five months to get the 1965 Voting Rights Act through Congress, its passage was never really in doubt. Even several of the southerners indicated to Clarence Mitchell that they had resigned themselves to the law and might as well support it. Indeed, four senators from southern states not covered by the Act eventually voted for the administration's bill. On August 6, 1965, President Johnson signed the law in the same room of the White House where Lincoln had promulgated his Emancipation Proclamation. Many of those who were present at the ceremony, including the leaders of the civil rights movement, believed that the Voting Rights Act was of no lesser historical significance.[73]

The more militant civil rights activists, however, were unwilling to wait until the law became effective and insisted on crushing the political power of white supremacists immediately. As it had promised after the Atlantic City convention, the MFDP had held "freedom elections" in Mississippi in November 1964 in which Fannie Lou Hamer and two other black women were "elected" to Congress. Arguing that the official elections had been illegal due to the continued disfranchisement of black voters, the MFDP decided to challenge the elections and to petition the U.S. House of Representatives to deny seating to the official congressional delegation from Mississippi. The challenge dragged on for ten months and at times became more important for SNCC and the MFDP than working for the passage of the Voting Rights Act. Although he did not believe in the ultimate success of the campaign, SNCC activist Robert Moses insisted that the Mississippi movement had to take a stand for morality and legitimacy as opposed to politics and legality: "You say we're not legal because we don't abide by Mississippi laws, but the laws of Mississippi are illegal. . . . They had the mock election, We had the *real* election."[74]

Most of the liberal supporters of the civil rights movement agreed that a good case could be made for challenging the official elections in Mississippi, which had excluded more than 90 percent of the eligible black electorate. When the new Congress assembled in January 1965, 149 congressmen, more than one-third of all members of the House, voted to deny seating to their colleagues from Mississippi. However, very few liberals accepted the tenuous proposition that the candidates who had been elected in the "freedom vote" were entitled to these seats. The White House, fearing the rebellion of white southern congressmen, declined to support the challenge, arguing that this was a matter falling solely under the jurisdiction of the House itself.[75]

The NAACP leaders also did not believe in the legal and political merits of the MFDP challenge to unseat the representatives from Mississippi. The claims of the "freedom" candidates had no precedent in congressional history, the association's legal expert noted, and obtaining a two-thirds majority was simply inconceivable. NAACP assistant secretary John Morsell advised the local branches that the association did not endorse the MFDP campaign and had not authorized any fund-raising efforts. In a meeting of the Leadership Conference on Civil Rights, Clarence Mitchell pleaded against official support for the MFDP, but to no avail.[76]

The MFDP eventually dropped its demand that the congressional seats of Mississippi be given to Mrs. Hamer and her colleagues. However, it insisted on new elections based on the overwhelming evidence of racial disfranchisement in the Magnolia state that it presented in another petition to the House in May 1965. Nevertheless, most of the congressmen remained unwilling to impose the drastic sanction of unseating representatives who could not be held individually responsible for the political discrimination against African-Americans. Understandably, the MFDP activists were bitterly disappointed by what they saw as hypocritical legalism. "I am not crying for myself today," Fannie Lou Hamer apologized for her tears, "but I'm crying for America. I cry that the Constitution of the United States . . . applies only to white people." Still, she added: "But we will come back year after year until we are allowed our rights as citizens."[77]

The MFDP activists had not overlooked that the NAACP considered its challenge to unseat the segregationists from Mississippi unnecessary and a distraction from the more important goal of securing the Voting Rights Act. With the new law taking effect, the association's leaders were convinced that the civil rights movement should focus on mobilizing black voters for the next congressional elections in 1966. This seemed plausible enough. Since almost half of Mississippi's voting-age population was black, the political landscape of the state was bound for fast changes, many black Mississippians believed. As it turned out, they had all underestimated the ingenuity of white supremacists. Right after the signing of the Voting Rights Act, the state legislature began diluting black electoral strength by enacting elaborate schemes of racial gerrymandering and other manipulations of the electoral process. Although black registration in Mississippi skyrocketed from less than 7 percent in 1964 to almost 60 percent in 1971, it took until 1986, more than twenty years after the signing of the Voting Rights Act, for the first black representative from Mississippi to be elected to the U.S. Congress.[78]

The Voting Rights Act, to be sure, did not end the discrimination of black voters overnight. Intimidation, economic pressures, and threats of violence did not cease immediately, and the guardians of white supremacy continued to devise electoral laws aimed at minimizing the Act's political impact. Nevertheless, the Voting Rights Act is rightly ranked among the most important and effective pieces of legislation in American history. Its short-term impact was spectacular, pushing black registration in the South close to the level of whites within a few years. A hundred years after the ratification of the Fifteenth Amendment, the Act finally enforced the constitutional protections of this instrument. It was a truly radical reversal of the federal system, but, as Chief Justice Earl Warren observed in declaring the Act constitutional, "exceptional conditions can justify legislative measures not otherwise appropriate."[79]

The historical developments that culminated in the Civil Rights Act of 1964 and the Voting Rights Act of 1965 seemed to vindicate the NAACP's long-standing conviction that eventually the federal government would have to take responsibility for enforcing the civil and political rights of black citizens. It needs to be emphasized, however, that these goals were achieved in a way that was remarkably different from what most of the association's leaders had envisioned. Although President Johnson enthusiastically praised Roy Wilkins for his "statesmanlike leadership" and the NAACP's "thoughtful and orderly approach to problems of race relations," there can be no doubt that nonviolent mass protests and the violent response by the forces of white supremacy created the political momentum that led to the abolition of de jure segregation and the securing of black voting rights. Yet it would also be misleading to depict the NAACP as a conservative force. Claiming the position of the liberal center within the civil rights movement, the association sought to mediate between the moral radicalism of groups like SNCC and the MFDP and the imperatives of liberal coalition politics. As long as there was a broad consensus on the movement's basic goals, the inevitable tensions and conflicts between moderates and militants may even be seen as part of a fruitful division of labor. As soon as these goals had been achieved, however, the consensus between the NAACP and the radical wing of the civil rights movement unraveled. Much to the surprise and disappointment of racial liberals, civil rights reform did not lead to the pacification of race relations.[80]

9

Black Power–White Backlash

The broad national consensus in favor of desegregation and voting rights that emerged in the early 1960s was predicated upon the expectation that these reforms would lead to a swift "solution" of the race question and allow Americans to return to "normalcy." The leaders of the civil rights movement deliberately nurtured these expectations. "Give us the ballot," Martin Luther King Jr. proclaimed in 1957, "and we will no longer have to worry the federal government about our basic rights." If only blacks had full and free access to the vote, Roy Wilkins wrote to the *New York Times* in 1960, "following a period of transition and training, many aspects of civil rights now considered ponderously in Washington will plague the Hill less and less as the state capitols and county courthouses will take over. The Hill can then concern itself with the myriad 'normal' problems of federal state relationships, budget, defense, foreign policy, and space."[1]

Tragically, however, this vision of gradual and orderly change did not materialize. The passing of the 1964 Civil Rights Act was followed by a first wave of violent ghetto riots in New York, New Jersey, and other metropolitan areas of the Northeast. Only five days after Lyndon Johnson had signed the Voting Rights Act in the summer of 1965, riots erupted in the Watts district of Los Angeles that left thirty-four African-Americans dead. Over the next three years most of the big cities outside of the South lived through a series of "long hot summers" of violent unrest in the black ghettoes. When Detroit exploded in July 1967, forty-three persons, including thirty-three blacks, lost their lives. The police and the National Guard had recklessly made use of their firearms. When Martin Luther King Jr. was assassinated on April 4, 1968, racial riots, especially ferocious in the nation's capital, broke out in 170 cities, leaving dozens of people dead and thousands injured. Racial civil war seemed imminent. The United States, one black political analyst commented, stood "on the threshold of the most critical period in its history since the first shot was fired on Fort Sumter in 1861."[2]

Typically, the riots were triggered by acts of brutality by white police officers against black ghetto dwellers. However, most analysts agreed that the outbursts of violence had much deeper roots. The civil rights movement had raised the consciousness and expectations of all African-Americans, but its focus on desegregation and political rights did not address the social and economic plight of the increasingly impatient black population of the urban ghetto. The National Advisory Commission on Civil Disorders, which had been established by President Johnson after the riots in Detroit, somberly announced in its final report of February 1968 that the American nation was "moving toward two societies, one black, one white—separate and unequal." The commission, which included NAACP leader Roy Wilkins, held "white racism . . . essentially responsible for the explosive mixture which has been accumulating in our cities since the end of World War II." Calling for "unprecedented levels of funding and performance," the report asked the federal government to create 2 million new jobs in both the private and public sectors and to build 6 million new housing units for low-income families within five years. If necessary, these programs would have to be financed by tax increases.[3]

Despite all its gloomy rhetoric, the Kerner Report, named after the commission chairman, Illinois governor Otto Kerner, confidently espoused the liberal creed that racial tensions could be brought under control by federal antidiscrimination legislation and generous spending on economic stimulus and welfare programs along the lines of LBJ's "Great Society." By 1968, however, the political and economic support for a reform effort of the kind and magnitude that the report demanded had long since eroded. Not only was the war in Vietnam draining the resources away from the war on poverty, but the liberal consensus had given way to a polarization of American society at large and of the races in particular. In the public discourse the terms *Black Power* and *White Backlash* signified a political and cultural confrontation between a young generation of black protesters who turned their backs on the ideals of nonviolence and integration in favor of a militant and separatist nationalism and the white mainstream calling for "law and order." As the leading moderate civil rights organization, the NAACP, now more than ever, tried to stem the tide of black radicalization and to continue its struggle for racial reform.

The Split of the Civil Rights Movement

Throughout its history of more than fifty years, the NAACP had consistently rejected all variants of black separatism and stuck to the goal of integrating African-Americans into the mainstream of American life. The association took pride in the achievements of outstanding black individuals and in the contributions of black Americans to the nation at large, but it remained firmly committed to the universalist ideals of the American creed and to a traditional understanding of loyalty and patriotism. As has been described in several of the previous chapters, the NAACP's confidence in integration was never uncontroversial. Its numerous critics derided it as either self-delusion or, worse, racial treason.[4]

In the late 1950s and early 1960s, the most radical manifestation of black separatism was espoused by the Nation of Islam, an all-black Muslim group founded in Detroit around 1930, preaching an esoteric doctrine of a black original creation and white devils and isolating itself from white society as much as possible. Its appeal among African-American ghetto residents was largely due to its charismatic spokesman, Malcolm X, who acquired notoriety as an eloquent critic of the nonviolent civil rights movement, which he saw as being controlled by whites.[5]

Not surprisingly, the NAACP strictly disassociated itself from the Black Muslims and Malcolm X. Roy Wilkins received several invitations from the Muslim minister to discuss a "united front" against the "common enemy," but politely declined, citing his busy schedule. Among other reservations, the NAACP leader was angered by the fascination of white audiences with Malcolm's call for black retaliatory violence, which in Wilkins's opinion had been rendered irrelevant by the achievements of the civil rights movement. The "Malcolms," he assured the readers of his weekly syndicated column in early 1965, came too late. "The forces under the banner of non-violence have at last aroused the nation. . . . If they [African-Americans] did not reach for shotguns and rifles when lynchings were at a twice-a-week average and when segregation and discrimination were in humiliating flower, they are not about to immolate themselves now, when things are improving." When Malcolm X was assassinated a month later, presumably because of his earlier breach with the Nation of Islam, Wilkins took the murder as another "shocking and ghastly demonstration of the futility of resorting to violence."[6]

While Wilkins believed that black Americans had found new confidence in the democratic process, he increasingly worried about the danger of a "backlash" among disaffected whites. When the NAACP reorganized in Alabama in the fall of 1964, after the ban by the state had finally been struck down by the U.S. Supreme Court, the executive secretary cautioned his audience against the temptations of triumphalism: "Please remember you are going to have to live with white people. No matter how thrilling it is for you to win and for them to lose, don't leave any more scars than you have to leave." The struggle for civil rights was far from over. It merely entered a new phase, in which making civil rights and racial equality a social reality would be the order of the day. At the same time, the association's leaders realized that the NAACP would once again have to shift its focus. When the legislative struggle for the ballot was drawing to a close in the summer of 1965, the NAACP's director of publications, Henry Lee Moon, candidly acknowledged that the rhetoric of equal opportunity would no longer suffice. "Basic to the concept of the NAACP since its founding," he wrote to Wilkins, "has been the conviction that once the racial barriers shall have been leveled, the problem will be solved and our goal attained. . . . The need for special effort on behalf of Negroes, as Negroes, would no longer exist. . . . It now appears that at least half the race is totally unprepared, psychologically and emotionally, as well as vocationally, to take advantage of new opportunities."[7]

Militant rhetoric by black radicals, let alone violent action, the association's leadership feared, threatened to undermine the broad liberal consensus needed to sustain race-based economic programs at a moment when the political prospects for such an effort had never been better. Most important, President Johnson appeared to be seriously committed to his vision of a "Great Society." After centuries of enslavement and discrimination, legal rights and equality of opportunity would simply not do, LBJ declared in a speech at Howard University in June 1965. To overcome the historical burden of racism, America needed "equality as a right and result." In his State of the Union message of January 1966, he announced his plans for a new civil rights bill that would include a ban on racial discrimination in housing. Although the American military effort in Vietnam set limits on what could be done, Johnson boasted that America was strong enough "to pursue our goals in the rest of the world while still building a Great Society at home." Roy Wilkins's telegram enthusiastically cheered LBJ on: YOUR CALL FOR CARRYING ON DOMESTIC CRUSADE FOR THE GREAT SOCIETY PROJECTS INCLUDING ALL ASPECTS OF ANTI-POVERTY PROGRAM ALONG WITH FULFILLING OUR NATION'S COMMITMENT IN VIETNAM IS THE RIGHT CALL AND IS A CHALLENGE FOR EVERY AMERICAN.[8]

In the eyes of the NAACP leadership, support for Johnson's Vietnam policy did not seem to be too high a price to pay for the continuation of the administration's liberal civil rights and social welfare policies. It also reflected the association's traditional commitment to patriotic wartime loyalty and anticommunism. Of course, the NAACP did not take a hawkish stand on the war itself. Rather, for the duration of the Johnson presidency it insisted that civil rights and the war were separate issues and that the association was only concerned with the former. Unlike all previous twentieth-century wars with U.S. involvement, when the NAACP had vigilantly monitored and protested racial discrimination in the armed forces, there was no systematic investigation of conditions in Vietnam. An African-American sergeant who had inquired about this issue was told that the NAACP had received no complaints from black soldiers and that "[w]hatever discomforts they have to endure and whatever sacrifices they are called on to make appear to be the same as those which confront all American servicemen in the area."[9]

This patriotic image of blacks and whites fighting side by side celebrated racial progress and integration under the star-spangled banner. It omitted the sordid fact that African-Americans were paying a high price for integration. Facing almost exclusively white selective service boards, they were twice as likely to be drafted than their white peers, disproportionately assigned to combat units, and suffered a casualty rate vastly in excess of their overall proportion among the U.S. troops in Vietnam. The high death toll and the inequities of the draft soon became a serious concern for many NAACP members. In the spring of 1966, the NAACP New Jersey state conference asked the national office to determine an official position "in light of . . . the high mortality rate of our Negro fighting men." Wilkins, however, dodged the issue, arguing that theirs was not a peace organization and that members were free to express themselves through other groups. A few months later, the Greenwich Village, New York, branch introduced a resolution to the upcoming annual convention asking, rather meekly, "that this convention acknowledge the fact of detrimental effects that the defense and military activities have upon the Civil Rights Movement" and that the local branches "be encouraged to consider and debate these issues." The resolution was safely voted down by the convention.[10]

While criticism of the Vietnam War remained largely muted among the NAACP membership, the nonviolent activist wing of the civil rights movement began to speak out against the war early on. In July 1965, Martin Luther King Jr. publicly declared that communism could not be defeated by bombs and that the war had to be stopped by negotiating with the Vietcong. Roy Wilkins instantly dismissed the statement as "a tactical error." In the same month, members of the Mississippi Freedom Democratic Party, after one of their fellow activists had been killed in Vietnam, urged blacks to resist the draft so they would not be looked upon as traitors "by all the colored people of the world." Spokespersons for the party hastened to state that the widely publicized declaration did not represent official policy, but added: "It is easy to understand why Negro citizens of McComb, themselves the victims of bombings, Klan-inspired terrorism, and harassment arrests, should resent the death of a citizen of McComb while fighting in Viet Nam for 'freedom' not enjoyed by the Negro community of McComb."[11]

With the congressional struggle for the Voting Rights Act in its final stage, Roy Wilkins condemned the call for draft resistance as "child-like and mischievous in the extreme." In his weekly syndicated column, he lashed out at the MFDP for "tinker[ing] with patriotism at a time when their country is engaged in an armed conflict," and pontificated on black heroes from the War of Independence to Pearl Harbor who had done infinitely more for their race than the "young squirts" down in Mississippi. In essence, the NAACP secretary was demanding that black men fight and die in Vietnam so that civil rights leaders could put their "loyalty, heroic service and sacrifice . . . on the bargaining table." But the young and increasingly radical activists were no longer prepared to accept this kind of bargain and fight for a country that denied their basic rights as citizens. In January 1966, SNCC crossed the line to open protest after one of its registration workers was murdered in Tuskegee, Alabama, for trying to use a "whites only" restroom. In an angry statement, it accused the U.S. government of hypocrisy in its professed concern for the freedom of both the Vietnamese people and African-Americans, equating the violence in Alabama to that in Vietnam: "Sammy Younge was murdered because United States law is not being enforced. Vietnamese are being murdered because the United States is pursuing an aggressive policy in violation of international law." SNCC declared its support for draft resisters unwilling "to contribute their lives to United States aggression."[12]

Not surprisingly, the NAACP immediately distanced itself from the SNCC statement. In a private meeting with Vice President Hubert Humphrey, Wilkins, Clarence Mitchell, and National Urban League (NUL) leader Whitney Young protested that the White House seemed to "treat all of the civil rights leaders alike when the SNCC outfit engages in the most outrageous attacks on the President and the Administration." The complaint referred to a presidential pet project, the White House Conference on Civil Rights, which was scheduled for the coming spring and was designed to reaffirm support for Johnson's "Great Society." The list of more than two thousand participants, although clearly dominated by moderates, included SNCC and several other militant groups.[13]

In a preparatory meeting for the White House Conference that included representatives of all major civil rights organizations, except SNCC, the NAACP leaders successfully pressed for an agreement that the civil rights movement would take a stand on Vietnam only as it affected the "Great Society" programs, "in order that Negro boys returning from Vietnam will return to better working conditions here at home." SNCC, however, was no longer willing to accept compromises on the war. It categorically refused to "meet with the chief policy maker of the Vietnam war to discuss human rights in this country when he flagrantly violates the human rights of colored people in Vietnam." In the absence of SNCC, the delegates of the Congress of Racial Equality (CORE) tried to raise the issue at the White House Conference, which took place in June 1966. Since America had not yet "demonstrated its ability and willingness to afford both 'guns and butter,'" CORE demanded that it make "equal opportunity for its minority citizens the number one priority . . . and cease its involvement in Vietnam." This was of course totally unacceptable for the administration. The CORE resolution was voted down and replaced by a formula that urged the president "to continue and intensify his efforts to bring the war in Vietnam to an early and honorable end so that the same and even a much greater level of Federal funds and Federal leadership can be focused to fulfill these rights today."[14] While opposition among black civil rights groups grew as the war escalated, including harsh condemnations by Martin Luther King Jr., the NAACP leadership maintained its "separate issues" doctrine throughout the Johnson administration, despite considerable rumblings among the membership.[15]

Yet the war in Vietnam was only one of several controversies fueling the polarization within the civil rights movement. Equally important was the predictable disappointment that the new civil rights laws did not quickly translate into visible political and social change. More and more activists began to question the wisdom of operating within political structures that continued to be dominated by white supremacists. In Lowndes County, Alabama, where disfranchised blacks were a large majority of the eligible voters, SNCC, since the spring of 1965, had begun to build an independent African-American political party: the Lowndes County Freedom Organization, which used a black panther as its emblem. The founding of the LCFO did not follow a deliberately separatist program—there simply were no whites willing to join—but, unlike the Mississippi Freedom Democrats, the LCFO had no interest in working under the label of the Democratic Party of Alabama. In the spring of 1966, SNCC activist Stokeley Carmichael called upon the black residents of Lowndes County to boycott the upcoming Democratic primary because it was "as ludicrous for Negroes to join [the Democratic Party] as it would have been for Jews to join the Nazi Party in the 1930s."[16]

In the eyes of the NAACP leadership, calls for boycotting an election were as irresponsible as calls for draft resistance. NAACP director of branches Gloster Current implored black Alabamians "to ignore the silly advice of SNCC . . . and turn out a large vote for whatever liberal candidates" they could support; where there were only "two equally bad candidates," they should at least vote against the incumbent. Given the overwhelming edge whites had in numbers and resources, Roy Wilkins argued that to "choose the path of black party organization . . . is to choose political suicide." Wilkins conveniently ignored the fact that Carmichael's call to boycott the Democratic primary extended only to the Alabama Black Belt and did not constitute a general repudiation of interracial coalition politics. Moreover, the results of the 1966 Democratic primary underscored that Carmichael had a point. Lurleen Wallace, the stand-in candidate for her husband, George Wallace, handily won the nomination for governor. Most of the candidates whom black voters had supported lost. Wilkins commented meekly that black voters needed not to be discouraged, as their numbers would certainly grow and racial polarization at the ballot box subside.[17]

When Stokeley Carmichael was elected the new chairman of SNCC in May 1966, this was widely seen as a victory for the adherents of a separatist black nationalism. Carmichael himself denied being a nationalist, but, pointing to the recent elections in Alabama, he insisted that in these circumstances integration was meaningless and that blacks really needed "political and economic power." Roy Wilkins nevertheless publicly accused SNCC of having chosen "a racist course." At least the separatists had cleared the air. In the future there would be no more cooperation with SNCC. Gloster Current even speculated that SNCC might break up and that the "mature and balanced young people associated with the student group" could be recruited into the ranks of the association.[18]

With a good deal of justification, SNCC leaders complained that the media distorted their message of black self-help and autonomy as separatism. But Carmichael and other activists also could not resist playing the "bad boys" for the white media by making all kinds of provocative statements. Moreover, SNCC deliberately chose to disassociate itself from white liberals and the moderate wing of the civil rights movement, especially the NAACP. The conflict came to a head in June, when James Meredith, the black student who had integrated the University of Mississippi in 1962, began his "March against Fear" from Memphis, Tennessee, to Jackson, Mississippi, and was wounded by sniper bullets upon entering the Magnolia state. The leading civil rights organizations decided to continue the march and tried to agree on a common theme. Predictably, Roy Wilkins proposed to make it into a pageant for voter registration and civil rights legislation. The representatives of SNCC and CORE, however, insisted on direct action and, in order "to put President Johnson on the spot," drew up a "manifesto" that was highly critical of the administration and then demanded that Wilkins sign it without even discussing changes. The NAACP patriarch was shouted down and SNCC members bluntly told him that it was time for him to retire and write his memoirs. Joined by NUL leader Whitney Young, Wilkins left the scene in disgust.[19]

Although he was worried about the militant rhetoric and the repudiation of nonviolence by the SNCC and CORE activists, Martin Luther King Jr. decided to stay. Apparently he hoped to retain some influence with the marchers, and perhaps he also did not wish to be in the same boat with Roy Wilkins, whom he cordially disliked. The SNCC and CORE leaders, for their part, did not want to break with the popular minister. As the marchers were constantly harassed by white mobs and the Mississippi state police, King's message of nonviolence was eclipsed by calls for armed self-defense. When the march reached Greenwood, Mississippi, where SNCC workers had been the target of brutal abuse during earlier registration campaigns, Stokeley Carmichael and his fellow activist Willie Ricks began to intonate the chant "What do we want? Black Power!," evoking enthusiastic responses from many of the marchers. Although the slogan unmistakably repudiated the ethics of nonviolence, Martin Luther King Jr. resolved to avoid friction. The march ended on 26 June in Jackson with a peaceful rally of fifteen thousand African-Americans.[20]

Despite the attacks on its executive secretary, the NAACP did not entirely withdraw from the Meredith march. NAACP members were informed that they were free to join the marchers on an individual basis. After the march, Roy Wilkins noted an increase in voter registration and condescendingly acknowledged: "The 800,000 Negro citizens of the state will benefit from the march, even from some of the childish, but understandable, antics of some of the marchers." But when SNCC dismissed President Johnson's new proposal for an open housing bill as "hypocrisy" and as "totally useless and totally unnecessary," the NAACP leadership ran out of patience. At the association's annual convention in July the break with SNCC was finally made official. A long memorandum told the delegates how the radicals had deceived, attacked, and financially exploited the NAACP during the early 1960s. Despite the provocations against the association's secretary, the Mississippi branches had provided much-needed logistical support during the march and shown up in large numbers at the concluding rally. But Charles Evers, the NAACP's field secretary in Mississippi, himself a proponent of more aggressive civil rights strategies, was barred from the speakers' platform, and the name of his martyred brother was not even mentioned. In his keynote address to the NAACP convention, Wilkins condemned the Black Power slogan in the harshest possible words: "No matter how endlessly they try to explain it, the term means antiwhite power . . . a reverse Mississippi, a reverse Hitler, a reverse Ku Klux Klan."[21]

The genie was out of the bottle, however, and it could not be put back. Over the next few years Black Power would shape much of the public discourse on race relations. And even the NAACP implicitly acknowledged that the term articulated a legitimate problem: How could blacks assert their claim to participation, autonomy, and identity in a society dominated by whites. The association's annual convention passed a resolution that reaffirmed the goal of "political power, based on the effective use of the ballot," but also emphasized that this power had to be rooted in the collective interests and identity of the African-American community:

> Although the NAACP has carefully plotted the demise of racial discrimination, at no time have we contemplated ethnicide. Ethnic continuity as well as ethnic unity are not only desirable, but perhaps indispensable in a pluralistic society. We can no more reject the idea of Negroes, as a unified group, constituting a viable force within the democratic scheme of things than we can reject the clear and obvious fact that every other ethnic and nationality group in our society has sought to use its common identity as a means of generating social, economic and political power and has used that power to attain and elevate its place within the mainstream of American life.[22]

The NAACP's 1966 resolution set the tone for the ensuing ideological confrontation with the advocates of Black Power. Along with its uncompromising opposition to black separatism, the association tried to establish a respectable pluralistic definition of the ominous term that it hoped would be acceptable both for the large majority of African-Americans and for white liberals.

Ideological Challenge and Organizational Self-Assertion

While Black Power quickly caught on with many young black activists, it never represented a clear political or ideological program. Although they dramatically presented their analysis as "the last reasonable opportunity for this society to work out its racial problems short of prolonged guerilla warfare," the 1967 book *Black Power: The Politics of Liberation in America* by Stokely Carmichael and political scientist Charles Hamilton remained curiously vague and offered a surprisingly conventional analysis of American politics. Hamilton candidly conceded that a comprehensive definition of Black Power was impossible.[23]

By and large, there were two major camps of "Black Powerites." "Pluralists" continued to acknowledge the larger framework of American society and politics but focused on "community control" of black institutions and businesses and on building a black political power base not dominated by white allies. "Nationalists," in contrast, drew more far-reaching consequences from defining African-Americans as a nation separate from whites. Some actually advocated a separate state or at least separate territories as enclaves within the United States, while others celebrated black cultural distinctiveness and identity as the foundations of nationhood. And although in its criticism of American capitalism Black Powerites drew heavily on Marxist terminology, many Marxists tended to be unhappy with the theoretical vagueness of a concept that clearly assigned priority to race rather than class.[24]

While Black Power was not a coherent ideology, the term nevertheless delineated a discursive battlefield in defining the black agenda in the late 1960s. To the movement's followers it meant:

- Celebrating blackness and the African cultural heritage.
- Defining the African-American community as an "internal colony" and their freedom struggle as part of a global anti-colonial revolution.
- Repudiating the goal of racial integration.
- Demanding autonomous black institutions and organizations.
- Retreating from the ideal of nonviolence.
- Abandoning the political process and party politics.

Each of these positions, either explicitly or implicitly, challenged the traditional ideological orientation of the NAACP, which was once again confronted with the questions of whether and to what extent it should adapt to the new zeitgeist. Predictably, the association's willingness to do so was very limited.

The cult of blackness and African heritage met with incomprehension and amusement from the association's leaders, who scoffed at Afro-style hairdos, the persistence of tribalism in Africa, and lofty ideas of unity with people whom Roy Wilkins called "cousins, 350 years removed." Racial pride was necessary to overcome the deformations of racism, but it was defined within the framework of American values. Rather than promulgating a "compensatory nationalism" for the black masses, the NAACP aimed at "enhancing the dignity of the individual Negro . . . thus instilling a pride in himself as a person and an American."[25]

Traditionally, the NAACP had supported decolonization and self-determination for nonwhite nations. Yet international racial solidarity never superseded its loyalty to the United States, especially not if the nonwhites happened to be communists. The appeal to racial brotherhood fell on deaf ears with a devout American patriot such as Roy Wilkins, who rebuffed it as the "color gambit" and declared: "[A]ll men are my brothers, but [Chinese] Premier Chou En-lai, for example, is no close relative." While black critics of the Vietnam War lamented that African-Americans and Vietnamese were killing each other for the sake of "international white supremacy," the NAACP denied the racial dimensions of the war.[26]

The goal of racial integration was of course central to the NAACP's history and program. Integration, its resolutions and public statements repeated over and over again, meant "full participation in all phases of American life." It did not, however, mean that blacks should give up their ethnic identity or renounce unity and solidarity. But the idea of a separate black nation pitted against the rest of the American people struck the NAACP leaders as absurd and outright suicidal.[27]

Nevertheless, the NAACP could not easily dismiss the demand for autonomous black institutions and organizations as separatism, since it prided itself in its 90 percent black membership and its close ties to black churches, colleges, and labor unions. But from the association's point of view, it was one thing to recognize the legitimacy of historically black institutions and the quest for maximum participation in decisions that affected black people. It was quite another to actively advocate a new color line under the banner of self-determination. When African-American students raised the demand for separate dormitories, Roy Wilkins instantly threatened to take them to court. The same policy applied within the association. An attempt to form an all-black NAACP branch in Tampa, Florida, was immediately suppressed. Whereas SNCC and CORE eventually excluded whites from their ranks, the NAACP upheld the ideal of an integrated civil rights movement. After all, as Roy Wilkins wrote to black congressman Adam Clayton Powell, whites who were responsible as a group for the plight of blacks "owe[d] it to themselves and to the nation to help rectify racial wrongs."[28]

Unlike the adherents of nonviolent direct action, the NAACP had never subscribed to an ideal of unconditional nonresistance, and it defended many blacks in court who had resorted to force to protect their lives and homes. Collective violence as either revenge or political strategy, however, was seen as doomed to failure and would only provide white racists with a welcome pretext for violent repression. When Robert F. Williams, president of the Monroe, North Carolina, NAACP branch began arming his group in 1959, the national secretariat immediately expelled him from the association, though not without vocal protests from many members. The Williams affair, though reflecting a strong tradition of self-defense among southern blacks, did not seriously affect the nonviolent image of the civil rights movement. During the first half of the 1960s, the civil rights struggle continued to draw much of its moral appeal from its firm commitment to nonviolence even in the face of brutal racist oppression.[29]

In the second half of the decade, however, the picture changed dramatically. Former paragons of nonviolence gradually repudiated their ideals and self-styled guerillas preached armed struggle. More than anything else, the violent eruption of the northern black ghetto seemed to lend credence to the revolutionary rhetoric that a few years earlier could have been dismissed as sheer fantasy. In 1966, CORE still denied that Black Power meant violence; a year later, the group celebrated "the explosions of this summer as the beginning of the Black Revolution," and attacked "certain Civil Rights Leaders" for condemning the riots. And long before SNCC dropped the term "Nonviolent" from its name in 1968, the celebration of retaliatory violence became a standard tenet of its rhetoric.[30]

No group, however, frightened the American public more than the Black Panthers. Founded in Oakland, California, in the fall of 1966, the Panthers quickly became the epitome of black militancy, publicly wielding guns and sporting paramilitary black uniforms that Roy Wilkins found "painfully reminiscent of the Hitler and Mussolini type of fascism." Seeking an ideological synthesis of black nationalism and revolutionary Marxism, the Panthers posed as the vanguard of the black revolution. They approved of the ghetto riots only as a first step that was, in their words, "sporadic, short-lived, and costly," and called upon the "masses" to follow the "guerilla warfare method." Such boastful rhetoric notwithstanding, there is little evidence to link the urban unrest during the "long hot summers" of the 1960s directly to the Panthers or other black militants. But it would be equally misleading to dismiss the riots simply as "blind anger," since acts of violence and looting were predominantly directed against the representatives of the "white order," that is to say the police and white-owned businesses. Moreover, it could not be denied that the riots forced the city, state, and federal governments to negotiate with black community leaders.[31]

For the NAACP, which had hoped for an easing of racial tensions as a consequence of civil rights and social reform, the violent unrest came as a shocking surprise. Predictably, the association blamed the riots on the living conditions in America's inner cities but at the same time condemned them as self-destructive and detrimental to black interests. The legitimate and understandable grievances and anger among the black community, its leaders incessantly told their audiences, had to be funneled into the constructive channels of the political process, most importantly into increased voter registration, in order to build the necessary electoral support for a determined reform effort, while throwing rocks and bottles would only fan the backlash.[32]

That many advocates of Black Power proposed to give up on traditional liberal coalition politics in favor of independent all-black parties and candidates struck the NAACP as outright foolishness. This strategy would inevitably polarize the electorate along racial lines and lock the black vote into a permanent minority position without any chance to hold the balance of power. In 1967, the association's annual convention, recalling the long, hard fight against the white primary, declared its firm opposition to "political segregation whether in all-white or all-Negro parties." The goal remained "to integrate Negroes into the existing political parties as voters, candidates, and party officials."[33]

In the debate over interracial political alliances, both sides had plausible arguments. The protagonists of Black Power did not reject cooperation completely, but they insisted that first an independent black base had to be built in order to prevent white domination. In their book, Carmichael and Hamilton ridiculed "the myth" of a moral coalition between poor African-Americans and affluent white liberals. Viable coalitions must not be built on sentimental paternalism, they demanded, but on the mutual recognition of self-interest and autonomy and on "specific and identifiable goals" from which both parties would equally benefit. Obviously, in the Black Belt of the South, there were no partners for this kind of cooperation. Here the need to build independent black organizations had to take precedence over interracialism, so the local black people could finally begin to develop an awareness of their real political and economic interests. The authors interpreted the fact that the Lowndes County Freedom Organization had not been able to elect a single of their candidates in the 1966 general elections, even though black voters were now a majority, as evidence of the continued material and mental dependency of rural blacks on white elites. Once again the plantation owners had herded "their niggers" to the polls.[34]

In contrast, the supporters of interracial coalitions viewed the election outcome as a clear indication that black voters rejected the "separatist" strategies of the LCFO and SNCC. In Selma, Alabama, for example, the newly enfranchised African-Americans had been crucial in the defeat of Sheriff Jim Clark, the villain of the 1965 voting rights campaign, by a white "moderate." While the mid-term elections of 1966 were widely seen as a "backlash vote" due to the heavy losses of the Democrats in Congress, Roy Wilkins spoke of a "Negro Frontlash" because black voters and candidates had made remarkable progress. In Massachusetts, a state with a comparatively small African-American population, black Republican Edward Brooke was elected to the U.S. Senate, the first black member of this body since Reconstruction. In Jefferson County, Mississippi, the first African-American won a seat on the local school board, a victory in which NAACP leader Charles Evers had played a significant part. Instead of relying on "black strength," as Stokely Carmichael had recommended, Wilkins rejoiced that black voters had entered "the American political game." Moreover, the NAACP leader noted a considerable decline in race-baiting among white politicians and voters. Even in Mississippi, more and more whites began to break free from the "prison" of racism.[35]

Even though successful interracial alliances would remain rare exceptions in southern politics for a long time to come, the NAACP remained steadfast in its views and refused to blame their repeated failures exclusively on the weakness and volatility of white liberals. When in 1970 Andrew Young, a former close aid of Martin Luther King Jr., missed election to the U.S. House of Representatives in his Atlanta, Georgia, district by twenty thousand votes, Roy Wilkins sharply rebuked black analysts for turning on "their favorite whipping boy, the white liberal." They better ask themselves, the NAACP secretary suggested, why more than thirty thousand registered black voters had not even cast a ballot. Flamboyant condemnations of "decadent white politics" could not alter the fact that blacks would always need white support in order to get elected or pass the laws they favored. In contrast, black politician Tom Bradley demonstrated the right way to play politics, according to Wilkins, when he forged a coalition of black, Hispanic, and white voters in the 1973 mayoral race in Los Angeles. Although African-Americans represented no more than 18 percent of L.A. voters, Bradley managed to get himself elected as the city's first black mayor. This was "a performance strictly in the tradition of every candidate of an American minority," the NAACP leader observed with great satisfaction.[36]

From hindsight, there can be little doubt that the position of the NAACP had much more realism than that of the Black Powerites. The latter certainly had a point in complaining that whites normally dominated interracial coalitions, but their own ideas more or less envisioned a reversal of the political roles. In fighting for black interests, whites might play an auxiliary part, but they had to subordinate to black leadership. "When we need white people, we will call you," a Black Power manifesto from Chicago proclaimed. This hardly squared with Black Power's claim that coalitions could only be based on cold, hard interests. Instead it reintroduced, through the backdoor, the character of the white idealist who had just been exiled with great fanfare. To be sure, leftist students, ridden by white guilt, might be willing to bow to the "dictatorial power" demanded by the "Black Power cabal," as Roy Wilkins said, mocking an interracial "New Left Conference" held in 1967. But they were certainly not representative of any significant part of the white electorate. In contrast, the coalition between white liberals and African-American voters that black radicals off-handedly dismissed would show a remarkable resilience over the next decades.[37]

Nonetheless, in rejecting Black Power, the NAACP leaders often displayed the same rigid dogmatism for which they faulted their antagonists. For example, their uncompromising disapproval of all-black political associations conveniently ignored the fact that especially in the Deep South there were very few whites willing to accept blacks as equal partners in a political alliance. That black activists felt a deep aversion against working within the Democratic Party organizations of Mississippi and Alabama was perfectly understandable and certainly not tantamount to separatism. To be sure, appeals to vote only for black groups and candidates offered few political prospects, but when Roy Wilkins suspected even the Black Congressional Caucus, formed in 1973, of trying to establish a separate black party and warned against "forcible conformity" and "dictatorship," this clearly bordered on irrational alarmism.[38]

Among the many reasons for the NAACP's intransigence toward the Black Power movement, the generation gap obviously played a major role. Born in 1922, CORE director Floyd McKissick was the oldest among the leading radicals; most of the others, like SNCC leaders Stokely Carmichael and Hubert "Rap" Brown, were in their mid- to late twenties. The association's national leaders, in contrast, were men (and some women) in their fifties and sixties who were immensely proud of their achievements and liked to look down on the "young smart-alecks of both races [whose] history of Negro-white relations begins in 1960," as Roy Wilkins, born in 1901, scolded the new generation of protesters. For their part, the radicals retaliated with the customary "Uncle Tom" epithet and gratuitously declared the NAACP's goals and methods "irrelevant." Roy Wilkins even became the target of an alleged murder plot by black militants and had to put up with bodyguards for a while.[39]

Moreover, the veterans of the civil rights struggle were frustrated that their own message of "responsible militancy," as Henry Lee Moon put it, was eclipsed by inflammatory one-liners, such as "Violence is as American as Cherry Pie," for which especially Carmichael and "Rap" Brown acquired notoriety. Moon blamed the resonance of Black Power on the sensationalism of the media, which seemed to convey the message that only those who preached revolution and violence would be heard. Ironically, the radicals also complained about the white media for focusing on violence and separatism while ignoring Black Power's message of self-respect and racial solidarity.[40]

Still, the most important reason for the association's uncompromising opposition to Black Power" went beyond age or vying for public attention. The NAACP perceived a genuine ideological gap between its own long-standing goals and values and those of "Black Power," a gap that it believed it could not bridge without betraying its history and identity. Unlike the strategy debates of the early 1960s, the conflict was no longer about different ways and means to a common goal. It was now about fundamentally different visions of the place African-Americans ought to take in society and about the character of American society itself. While the radicals came to see the United States as inherently and unalterably racist, leaving separation as the only way of survival for black people, the NAACP remained committed to the vision of a color-blind society and to the American Dream of upward mobility through hard work. "In the present climate," Roy Wilkins thundered in a 1967 letter to *LOOK Magazine*, "it is practically useless to try to urge the slow, hard, trial-and-failure route that is the inevitable requirement for emergence and attainment. It is worse than useless to talk about excellence. The now familiar wail of deprivation greets anyone who counsels 'study, work, compete, prepare, try and try again.'"[41]

Such jeremiads surely sounded hollow and meaningless to the new generation of black militants. But in coping with the challenge from "Black Power," the NAACP did not depend on ideological appeals in the first place, but on its time-tested organizational strength, which its director of branches, Gloster Current, without the slightest trace of irony, compared to the Pentagon. The "power created by organization," celebrated by the 1967 annual convention, was no empty catchphrase. In more than half a century, the NAACP had built an organizational structure that had shielded it against all ideological and political challenges that had come from either white supremacists or black nationalists. Black Power would be no exception.[42]

First of all, strength lay in sheer numbers. Unlike SNCC and CORE, which were basically small and volatile bands of activists with a few local strongholds, the NAACP counted roughly 1,800 local branches and youth and college chapters nationwide. Its numerical strength peaked in 1963, the exceptional year of the March on Washington, with an official number of 535,000 dues-paying members. CORE never exceeded 5,000, according to the estimate by August Meier and Elliot Rudwick. The claims by radical critics that the NAACP had become "irrelevant" to the black freedom struggle were hardly corroborated by the development of its membership figures. Despite some ups and downs, the association gained a net of 20,000 members between 1965 and 1969, before its membership plummeted by 100,000 in 1970, a decline that was clearly triggered by the doubling of annual dues. With figures slowly recovering, the NAACP could again claim well over 400,000 members in the early 1970s.[43]

Of course, this is not to say that all members unanimously supported the national leadership on such critical issues as the war in Vietnam and Black

Power. There were numerous protests by members against the official stand on both issues, and several branches passed resolutions at variance with the national leadership, although it is difficult to determine how representative these voices were for the membership at large.[44] Even before Vietnam and black power became controversial within the association, an internal opposition had formed against the conservatism and the hierarchical structure of the national leadership, particularly against Roy Wilkins's autocratic style. The insurgents, who formed an informal circle in 1962 and were led by Chester Lewis of the NAACP branch of Wichita, Kansas, generously called themselves the "Young Turks," although most of them were already middle-aged. They demanded more organizational democracy and a generational change within the NAACP, especially the resignation of the executive secretary, NAACP president Arthur Spingarn, and the chairman of the board of directors, Bishop Stephen Spottswood. They also criticized what they saw as a disproportionate influence of white liberals, specifically of Walter Reuther, president of the powerful United Auto Workers, who served on the NAACP board of directors and was regarded as one of Wilkins's staunchest supporters.[45]

The "Young Turks," whose strongholds were to be found in the Midwest and the West, sought to commit the association to a much more radical policy that would have openly challenged the NAACP's corporate donors, who only gave money "to keep the natives quiet," as Chester Lewis told a conference of branches in 1967. He also called for a "national black-oriented party" and a clear focus on the problems of the ghetto. The strength of the "Young Turks" reached its peak in 1968, when they came out with a program that drew heavily on black power rhetoric but was mostly concerned with an organizational reform and the rejuvenation of the association. The leadership, they charged, had lost the "respect and confidence of the black masses" and failed "to appreciate the historical but ominous implications of the rebellions in our cities and the constructive implications of Black Power." At the 1968 annual convention, the "Young Turks" mustered the support of roughly one-third of the delegates, and after heated discussions they staged a walkout. The majority rejected the opposition's program, but eventually passed a resolution that officially approved of black power defined as "control of economic, educational, and political institutions within the black community." This was little different from the position the convention had taken two years earlier.[46]

Despite the unprecedented strength of the opposition, the national leadership managed to control dissent and keep the rank and file in line. In defending his power, Roy Wilkins had not exactly been particular in his methods.

There was serious tampering with procedural rules that made sure that all proposals by the opposition were tabled. When his incensed critics resorted to staging demonstrations, the NAACP secretary did not hesitate to call the police. After the convention, many of the insurgents gave up on the NAACP and the "Young Turks" disintegrated. How serious and personal Wilkins took the onslaught becomes clear from his vindictive reaction to the resignation of "Turk" leader Chester Lewis from the NAACP. Wilkins indeed ordered that "his [Lewis's] name, the names of his three children and the name of his wife are to be removed from any and all card files, or continuing records of any nature." Nevertheless, the national secretariat was fully aware that a dialogue with the dissenters and the membership was urgently needed. Even Wilkins conceded that the defeat of the "Young Turks" was a "last opportunity" to come up with a "productive program" or else the leadership would be supplanted at the next convention.[47]

That Wilkins faced criticism within the association could hardly come as surprise. For more than thirty years, he had been a key figure in the NAACP leadership whose influence continued to grow unabatedly. Many of his detractors saw him as a leftover from another day whose retirement was overdue. Yet Wilkins survived the Black Power challenge and held on to his position as the executive secretary of the NAACP until 1977, when he finally stepped down at the age of seventy-six after fifty years in the service of the association. His long endurance at the helm testifies to his skills as an organizational man and his close rapport with the board of directors. But Roy Wilkins was also quite popular among the majority of the NAACP membership and among the African-American population at large. Although he lacked personal charisma, the NAACP leader enjoyed about the same 60 percent approval rate as Martin Luther King Jr. among blacks, while whites, not surprisingly, perceived him as distinctly more moderate. The centralized style of leadership and decision-making that Wilkins represented often was a source of discontent among members and supporters, but it clearly was conducive to organizational stability. Within the framework of the NAACP, it was inconceivable that an oppositional faction could simply oust the leadership and commit the entire organization to a new political line, as had happened to SNCC in May of 1966, when Carmichael and his followers defeated chairman John Lewis on a questionable second ballot.[48]

Another factor that enhanced the NAACP's organizational strength was its strong middle-class orientation, which many critics—and sometimes even leading officers of the association—tended to view as a serious weakness. The national officers were middle-aged, often college-educated professionals with long-standing commitments to the association and proven organizational skills. The typical branch official, an internal study of 1967 found, was in his or her forties, had a secure income, mostly from white-collar work, was southern-born, and had a strong church affiliation. Black churches, fraternal orders, colleges, business leagues, and unions provided a solid base of support and recruitment. The NAACP was undoubtedly an organization of the black middle-class, but what radicals intended as a pejorative epithet in fact counted to its advantage. It was much harder to organize the urban and rural poor, who lacked the resources to become permanently involved in political activities.[49]

In addition to its middle-class character, the strong southern base of the association—half of its branches were below the Mason-Dixon line—worked against radicalization. According to Gloster Current, the southern branches remained firmly committed to integration, while northern affiliates were influenced to a degree by separatist ideology. Whether the fact that southern communities were largely spared by the race riots of the 1960s was attributable to the NAACP's moderating influence, as some of its officers boldly claimed, is certainly questionable. However, it seems safe to say that few black southerners considered the cause of civil rights "irrelevant," as a 1967 CORE manifesto pontificated.[50]

Advocates of black power liked to attack the NAACP as "guided, financed, and controlled by whites." As far as the race of its members and leaders was concerned, this charge seemed spurious. Ironically, its 90 percent African-American membership largely spared the association from the internal racial tensions that shattered both CORE and SNCC, with their much higher proportions of white members and activists. Until 1964, the membership of CORE was, in fact, white. When the Philadelphia chapters of CORE and the NAACP clashed in a nasty feud in 1965, the NAACP branch president ridiculed CORE as being composed of "90 percent insincere, exhibitionist, frustrated, beatnik white intellectuals." The much-debated conflicts over class and race, namely that well-educated whites should not be allowed to dominate poor blacks, which eventually led to the exclusion of whites from CORE and SNCC, never became much of an issue within the NAACP.[51]

The NAACP leadership also could hardly be described as being dominated by whites, although the ceremonial position of the NAACP president was traditionally held by a white member. Because Arthur Spingarn, a Jew, retained this office for many decades, Malcolm X claimed that "the NAACP is not a Negro organization . . . it's a Jewish organization." As a matter of fact, the national secretariat had been virtually all-black since the 1930s. The supervising national board of directors still showed a 22 percent share of whites in the early 1960s, which, however, dropped to 12 percent by the end of the decade, roughly commensurate with the membership at large.[52]

The charge of white domination thus primarily referred to the alleged influence wielded by white donors. In 1967, for example, Jackie Robinson, baseball hero, former NAACP board member, and supporter of the "Young Turks," publicly accused the NAACP leaders of being more concerned with gaining money from the Ford Foundation than the respect of young African-Americans. Undeniably, moderation paid off for the association. Like other moderate groups, it dramatically increased its outside income during the late 1960s, as contributions to CORE and SNCC simultaneously dwindled. From 1966 to 1967, the year the call for Black Power conquered the media, the association's external income more than doubled. Liberal institutional donors, such as the Ford, Rockefeller, and Carnegie foundations, increased their contributions substantially in order to strengthen the moderate groups, especially the NAACP, the Legal Defense and Education Fund, and the Urban League. By 1968, grants and donations, mostly from foundations and corporations, made up more than half of the NAACP's total revenues of about $3.5 million.[53]

However, if the amount of outside funding is taken as an indicator of white influence, SNCC, CORE, and the SCLC all must have been heavily "white controlled" during the mid-1960s. Between 1963 and 1965, each of these groups, although much smaller than the NAACP, actually raised a higher total of external contributions. In 1964, the NAACP received $292,738 in outside income, while SNCC collected $631,439 and CORE $694,588. While the NAACP openly touted its anti–Black Power stance in its fund-raising letters, it would be a far-fetched conclusion that the association's opposition to Black Power was bought by foundation money. The NAACP, to be sure, did nothing to offend its benefactors, but it did not have to sell its soul to accept money to be spent on voter education or civil rights litigation. For their part, the large donors were obviously persuaded that the NAACP still represented the vast majority of African-Americans, who wanted integration and equality and rejected violence and separatism.[54]

It is hard to determine whether this claim was still justified. Surveys among blacks showed that the overwhelming approval that the association had enjoyed in the early 1960s had eroded considerably by the end of the decade. In 1969, only one-fifth of those surveyed thought the NAACP was doing an excellent job, compared to four-fifths six years earlier. Support for black nationalism had grown correspondingly. Fifty-nine percent of African-

Americans approved of the idea of Black Power, and 18 percent even supported a separate black nation. Half of the respondents thought the riots had been useful, while one-third believed violence would also be necessary in the future. Even so, these data should not be exaggerated. The changing mood among the black community certainly reflected a great deal of disillusionment with the traditional civil rights agenda, but it did not translate into political support for radical nationalist groups, which already were in sharp decline. By the end of the decade, SNCC and CORE had disintegrated. The NAACP's loss in confidence and prestige, on the other hand, appears to have been more relative than absolute. Its members were perhaps disgruntled, but most of them did not leave the association. Supporters became more critical, but they were unwilling to write off America's oldest black civil rights group as "irrelevant." Most importantly, the association managed to avoid internal schisms and preserved its organizational stability. This was definitely no small feat in the volatile political climate of the late 1960s.[55]

It is true that the NAACP's response to the challenge of Black Power was intellectually uninspiring and largely defensive. Basically, it defended its historical mission and goals and kept the radicals at arm's length. For example, the NAACP made a point of not participating in the Black Power conferences of 1966 and 1967. In 1968, however, Roy Wilkins and NUL leader Whitney Young both spoke at the CORE annual convention held under the banner of "Black Nationalism: CORE's Philosophy for Survival." The NAACP secretary dutifully acknowledged the need to build black self-confidence, economic independence, and political muscle, but he left no doubt that the association would never be converted to separatism. That Whitney Young, in contrast, paid his respect for "those who choose a segregated living" struck the NAACP officials as a despicable attempt "to court favor with the extremists."[56]

Nevertheless, the association's leaders also realized that they had neglected the grievances of urban blacks and needed to reach out to the ghetto, to black youths, and to critical voices within its own ranks. Among the national officers, Director of Branches Gloster Current, though basically a bureaucrat, was most acquainted with these problems and kept on urging for serious study and discussion. He even suggested the creation of "a new type of branch in the ghetto," led by "bartenders and barbers and persons of that type," that is by people who would not be identified with the reverend, lawyer, and business-man type that dominated most NAACP groups. As a matter of principle, however, the association remained firmly opposed to the romanticized notions of the ghetto as the place for black self-development and self-determination espoused by much of the Black Power rhetoric. In 1972, the National Black Political Convention—with eight thousand participants, the largest political meeting of African-Americans of the era—gathered in Gary, Indiana. The NAACP sent delegates but immediately distanced itself when the convention embraced an "openly separatist and nationalist agenda." What the NAACP wanted, Roy Wilkins explained to black congressman Charles Diggs, was "an equitable black share of control in institutions and agencies now controlled and dominated by whites," whereas "focusing . . . upon controlling the meager, poverty-ridden institutions of the ghetto . . . would fetter black America forever into the poorest and least influential sectors of the national life." Despite an increasing awareness of ghetto problems, no sweeping changes took place in NAACP programs, which continued to concentrate on lobbying for civil rights legislation and on voter registration and education.[57]

Fighting the Backlash

While the protagonists of Black Power hoped for "a new spirit of independence" among African-American voters, most blacks continued to see the liberal wing of the Democratic Party as their political home. In the 1968 and 1972 presidential elections, black voters cast their ballots for the defeated Democratic candidates in approximately the same proportions as they had voted for Lyndon Johnson in 1964. In contrast, the political and cultural polarization of the 1960s had a profound impact on the political orientation and voting behavior of white Americans. In particular, the ethnic working and lower middle-classes of the urban North who feared that black gains would come at their expense began to desert the Democratic Party in droves. Among these voters, racial liberalism and integration were widely perceived as a threat to their own social status and cultural identity.[58]

Yet it would be too facile to depict the infamous backlash simply as a reaction to the rights revolution of the 1960s. As historian Thomas Sugrue and others have demonstrated, the militant resistance against the integration of white ethnic residential areas had already been a major factor of political mobilization in cities like Chicago and Detroit during the 1940s and 1950s, setting tight limits to the liberal consensus on race to begin with. In 1963, before the ghetto riots had begun, local elections in Boston and Philadelphia showed massive defections by Italian and Irish voters from the Democratic Party as a response to efforts to desegregate the public school systems, prompting a delighted comment from Alabama governor George Wallace that in North too "there are many other people who believe about segregation as I do."[59]

It was no coincidence, therefore, that the first major political victory for the white backlash was the defeat of President Johnson's open housing bill in the Senate in September 1966. The proposed ban on racial discrimination in selling and renting apartments and houses was not primarily targeted at the South, but directly affected the North and sparked deep-seated fears of a forcible integration of all-white neighborhoods. During the open housing marches through Chicago's white working-class neighborhoods in 1966, Martin Luther King Jr. and the SCLC encountered violent hatred not unlike what they had experienced in Selma, Alabama, the preceding year. Unlike the Civil Rights Act of 1964 and the Voting Rights Act of 1965, the open housing bill of 1966 was not backed by a broad moral consensus that would compel lukewarm lawmakers to vote for it. Only after Martin Luther King Jr. had been assassinated in 1968 did Congress pass a diluted version of the bill as a tribute to the slain civil rights leader. The new law's implementation, however, remained weak.[60]

The congressional elections of November 1966 unmistakably signaled that LBJ's liberal racial and welfare policies were quickly losing ground among the American electorate. The Democrats lost forty-seven seats in the House and three in the Senate, more than they had gained in their landslide victory two years before. Of course, race had not been the only factor in the outcome of the elections. The NAACP denied that liberal candidates had been defeated because of their stand on civil rights and pointed out that several staunch allies of the civil rights cause who had been supported by the association had actually won reelection. However, without naming King personally, Roy Wilkins blamed the defeat of Illinois senator Paul Douglas on "the provocative activities of a civil rights group last summer." Despite the modest progress of black candidates in the 1966 elections, the NAACP was clearly worried that black radicalism might fan a white backlash at the polls.[61]

In order to counteract this danger, the association did its best to contain the radicalization among African-Americans and to convince white audiences that the overwhelming majority of blacks supported neither violence nor separatism. In addition to denouncing Black Power, the national secretariat continued to call upon its local branches to do everything within their power to prevent the outbreak of riots. Although a Johns Hopkins University sociologist attested to "a strong negative relation between the size of NAACP membership of branches and the incidence of riots" in the large northern cities, the NAACP officers knew well that they had little influence among black ghetto youth. The root causes of the riots, the social disintegration of young ghetto residents, could only be removed by a determined reform effort along the lines of the "Great Society." The worst enemy of this policy, the

NAACP leaders were convinced, was an unholy alliance between white conservatives and black militants.[62]

Understandably, the association looked at the forthcoming presidential elections with considerable anxiety. Again George Wallace emerged as the political champion of the white backlash and was able to stage a well-organized and -financed campaign. His American Independent Party qualified for the ballot in all fifty states, and his aggressive "law and order" rhetoric resonated strongly among many Americans frightened by racial and political violence. Interestingly, the core of Wallace's constituency outside of the South consisted of young, white, working-class males—a mirror image of the Black Power movement in terms of age, class, and gender. Two months before the elections, polls reported Wallace's approval rating at more than 20 percent. The Republican nominee, Richard Nixon, who had made an astounding political comeback, also appealed to the "silent majority" of law-abiding citizens and ran a "southern strategy" of skillfully catering to the anti-desegregation mood among white southerners.[63]

In this situation, the NAACP more or less openly backed Vice President Hubert Humphrey's presidential bid, after LBJ had declared that he would not seek reelection. Humphrey had been a reliable supporter of civil rights since the 1940s and promised to carry on with Johnson's "Great Society" programs. In contrast, Senator Eugene McCarthy of Minnesota, who emerged as Humphrey's principal rival for the Democratic nomination after the murder of Robert Kennedy, was viewed with suspicion for his anti-war message. When McCarthy invited himself to the 1968 NAACP convention, Roy Wilkins made it clear to him that he was not welcome. The NAACP leader still considered criticism of the Vietnam War to be a dangerous wedge that would split the liberal forces. As in 1964, the NAACP organized nationwide voter registration drives, which it claimed resulted in 1 million new black voters. In its appeals to register and vote, the association reminded African-Americans of the tremendous progress that had been made thanks to the civil rights legislation of the mid-1960s. Apathy or senseless radicalism would only jeopardize this progress. Rather than waste their time heckling at Wallace rallies, black activists should focus on getting out the anti-Wallace vote. The association did not attack Richard Nixon directly but kept him at arm's length. When black Republican senator Edward Brooke arranged for a meeting between Nixon and black leaders, Roy Wilkins politely declined the invitation.[64]

For their part, Humphrey and the national Democratic Party stuck to the liberal civil rights coalition and did not try to placate the potential Wallace voters. The Democratic convention made good on the promise made to the

Mississippi Freedom Democrats four years earlier and seated an interracial delegation from the Magnolia state. The party's platform proudly cited the civil rights acts passed during the Johnson administration, including the unpopular open housing law, and endorsed the recommendations of the Kerner Report. Although vilified by black radicals, liberals by and large did not turn their backs on civil rights, even if this had become a liability with many white voters.[65]

To some degree the outcome of the 1968 election reflected a normalization of American politics following LBJ's extraordinary triumph four years earlier. But there was also undeniable evidence that the ominous racial backlash had played a significant role. Richard Nixon only won by a razor-thin plurality of the popular vote, yet Wallace carried five states of the Deep South and polled 13.5 percent of the nationwide vote. His strong showing among the northern and midwestern white ethnic working class chipped away at a cornerstone of the Democratic coalition and helped Nixon win narrow pluralities in key states, such as Ohio, Illinois, and New Jersey. Humphrey only carried a total of fourteen states and lost 12 million votes compared to Johnson's tally of 1964. That this dramatic decline had much to do with the race issue was reflected in the fact that voters were sharply divided along racial lines. Whereas nine out of ten blacks cast their ballot for Humphrey, only 40 percent of whites supported the Democratic candidate. There was no denying that African-Americans had come down on the losing side and in the future would again face an administration that owed no debts to black constituencies. At least the Democrats had defended their majorities in both houses of the Congress, which limited the new president's ability to undo the achievements of the civil rights movement, in case that should be his plan.[66]

The NAACP considered Richard Nixon's ascent to the White House "bad luck" and had a hard time adjusting to the new situation. Roy Wilkins could not overcome his distaste for the new chief executive and stayed away from his inauguration, despite a personal invitation from Nixon. But there was also a positive side to the change in the Oval Office. After the association, at considerable political cost, had shielded LBJ for years against the attacks from black radicals, it eagerly seized the opportunity to gain a new profile as a critic of the Nixon administration. Now the NAACP even went on record with statements against the Vietnam War. When four students were killed in May 1970 by rampant National Guardsmen at Kent State University, the NAACP secretary placed the dead on the same level as victims of the black civil rights struggle and applauded the outrage over both the killings and the military escalation in Indochina. A few months later, a joint declaration by the NAACP and the Urban League demanded the immediate termination of the war, and in 1972 Wilkins finally made the claim that "an end to U.S. involvement in the Indochina war" had "long been integral to NAACP policies and programs."[67]

Most importantly, the association was extremely critical of Nixon's civil rights policies. Wilkins publicly attacked them as "hostile to the interests of minorities" and intended "to slow down the creeping Negro." At the 1972 NAACP annual convention, several of the association's leaders, including the chairman of the board of directors, Bishop Spottswood, accused the president of openly joining "with the enemies of black people." Black Republicans had difficulties preventing a resolution against a second term for Nixon, bitterly complaining that the leadership had turned the convention into an openly partisan affair. When Nixon won reelection by an overwhelming margin, Wilkins attributed the president's triumph to his skillful courting of former supporters of George Wallace, who had dropped out of the race after an assassination attempt left him bound to a wheelchair. Nixon's victory only aggravated an already "muddy civil rights picture," the secretary mused after the elections.[68]

There was much to criticize about Nixon's civil rights policy, to be sure. The president clearly indicated his sympathies for those whites, in the North and in the South, who opposed "forced" integration of schools, neighborhoods, and the workplace. But facing a Democratic majority in Congress, the liberal wing of the Republican Party, and a federal judiciary committed to desegregation, the Nixon administration was in no position to turn back the clock. In fact, Nixon's attempts to appoint conservative southerners to the U.S. Supreme Court were twice blunted by the Senate, in 1969 and 1970. Roy Wilkins gleefully drew parallels to the association's glorious fight against Judge John J. Parker in the 1930s.[69]

Nixon's courtship of the white South, however, could easily obscure the fact that his administration's civil rights record was highly ambivalent and in some respects astounding. While it actively opposed the busing of schoolchildren for the purpose of educational desegregation, the proportion of black children attending segregated schools in the South plummeted from 68 percent to 8 percent between 1968 and 1972, a lower figure than for the rest of the nation. Equally surprising, it was the Nixon administration that first enacted federally mandated racial quotas in employment, which, much to Nixon's satisfaction, pitted the NAACP against the labor unions.[70]

Perhaps no other issue was more significant in demonstrating that the Second Reconstruction could not be undone than the renewal of the Voting

Rights Act in 1970. Several of its key stipulations, including the "preclearance" requirement for new voting laws and the suspension of literacy tests, had been limited to five years. Since black registration in the jurisdictions covered by the Act had skyrocketed after 1965, spokesmen for the white South claimed that the law had served its purpose and should be allowed to expire. Civil rights advocates, on the other hand, complained about continuing obstruction in many parts of the South and warned against the return of racial disfranchisement if the law were not renewed. To demonstrate its open ears for the complaints about the allegedly stigmatizing sectional character of the law, the Nixon administration proposed to extend the ban on literacy tests to the entire United States. In exchange for this largely symbolic gesture, it offered to strike down the "preclearance" requirement, a cornerstone of the 1965 legislation. Much to the shock of the liberals, the administration's bill received a narrow majority in the House of Representatives in late 1969.[71]

Facing the dilution of its major legislative achievement, the civil rights lobby, with the NAACP's Clarence Mitchell vigorously taking the initiative, managed to turn this setback into a substantial victory. To alleviate southern resentment, the liberals agreed to a nationwide ban of literacy tests but proposed another five-year renewal for all other parts of the Voting Rights Act, which was finally passed by the Congress in June 1970. Since the law also mandated a uniform voting age of eighteen, which was constitutionally suspect, President Nixon at first considered a veto. Eventually he decided to sign the bill, because, among other reasons, a veto would be viewed as a "gross and gratuitous slap in the face of black America," as one of his advisers warned.[72]

In the early 1970s, it could hardly be overlooked that the struggle for black civil rights had lost much of its earlier momentum. Nevertheless, fears that the Second Reconstruction would suffer the same tragic fate as the first one turned out to be vastly exaggerated. The polarization of race relations, to be sure, was a key factor in the demise of the New Deal coalition and the rise of a hegemonic conservatism. Still, the major victim of these developments was not civil rights, but the liberal welfare state. True enough, the debates on the welfare state over the past forty years have often had a fairly racist subtext. This should not obscure the fact, though, that the rights revolution triggered by the African-American civil rights movement has shaped American political culture in profound ways and is deeply anchored in American institutions.[73]

In the late 1960s, however, this was difficult to foresee. The NAACP's attitude toward Black Power and the white backlash was based on the conviction, rooted in the association's history, that blacks would always be a vulnerable minority that could not attain its goals and interests without strong support from whites. The black militants, Roy Wilkins predicted in 1967, would either recognize this historical fact or perish. As far as the political message of the Black Power movement is concerned, this skepticism was well-founded. But while Black Power as a political rallying cry subsided in the 1970s, its claims for the recognition of an autonomous black culture within a wider pluralist framework were bound to make much headway as American society became more multicultural in the late twentieth century. In contrast, the NAACP's traditional ideal of a color-blind society would lose much of its earlier integrating force.[74]

Conclusion

The Ticket to Freedom?

In Search of Political Integration

Around 1970, the reenfranchisement of southern blacks appeared to be firmly secure due to the implementation of the Voting Rights Act and the tireless voter registration efforts of the civil rights movement. By then, the NAACP looked back at sixty years of struggle for the ballot. Although the resistance of white supremacists against "first-class citizenship" for African-Americans often seemed to be insurmountable throughout these decades, the association never lost its faith that the egalitarian and liberal ideals of American democracy would eventually prevail over the forces of racism. Despite numerous setbacks and vitriolic attacks from its critics, the NAACP tenaciously stuck to its basic methods and principles. "It cannot be said too often," board member Edward Muse stated, affirming his opposition to Black Power in 1968, "that the goal of the NAACP is integration; that is the creation of a society where race is irrelevant in human affairs."[1]

It may be true, as critics of the association frequently insinuated, that the commitment to a "color-blind" society to some degree reflected the interest of the NAACP leaders in social recognition and upward mobility. As described above, the national, regional, and local officials of the association were largely drawn from the black middle class that had acquired the professional skills necessary for running a large and stable organization. As long as Jim Crow laws and segregated labor markets barred most qualified blacks from adequate employment in the larger economy, a position with the NAACP, the Urban League, or other black self-help organizations offered an attractive alternative for aspiring and self-confident African-Americans. Ironically, when the civil rights movement succeeded in breaking down the racial barriers in the private and public sectors, the recruitment of qualified employees became more difficult for the NAACP.[2]

It would be grossly misleading, however, to dismiss the persistence of the association's integrationism as being rooted in the special interest of a small group of relatively privileged members of the black middle class. For one thing, the overwhelming majority of NAACP members and activists worked on a voluntary basis with few prospects of personal gain or advancement but often at considerable personal risk. Although there was much disagreement over strategy and methods, the struggle against segregation and disfranchisement constituted a unifying interest of all African-Americans, regardless of social status. Moreover, since the early 1930s, the NAACP also promoted the economic interest of black Americans and did not confine its activities to securing legal and political rights. Its economic program, however, never aimed at a radical transformation of American capitalism but remained reformist in a dual sense: First, all racial barriers against equal opportunity in business, employment, and education had to be removed. Second, the liberal welfare state had to be extended at all levels in order to fight poverty, unemployment, ignorance, and other social evils that afflicted the black minority more than any other racial or ethnic group in America. In the mid-1960s, Lyndon Johnson's vision of a "Great Society" seemed to start off the reform effort that many NAACP leaders hoped would bring the United States closer to the model of the Western European welfare state.[3]

In its efforts to reform American society, the NAACP remained closely wedded to the institutional framework of the American political system. Collective violence as a strategy to force social change was strictly rejected. Nonviolent direct action and mass protests were condoned as legitimate tactics to exert pressure, but the association never left a doubt that it preferred legal action and the political process. The right to vote, both as a symbol of "first-class citizenship" and as an instrument for advancing collective interests, remained at center stage of the NAACP's strategic approach. Unrestricted access to the polls and the "intelligent" use of the ballot would provide the black minority with a potent weapon to win inclusion into the democratic and egalitarian promise of America. The struggle against racial discrimination, moreover, would not only benefit African-Americans, but American society as a whole.[4]

What is more surprising than the NAACP's general commitment to the American creed, however, is its conspicuous lack of interest in alternatives to the American electoral system. Of course, the association attacked the institutional pillars of disfranchisement in the South, including the grandfather clause, the white primary, and the poll tax. But even its opposition to literacy tests, widely used as a qualification for voting outside of the South, remained limited to the demand for an impartial administration. Institutional changes that might have transcended the American electoral system at large were not part of the NAACP agenda at all. For example, the association never seriously considered a switch from the American winner-takes-all system, based on single-member districts, to European-style systems of proportional represen- tation, although the latter are clearly more conducive to the political represen- tation of distinct minorities. To be sure, alternatives to the traditional Ameri- can system of single-member districts have never enjoyed broad support and the prospects for enacting reforms have always been very slim. But the fact that the NAACP never even considered such alternatives reaffirms that in its political thought and outlook it was as American as apple pie.[5]

The goal to promote the civil rights and economic interests of African-Americans through the ballot continued to enjoy a very high priority for the NAACP in the years after 1970. The voter registration efforts, in particular, were maintained at a constantly high level. When W. C. Patton retired as the director of the NAACP voter registration committee in 1977, he was suc- ceeded by Joseph Madison, a twenty-seven-year-old activist from Dayton, Ohio, who vigorously set out to adapt the registration work to the require- ments of the post–civil rights era. The headquarters of the NAACP registra- tion committee were relocated from Birmingham, Alabama, to Detroit, Michigan, because the North had begun to trail the South in black registra- tion. Moreover, because young people could be more easily reached at pop concerts than at church services, Madison persuaded African-American pop stars, such as singer Michael Jackson, to allow NAACP registration workers at their concerts.[6]

Joseph Madison has estimated that about a half million new black voters were registered while he was in charge of the association's voter registration and education programs. Like his predecessors, John Brooks and W. C. Patton, Madison wanted to retain control over the activities of the local branches and especially over their use of financial contributions. As in the past, money was always tight, but the large institutional donors, including philanthropic foundations and labor unions, continued to underwrite the NAACP's voter education projects. Although the association reaffirmed its traditional nonpartisanship, its campaigns were launched to benefit black candidates and white liberals friendly to black interests. According to Joseph Madison, the NAACP registration work was immensely helped by the candi- dacy and ensuing presidency of conservative Republican Ronald Reagan. As early as 1965, an NAACP official had described Reagan, who was then running for governor of California, as "a threat to the entire country" that should best be stopped right away. As president, Ronald Reagan was the "devil" that the registration activists needed for a large African-American voter turnout. Although Reagan won the White House twice, Madison has maintained that black voters at least helped the Democrats defend their congressional majorities.[7]

Nevertheless, the continuing effort to educate and mobilize black voters could not prevent the political predominance of a resurgent conservatism that cared little about the specific social and economic problems of the black community. At the same time, the overall rates of registration and voting among African-Americans showed signs of stagnation. In 1968, more than 57 percent of eligible blacks reported that they had actually cast a ballot, while in 1992 only 54 percent said so. Not surprisingly, the enthusiasm for registration work that had inspired the NAACP during the civil rights era began to subside. After Joseph Madison left his position in 1986, the office of the voter registration committee was merged into the national secretariat, which moved from New York to Baltimore, Maryland. Voter registration thus lost the independent and prominent role it had played among the manifold activities of the association since the 1950s. Following this transition, the NAACP voter education department mostly concerned itself with the development of educational programs, while the registration work was again left to the local branches without much coordination or control from the national secretariat.[8]

The Impact of the Ballot

In the wake of the Second World War, a young NAACP worker from South Carolina proclaimed that "the ballot holds the answer to 99 percent of our present worries. It will establish equal opportunity to learn; it will remove the head-whipping police officers; it will enact such laws as may be necessary to destroy lynching mobs, the poll tax restriction and it will make both sides of the railroad track livable."[9] Many of these high hopes would be bitterly disappointed over the years to come. But then again, 99 percent is hardly a fair measure for assessing the achievements of the NAACP's struggle for the vote. As in most political movements, disappointment and disillusionment were inevitable and were keenly felt by those who had waged the fight. Still, from a long-term perspective we have to ask whether the association's unwavering belief in the ballot and the political process turned out to be justified.

To begin with, it is obvious that laws to abolish segregation and other forms of racial discrimination did not come as a direct consequence of black electoral power, as the NAACP had preached for decades. Desegregation was primarily brought about by a series of legal victories, beginning in the 1930s, and by the dramatic mass protests of the civil rights movement. It was non-violent direct action, more than anything else, that forced the U.S. Congress to enact the Civil Rights Act of 1964 and the Voting Rights Act of 1965, two laws that most Americans considered to be radical departures from the traditional federal-state relationship of the American political system.

Its many accomplishments in the struggle for the ballot notwithstanding, the great breakthrough for which the NAACP continued to hope took painfully long to occur. The ban on the grandfather clause, the end of the white primary, the decline of the poll tax, and the untiring registration work of the association and other civil rights groups all weakened but could not destroy the political system of white supremacy in the South. In the North, the association's ritualistic balance-of-power rhetoric did not have much of an impact on politicians hostile to black interests. Indeed, very few of them could be successfully punished at the polls. To be sure, the growth of the black electorate in the North made the liberal wing of the Democratic Party more responsive to African-American voters, but even when they provided the crucial margins for Harry Truman and John F. Kennedy to win the White House, their rewards were rather meager. As long as the southerners held a de facto veto power in the U.S. Senate, all meaningful federal civil rights legislation was doomed. Only when the civil rights movement staged a major national crisis in the early 1960s did this situation change.

Although the ballot was no magical political weapon, the NAACP's struggle for the right to vote had many important long-term consequences. During the first half of the twentieth century, white supremacy was deeply entrenched in the South and enjoyed much support in the rest of the nation as well. That the NAACP—and many other organizations and individuals—firmly asserted and defended the African-American claim to first-class citizenship and democratic participation against this hegemonic culture of racism can hardly be overstated, even though the concrete results were often wanting. Its interracial character and integrationist creed allowed the association to reach sympathetic white audiences and to confront white Americans with the blatant contradiction between their self-congratulatory celebration of democracy and the ugly reality of racism.

Equally important were the NAACP's incessant efforts for the political education and mobilization of African-Americans. Voter registration, in particular, became a major field of action for the association and its local branches. No other organization had a greater part in increasing black registration in the South from a minuscule 150,000 in 1940 to more than 1.2

million in 1952.[10] This groundwork set the stage for the growing politicization of southern blacks in the late 1950s and early 1960s, when the civil
rights movement launched its crucial assault on Jim Crow. Even during the
nonviolent action phase of the civil rights struggle the vote remained the
movement's second strategic pillar. That many activists were willing to risk
life and limb in working for first-class citizenship is impressive testimony to
their belief in the transformative power of the ballot. At the same time, the
demand for the franchise communicated a "constructive" message to the
white majority: Black reenfranchisement held the promise of a peaceful and
orderly solution to the race issue. While this message was most vocally articulated by the NAACP, many supporters of nonviolent direct action basically
agreed.

The hopes for a swift pacification of the racial conflict through civil rights
reforms evaporated in the riotous "long hot summers" of the late 1960s. Nevertheless, desegregation and the protection of the right to vote led to profound changes in the political and social status of African-Americans in the
South and in the rest of the United States. Most obviously, the political system of white supremacy that had prevailed in the South for almost a hundred
years began to fade away, even though attempts to prevent blacks from registering and voting did not cease immediately. Often grudgingly, white southerners learned to accept the end of public segregation and to respect the right
of their black fellow-citizens to political participation. Racial demagoguery,
the lifeblood of southern politics for many decades, was no longer a dominant discourse. The region saw the rise of moderate progressives, such as
Georgian Jimmy Carter, who promised a better life for all citizens in a truly
New South of prosperity and opportunity. When Carter ran for president of
the United States in 1976, the unanimous support of black voters in the
South pushed him over the top in ten of the eleven states of the former Confederacy. After a close lead in Mississippi eventually sealed Carter's victory,
civil rights leader Andrew Young jubilated: "The hands that picked the cotton
finally picked the president."[11]

In the seven southern states covered by the 1965 Voting Rights Act, black
registration increased from 31.4 percent in 1964 to 57.7 percent in 1982; in
Mississippi it went up from 6.7 percent to 75.8 percent. This not only meant
that white politicians were actively seeking black support, but also that African-Americans could be elected to public office, often for the first time in the
twentieth century. In many places these victories built on the registration
work of the NAACP, as, for example, when the first African-American was
elected to the Virginia legislature in 1967. These "firsts" quickly added up to
sizeable numbers, although from a very low baseline. In 1964, the total num-

ber of black elected officials in the entire South had been lower than 25, but by 1970 it had increased to roughly 700; over the next decade it grew to 3,140 in 1982. With 426 elected black officeholders, Mississippi led all other states of the Union. Moreover, beginning with Maynard Jackson's election as mayor of Atlanta in 1973, a good number of the major southern cities elected black politicians to their top executive post, including New Orleans, Birmingham, Charlotte, North Carolina, and Richmond, Virginia. As voters and as candidates, African-Americans have become widely accepted actors in southern politics.[12]

From Disfranchisement to Minority Vote Dilution

The reenfrachisement of southern blacks also led to the return of the two-party system to the region. To be sure, this did not make southern politics interracial, let alone "color-blind." Following up on the southern strategies of Goldwater and Nixon in the 1960s, the Republicans established themselves as the party of conservative whites, while the Democrats became widely perceived as the home of black voters and white liberals.[13] Under the surface of black progress, many analysts and civil rights advocates argued, white resentment lingered on. Only a minority of white voters, they found, would be willing to cast a ballot for a black candidate. Black lawmakers therefore almost always represented electoral districts where black voters were in a sizeable majority. A collaborative research project, published in 1994, stated an "almost perfect correlation" between majority-black districts and black officeholding in state legislative and congressional districts. "For blacks to win," the authors concluded, "it is therefore still necessary in the South to draw districts in which blacks are a majority or a supermajority of the population."[14]

The observation that black candidates could only win in black-majority districts and that nowhere did their numbers come close to the 20 percent share of African-Americans in the overall population of the South was not a new one. Following the enactment of the Voting Rights Act, southern legislatures began to devise new electoral schemes in order to dilute the value and impact of black ballots. The most important methods were the racial gerrymandering of electoral districts and the introduction of at-large elections to insure that black candidates would always face a majority of white voters. Unlike the outright denial of the ballot, however, minority vote dilution is an elusive concept that raises numerous controversial issues: Does it require proof that an electoral system or districting plan was adopted with a discriminatory intent or is it enough to demonstrate that it has disproportionate results? Are racial and ethnic minorities entitled to representation in proportion to their overall share in the voting-age population? Can minorities only be represented by minority candidates? For more than thirty years now, courts and legislatures have grappled with these questions, but they are far from being settled.[15]

The political and legal consensus that had generated the Voting Rights Act also held against the attempts to dilute the law's impact. Most importantly, in a 1969 landmark decision the U.S. Supreme Court ruled that the "preclearance" requirement of the Act reached practically all changes in the electoral system of a covered state, including the drawing of new districting plans and the introduction of at-large elections. This led to a dramatic increase in both preclearance reviews by the Department of Justice—an estimated 190,000 until 1991—and lawsuits alleging minority vote dilution. But so far, no workable criteria for minority vote dilution had been established. In a 1973 ruling, the Supreme Court defined the term broadly, as meaning that minority voters "had less opportunity than did other residents to participate in the political process and to elect legislators of their choice." Decisions had to be based on "the totality of circumstances," which might include a history of racial discrimination and polarization and other "cultural and economic realities."[16]

Subsequently, however, the Supreme Court's conservative members began to set limits to the expansion of the Voting Rights Act. In 1976, a majority held that the purpose of preclearance was to "insure that no voting-procedure changes would be made that would lead to a retrogression in the position of racial minorities." This meant that a districting plan was constitutionally permissible as long as it did not diminish the opportunities for black candidates, even though it might leave black voters underrepresented in regard to their population share. Moreover, in the 1980 case of *City of Mobile v. Bolden*, the Court held that in order to establish unconstitutional vote dilution disproportionate effects were not enough, but plaintiffs had to show discriminatory intent. Since the intent standard was difficult to meet, voting rights activists feared that *Bolden* might once again open the doors to ostensibly color-blind practices that resulted in the de facto exclusion of blacks from meaningful participation and representation.[17]

In response to *Bolden*, the civil rights community successfully lobbied Congress to reverse the Supreme Court. In 1982, the Voting Rights Act was not only extended for another twenty-five years but also significantly amended. The Act now prohibited the use of any voting qualification or practice resulting in abridging the political opportunities of racial minorities, thereby eliminating the intent standard of *Bolden*. Still, it also explicitly did not establish a right to minority representation equal to their proportion in the population. When the Supreme Court first had to interpret the new law in 1986 in the case of *Thornburgh v. Gingles,* Justice William Brennan announced three key criteria for establishing illegal minority vote dilution: (1) a minority group must be sufficiently large and geographically compact; (2) it must be politically cohesive; and (3) white majorities must vote as a bloc to enable it usually to defeat the minorities' preferred candidate. The five-to-four *Gingles* Court, however, was deeply divided, with the dissenters complaining that the ruling, in effect, created a right to proportional representation.[18]

While Congress and the Supreme Court made it easier to challenge minority vote dilution, the federal Justice Department also adopted a tougher policy in protecting black electoral opportunity. When the states began reapportioning their congressional districts after the census of 1990, the DoJ insisted that the states covered by the Voting Rights Act create more districts with a black majority of the population. And indeed, in the 1992 elections thirteen additional southern blacks were elected to the U.S. House of Representatives, all of them from newly drawn majority-black districts. Since many of these districts had a bizarre geographical shape that easily matched Elbridge Gerry's famous "salamander," they provoked bitter controversy and protracted litigation. Now white voters claimed to be victims of reverse racial gerrymandering, because traditional principles of districting, such as geographical compactness and common economic interests, had allegedly been disregarded for the sole purpose of ensuring the election of a black candidate.[19]

The first ruling on the constitutionality of majority-black congressional districts under the Voting Rights Act was the 1993 case of *Shaw v. Reno,* involving a reapportionment plan by North Carolina that contained a bizarre-looking majority-black district that stretched for about 160 miles along Interstate 85. Justice Sandra Day O'Connor argued for the majority that such "dramatically irregular" districts violate the equal protection clause of the Fourteenth Amendment. Even for remedial purposes, racial gerrymandering was impermissible, because it reinforced racial stereotypes and threatened to establish a new form of "political apartheid." Two years later, in *Miller v. Johnson,* the Supreme Court further tightened the limits on drawing majority-black districts. A district did not have to look bizarre on its face to violate the Constitution, the Court held. It was enough to show that "race was the predominant factor motivating the legislature's decision to place a significant number of voters within or without a particular district." Since the state legislatures had drawn these race-conscious plans in order to comply with the

Voting Rights Act, *Shaw, Miller,* and similar rulings implied that the majority believed the Act itself to be unconstitutional.[20]

In virtually all of the major cases involving minority vote dilution, the Court was sharply divided by a five-to-four ratio. The civil rights community was especially incensed by the fact that the crucial vote for the majority came from Justice Clarence Thomas, the African-American member of the Court who had replaced the legendary Thurgood Marshall in 1991. In fact, Thomas has been the most outspoken critic of a broad construction of the Voting Rights Act. In his concurring opinion to the 1994 case of *Holder v. Hall,* brought by an NAACP branch from Georgia, Thomas called for overruling *Gingles* and for limiting the Act to the individual right to cast a ballot and have it fairly counted.[21]

Shaw v. Reno and its progeny have triggered an avalanche of criticism from the dissenting minority of the Court, the civil rights community, and many scholars. Race, the critics contend, is a legitimate factor in redistricting and white voters suffer no harm from residing in a majority-black district. Given America's long tradition of gerrymandering for partisan purposes, there are no "traditional principles of districting" that oddly shaped districts could violate. The notion of a color-blind political process, as espoused by *Shaw,* is dismissed as fictitious and as a subterfuge for transforming the Voting Rights Act from an instrument to prohibit disfranchisement and vote dilution into a device to diminish minority political power. The NAACP's Washington Bureau chief predicted "the resegregation of American electoral democracy." In his book *Colorblind Injustice: Minority Voting Rights and the Undoing of the Second Reconstruction,* historian J. Morgan Kousser concluded that *Shaw* was "as wrong as *Plessy,* as wrong as *Dred Scott.*"[22]

These are damning historical analogies, indeed, but they are not substantiated by numerical evidence. In 1996, five black representatives from the South whose majority-black districts had been redrawn as a result of *Shaw* and *Miller* had to run in districts with a white majority. Surprisingly, all five of them, including three black women with strong liberal reputations, won handily. Even if these results primarily reflected the power of incumbency, as critical observers insinuated, the fact that incumbency worked for black candidates among a substantial part of the white electorate appears remarkable enough. Ten years after *Shaw v. Reno,* the numbers do not bear out any negative impact. In 1992, the southern states covered by the Voting Rights Act had a total of thirteen black representatives in Congress. Following the election of 2000, the number was twelve, hardly a precipitous decline. During the same period the number of black members of the respective state legislatures increased from 155 to 245. According to the figures of the Joint Center for Political and Economic Studies, the leading African-American think tank, the total number of black elected officials in the United States has continuously grown from 7,370 in 1990 to 9,101 in 2001. Whatever the merits of the constitutional arguments brought by the Court's critics may be, their gloomy predictions have not materialized. If the Supreme Court's capacity for promoting social and political reform must not be overestimated, as recent scholarship has suggested, perhaps we should also not overestimate its capacity to turn back the clock.[23]

Moreover, as its political costs have become evident, the strategy of maximizing black representation by drawing as many majority-black districts as possible has lost support even among many African-American politicians and civil rights advocates. Several analysts have alleged that the insistence of the Republican Department of Justice after 1990 on creating safe seats for southern black Democrats was based on the calculation that packing large numbers of loyal black Democratic voters into a few districts would pave the way for white Republicans in the rest of the South. Incidently, this is what happened in the so-called 1994 "Republican Revolution." In majority-black districts African-Americans may get easily elected, but once in the legislature they face overwhelming opposition to their agendas from conservative Republicans. This is why analysts and some black politicians urge a shift from focusing on majority-black districts to so-called influence districts, in which black voters, though in a numerical minority, will still decisively influence the outcome of the elections. Whether a black candidate or a white candidate sympathetic to black interests is elected would be of secondary importance. Interestingly, recent conflicts over congressional redistricting in Georgia have pitted the state's Republican Party against civil rights veteran and black congressman John Lewis. The Republicans insist that the Voting Rights Act requires a maximum number of majority-black districts, while Lewis, a Democrat, has abandoned the "max black" principle and supports the drawing of black influence districts. In 2003, the Supreme Court upheld the redistricting plan of the Georgia legislature, which focused on creating such "influence districts" at the expense of slightly reducing the number of districts with a black majority. Once again the Republican Department of Justice had insisted on maximizing their number.[24]

Conservative and liberal authors have argued for a long time that extending the Voting Rights Act to the murky concept of minority vote dilution has distorted the traditional right to vote into a questionable group right to ethnic proportional representation. Others who have supported race-conscious remedies, such as majority-black districts, have nevertheless maintained the goal of a color-blindness and expressed their hopes that one day the Voting Rights Act will have outlived its usefulness.[25] On the other hand, the protagonists of a multicultural society based on group rights want to go on extending the Voting Rights Act beyond the drawing of majority-black districts. In the early 1990s, law professor Lani Guinier, a former lawyer for the NAACP Legal Defense and Education Fund, advocated electoral reforms based on varieties of European-style proportional representation that would allow minorities to elect candidates of their own choice in jurisdictions with large majorities of white voters. Even more controversial, Guinier proposed what she called "interest representation" for minorities, that is a preferential and institutionalized influence of minority lawmakers on all legislative issues that affect minorities in order to secure material results favorable to their constituents. It was time, she argued, to discard the "chimera of physically integrated legislatures in a color-blind society" and to embrace the ideal of "a fair and just society" for which the civil rights movement had fought. When President Bill Clinton nominated Guinier as the head of the DoJ's Civil Rights Division in 1993, this provoked a storm of protests in Congress and the media against the alleged "quota queen." Clinton withdrew Guinier's name without giving her an opportunity to defend her views in the U.S. Senate.[26]

After Civil Rights

It has certainly been a long way from the unwavering belief in a "color-blind democracy," held by NAACP leaders like Walter White or Roy Wilkins, to the notion of "interest representation" in a multicultural society. Certainly, the observation that electoral success did not directly translate into socioeconomic advancement was one important reason why the traditional notion of the vote as the ticket to freedom and equality has lost much of its earlier appeal. In many of America's big cities, black politicians have been elected as mayors or have held other key administrative positions. In 2001, forty-nine cities with more than fifty thousand residents had black majors, and more than half of them have no black majority of the population. Black mayors have opened up the public sector to black employees at all levels, but a shrinking tax base and the flight of the white and black middle classes to the suburbs have set limits to their ability to solve the problems of the inner cities. Needless to say, given the nature of urban machine politics, black mayors and city councils are no guarantee for the fair distribution and efficient use of scarce resources.[27]

The continuing economic deprivation of many African-Americans, despite affirmative action and other efforts to make up for the history of slavery and racism, remains the most controversial issue of American race relations to date. Even though the black middle class has grown impressively over the past decades, the official poverty rate of 24.1 percent among African-Americans is still twice the national average. Most importantly, the urban black underclass is trapped in a nightmarish world of gang violence, street crime, drugs, and dependency on welfare programs that have been cut substantially since the 1990s. Also, the black family has undergone a dramatic decline. In the mid-1990s, about three-fourths of all black children were born out of wedlock, most of whom were doomed to grow up in poverty.[28]

The reasons for the continuing plight of the black underclass and the significant social disadvantagement of the African-American population at large are, of course, highly controversial. Many authors on the left see it as irrefutable proof of the persistence of a structural racism in American society, despite the limited gains of the civil rights era. "Racism," the black writer Derrick Bell states, "is an integral, permanent and indestructible component of this society."[29] Others, like black sociologist William Julius Wilson, have argued that the economic problems of urban blacks can no longer be adequately explained by racism, but stem from the larger forces of a postindustrial and globalized economy.[30] While Wilson advocates social democratic strategies of job creation and social policies, many conservatives blame the emergence of what they see as a "dysfunctional" ghetto culture of crime, poverty, and self-segregation on the welfare state. Liberal welfare paternalism combined with the radical negativism of the 1960s, authors such as Charles Murray, Lawrence Mead, and Dinesh D'Souza maintain, only increased the dependency of poor blacks and destroyed middle-class values and work ethics among African-American ghetto residents.[31] Others, however, have criticized the widespread tendency to "let the underclass define our notion of black America," as Abigail and Stephan Thermstrom write. After all, they contend, the past fifty years have brought tremendous racial change and progress that few people could have imagined in the age of Jim Crow. Rejecting what he calls "the overracialization of American life," sociologist Orlando Patterson finds that "the real Afro-Americans are diverse, surprisingly happy, and very American."[32]

Like Patterson, other black intellectuals, often regarded as conservatives, including Thomas Sowell, Shelby Steele, and John McWorther, have become highly critical of the so-called civil rights establishment for habitually blaming all problems of black America on white racism, thus perpetuating a mental victim status that amounts to "self-sabotage." In this perspective, the noble cause of civil rights has been perverted into a racial spoils system to insure privileges for those who do not need them.[33] Ironically, authors on the left, such as historian Manning Marable, also lament a crisis of black leadership due to the alleged opportunism of a black elite that combines an authoritarian style with ingratiating itself to white corporate America. The void opened by this lack of real leadership, Marable argues, paved the way for Louis Farrakhan, the leader of the Nation of Islam, who succeeded in attracting hundreds of thousands of black men to his 1995 "Million Man March" in Washington, D.C.[34] Few commentators failed to point out the sharp contrast between the integrationist message that had inspired the 1963 March on Washington and the Nation of Islam rally that excluded not only whites but also women.

Not surprisingly, the crisis of leadership profoundly affected the NAACP, and its relationship with Farrakhan and the Nation of Islam played an important part in the turmoil that afflicted the association in the mid-1990s. Trying the stem the loss of members and to attract more young people, the NAACP's executive director, Benjamin Chavis, elected in 1993, tried to open up the association to black nationalism. At "summit meetings" of black leaders in 1993 and 1994 that included Chavis, the Reverend Jesse Jackson, and Louis Farrakhan, the participants agreed on the need for "maximum unity," despite Farrakhan's well-known racism and anti-Semitism. Predictably, Chavis's new line led to heated controversy within the NAACP. When the executive director had to admit to the personal misuse of association funds, he was finally ousted in the summer 1994, along with the chairman of the board of directors.[35]

Many observers viewed the NAACP's political and financial troubles as most unfortunate, because its paralysis coincided with the triumph of the conservative "Republican Revolution." Less benevolent commentators saw the association's corruption and immobility as beyond redemption and called for an "institutional mercy killing" to facilitate a new beginning under a new name.[36] Such swan songs were, however, premature. In 1995, the NAACP managed to consolidate its finances and initiate an overhaul of its leadership. The election of Myrlie Evers-Williams, widow of the martyred Mississippi civil rights leader, as chairwoman of the board of directors was widely seen as signal to restore the association's credibility. Large donors who had been angered by the advances toward black nationalism began to open their pockets again. Moreover, the election of Evers-Williams also ratified the overdue recognition of the role of women, who are a majority among the NAACP members.[37]

In late 1995, the board of directors voted to appoint Kweisi Mfume, a prominent Democratic congressman from Baltimore and former chairman of the Congressional Black Caucus, as both the new president and the new chief executive officer of the NAACP. Although Mfume entertained friendly relations with Louis Farrakhan, he announced that he would again reach out to the NAACP's historic allies in the corporate and white communities, including Jewish organizations. Mfume, a former school dropout and street hustler who had turned his life around, was widely hailed as an energetic leader with the ability to unite the different factions within the association.[38]

In the post–civil rights era, the NAACP is often viewed as representing a special interest rather than the universal ideals of American democracy. Many Americans are no longer prepared to see the nation's racial conflicts as a historical legacy and burden. The race issue no longer conveys the same moral clarity that it did in the age of Jim Crow. At the same time, racial discrimination continues to be a fact of life, and safeguarding the civil rights and social interests of African-Americans will remain an important concern. Some hope for a Third Reconstruction that will address the issue of economic inequality, perhaps based on a resurgence of nonviolent protests or even ghetto rebellions.

Still, as in the past, there will be few viable alternatives to the political process, and politics, of course, will remain a tedious and frustrating affair. When this author asked former NAACP voter registration director Joseph Madison whether, all things considered, the ballot had been black America's ticket to freedom, he replied: "It has been the ticket to the train but the train has not arrived at the final destination which would be the sharing of wealth and power. The great problem is that in many black communities there is not even a stop to board the train."[39]

Notes

Introduction: Writing the History of the NAACP

1. Meier, "Epilogue: Toward a Synthesis of Civil Rights History," 212.

2. Eagles, "The Civil Rights Movement," 465; on the other groups, see the leading accounts by Carson, *In Struggle*; Meier and Rudwick, *CORE*; Weiss, *The National Urban League*; Fairclough, *To Redeem the Soul of America*.

3. Kellogg, *NAACP*; several important essays on the NAACP by Meier and Rudwick are collected in their volume *Along the Color Line*.

4. For case studies of limited scope and time-range, see Ross, *J. E. Spingarn and the Rise of the NAACP*; Tushnet, *The NAACP's Legal Strategy against Segregated Education*; Zangrando, *The NAACP Crusade against Lynching*; Goings, *The NAACP Comes of Age*; Cortner, *A Mob Intent on Death*. For outdated or unsatisfactory overviews, see St. James, *The National Association for the Advancement of Colored People*; Hughes, *Fight for Freedom*; Finch, *The NAACP*; Harris, *History and Achievement of the NAACP*.

5. See esp., Ovington, *The Walls Came Tumbling Down*; Johnson, *Along This Way*; White, *A Man Called White*; Wilkins with Mathews, *Standing Fast*; see also Watson, *Lion in the Lobby*, a book that started out as an autobiography of NAACP lobbyist Clarence Mitchell and was continued by Mitchell's former aide after his death.

6. In 1987, Robert Zangrando estimated that the NAACP Records in the LoC comprised at least 2 million documents (see Zangrando, "Manuscript Sources for Twentieth Century Civil Rights Research," 244). Since then, many more documents have been processed.

7. The most important King biographies are Lewis, *King*; Oates, *Let the Trumpet Sound*; Garrow, *Bearing the Cross*; also see the monumental multi-volume narrative by Branch, *Parting the Waters: America in the King Years, 1954–63* and *Pillar of Fire: America in the King Years, 1963–1965*. For a critical perspective on the "Montgomery to Memphis" paradigm, see Fairclough, "Historians and the Civil Rights Movement," 387–90. Fairclough himself has also written a very readable biography of King (see Fairclough, *Martin Luther King, Jr.*).

8. Franklin and Meier, eds., *Black Leaders of the Twentieth Century*, includes, however, an article on NAACP executive secretary James Weldon Johnson (see Levy, "James Weldon Johnson and the Development of the NAACP").

9. Carson, "Civil Rights Movement"; Carson, "Civil Rights Reform and the Black Freedom Struggle"; Carson, "Martin Luther King, Jr."; for a harsh critique of the "top-down" paradigm, see Payne, *I've Got the Light of Freedom*, 413–41.

10. For pioneering local studies, see Chafe, *Civilities and Civil Rights*; Morris, *The Origins of the Civil Rights Movement*; Norrell, *Reaping the Whirlwind*. The two most outstanding civil rights studies on the state level are Dittmer, *Local People*; Fairclough, *Race and Democracy*. Both authors emphasize the importance of the NAACP. For other local- and state-centered studies that stress the role of the NAACP, see Wright, "The Civil Rights Movement in Kentucky, 1900–1970"; Dulaney, "Whatever Happened to the Civil Rights Movement in Dallas, Texas?"; Gavins, "The NAACP in North Carolina during the Age of Segregation"; Reed, *The Chicago NAACP and the Rise of Black Professional Leadership, 1910–1966*; Eick, *Dissent in Wichita*; also see Tuck, *Beyond Atlanta*.

11. Quoted in Ransby, *Ella Baker and the Black Freedom Movement*, 139.

12. See, e.g., Bates, "A New Crowd Challenges the Agenda of the Old Guard in the NAACP, 1933–1941." Bates's essay is an important contribution to the history of the NAACP, but it suffers from a vague use of key concepts, such as "the masses," "the black working class," and "the middle class."

13. See esp. chapters six and seven.

14. Fairclough, *Race and Democracy*, esp. xiv–xvi; Fairclough, *Better Day Coming*, esp. 67–85, 181–201.

15. Schneider, *We Return Fighting*, 4.

16. Janken, *White*. For another recent biography of an important civil rights activist who served for some time with the national secretariat of the NAACP, see Ransby, *Ella Baker and the Black Freedom Movement*, esp. 105–47.

17. See Anderson, *Eyes off the Prize*, esp. the introduction (1–7) and conclusion (271–76). For my own account of the NAACP's role in the early Cold War, see chapter five.

18. See Berg, *The Ticket to Freedom*; also Berg, "Guns, Butter, and Civil Rights"; Berg, "Black Power"; Berg, "Activists, Leaders, and Supporters"; Berg, "Individual Right and Collective Interest."

19. For historians dedicated to international cooperation this is sometimes frustrating. For example, the recent and otherwise excellent historiographical guide by Agnew and Rosenzweig, *A Companion to Post-1945 America*, lists but a handful of foreign-language entries among roughly one hundred pages of bibliography, although there is a large and vibrant international scholarly community doing research on contemporary American history.

20. Fairclough, "Segregation and Civil Rights," 158.

21. For a general account of the struggle for black voting rights that largely focuses on legislation and litigation, see Lawson, *Black Ballots*; Lawson, *In Pursuit of Power*. Both of these books pay a good deal of attention to the activities of the NAACP; on the ensuing debates about minority vote dilution, see the conclusion of this book.

22. "Some Reasons Why Everybody Should Register and Vote" (1965), NAACP

Records, Library of Congress, Manuscript Division, part 3, series A, box 270. On the symbolic function of the vote, see Shklar, *American Citizenship,* 25–62; the first modern history of the suffrage in American history has only been published a few years ago (see Keyssar, *The Right to Vote*).

23. See esp. chapter seven.

24. On Thurgood Marshall's legal achievements, see the two volumes by Tushnet, *Making Civil Rights Law* and *Making Constitutional Law;* also see McNeil, *Groundwork;* on the history of the NAACP LDF, see the memoirs of its longtime director Jack Greenberg, *Crusaders in the Courts.*

25. For an earlier account, see Hine, *Black Victory.*

26. For a skeptical view, see Rosenberg, *The Hollow Hope.*

27. See chapters six, seven, and nine.

28. For a systematic account of the social reform agendas of major civil rights organizations that contests the notion of a "narrow" focus on civil rights, see Hamilton and Hamilton, *The Dual Agenda.*

29. For pronounced summaries of this interpretation of the civil rights movement, see Carson, "Civil Rights Reform and the Black Freedom Struggle"; Chafe, "The End of One Struggle, the Beginning of Another"; also see the influential textbook by Marxist historian Manning Marable, *Race, Reform, and Rebellion;* for an argument that sees historical integration as a failure for most African-Americans and pleads for "limited separation," see Brooks, *Integration or Separation?*

Chapter 1. The Making of an Integrationist Civil Rights Organization

1. For the most comprehensive analysis of the Springfield riots, see Senechal, *The Sociogenesis of a Race Riot,* esp. 15–54; Walling, "The Race War in the North."

2. Newton and Newton, *Racial and Religious Violence in America,* 290–335.

3. Walling, "The Race War in the North," 531.

4. On the aftermath of the riot, see Senechal, *The Sociogenesis of a Race Riot,* esp. 160–73.

5. Walling, "The Race War in the North," 529, 534.

6. Ovington, *The Walls Came Tumbling Down,* esp. 100–104; for the most comprehensive account of the NAACP's founding, see Kellogg, *NAACP,* 9–30.

7. *The Call* and a list of the original signers are printed in Kellogg, *NAACP,* 297–99; Villard, *Fighting Years,* 191–94.

8. *Proceedings of the National Negro Conference 1909,* esp. 14–66, 197, 222–26 (resolutions).

9. Kellogg, *NAACP,* 37–45, 91; "Articles of Incorporation and Bylaws of the NAACP," *Crisis* 2 (September 1911): 193–94; Rudwick and Meier, "The Rise of the Black Secretariat in the NAACP, 1909–1935."

10. "N.A.A.C.P.," *Crisis* 1 (December 1910): 16–17.

11. "Agitation," *Crisis* 1 (December 1910): 11.

12. Jane Addams, "Social Control," *Crisis* 1 (January 1911): 22–23; on the origins of the NAACP in the progressive movement, see Meier and Bracey, "The NAACP as a Reform Movement"; Reed, "Organized Racial Reform during the Progressive Era."

13. Ovington, *The Walls Came Tumbling Down*, 111–12; Weiss, *The National Urban League 1910–1940*, esp. 47–60.

14. Washington, *Up from Slavery*, 218–25 (Atlanta speech), 234; on Booker T. Washington, see Harlan, *The Making of a Black Leader*, esp. 216–28; Harlan, *The Wizard of Tuskegee*; Meier, *Negro Thought in America, 1880–1915*.

15. Du Bois, *The Souls of Black Folk*, 43.

16. Ibid.; Aptheker, ed., *Pamphlets and Leaflets by W.E.B. Du Bois*, 55–58; on the relationship between Du Bois and Washington and on the Niagara Movement, see Lewis, *W.E.B. Du Bois: Biography of a Race*, 297–342.

17. "Our Own Consent," *Crisis* 5 (January 1913): 129; on the growth of *The Crisis*, see the various reports by Du Bois in Aptheker, ed., *Pamphlets and Leaflets by W.E.B. Du Bois*, 105–6, 137–39, 153–60.

18. On the relationship between the NAACP and Booker T. Washington, see Kellogg, *NAACP*, 67–88; Meier, "Booker T. Washington and the Rise of the NAACP."

19. Villard, *Fighting Years*, 4–9; Ovington, *The Walls Came Tumbling Down*, 5–8; Hixson, *Moorfield Storey and the Abolitionist Tradition*; McPherson, *The Abolitionist Legacy*, 368–93.

20. Ross, *J. E. Spingarn and the Rise of the NAACP*; on the role of Jews in the early NAACP, see Diner, *In the Almost Promised Land*, 118–54, 122; Lewis, "Parallels and Divergences."

21. Kellogg, *NAACP*, 21–24.

22. On the dissatisfaction with Du Bois's administrative work, see, e.g., Joel E. Spingarn to Villard, 7 April 1911; Villard to Spingarn, 16 April 1914, both in Joel E. Spingarn Papers, box 95–11.

23. Quoted in Kellogg, *NAACP*, 96. On Du Bois's work as editor of *The Crisis* and his quarrels with the board of directors, see Lewis, *W.E.B. Du Bois: Biography of a Race*, 408–24, 466–500. On the role of whites in the NAACP, see Berg, "Activists, Leaders, and Supporters."

24. Johnson, *Along This Way*, 308–10; Ross, *J. E. Spingarn and the Rise of the NAACP*, 79–80; Avery, *Up from Washington*, 54–57; White, *A Man Called White*, 35–38; Rudwick and Meier, "Integration vs. Separatism," 257.

25. On the Boston NAACP during its first decade, see Schneider, *Boston Confronts Jim Crow, 1890–1920*, 133–59; Reed, *The Chicago NAACP and the Rise of Black Professional Leadership, 1910–1966*, 17–43; Reed, "Organized Racial Reform during the Progressive Era."

26. Kellogg, *NAACP*, 118; NAACP, *Annual Report*, 1914; "N.A.A.C.P.," *Crisis* 19 (March 1920): 243; see, for example, the interviews with Lucille Black, longtime membership secretary of the NAACP, and Gloster Current, longtime director of branches, RJBOHC, interviews nos. 70 and 167.

27. Ross, *J. E. Spingarn and the Rise of the NAACP*, 52–58; see Moorfield Storey to NAACP secretary Roy Nash on his expenses in regard to NAACP cases, Joel E. Spingarn Papers, box 95-11.

28. Du Bois, *Dusk of Dawn*, 227.

29. Ross, *J. E. Spingarn and the Rise of the NAACP*, 53.

30. Undated memorandum (1913) by Du Bois to the NAACP board of directors, Aptheker, ed., *Pamphlets and Leaflets by W.E.B. Du Bois,* 116–22, 119.

31. Minutes of the Executive Committee Meeting, 29 November 1910, Joel E. Spingarn Papers, box 95-14; Articles of Incorporation in *Crisis* 2 (September 1911): 194; on the development of branch policies and individual branches during the NAACP's first decade, see Kellogg, *NAACP,* 117–37.

32. See the interviews with Lucille Black and Gloster Current, RJBOHC, interviews nos. 70 and 167.

33. See Johnson, *Along This Way,* 314–16, 356–57.

34. Kellogg, *NAACP,* 142–45, 221–35; NAACP, ed., *Thirty Years of Lynching in the United States*; Zangrando, *The NAACP Crusade against Lynching.*

35. See Mary Ovington to Joel Spingarn, 28 February 1917, Joel Spingarn Papers, box 95-9; Kellogg, *NAACP,* 247–50.

36. Ross, *J. E. Spingarn and the Rise of the NAACP,* 84–97; Kellogg, *NAACP,* 250–57.

37. "The Perpetual Dilemma," *Crisis* 13 (April 1917): 270–71; "Close Ranks," *Crisis* 16 (July 1918): 111; Du Bois, *Dusk of Dawn,* 253–58. The background of "Close Ranks" and the charge of opportunism remain controversial to date. See Lewis, *W.E.B. Du Bois: Biography of a Race,* 553–60; Jordan, "'The Damnable Dilemma'"; Ellis, "W.E.B. Du Bois and the Formation of Black Opinion in World War I."

38. Kellogg, *NAACP,* 256–66; Du Bois, *Dusk of Dawn,* 260–62; Schneider, *We Return Fighting,* 7–16; "Documents of the War," *Crisis* 18 (May 1919): 16–21; "Returning Soldiers," *Crisis* 18 (May 1919): 13–14.

39. "NAACP and Xmas," *Crisis* 21 (January 1922): 105.

40. Quoted in *Crisis* 2 (May 1911): 24.

41. On the genesis of the southern political system, see Kousser, *The Shaping of Southern Politics*; Perman, *Struggle for Mastery.*

42. Porter, *A History of Suffrage in the United States,* 220–21.

43. See the NAACP press release of 23 August 1929, NAACP Records I C 390.

44. See White's report, "Election Day in Florida," *Crisis* 21 (January 1921): 106–9; "Disfranchisement in Congress," *Crisis* 21 (February 1921): 165; letter and memorandum by Walter White to the chairman of the House Committee on the Census, Isaac Siegel (R-N.Y.), 3 December 1920; NAACP press release of 31 December 1920; NAACP booklet "Disfranchisement of Negro Americans in the Presidential Election of 1920," all in NAACP Records I C 284; Walter White to Dr. Seth Hills of Jacksonville, Florida, 6 January 1921, NAACP Records I C 389.

45. On the origins of the Fourteenth Amendment, see Foner, *Reconstruction,* 252–56.

46. Joseph C. Manning, "Suffrage Conditions in Democratic and Republican States Compared," *Crisis* 4 (October 1912): 304–8.

47. Albert Pillsbury, "Negro Disfranchisement as it Affects the White Men," *Proceedings of the National Negro Conference 1909,* 180.

48. Moorfield Storey to Mary C. Nerney, 6 August 1915, Arthur B. Spingarn Papers, box 28; see also Du Bois, "Reduced Representation in Congress," *Crisis* 21 (February 1921): 149–50.

49. Sherman, *The Republican Party and Black America,* 18, 75–77.

50. Telegram by Mary White Ovington to the chairman of the Census Committee, Isaac Siegel (R-N.Y.), 8 November 1920; James Weldon Johnson to Siegel, 3 December 1920; "Congressman to Wage Attack on Anti-Negro Election Legislation," *New York Call,* 6 December 1920, all in NAACP Records I C 284.

51. For the material, which was prepared by Du Bois, see "The Election and Democracy," *Crisis* 21 (February 1921): 156–60.

52. "Tinkham Presses Fight on Representation," *New York Times,* 5 January 1921; "House to Have 483 by New Measure," *New York Herald,* 7 January 1921, copies in NAACP Records I C 399; letters of 11 and 14 January 1921 by Walter White to Tinkham, NAACP Records I C 399; "House Delays Inquiry Into Negro Vote Charges," *New York Tribune,* 7 May 1921, copy in NAACP Records I C 285.

53. Sherman, *The Republican Party and Black America,* 169–71.

54. *Williams v. Mississippi,* 170 U.S. 213 (1897); *Giles v. Harris,* 189 U.S. 475 (1903); *Giles v. Teasley,* 193 U.S. 146 (1904).

55. Pillsbury, "Negro Disfranchisement as it Affects the White Men," *Proceedings of the National Negro Conference 1909,* 181; Moorfield Storey to Mary C. Nerney, 6 August 1915, Arthur B. Spingarn Papers, box 28.

56. Du Bois, *The Souls of Black Folk,* 46; Du Bois, "Reduced Representation in Congress," *Crisis* 21 (February 1921): 149–50.

57. See Stevens, *Literacy, Law, and Social Order,* esp. 64–83.

58. Walter White to Carter Glass, 12 September 1938, NAACP Records I C 285.

59. Tushnet, *The NAACP's Legal Strategy against Segregated Education, 1925–1950.*

60. Logan, *The Attitude of the Southern White Press toward Negro Suffrage,* 68.

61. "Decision for the South to Ponder," *New York Evening World,* 9 March 1927; "Nullification in Texas," *New York World,* 26 July 1927, copies in NAACP Records I D 64; circular letter by James Weldon Johnson to newspapers editors, 18 November 1927, NAACP Records I C 390.

62. Mary Church Terrell, "The Justice of Woman Suffrage," *Crisis* 4 (September 1912): 243–45; Ellen DuBois, *Feminism and Suffrage,* 60–63, 162–80.

63. Du Bois, "Votes for Women," *Crisis* 4 (September 1912): 234; Adella Hunt Logan, "Colored Women as Voters," *Crisis* 4 (September 1912): 242; Martha Gruening, "Two Suffrage Movements," *Crisis* 4 (September 1912): 245–46; Du Bois, "Votes for Women," *Crisis* 15 (November 1917): 8.

64. Ida Husted Harper to Elizabeth C. Carter, 18 March 1919, NAACP Records I C 407.

65. "Denies South Carolina Negro Women Want Vote," *World,* 18 February 1919, copy in NAACP Records I C 407; John Shillady to Alice Paul, 21 March 1919; Paul to Shillady, 28 March 1919; Paul to Mary Ovington, undated; Paul to the editor of the NAACP Branch Bulletin, 30 March 1919; NWP, "Facts About the Suffrage Amendment," undated (1919), all in NAACP Records I C 407; on Alice Paul and the NWP, see Lunardini, *From Equal Suffrage to Equal Rights.*

66. Resolution by Senator Gay of Louisiana, 13 February 1919; Resolution by Senator Jones of New Mexico, 28 February 1919; John Shillady to Carrie Chapman Catt, 9 April 1919 (quotations); Shillady to Alice Paul, 10 April 1919; Catt to Shillady, 6 May 1919;

Shillady to Charles Nagel, 19 May 1919; Nagel to Shillady, 22 May 1919, all in NAACP Records I C 407.

67. "Votes for Women," *Crisis* 15 (November 1917): 8; NAACP release, 15 September 1920; Chas. A. J. McPherson to the New York office of the NAACP, 18 November 1920; W. E. Morton to the New York office of the NAACP, 25 November 1920, all in NAACP Records I C 284. The box contains numerous other reports of discrimination against black women voters in the South.

68. Mary Ovington to Florence Kelley and fifty other members of the NWP advisory board, 6 December 1920; Florence Kelley to Ovington, 22 December 1920; Ovington to Mary Talbert, 30 December 1920; Ovington to Alice Paul, 4 January 1921, all in NAACP Records I C 384; Ovington to Charlotte Atwood, 17 January 1921; Ovington to Alice Paul, 24 January 1921; Addie W. Hunton to A. H. Grimke, 29 January 1921; Hunton to James Weldon Johnson, 7 February 1921; Mary Church Terrell's speech, undated; official program of the NWP convention, 15–18 February 1921, all in NAACP Records I C 407; Ella Rush Murray, "The Woman's Party and the Violation of the 19th Amendment," *Crisis* 21 (April 1921): 259–61; Walter White to Gaeta W. Boyer, 4 September 1924, NAACP Records I C 278.

69. Florence Kelley to James Weldon Johnson, 19 April 1921; Addie Hunton to Johnson, 20 April 1921; Hunton to Mrs. Louis F. Slade, 16 May 1921, all in NAACP Records I C 407.

70. Walter White to Alice Paul, 18 August 1924, NAACP Records I C 278. The background was a memorial service for Inez Milholland (1886–1916), a devoted NWP suffragist and daughter of NAACP cofounder John Milholland, at which the NWP allegedly tried to prevent black guests from speaking. See the materials in ibid.

71. On Garvey and the UNIA, see Cronon, *The Story of Marcus Garvey and the Universal Negro Improvement Association*; Stein, *The World of Marcus Garvey*; Levine, "Marcus Garvey and the Politics of Revitalization."

72. "The U.N.I.A.," *Crisis* 25 (January 1923): 122; for a skeptical view on the UNIA's inflated membership figures, see also Schneider, *We Return Fighting*, 140–41.

73. "The Rise of the West Indian," *Crisis* 20 (September 1920): 214–15. For a comprehensive account of the ideological and personal rift between Garvey and Du Bois, see Lewis, *W.E.B. Du Bois: The Fight for Equality and the American Century*, 50–84.

74. Lewis, *W.E.B. Du Bois: The Fight for Equality and the American Century*, 72; Du Bois, "Marcus Garvey," *Crisis* 21 (December 1920): 58–60, and (January 1921): 112–15.

75. James Weldon Johnson to Marcus Garvey, 20 January 1922; Garvey's angry reply, 21 January 1922, both in NAACP Records I C 304.

76. Cronon, *The Story of Marcus Garvey and the Universal Negro Improvement Association*, 105–10, 187–91; Stein, *The World of Marcus Garvey*, 153–61.

77. Pickens to Garvey, July 1922; draft of the letter to U.S. Attorney General Henry Daugherty, 15 January 1923, both in NAACP Records I C 304; Du Bois, "Demagog," *Crisis* 23 (April 1922): 252; Du Bois, "The Black Star Line," *Crisis* 24 (September 1922): 210–14; Du Bois, "UNIA," *Crisis* 25 (January 1923): 120–22; Du Bois, "Back to Africa," *Century Magazine* (February 1923), quoted in NAACP press release, 25 January 1923, NAACP

Records I C 304; Garvey quoted in Lewis, *W.E.B. Du Bois. The Fight for Equality and the American Century*, 80, 82.

78. NAACP press releases, 18 May and 22 June 1923, NAACP Records I C 304; Du Bois, "A Lunatic or a Traitor," *Crisis* 28 (May 1924): 8–9; Cronon, *The Story of Marcus Garvey and the Universal Negro Improvement Association*, 192.

79. "The Drive," *Crisis* 22 (May 1921): 8.

80. Membership figures according to a memorandum by R. Williams to Gloster Current, 15 June 1954, NAACP Records II A 202.

81. On Weber's definition and concept of charismatic authority, which I use loosely here, see Weber, *Wirtschaft und Gesellschaft*, 140–48.

Chapter 2. Educating Black Voters and White Politicians

1. *Proceedings of the National Negro Conference 1909*, 224; Smith and Horton, *Historical Statistics of Black America*, 2:1589–90.

2. On the Republican retreat from the southern states, see Vallely, "National Parties and Racial Disfranchisement"; Sherman, *The Republican Party and Black America*.

3. James Weldon Johnson, "The Gentlemen's Agreement and the Negro Vote," *Crisis* 28 (October 1924): 260–64.

4. Smith and Horton, *Historical Statistics of Black America*, 2:1319–20, 1505–6.

5. See the quote from the *New York Evening Post* and Johnson's reply in the NAACP press release of 15 April 1927, NAACP Records I C 390.

6. Du Bois, "Lessons in Government," *Crisis* 12 (October 1916): 269.

7. See, e.g., Du Bois, "Voting," *Crisis* 1 (December 1910): 11; editorial, "Colored Votes," *Crisis* 25 (January 1923): 117–18.

8. See, e.g., the NAACP press release of 5 October 1930 on its campaign against Senator Roscoe McCullock (R-Ohio), NAACP Records I C 391; Walter White to Nathan Strauss, 16 September 1920 and 26 October 1920, NAACP Records I C 284.

9. Du Bois, "The Harding Political Plan," *Crisis* 23 (January 1922): 106; Kellogg, *NAACP*, 127; Du Bois, "Political Rebirth and the Office Seeker," *Crisis* 21 (January 1921): 104; see various resolutions cited by Walter White in his decline to join a committee for Roosevelt and Wallace, letter to Helen Hall of 29 October 1940, NAACP Records II A 476.

10. See William English Walling, "Salvation by the Ballot," *Crisis* 32 (September 1926): 227–30.

11. In 1948, the NAACP director of public relations, Henry Lee Moon, published his *Balance of Power: The Negro Vote*. For a critique of Moon, see Chuck Stone, *Black Political Power in America*, esp. 42–44.

12. Du Bois, "Where We Are," *Crisis* 28 (October 1924): 247–48; Du Bois, "The Elections," *Crisis* 28 (December 1924): 55–56; U.S. Department of Commerce, *Historical Statistics of the United States: Colonial Times to 1970*, 2:1071–72.

13. Du Bois, "Mr. Taft," *Crisis* 2 (October 1911): 243; editorial, "Mr. Roosevelt," *Crisis* 4 (September 1912): 235–36; Sherman, *The Republican Party and Black America*, 104–9.

14. Jane Addams, "The Progressive Party and the Negro," *Crisis* 5 (November 1912): 30–31; Du Bois, "The Last Word in Politics," *Crisis* 5 (November 1912): 29.

15. Du Bois, "The Election," *Crisis* 5 (December 1912): 75–76; "An Open Letter to Woodrow Wilson," *Crisis* 5 (March 1913): 236–37; Villard, *Fighting Years*, 236–41; Kellogg, *NAACP*, 159–65.

16. See the open letters of 15 August 1913 and September 1913, printed in Aptheker, ed., *Writings by W.E.B. Du Bois in Periodicals Edited by Others*, 3:66; Kellogg, *NAACP*, 164–77.

17. Du Bois, "Political," *Crisis* 4 (September 1912): 233; editorial, "Mr. Roosevelt," *Crisis* 4 (September 1912): 236; editorial, "The Election," *Crisis* 5 (December 1912): 75–76; "An Open Letter to Woodrow Wilson," *Crisis* 5 (March 1913): 236–37.

18. Du Bois, "The Presidential Campaign," *Crisis* 12 (October 1916): 268; quote from an undated speech by Hughes in Memphis, Tennessee, *Crisis* 13 (November 1916): 33–34; editorial, *Crisis* 13 (December 1916): 59.

19. See, e.g., James Weldon Johnson's telegram to Senator George Moses (R-N.H.), 11 December 1919; Mary White Ovington to Rep. Isaac Siegel (R-N.Y.), 8 November 1920, both in NAACP Records I C 284.

20. Walter White to the Republican National Committee, 30 July 1920; Jake Hamon (Ardmore, Oklahoma) to Ralph Sollitt (Republican National Committee), 21 August 1920; Walter White to Ralph Sollitt, 2 September 1920; report of the Sapulca, Oklahoma, NAACP branch, 11 October 1920, all in NAACP Records I C 284.

21. NAACP press release, 14 April 1920, NAACP Records I C 284; Schlesinger, *History of American Presidential Elections*, 3:2413; Johnson, *Along This Way*, 358–60; Johnson's report on his meeting with Harding, 9 August 1920, NAACP Records I C 388; Sherman, *The Republican Party and Black America*, 139–42.

22. NAACP press release, 15 September 1920, NAACP Records I C 284; Du Bois, "The Republicans and the Black Voter," *Nation* 110 (5 June 1920), printed in Aptheker, ed., *Writings by W.E.B. Du Bois in Periodicals Edited by Others*, 2:139–42.

23. Du Bois, "Political Rebirth and the Office Seeker," *Crisis* 21 (January 1921): 104; Du Bois's telegram to James W. Johnson, 11 January 1921; Johnson's report on his meeting with Harding, 15 January 1921, both in NAACP Records I C 389.

24. "Coolidge Tells Negroes of Aid Given by South," *Atlanta Constitution*, 20 January 1921; "Republicans Aim To Win Over the South, Says Hays," *New York Tribune*, 3 February 1921; William H. Taft, "Federal Offices for Negroes," *Boston Evening*, 8 January 1921; Robert R. Church to James Johnson, 27 May 1921; Johnson's reply, 1 June 1921, all in NAACP Records I C 389.

25. Du Bois, "The Harding Political Plan," *Crisis* 23 (January 1922): 105–6; "Third Parties," *Crisis* 25 (January 1923): 105. On the GOP purges in the South, see Sherman, *The Republican Party and Black America*, 152–58.

26. For the NAACP's protests against the political influence of the Klan, see the press releases of 20 November 1923 and 11 December 1923, NAACP Records I C 389; press release of 26 May 1924; open letter to Coolidge of 31 May 1924; letter by James W. Johnson to the Republican Committee on Resolutions, 9 June 1924; open letter to Coolidge, 16 September 1924, all in NAACP Records I C 390; on the parties' and candidates' stand on the Klan, see Sherman, *The Republican Party and Black America*, 205–8; Du Bois, "Vote," *Crisis* 28 (July 1924): 104.

27. Du Bois, *Dusk of Dawn*, 234–35; "The Presidential Election," *Crisis* 12 (October 1916): 268.

28. NAACP press releases, 3 July 1924, 11 July 1924, NAACP Records I C 390; Du Bois, "La Follette," *Crisis* 28 (August 1924): 154.

29. See the press releases of the La Follette for President Committee, 6 and 11 August 1924; G. Victor Cools to James W. Johnson, 6 August 1924; NAACP press release, 25 July 1924; Pickens to Gilbert E. Roe, 7 August 1924; Pickens to Victor Cools, 11 August 1924; Pickens to Myrtle Foster Cook, 6 October 1924 (quote), all in NAACP Records I C 390; "How Shall We Vote? A Symposium," *Crisis* 29 (November 1924): 13.

30. Walter White to Victor Cools, 14 August 1924; White to Ernest Gruening, 17 September 1924 (quote); James W. Johnson to Ernest Gruening, 18 September 1924, all in NAACP Records I C 390.

31. James Weldon Johnson, "The Gentlemen's Agreement and the Negro Vote," *Crisis* 28 (October 1924): 260–64.

32. Du Bois, "The Election," *Crisis* 29 (December 1924): 55.

33. William Borah, "Negro Suffrage," *Crisis* 33 (January 1927): 132.

34. White, *A Man Called White*, 80–81; Du Bois, "Postscript," *Crisis* 35 (May 1928): 168.

35. Resolutions of the 1924 NAACP annual convention, press release of 3 July 1924, NAACP Records I C 390.

36. White, *A Man Called White*, 99–101; Weiss, *Farewell to the Party of Lincoln*, 7–9.

37. Du Bois, "Is Al Smith Afraid of the South?" *Nation* 127 (17 October 1928), printed in Aptheker, ed., *Writings by W.E.B. Du Bois in Periodicals Edited by Others*, 2:296–301; "How Shall We Vote? A Symposium," *Crisis* 35 (November 1928): 168, 186.

38. Weiss, *Farewell to the Party of Lincoln*, 9–11.

39. White, *A Man Called White*, 104; for an interpretation of Hoover's racial policies that stresses his progressive visions, see Lisio, *Hoover, Blacks, and Lily-Whites*, esp. xiii–xix. Lisio concedes, however, that Hoover's ignorance and silence on racial matters caused his vision to founder badly. For a less benign view of Hoover, see Sherman, *The Republican Party and Black America*, 224–51; and for a very critical view, see O'Reilly, *Nixon's Piano*, 102–8.

40. On the legislative history of the Dyer bill, see Zangrando, *The NAACP Crusade against Lynching*, 51–71; Sherman, *The Republican Party and Black America*, 178–99; Du Bois, "The Harding Political Plan," *Crisis* 23 (January 1922): 106.

41. James Johnson to Moorfield Storey, 4 February 1922; William Borah to Moorfield Storey, 9 February 1922; Johnson to Storey, 18 May 1922; Borah to Storey, 1 June 1922, all in Moorfield Story Papers, box 2.

42. NAACP press releases of 22 September 1922 and 6 October 1922; Walter White to Oscar Baker, 5 October 1922, all in NAACP Records I C 389; see also the summary by Du Bois, "Colored Votes," *Crisis* 25 (January 1923): 117–18.

43. Walter White to David Minahan, 14 October 1922; James Johnson to R. W. Stewart, 24 October 1922; NAACP press release, 9 November 1922, all in NAACP Records I C 389.

44. Dyer to James Johnson, 10 October 1922; Johnson's reply, 11 October 1922; Geo L. Vaughn to Johnson, 16 October 1922; Dyer to Johnson, 21 October 1922, all in NAACP Records I C 389.

45. NAACP press release, 17 November 1922, NAACP Records I C 389; Du Bois, "Colored Votes," *Crisis* 25 (January 1923): 117.

46. Du Bois, "The Dyer Bill," *Crisis* 25 (January 1923): 118–19.

47. Du Bois, "Colored Votes," *Crisis* 25 (January 1923): 118; "Political Straws," *Crisis* 26 (July 1923): 124–25.

48. NAACP press release, 28 March 1930, NAACP Records I C 397. For an exhaustive treatment of the Parker fight, see Goings, *The NAACP Comes of Age*. Goings, however, tends to exaggerate the impact of the NAACP's opposition. See also Lisio, *Hoover, Blacks, and Lily-Whites*, 205–31; Sherman, *The Republican Party and Black America*, 239–46. The NAACP's lobbying efforts are documented in the NAACP Records I C 397 and 398.

49. White, *A Man Called White*, 104–11; Goings, *The NAACP Comes of Age*, 37–53; Lisio, *Hoover, Blacks, and Lily-Whites*, 228–30; NAACP press release, 23 May 1930, NAACP Records I C 397; Du Bois, "The Defeat of Judge Parker," *Crisis* 37 (July 1930): 225–27, 248.

50. Walter White's circular letter to the NAACP branches, 8 May 1930, NAACP Records I G 224; Du Bois, "The Defeat of Judge Parker," *Crisis* 37 (July 1930): 225; Goings, *The NAACP Comes of Age*, 57–59.

51. Minutes of the board of directors' meeting, 14 July 1930, NAACP Records I A 2.

52. "Finish of the Parker Fight," *Crisis* 41 (December 1934): 364; NAACP press release, 9 November 1934, NAACP Records I C 392; White, *A Man Called White*, 113.

53. NAACP press release, 5 October 1930, NAACP Records I C 391; William Pickens, "The Negro Voter and Allen," *Crisis* 37 (October 1930): 338; Goings, *The NAACP Comes of Age*, 59–69.

54. "Finish of the Parker Fight," *Crisis* 41 (December 1934): 364.

55. See the folders "Politics General" in NAACP Records I C 391, 392, 393.

56. NAACP press releases, 29 May 1932 and 24 June 1932, NAACP Records I C 391.

57. Schlesinger, *History of American Presidential Elections*, 3:2741–83, 2759; Walter White to Franklin D. Roosevelt, 20 June 1932; response by Roosevelt's secretary, 21 June 1932, NAACP Records I C 391.

58. "Socialists and Communists Bid for the Negro Vote," *Crisis* 39 (September 1932): 279–80, 300; "Vote for Hoover," *Crisis* 39 (October 1932): 313–14, 332; "Why Vote for Roosevelt," *Crisis* 39 (November 1932): 343–44.

59. NAACP press release, 17 October 1932, NAACP Records I C 391; Weiss, *Farewell to the Party of Lincoln*, 29–33.

60. NAACP press releases, 9 November 1932, 11 November 1932 (quote), 18 November 1932, NAACP Records I C 391.

61. Walter White to Franklin Roosevelt, 4 January 1933; response by Roosevelt's secretary, Marvin McIntyre, 22 February 1933, NAACP Records I C 78; White, *A Man Called White*, 168–70. White mistakenly dates the appointment in 1935. See Weiss, *Farewell to the Party of Lincoln*, 105–6.

62. NAACP, *Annual Report*, 1931, 1932, 1933; Walter White to Fred Knollenberg, 20 December 1932, NAACP Records I D 63; Bates, "A New Crowd Challenges the Agenda of the Old Guard in the NAACP, 1933–1941," 357–59. On the black plight during the Great Depression, see Wolters, *Negroes and the Great Depression: The Problem of Economic Recov-*

ery; Sitkoff, *A New Deal for Blacks*; Kirby, *Black Americans in the Roosevelt Era*; Sullivan, *Days of Hope*.

63. Du Bois, "Segregation," *Crisis* 41 (January 1934): 20.

64 .William H. Hastie, "DuBois, Ex-Leader of Negroes," *New Negro Opinion*, 25 January 1934, copy in NAACP Records I C 287; Walter White to Du Bois, 15 January 1934; Du Bois to White, 17 January 1934, both in NAACP Records I C 287.

65. Du Bois, "The NAACP and Segregation," *Crisis* 41 (February 1934): 52.

66. "Segregation—A Symposium," *Crisis* 41 (March 1934): 79–82.

67. Minutes of the NAACP board meetings, 12 December 1932 (quote), 9 January 1933, NAACP Records I A 3. For a comprehensive account of Du Bois's motivations and activities before breaking with the NAACP, see Lewis, *W.E.B. Du Bois: The Fight for Equality and the American Century*, 302–48, esp. 316–17, 335–48, 339 (quote).

68. Du Bois, "Segregation in the North," *Crisis* 41 (April 1934): 115–17. On White's vulnerability to the charge of "passing," see the exchange between him and Joel Spingarn. Joel Spingarn to White, 12 January 1934; White to Spingarn, 15 January 1934, both in NAACP Records I C 287. White insisted that he could have "stopped living as a Negro and passed as white" long ago. See also Janken, *White*, 188–91.

69. Minutes of the NAACP board meetings, 9 April 1934, 23 April 1934, 14 May 1934, 9 July 1934, all in NAACP Records I A 3; Du Bois, "Segregation," and "The Board of Directors on Segregation," *Crisis* 41 (May 1934): 147, 149; see also Du Bois, "Counsels of Despair," *Crisis* 41 (June 1934): 182; Du Bois to the board of directors, 1 June 1934, 26 June 1934, both in NAACP Records I C 287; "Dr. Du Bois Resigns," *Crisis* 41 (August 1934): 245.

70. "Dr. Du Bois Resigns," *Crisis* 41 (August 1934): 245; Minutes of the NAACP board meeting, 9 July 1934, NAACP Records I A 3.

71. "Address to the Country," Twenty-third Annual Conference of the National Association for the Advancement of Colored People, Washington, D.C., May 17–22, 1932, Arthur B. Spingarn Papers, box 26; see the draft of the economic program by Arthur Spingarn, Herbert Seligman, and Du Bois, Arthur Spingarn Papers, box 28.

72. Mary Ovington to Joel Spingarn, 22 August 1933, Joel E. Spingarn Papers, box 95-9; Ross, *J. E. Spingarn and the Rise of the NAACP*, 169–85; Du Bois, *Dusk of Dawn*, 299–302; Sitkoff, *A New Deal for Blacks*, 251–53; Francis Q. Morton, "Segregation," *Crisis* 41 (August 1934): 244–45.

73. Minutes of the NAACP board meeting, 9 July 1934, NAACP Records I A 3; Walter White to Abram Harris, 12 July 1934; "Future Plan and Program of the NAACP," both in NAACP Records I A 29.

74. Mary Ovington to Joel Spingarn, 23 September 1934; Memorandum by Roy Wilkins to Walter White, 19 September 1934, both in NAACP Records I A 29.

75. See the final Report of Future Plan and Program of the NAACP and the memorandum to the delegates of the 1935 annual conference, 14 June 1935; NAACP press release, 30 June 1935; NAACP press release, 28 June 1935, all in NAACP Records I B 11; Bates, "A New Crowd Challenges the Agenda of the Old Guard in the NAACP, 1933–1941," 352–56, exaggerates the resistance against addressing economic issues within the NAACP leadership.

76. Sitkoff, *A New Deal for Blacks*, 256–57; Bates, "A New Crowd Challenges the Agenda of the Old Guard in the NAACP, 1933–1941," 368–77; Zieger, *The CIO*, 122–24; Hamilton and Hamilton, *The Dual Agenda*, esp. 8–42.

77. On the attitude of the American communists toward the race question, see the useful synthesis by Hutchinson, *Blacks and Reds*, esp. 29–136; also see Fried, *Communism in America*, 103–6, 146–58; on the black Alabama communists, see Kelley, *Hammer and Hoe*.

78. On the Scottsboro case, see the standard account by Carter, *Scottsboro*.

79. "NAACP Joins the Lynching Mob," *Southern Worker*, 13 June 1931; Harry Haywood, "The Road to Negro Liberation. Report to the Eighth Convention of the Communist Party of the USA, Cleveland, April 2–8, 1934," both in Foner and Shapiro, *American Communism and Black Americans*, 125–46, 262–64; Fried, *Communism in America*, 150–54; Carter, *Scottsboro*, 51–103; for an account that is highly critical of Walter White's maneuvering in the case, see Janken, *White*, 148–55.

80. Resolutions of the 24th annual convention of the NAACP in Chicago, 29 June–2 July 1933, Arthur B. Spingarn Papers, box 26.

81. See, e.g., White's reports for the board meetings of September and October 1933, NAACP Records I A 17; telegram by the board of directors to FDR, 11 February 1935, NAACP Records I A 3; NAACP press release, 14 June 1935; resolutions of the NAACP annual conference, 25–30 June 1935, both in NAACP Records I B 11; on racial discrimination under the New Deal, see Sitkoff, *A New Deal for Blacks*, 42–57.

82. Sitkoff, *A New Deal for Blacks*, 58–83; Weiss, *Farewell to the Party of Lincoln*, 142–56; Kirby, *Black Americans in the Roosevelt Era*, 106–51; Sullivan, *Days of Hope*, 41–67.

83. M. Dunell to Harry Hopkins, 21 May 1938; on the background, see Hopkins's letter to the WPA workers, 5 May 1938; Alfred Smith to Walter White, 6 October 1938; George Murphy to White, 12 October 1938, all in NAACP Records I C 285. There are many other letters to Hopkins in the same records.

84. NAACP press release, 10 January 1936, NAACP Records I C 392; Walter White, "An Estimate of the 1936 Vote," *Crisis* 43 (February 1936): 46–47.

85. See Walter White's letter to GOP candidates, 5 March 1936; NAACP catalogue of demands to the parties, 9 and 23 June 1936; Walter White to Franklin Roosevelt, 26 June 1936, all in NAACP Records I C 392; Schlesinger, *History of American Presidential Elections*, 3:2851–56; Weiss, *Farewell to the Party of Lincoln*, 180–203; Francis R. Rivers, "The Negro Should Support Landon," *Crisis* 43 (October 1936): 296–97; "Roosevelt the Humanitarian," *Crisis* 43 (October 1936): 298–99.

86. NAACP press release, 9 October 1936; White to Landon, 14 October 1936; NAACP press release, 26 October 1936, all in NAACP Records I C 392; on the NAACP's electoral politics in the 1930s and 1940s and the issues of nonpartisanship, also see the recent, though rather superficial, essay by Topping, "'Supporting Our Friends and Defeating Our Enemies': Militancy and Nonpartisanship in the NAACP, 1936–1948."

87. NAACP press release, 10 October 1936; Charles White to Walter White, 17 October 1936 (and numerous other protests); White's reply, 19 October 1936, all in NAACP Records I C 392.

88. Weiss, *Farewell to the Party of Lincoln*, 205–8; Walter White to Congressman Bolton (R-Ohio), 5 November 1936, NAACP Records I C 392.

89. NAACP press release, 6 November 1936; telegrams by Joel Spingarn and Walter White to FDR, 4 November 1936, all in NAACP Records I C 392.

90. On the growing resistance among southern lawmakers against the New Deal, see Egerton, *Speak Now against the Day*, 110–20; Sikoff, *A New Deal for Blacks*, 102–23; Zangrando, *The NAACP Crusade against Lynching*, 98–165.

91. NAACP press release, 4 February 1940, NAACP Records II A 473; Weiss, *Farewell to the Party of Lincoln*, 286–95.

92. Weiss, *Farewell to the Party of Lincoln*, 209–35, 212.

93. Du Bois, "The Harding Political Plan," *Crisis* 23 (January 1922): 105–6.

94. Rosenstone and Hansen, *Mobilization, Participation and Democracy in America*, 5.

95. Du Bois, "Political Rebirth and the Office Seeker," *Crisis* 21 (January 1921): 104.

Chapter 3. Chasing the Rainbow? Black Voting Rights in the Courts

1. Du Bois, "Segregation in the North," *Crisis* 41 (April 1934): 115. For the controversy on voluntary segregation, see chapter two. Bunche, "A Critical Analysis of the Tactics and Programs of Minority Groups," 308–20; on the debate between the "legalists" and the "economic instrumentalists" in the NAACP, see Tushnet, *The NAACP's Legal Strategy against Segregated Education*, 8–13.

2. See the letter by A. G. Perkins to J. B. Grigsby and O. P. Dewalt, NAACP leaders from Houston, Texas, 24 July 1928, NAACP Records I D 64.

3. See Rosenberg, *The Hollow Hope*, esp. the conclusions, 336–43. In August 1955, NAACP lawyer Thurgood Marshall complained that after the two *Brown* decisions by the Supreme Court, "our supporters are under the impression that the fight is over." Marshall's circular letter to the editors of black newspapers, 18 August 1955, *Birmingham World* Correspondence, 1102.1.6; on the backlash from white racists after *Brown*, see Bartley, *The Rise of Massive Resistance*; Klarman, "How *Brown* Changed Race Relations."

4. Rosenberg, *The Hollow Hope*, 57–63.

5. Ibid., 145–50, 340–41.

6. Klarman, "Is the Supreme Court Sometimes Irrelevant? Race and the Southern Criminal Justice System in the 1940s," esp. 119, footnote 1, which documents the controversy over Gerald Rosenberg's book, 120 (quote), 143–48, 149–53.

7. On the structural preconditions of the civil rights movement, see McAdam, *Political Process and the Development of Black Insurgency*; on the dominance of the race issue in the South, see V. O. Key's classic study, *Southern Politics in State and Nation*; on lily-white Republicanism, see chapter two.

8. "The N.A.A.C.P.," *Crisis* 2 (May 1911): 25.

9. "Pink Franklin's Reprieve," *Crisis* 1 (February 1911): 15; Kellogg, *NAACP*, 57–65, 293; see also the interview with Arthur Spingarn, who coordinated the NAACP's legal work from 1910 to 1936, RJBOHC, interview no. 165.

10. *Moore v. Dempsey*, 261 U.S. 86 (1923); for a comprehensive account of the so-called Arkansas riot cases, see Cortner, *A Mob Intent on Death*; for the limited impact of the

Court's criminal justice decisions on the treatment of black defendants in the South, see Klarman, "Is the Supreme Court Sometimes Irrelevant?" 120–38.

11. On the Sweet trials, see Ovington, *Walls Came Tumbling Down*, 198–213; Schneider, *We Return Fighting*, 301–17; for a new comprehensive account, see Boyle, *Arc of Justice*.

12. *Plessy v. Ferguson*, 163 U.S. 537 (1896); *Williams v. Mississippi*, 170 U.S. 213 (1897); *Giles v. Harris*, 189 U.S. 475 (1903); *Giles v. Teasley*, 193 U.S. 146 (1904).

13. *Guinn v. United States*, 238 U.S. 347 (1915); Elliott, *The Rise of Guardian Democracy*, 71.

14. *Guinn v. United States*, 238 U.S. 347, 356 (1915); see the letter of Assistant U.S. Attorney General John B. Keenan to Walter White, 28 December 1934, NAACP Records I C 285.

15. Storey's brief in *Guinn v. United States*, 238 U.S. 347 (1915), 353.

16. *Buchanan v. Warley*, 245 U.S. 60 (1917); Kellogg, *NAACP*, 183–87; *Shelley v. Kramer*, 334 U.S. 1 (1948).

17. See the folders "Voting Discrimination" in NAACP Records I C 284, 285, 286, which contain a host of legal material related to disfranchisement in the period from 1920 to 1936. The following is a digest of this material.

18. See, e.g., the letter by Walter White to E. F. Sanders of High Point, North Carolina, 14 August 1922, NAACP Records I C 389.

19. See the letter by Butler W. Nance of Greenwood to Moorfield Storey, 14 April 1919; John Shillady to Storey, 19 April 1919, NAACP Records I C 284.

20. NAACP special legal assistant William T. Andrews to W. H. Harrison, 17 April 1928, NAACP Records I C 390; also see a similar letter by Andrews to Mack Holiman of Hattiesburg, Mississippi, 30 January 1928, NAACP Records I C 285.

21. See the letter from R. H. Hines to Shillady, 14 September 1918; reply and memorandum by John Shillady, 5 October 1918; circular letter to all Texas branches, 21 October 1918; "Judge Erwin Clark Holds Negroes May Vote in City Primary, Feb.18," *Waco Times*, 16 February 1919, NAACP Records I C 284.

22. John A. Hibbler of Little Rock to William Andrews, 30 August 1929; Walter White to Hibbler (quote), 5 September 1929; Walter White to Luther Moore of Little Rock, 13 November 1929, NAACP Records I D 44; Roy Wilkins to Alonzo P. Holly of Miami, Florida, 25 May 1932, NAACP Records I C 285.

23. On the NAACP's relationship with the Garland Fund and the Margold report, see Tushnet, *The NAACP's Legal Strategy against Segregated Education*, 7–8, 13–20, 25–29; Tushnet, *Making Civil Rights Law*, 11–13.

24. Hixson, *Moorfield Storey*, 134–45; interview with Arthur B. Spingarn, RJBOHC, interview no. 165; Meier and Rudwick, "Attorneys Black and White," 128–73, esp. 130–36.

25. Arthur Spingarn's letter to Nathan Margold, 16 October 1930, Arthur B. Spingarn Papers, box 33; Grand Master Florida Ku Klucks to W. R. O'Neal, 28 October 1920, NAACP Records I C 285; see also *Crisis* 21 (January 1921): 107.

26. Du Bois, "Disfranchisement," *Crisis* 30 (June 1930): 62–63.

27. Argersinger, "Electoral Processes," 506–7.

28. See John Shillady to R. H. Hines, 5 October 1918, NAACP Records I C 284; Hine, *Black Victory*, 54–59.

29. Hine, *Black Victory*, 25–42; Kousser, *The Shaping of Southern Politics*, 196–209.

30. Quoted in "The White Primary," *Crisis* 30 (May 1925): 33–34.

31. Hine, *Black Victory*, 72–79; NAACP press releases, 3 April 1925 (quote), 16 October 1925, NAACP Records I D 63; Du Bois, "The White Primary," *Crisis* 30 (May 1925): 33–34; "The 'White Primary' Fight," *Crisis* 30 (July 1925): 123–24; "The White Primary Fight," *Crisis* 31 (December 1925): 72.

32. *Nixon v. Herndon*, 273 U.S. 536 (1927), 536–39; NAACP press releases, 3 January 1927, 25 February 1927, NAACP Records I D 64; "The White Primary," *Crisis* 34 (March 1927): 9–10.

33. *Nixon v. Herndon*, 273 U.S. 536 (1927), 540–41.

34. "An Invited Slap," *Columbia Record*, 10 March 1927; "Texas Plans Modified Primary Law to Replace One Thrown Out by Court," *Columbia Record*, 8 March 1927, copies in NAACP Records I D 64.

35. NAACP press release, 8 March 1927, NAACP Records I D 64; Walter White, "The Supreme Court and the NAACP," *Crisis* 34 (May 1927): 82–83; "The N.A.A.C.P. Battle Front: The Year's Work," *Crisis* 35 (February 1928): 49.

36. See the overview in Hine, *Black Victory*, 90–108; on the Virginia case *West v. Bliley*, see NAACP press releases 24 January 1930, 21 March 1930, 13 June 1930 (quote), NAACP Records I D 68; P. B. Young of Norfolk, Virginia, to Thurgood Marshall, 9 April 1937; H. E. Fauntleroy of Petersburg, Virginia, to Thurgood Marshall, 23 April 1937, NAACP Records I C 285.

37. NAACP press release, 27 July 1928, NAACP Records I D 64; Hine, *Black Victory*, 109–17.

38. Walter White to Knollenberg, 20 August 1930; Knollenberg's reply, 23 August 1930; Arthur Spingarn to Nathan Margold, 16 October 1930, all in Arthur Spingarn Papers, box 33.

39. See *Nixon v. Condon*, 286 U.S. 73 (1932), 74–79, 81–89, 89–106.

40. Circular letter by Walter White to the press, 3 May 1932; NAACP press release, 6 May 1932, NAACP Records I D 63. On the Parker fight, see chapter two.

41. William Pickens, "Next Step in the Primary Voting Fight," NAACP press release, 7 May 1932, NAACP Records I D 63.

42. NAACP press release, 13 May 1932; Carter Wesley to Fred Knollenberg, 30 May 1932, NAACP Records I D 63.

43. NAACP press release, 29 July 1932; "Houston Editor Finds Wife's Bed Ablaze," *Dallas Express*, 5 August 1932; NAACP press release, 28 October 1932, NAACP Records I D 63.

44. NAACP, *Annual Report*, 1931, 1932; NAACP press release, 25 March 1927, NAACP Records I D 64; NAACP press release, 31 May 1932; Walter White to Fred Knollenberg, 20 December 1932, NAACP Records I D 63.

45. NAACP press release, 9 February 1934; Fred Knollenberg to Walter White, 21 September 1934, NAACP Records I D 92.

46. Walter White to L. W. Washington of El Paso, 1 March 1932; Herbert Seligman to Carter Wesley of the *Houston Informer*, 10 May 1932; Wesley to Seligman, 20 May 1932;

Seligman to Wesley, 26 May 1932, NAACP Records I D 63; on the background of the Houston opposition, see Hine, *Black Victory*, 126–37, 144–52.

47. *Grovey v. Townsend*, 295 U.S. 45 (1935), 55.

48. Fred Knollenberg to Jack Atkins, 4 April 1935; NAACP press release, 12 April 1935, NAACP Records I D 92.

49. *Grovey v. Townsend*, 295 U.S. 45 (1935), 55.

50. Jack Atkins to Charles Houston, 12 May 1935, NAACP Records I D 92.

51. Meier and Rudwick, "Attorneys Black and White," 147–54; on Houston and Marshall, see McNeil, *Groundwork*; Tushnet, *Making Civil Rights Law.*

52. See the background reports by Roscoe Dunjee of Oklahoma City, 2 and 3 April 1933, NAACP Records I G 171; Thurgood Marshall to the American Civil Liberties Union, 1 November 1937; Charles Chandler of Muskogee, Oklahoma, to Thurgood Marshall, 26 September 1938, NAACP Records I D 60.

53. *Lane v. Wilson*, 307 U.S. 268 (1939), 275.

54. *Lane v. Wilson*, 307 U.S. 268 (1939), 276; on Frankfurter's attitude toward his NAACP affiliation as a Supreme Court Justice, see Tushnet, *Making Civil Rights Law*, 68.

55. NAACP press release, 26 May 1939, NAACP Records II A 473; Thurgood Marshall, "Equal Justice Under Law," *Crisis* 46 (July 1939): 199–201.

56. Meier and Rudwick, "Attorneys Black and White," 146; H. W. Robinson of New Orleans to William T. Andrews, 3 August 1931; Nathan Margold to H. W. Robinson, 24 September 1931, Arthur B. Spingarn Papers, box 32; Charles Houston to F. B. Smith of New Orleans, 16 October 1935, NAACP Records I C 392.

57. NAACP press release, 15 March 1934, NAACP Records I C 392; see note 3.35, above. On the Wilkesboro, North Carolina, case, see Walter White to U.S. Attorney General Homer Cummings, 30 August 1935; Charles Houston to Cummings, 16 October 1935; Charles Houston to U.S. Attorney Carlisle Higgins, 11 November 1935; Houston to Cummings, 18 November 1935; "Charge that Cashion Denied Negroes Right to Register," *Greensboro News*, 3 December 1935; Higgins to Houston, 18 December 1935; Houston to Cummings, 25 May 1936; NAACP press release, 5 June 1936, all in NAACP Records I C 286; on the Alabama case, see Arthur Shores to Thurgood Marshall, 9 June 1939; NAACP press release, 7 July 1939; memorandum by Thurgood Marshall to the Alabama NAACP branches, 10 July 1939, NAACP Records I D 48.

58. Lawson, *Black Ballots*, 134; Rosenberg, *The Hollow Hope*, 61.

59. Charles Houston to Fred Knollenberg, 9 June 1938; Knollenberg to Houston, 2 July 1938; attorneys Mandell and Combs of Houston, Texas, to Thurgood Marshall, 25 October 1938, NAACP Records I D 92; Hine, *Black Victory*, 194–95.

60. Thurgood Marshall to Norman Lacey of Tampa, Florida, 16 December 1941, NAACP Records II B 210; Hine, *Black Victory*, 202.

61 *United States v. Classic*, 313 U.S. 299 (1941); Hine, *Black Victory*, 202–7; Tushnet, *Making Civil Rights Law*, 103–5

62. "Background Material on Texas Primary Case," 20 March 1944, NAACP Records II B 216; Hine, *Black Victory*, 212–17.

63. *Smith v. Allwright*, 321 U.S. 649 (1944), 669.

64. Tushnet, *Making Civil Rights Law*, 105–7.

65. *Smith v. Allwright*, 321 U.S. 649 (1944), 664–65.

66. See Marshall's public statement, 3 April 1944; Marshall to U.S. Attorney General Francis Biddle, 3 April 1944; Marshall to NAACP branches, 8 May 1944, NAACP Records II B 216; NAACP press release, 4 May 1944, NAACP Records II B 210; Tushnet, *Making Civil Rights Law*, 107.

67. See the compilation of the press reaction to *Allwright* in NAACP press release, 6 April 1944, NAACP Records II B 216; Hine, *Black Victory*, 223–29;

68. *Terry v. Adams*, 345 U.S. 461 (1953).

69. *Elmore v. Rice*, 72 F. Supp. 516 (1947), quoted after copy in Arthur Spingarn Papers, box 32; Tushnet, *Making Civil Rights Law*, 108.

70. *Davis v. Schnell*, U.S. District Court for the Southern District of Alabama, 7 January 1949, copy in NAACP Records II B 209; on the "Boswell" amendment, see Lawson, *Black Ballots*, 89–97.

71. Commentary by the *Jackson Daily News*, 14 June 1946, copy in NAACP Records II B 212; Bilbo quoted in Lawson, *Black Ballots*, 100–104.

72. See, e.g., the NAACP press release, 27 July 1944, NAACP Records II B 216; memorandum to the public relations department by the legal department, 6 November 1947, NAACP Records II B 213.

73. *Missouri ex rel. Gaines v. Canada*, 305 U.S. 337 (1938); Tushnet, *Making Civil Rights Law*, 121–22.

74. The term *realistic* is used here in its colloquial meaning. The academic movement known as *legal realism* was much more radical in its rejection of precedent and its embrace of political principles as the basis for legal decisions than any of the new Supreme Court justices. For an introduction, see Johnson, *American Legal Culture*, 122–50.

75. Bott, *Handbook of United States Election Laws and Practices*, 19–21.

Chapter 4. Protest and Loyalty: The NAACP in the Second World War

1. Myrdal, *An American Dilemma*, lxi, 997, 1016.

2. Wynn, *The Afro-American and the Second World War*, 55.

3. Smith and Horton, *Historical Statistics of Black America*, 2:1621; Wynn, *The Afro-American and the Second World War*, 60–78; Sitkoff, "Racial Militancy and Interracial Violence in the Second World War."

4. *The Public Papers of the Presidents of the United States: Franklin D. Roosevelt: 1944–45*, 32–42; *The Public Papers of the Presidents of the United States: Harry S. Truman: 1947*, 311; on the racial and gender implications of social rights, see Boris, "'The Right to Work is the Right to Live!'"

5. Quoted in Patterson, *Grand Expectations*, 23; Wynn, *The Afro-American and the Second World War*, 21–38; Sitkoff, "Racial Militancy and Interracial Violence in the Second World War," 668–70.

6. Myrdal, *An American Dilemma*, 1014, 1021.

7. See Eastland's statement, 31 January 1944, NAACP Records II A 473.

8. See, e.g., Plummer, *Rising Wind*; von Eschen, *Race against Empire*; Dudziak, *Cold War Civil Rights*.

9. "Charity Abroad," *Crisis* 3 (February 1912): 147–48.

10. Kellogg, *NAACP*, 282–83, Plummer, *Rising Wind*, 16–21; resolutions of the 1933 NAACP annual conference, 29 June–2 July 1933, Arthur B. Spingarn Papers, box 26.

11. Resolutions of the 1933 NAACP annual conference, 29 June–2 July 1933, Arthur B. Spingarn Papers, box 26; NAACP, *Annual Report*, 1935; "The Saga of Jesse Owens," *Crisis* 43 (September 1943): 267 (reprint from the *Cleveland Plain Dealer*); also see "Editorial," *Crisis* 43 (September 1943): 273.

12. Rabbi Stephen Wise, "Parallel Between Hitlerism and the Persecution of Negroes in America," *Crisis* 41 (May 1934): 127–29; Harold Preece, "Fascism and the Negro," *Crisis* 41 (December 1934): 355, 366; David H. Pierce, "Fascism and the Negro," *Crisis* 42 (April 1935): 107, 115; Elaine Ellis, "Sterilization: A Menace to the Negro," *Crisis* 44 (May 1937): 137, 155.

13. NAACP, *Annual Report*, 1935; resolutions of the 1936 NAACP annual conference, 3 July 1936, Arthur B. Spingarn Papers, box 26; for the general context, see Scott, *The Sons of Sheba's Race*; Plummer, *Rising Wind*, 37–56.

14. For condemnations of anti-Semitism, see Rabbi Edward L. Israel, "Jew Hatred Among Negroes," *Crisis* 43 (February 1936): 39; resolutions of the 1939 NAACP annual conference, 26 June–2 July 1939, Arthur B. Spingarn Papers, box 26; Roy Wilkins, "Hypocrisy," *Crisis* 45 (September 1938): 301; Plummer, *Rising Wind*, 68.

15. "Peace and War and the Negro," *Crisis* 45 (May 1938): 145; Walter Wilson, "Old Jim Crow in Uniform," *Crisis* 46 (February and March 1939): 42–43, 72–73, 82; "Defending Democracy," *Crisis* 46 (October 1939): 305.

16. George Padmore, "The Second World War and the Darker Races," *Crisis* 46 (November 1939): 327–28; "War and Dictatorship," *Crisis* 47 (July 1940): 211 (reprint from the *Chicago Defender*); Alfred Baker Lewis, "Dicatorship and Democracy," *Crisis* 47 (September 1940): 285.

17. Resolutions of the 1940 NAACP annual conference, 22 June 1940, Arthur B. Spingarn Papers, box 26.

18. NAACP, *Annual Report*, 1941; also see the overview in NAACP, *Annual Report*, 1940; "For Manhood in National Defense," *Crisis* 47 (December 1940): 375; "Jim Crow in the Army Camp," *Crisis* 47 (December 1940): 385, 388.

19. Smith and Horton, *Historical Statistics of Black America*, 2:1234–35; Nalty, *Strength for the Fight*, 125–42; Zieger, *The CIO*, 154–55.

20. White, *A Man Called White*, 186–87; "White House Blesses Jim Crow," *Crisis* 47 (November 1940): 350–51, 357; Pfeffer, *A. Philip Randolph*, 45–55; on the close cooperation between White and Randolph and the full support for the March on Washington by the NAACP, see Bracey and Meier, "Allies or Adversaries?"

21. Bracey and Meier, "Allies or Adversaries?" 13–17; White, *A Man Called White*, 190–93.

22. On the FEPC, see the study by Reed, *Seedtime for the Modern Civil Rights Movement*; Wynn, *The Afro-American and the Second World War*, 48–55.

23. Bracey and Meier, "Allies or Adversaries?" 16–17; Janken, *White*, 257–58, suggests that FDR would have been ready to make even more far-reaching concessions.

24. "Now is the Time Not to Be Silent," *Crisis* 49 (January 1942): 7; resolutions of the 1942 NAACP annual conference, 18 July 1942, NAACP, *Annual Report*, 1942; NAACP

press release, 23 January 1942; broadcasted speech by Walter White, 8 April 1942, NAACP Records II A 375.

25. Wynn, *The Afro-American and the Second World War*, 100.

26. See the letter to FDR, 5 February 1942, NAACP Records II A 512. Boxes II A 512 and 513 contain numerous other protests against racial discrimination in the military and defense industries sent to FDR.

27. Daniels, *The Decision to Relocate the Japanese Americans*, esp. 49–52, 113–14; Walter White to U.S. Attorney General Francis Biddle, 10 July 1942; NAACP press release, 27 April 1944, NAACP Records II A 325, where more materials on the NAACP's attitude toward the Japanese internment can be found.

28. Hill, *The FBI's RACON*, esp. introduction, 1–72.

29. Ibid., 406–14, 452–57.

30. Sitkoff, "Racial Militancy and Interracial Violence in the Second World War," 671–75, 673; White, *A Man Called White*, 224–30.

31. White, *A Man Called White*, 233–41, 235; Wilkins, *Standing Fast*, 183–84.

32. See the discussion of the poll tax in such classical works as Key, *Southern Politics in State and Nation*, 578–618, Myrdal, *An American Dilemma*, 481–84, Bunche, *The Political Status of the Negro in the Age of FDR*, 328–83.

33. On the legislative efforts to abolish the poll tax, see the comprehensive account by Lawson, *Black Ballots*, 55–85; "Georgia House Votes to Repeal Poll Tax, 141–51," *Herald Tribune*, 1 February 1945, copy in NAACP Records II A 474.

34. On the origins and founding of the SCHW, see Egerton, *Speak Now against the Day*, 177–97.

35. "The President and the Poll Tax," *Dallas Express*, 17 September 1938, copy in NAACP Records I C 285.

36. Lawson, *Black Ballots*, 61–62; press release by Lee Geyer, 7 August 1940; Geyer to Walter White, 15 May 1941; minutes of the NCAPT, 12 May 1941, all in NAACP Records II A 480.

37. See the NACPT "Poll Tax Fact Sheet" of late 1942, NAACP Records II A 386.

38. NAACP press release, 13 October 1942; Walter White to the NAACP branches, 23 October 1942; NAACP press release, 12 November 1942; Walter White to NAACP branch officers, 17 November 1942; NAACP press release, 27 November 1942, all in NAACP Records II A 479.

39. Speech by Walter White before the NCAPT, 9 March 1943, NAACP Records II A 386; NAACP press release, 12 November 1942, NAACP Records II A 479; see also the statement by Leslie Perry of the NAACP's Washington Bureau before the House Subcommittee on Elections, 2 July 1947, NAACP Records II A 478.

40. Lawson, *Black Ballots*, 66–68.

41. Ibid., 68–85; Watson, *Lion in the Lobby*, 172–75.

42. Guy Gillette to Walter White, 3 December 1943, NAACP Records II A 479.

43. *Breedlove v. Suttles*, 302 U.S. 277 (1937).

44. Marshall's memorandum for the ACLU, 5 March 1940, NAACP Records II A 480.

45. See Walter White to Senator James Mead (D-N.Y.), 20 May 1944, NAACP Records II A 479; statement by the NAACP Committee on Administration, 19 May 1944; NAACP

press release, 2 June 1944, NAACP Records II A 480; Walter White to Harry Truman, 11 April 1946, NAACP Records II A 478.

46. See, e.g., the following internal and public statements: Francis Pohlhaus, legal counsel of the NAACP's Washington Bureau, to Clarence Mitchell, 22 December 1954, NAACP Records II A 480; Mitchell's statement before the Subcommittee on Constitutional Amendments of the Senate Judiciary Committee, 13 April 1956, NAACP Records III A 72; Roy Wilkins to Dr. Darrell B. Carter, 19 January 1960; NAACP press release, 23 March 1962, NAACP Records III A 267.

47. Lawson, *Black Ballots*, 84; *Harper v. Virginia State Board of Elections*, 383 U.S. 663 (1966).

48. Walter White to Virginia Foster Durr, 15 March 1943, NAACP Records II A 386. The correspondence between the NAACP and the NCAPT is filed in NAACP Records II A 386, but unfortunately the record is rather fragmentary.

49. Walter White to Morris Milgram, 21 December 1942, NAACP Records II A 479.

50. See the memorandum on membership development since 1912 by R. Williams to Gloster Current, 15 June 1954, NAACP Records II A 201; for public claims, see the press release by the Detroit NAACP branch, 3 April 1947, NAACP Records II A 201; statement by Leslie Perry of the NAACP's Washington Bureau before the House Subcommittee on Elections, 2 July 1947, NAACP Records II A 478; Lucille Black in RJBOHC, interview no. 70; Myrdal, *An American Dilemma*, 822; memorandum by Roy Wilkins to the NAACP branch officers, 19 January 1944, NAACP Records II A 473; Oliver W. Harrington, NAACP director of public relations, to Emory Jackson, editor of the *Birmingham World*, 8 April 1947, BWC 1102.1.2.

51. Current quoted in Gavins, "The NAACP in North Carolina during the Age of Segregation," 105.

52. Tuck, "Black Protest during the 1940s," 68; Fairclough, *Race and Democracy*, 73; Gavins, "The NAACP in North Carolina during the Age of Segregation," 108–10; Dittmer, *Local People*, 29–30; Myrdal, *An American Dilemma*, 823.

53. See the memorandum on membership development since 1912 by R. Williams to Gloster Current, 15 June 1954, NAACP Records II A 201; Roy Wilkins to Hubert Delaney, 17 November 1949, Arthur B. Spingarn Papers, box 26; NAACP, *Annual Report*, 1948.

54. On the membership developments from the 1950s to the 1970s, see Rosenberg, *The Hollow Hope*, 154, table 4.4, and Marger, "Social Movement Organizations and the Response to Environmental Change," 23, table 1.

55. On the history of the LDF, see Greenberg, *Crusaders in the Courts*, esp. 19–25, 222–24, 478–86.

56. Watson, *Lion in the Lobby*, 152–86; see Mitchell's memorandum on his duties, 19 October 1951, Arthur B. Spingarn Papers, box 26.

57. On the organizational structure of the national office, see the various memoranda by the national staff that were compiled in October 1951: Henry Lee Moon (public relations) to Walter White, 5 October 1951; Thurgood Marshall (special counsel) to Earl Dickerson, 5 October 1951; Robert Carter (assistant special counsel) to White, 5 October 1951; Gloster Current (branches) to White, 18 October 1951; Clarence Mitchell (Washington Bureau), 19 October 1951; Walter White, 19 October 1951; Roy Wilkins to White, 19

October 1951, all in Arthur B. Spingarn Papers, box 26; also see the organization chart in St. James, *National Association for the Advancement of Colored People*, 164.

58. See RJBOHC interviews nos. 71 (Henry Lee Moon); 167 (Gloster Current); 70 (Lucille Black); see the cv of Gloster Current, 23 May 1958, NAACP Records II C 237.

59. On Marshall's life and career, see the two-volume biography by Tushnet, *Making Civil Rights Law* and *Making Constitutional Law*; White, *A Man Called White*; Wilkins, *Standing Fast*.

60. See Ransby, *Ella Baker and the Black Freedom Movement*, esp. 137–47, passim.

61. Wilkins, *Standing Fast*, 203–5, 219–20; Janken, *White*, 335–47, 361–72; Du Bois, "Segregation in the North," *Crisis* 41 (April 1934): 115–17; Walter White to Joel Spingarn, 15 January 1934, NAACP Records I C 287. Also see chapter two.

62. This happened after the 1968 showdown with the NAACP "Young Turks." See Eick, *Dissent in Wichita*, 156; see also chapter nine.

63. Hubert T. Delaney to Roy Wilkins, 9 November 1949, Arthur B. Spingarn Papers, box 26.

64. Wilkins's reply to Hubert Delaney, 17 November 1949, Arthur B. Spingarn Papers, box 26.

65. Myrdal, *An American Dilemma*, 826.

Chapter 5. Civil Rights and Liberal Anticommunism

1. White, *Rising Wind*, 155.

2. The literature on the McCarthy era and American anticommunism is voluminous. A standard reference remains Caute, *The Great Fear*; for historiographical introductions, see Richard M. Fried, *Nightmare in Red*; Schrecker, *The Age of McCarthyism*; Albert Fried, ed., *McCarthyism*; for a new synthesis on the impact of McCarthyism on American society, see Schrecker, *Many Are the Crimes*; for a long-term perspective on American anticommunism, see Heale, *American Anticommunism*; Powers, *Not Without Honor*, who defends the legitimacy of liberal anticommunism in the face of Soviet totalitarianism. For a new detailed study on southern anticommunism, see Woods, *Black Struggle, Red Scare*.

3. On the linkage between civil rights and the Cold War, see especially the work by Mary Dudziak, "Desegregation as a Cold War Imperative"; Dudziak, "Josephine Baker, Racial Protest, and the Cold War"; and Dudziak's recent synthesis, *Cold War Civil Rights*; also see the new book by Borstelmann, *The Cold War and the Color Line*.

4. Schlesinger, *The Vital Center*, ix, 30–50.

5. White, *A Man Called White*, 314–16, 334–35, 344–47; Wilkins, *Standing Fast*, 201–11, passim; Hughes, *Fight for Freedom*, 149–51; Record, *The Negro and the Communist Party*, esp. 260–68; Record, *Race and Radicalism*; Nolan, *Communism versus the Negro*, esp. 178–81; among recent historians, Reed, *The Chicago NAACP and the Rise of Black Professional Leadership*, 83–85, 133, has argued along these lines.

6. Marable, *Race, Reform, and Rebellion*, 26–32; Horne, "Commentary: Who Lost the Cold War?" 613–26, 614.

7. Anderson, *Eyes off the Prize*, 273. However, Anderson, whose recent book is the most comprehensive account so far, is no less critical of the black left because of its attachment to the CPUSA, 274; see also, Janken, *White*, 297–323, with an emphasis on Walter White's

personal opportunism; von Eschen, "Commentary: Challenging Cold War Habits," 634, speaks of a "stark and ultimately tragic choice." For a less fatalistic assessment of the NAACP's anticommunism, see Laville and Lucas, "The American Way."

8. Horne, *Black Liberation/Red Scare*, 228; Schrecker, *Many Are the Crimes*, 393, 543–44, footnote 89; Plummer, *Rising Wind*, 188, 190.

9. Schrecker, *Many Are the Crimes*, 369–70; for a very similar proposition, see Korstadt and Lichtenstein, "Opportunities Found and Lost," 811.

10. Roy Wilkins interview in RJBOHC, interview no. 550; also see Du Bois's undated [late 1948] memorandum "My Relations with the NAACP," NAACP Records II A 241; Lewis, *W.E.B. Du Bois: The Fight for Equality and the American Century*, 493–95; on Du Bois's ideological and political orientation after the Second World War, also see Marable, *W.E.B. Du Bois*; Horne, *Black and Red*. In contrast to Lewis, however, both authors tend to view Du Bois uncritically.

11. Resolution by the NAACP board of directors, 11 September 1944, NAACP Records II A 513; Du Bois, "Imperialism, United Nations, Colonial People," *New Leader* 27 (December 1944), printed in Aptheker, ed., *Writings by W.E.B. Du Bois in Periodicals Edited by Others*, 3:225–28; Lewis, *W.E.B. Du Bois: The Fight for Equality and the American Century*, 503–10; on the efforts of Du Bois and the black civil rights community at large to influence American policy toward the United Nations, also see Anderson, "From Hope to Disillusion," 531–42; Harris, "Racial Equality and the United Nations Charter," 131–45; Plummer, *Rising Wind*, 132–51; Logan, *The Negro and the Post-War World*, 76–88.

12. Anderson, "From Hope to Disillusion," 544–48; Anderson, *Eyes off the Prize*, 79–85; on the NNC, see Hutchinson, *Blacks and Reds*, 157–74, 177–91.

13. See the correspondence on the UN petition in Aptheker, ed., *The Correspondence of W.E.B. Du Bois*, 3:149–52, 160–65, esp. the memoranda by Du Bois to Walter White, 26 March 1946, 160–61, 1 August 1946, 163; also see these documents in NAACP Records II A 637.

14. Du Bois memorandum to White, 14 November 1946, Aptheker, ed., *The Correspondence of W.E.B. Du Bois*, 3:166–67; also see ibid., 180–84, for Du Bois's efforts to insure the reception of the petition; also see the undated chronology on the NAACP petition to the United Nations, prepared by Du Bois in 1948; Du Bois to Walter White, 17 October 1947, NAACP Records II A 637; Anderson, "From Hope to Disillusion," 553–59; Anderson, *Eyes off the Prize*, 92–112.

15. Quoted after the summary of the petition prepared by Du Bois; also see the statements by Walter White, Du Bois, and John Humphrey on the occasion of presenting the NAACP petition, NAACP Records II A 637.

16. Walter White to Du Bois, Harrington, and Wilkins, 24 October 1947; NAACP press release, 7 November 1947; memorandum by Julia Baxter to White, 18 December 1947; White to Bruce Bliven, 12 December 1947; NAACP circular letter to editors, civic leaders, and mailing list subscribers, 18 February 1948, all in NAACP Records II A 637; White, *A Man Called White*, 358–59; Du Bois to the editor of the *Morgantown Post* (West Virginia), 27 October 1947, Aptheker, ed., *The Correspondence of W.E.B. Du Bois*, 3:185–86.

17. Summary of the petition prepared by Du Bois, NAACP Records II A 637.

18. "UN Turns Down Petition," *Philadelphia Tribune*, 13 December 1948; "UN Group

Kills Probe of Bias on U.S. Negro," *Daily News,* 4 December 1948, both in NAACP Records II A 637; memorandum by Du Bois to Walter White, 1 July 1948, on his conversation with Eleanor Roosevelt, in Aptheker, ed., *The Correspondence of W.E.B. Du Bois,* 3:188–89; NAACP Records II A 241.

19. White, *A Man Called White,* 359.

20. On Du Bois's quarrels with the NAACP leadership, see Aptheker, ed., *The Correspondence of W.E.B. Du Bois,* 3:95–101; Du Bois, "My Relations with the NAACP," NAACP Records II A 241; Du Bois, "Common Objectives," in Aptheker, ed., *Writings by W.E.B. Du Bois in Periodicals Edited by Others,* 4:14–16; Du Bois, "The Winds of Time," in Aptheker, ed., *Newspaper Columns by W.E.B. Du Bois,* 2:644–45; Lewis, *W.E.B. Du Bois: The Fight for Equality and the American Century,* 508, 525.

21. Memorandum by Du Bois to the NAACP board of directors, 7 September 1948, in Aptheker, ed., *The Correspondence of W.E.B. Du Bois,* 3:243–45; NAACP Records II A 637.

22. See White's memorandum to Du Bois, 13 September 1948, NAACP Records II A 637. The secretary insisted, correctly, that he himself had proposed to send Du Bois. See White to the Committee on Administration, 13 July 1948, NAACP Records II A 241; Louis Wright, chairman of the NAACP board of directors, to Du Bois, 13 September 1948, in Aptheker, ed., *The Correspondence of W.E.B. Du Bois,* 3:246; Wilkins's memorandum for Walter White, 14 September 1948, on the board meeting, NAACP Records II A 241.

23. *The Public Papers of the Presidents of the United States: Harry S. Truman: 1947,* 311–13; White, *A Man Called White,* 347–48; on the growing international criticism of racial discrimination and violence in the United States, see Dudziak, *Cold War Civil Rights,* 18–46.

24. See the correspondence between the NAACP and the president's committee in President Truman's Committee on Civil Rights, reel 4, frames 186–247, esp. Robert Carter to Walter White, 12 March 1947; Walter White to Truman, 21 April 1947; Robert Carr to White, 10 April 1947; Robert Carr to White, 22 April 1947; also see NAACP Records II A 481. On the racial violence in the South, see Egerton, *Speak Now against the Day,* 359–75.

25. See the recommendations of the committee, *To Secure These Rights,* 151–73.

26. Walter White to Harry Truman, 28 October 1947, NAACP Records II A 481; Truman's statement, 29 October 1947, *The Public Papers of the Presidents of the United States: Harry S. Truman: 1947,* 479–80; Lewis, *W.E.B. Du Bois: The Fight for Equality and the American Century,* 529.

27. See Truman's special message to Congress, 2 February 1948, *The Public Papers of the Presidents of the United States: Harry S. Truman: 1948,* 121–26; Berman, *The Politics of Civil Rights in the Truman Administration,* 85, 116–18.

28. For a standard account that stresses the political motives and constraints behind Truman's civil rights policy, see Berman, *The Politics of Civil Rights in the Truman Administration;* for a rather critical interpretation, see O'Reilly, *Nixon's Piano,* 145–65; for an almost hagiographic account that sees only moral forces behind Truman's actions and denies that politics played any role, see Gardner, *Harry Truman and Civil Rights,* 202, passim.

29. Walter White to Eleanor Roosevelt, 7 July 1944, NAACP Records II A 512; White to Harold Young, 19 July 1944; White to Henry Wallace, 4 August 1944, NAACP Records II A 665; White, *A Man Called White*, 265–68.

30. Eleanor Roosevelt to Walter White, 3 August 1944, NAACP Records II A 512; White's telegram to Truman, 19 October 1944; Truman's response, 29 October 1944, NAACP Records II A 632; Wilkins, *Standing Fast*, 192–93.

31. See the undated "Call to Progressives"; White to the members of the Committee on Administration, 3 September 1946; Ruby Hurley to White, 4 September 1946; Gloster Current to White, 4 September 1946; Roy Wilkins to White, 4 September 1946; Madison Jones to White, 5 September 1946; program of the conference, held on 28 and 29 September 1946, all in NAACP Records II A 478; on the background of the initiative, see Boylan, *The New Deal Coalition and the Election of 1946*, 106–12.

32. See the resolution on Wallace's dismissal and the text of White's speech, 28 September 1946; NAACP chairman Louis Wright to William O. Walker of the *Cleveland Call and Post*, 16 November 1946, NAACP Records II A 478.

33. Boylan, *The New Deal Coalition and the Election of 1946*, 179–82; Hamby, *Beyond the New Deal*, 149–68.

34. Berman, *The Politics of Civil Rights in the Truman Administration*, 79–83; O'Reilly, *Nixon's Piano*, 155–58.

35. See White's memorandum to the NAACP staff, 25 February 1948, NAACP Records II A 241; also see White to the branch officers, 6 May 1948, NAACP Records II A 474.

36. Gloster Current to White, 24 February 1948; Wilkins to Lewis Booth, 23 April 1948; Miles Williamson to Wilkins, 12 May 1948; Leslie Perry to White, 2 March 1948; Clarence Mitchell to White, 2 March 1948; Will Alexander to White, 27 May 1948; Joseph Lohman to White, 18 June 1948, all in NAACP Records II A 665; "Candidate Wallace," *Crisis* 55 (February 1948): 40; Berman, *The Politics of Civil Rights in the Truman Administration*, 105; NAACP press release, 22 July 1948, NAACP Records II A 665.

37. "The Winds of Time," in Aptheker, ed., *Newspaper Columns by W.E.B. Du Bois*, 2:753–54; Du Bois to the NAACP board of directors, 8 March 1948, NAACP Records II A 241; Aptheker, ed., *The Correspondence of W.E.B. Du Bois*, 3:238–39. For Du Bois's political editorials in *The Crisis*, see esp. chapter two.

38. See Walter White to the Committee on Administration, 24 January 1948; Du Bois to the board of directors, 8 March 1948; White to Arthur Spingarn, 12 March 1948; White to Du Bois, 29 March 1948; Du Bois to Arthur Spingarn, 2 April 1948; Louis Wright to Du Bois, 28 May 1948, in NAACP Records II A 241; Aptheker, ed., *The Correspondence of W.E.B. Du Bois*, 3:238–42.

39. See "Du Bois Boosts Rainey," *Louisiana Weekly*, 26 June 1948, NAACP Records II A 240; excerpts from Du Bois's speech at a meeting of the Philadelphia NAACP branch, 16 June 1948; White to Du Bois, 9 July 1948; Du Bois to White, 9 July 1948; White to the Committee on Administration, 12 July 1948; Madison Jones to White, 20 July 1948; White to Arthur Spingarn, 28 July 1948, in NAACP Records II A 241.

40. On Du Bois's appearance before the board, see Wilkins to White, 14 September 1948; NAACP press release, 16 September 1948; Wilkins to branch officers, 15 Septem-

ber 1948, NAACP Records II A 241; "The Du Bois Incident: A Chronology," NAACP bulletin, October 1948; Wilkins to the president of the Pasadena, California, NAACP branch, 19 October 1948 (quote), in NAACP Records II A 240.

41. See numerous letters and resolutions by branches and individuals in NAACP Records II A 240, folders: W.E.B. Du Bois Dismissal; "Henry Wallace, Paul Robeson Condemn Dismissal of Dr. W.E.B. Du Bois by NAACP," *Shreveport News*, 2 October 1948 (quote); see also "Wallaceites Claim Dr. Du Bois Crucified," *Los Angeles Tribune*, 25 September 1948; "As We See It," *Daily Worker*, 13 September 1948, in NAACP Records II A 240.

42. George Schuyler, "Views and Reviews," *Pittsburgh Courier*, 9 October 1948, NAACP Records II A 240; Val. J. Washington, Republican National Committee, to Louis Wright, 27 September 1948; Louis Wright to the Committee on Administration, 1 October 1948; resolutions of the Committee on Administration, 5 October 1948, all in NAACP Records II A 241.

43. Moon, *Balance of Power*, 205; Wilkins, *Standing Fast*, 200; NAACP press release, 9 January 1948, NAACP Records II A 452; Clarence Mitchell to White, 20 May 1948, NAACP Records II A 633.

44. Walter White to James Roosevelt et al., 5 July 1948; White to Truman, 13 July 1948; White to Paul Fitzpatrick of the New York Delegation to the Democratic convention, 13 July 1948; NAACP press releases, 15 July 1948, in NAACP II A 225; on the background, see Berman, *The Politics of Civil Rights in the Truman Administration*, 106–14; Cohodas, *Strom Thurmond and the Politics of Southern Change*, 154–93.

45. See the undated "Survey of the Negro Vote in the 1948 Presidential Elections," NAACP Records II A 452; Henry Lee Moon, "What Chance for Civil Rights," *Crisis* 56 (February 1949): 42–45; memorandum by Moon for Walter White, 19 November 1948, NAACP Records II A 633; see Berman, *The Politics of Civil Rights in the Truman Administration*, 129–32.

46. White to Truman, 3 November 1948; NAACP press release, 4 November 1948; NAACP press release, 6 January 1949, in NAACP Records II A 633; *The Public Papers of the Presidents of the United States: Harry S. Truman: 1948*, 974; *The Public Papers of the Presidents of the United States: Harry S. Truman: 1949*, 1–7; on the demise of Truman's civil rights legislation, see Berman, *The Politics of Civil Rights in the Truman Administration*, 137–81.

47. Patterson, *Grand Expectations*, 157–58.

48. NAACP press release, 4 May 1944, NAACP Records II A 201.

49. Arthur Schlesinger Jr., "The U.S. Communist Party," *Life Magazine*, 29 July 1946, 84–96; Walter White to Henry Luce, 29 July 1946; John Billings to White, 7 August 1946; White to Billings, 16 August 1946; White's letter to the editor and Schlesinger's reply in *Life Magazine*, 2 September 1946, 7; Roy Wilkins to Milton Murray, 2 April 1947; Murray to Wilkins, 13 April 1947, Wilkins to Murray (quote), 30 April 1947, all in NAACP Records II A 201.

50. See White's protest against a red-baiting statement by Michigan governor Kim Sigler, NAACP press release, 4 April 1947; White's letter to Secretary of the Navy James V. Forrestal, 1 July 1947; Commodore Glass to White, 13 August 1947; White to Forrestal,

20 August 1947; Clarence Mitchell to White, 12 January 1948, all in NAACP Records II A 201.

51. See Walter White's statement on the martyred Florida NAACP leader Harry T. Moore, 2 October 1952; White to Attorney General Howard McGrath, 9 May 1951; McGrath's reply, 15 May 1951, in NAACP Records II A 202.

52. See Walter White's column, "A Real Program to Combat Communism," 2 January 1947; White to U.S. Attorney General Tom Clark, 14 April 1947; NAACP press release, 16 October 1947, NAACP Records II A 201; Mitchell's statement, 3 May 1950, quoted in "Information from the Files of the U.S. Committee on Un-American Activities"; HUAC, "The Negro and the Communist Party," 22 December 1954; Channing Tobias to Mitchell, 11 January 1955, all in NAACP Records II A 202.

53. Resolutions of the NAACP annual conference, 23 June 1950, Arthur B. Spingarn Papers, box 26; NAACP press release, 23 June 1950, NAACP Records II A 201; White's memorandum, 29 August 1950, NAACP Records II A 369.

54. Walter White to the NAACP branches, 15 January 1951; resolutions of the NAACP annual convention, 30 June 1951, NAACP Records II A 68; minutes of the meetings of the NAACP board of directors, 2 January 1951, 12 September 1951, NAACP Records II A 135; see the detailed "Procedure for Rejection or Expulsion of Membership NAACP," undated (1952), Arthur B. Spingarn Papers, box 26; Gloster Current to Thurgood Marshall, 7 November 1952, NAACP Records II A 128.

55. See the "Draft of Letter on Branch Policy," undated (1946); memorandum by Ruby Hurley to White, 7 January 1947; NAACP press release, 3 March 1949, NAACP Records II A 201; Roy Wilkins to Wilson Record, 21 December 1949, NAACP Records II A 202; Walter White to Morris Ernst, 3 January 1947, Arthur B. Spingarn Papers, box 28; White, *A Man Called White*, 346.

56. See the minutes of the Committee on Administration, 24 February 1947, NAACP Records II A 127; minutes of the meeting of the board of directors, 9 June 1947, NAACP Records II A 135; Alfred Baker Lewis to Walter White, 19 November 1947, NAACP Records II A 201; Gloster Current to NAACP branch officers, 10 December 1948, NAACP Records II A 369.

57. On the Richmond, California, branch, see NAACP Records II C 18, esp. the copy of the resolution on Greece, April 1947; Noah Griffin to Roy Wilkins, 7 August 1947; Griffin to Gloster Current, 19 November 1947, 9 December 1947; Bernard Evans et al. to Current, 18 December 1947; Current to Griffin, 19 December 1947; Griffin to Current, 22 December 1947; The People of Richmond, California, to the board of directors, 28 February 1949; Roy Wilkins to I. C. Mickins, 16 July 1949.

58. On the San Francisco branch, see NAACP Records II C 20: esp. Ella Baker to Elizabeth Williams, 21 June 1946; Noah Griffin to Walter White, 20 September 1946; White to Griffin, 20 September 1946; Madison Jones to White, 21 September 1946; Margery Pogue to Joseph James, 2 October 1946; Joseph James to White, 19 October 1946; Gloster Current to White, 26 November 1946; Griffin to Lucille Black, 18 February 1947; Wilkins to Griffin, 14 April 1947; Anthony Hart and Ethel Nance to Wilkins, 14 May 1947; Wilkins to Ethel Nance, 28 May 1947; Noah Griffin to Roy Wilkins, 14 July 1947; Wilkins to Griffin, 21 July 1947; Wilkins to Carlton Goodlet, 25 July 1947; Griffin to

Wilkins, 28 July 1947; Gloster Current to Walter White, 18 February 1948; Teresa Griffin to Roy Wilkins, 21 January 1949; Noah Griffin to Wilkins, 21 April 1949; Noah Griffin to Wilkins, 21 November 1949; Griffin to Wilkins, 23 November 1949; Griffin to Gloster Current, 23 December 1949; Wilkins to Cecil Poole, 30 December 1949; Wilkins to Poole, 22 March 1950; Walter White to Cecil Poole, 12 December 1950; Frank Williams to Gloster Current, 19 February 1951.

59. On the Great Neck, New York, branch, see NAACP Records II C 120: esp. Roy Wilkins to Anne Aldrich, 29 November 1949; Aldrich to Wilkins, 6 December 1949; Gloster Current to Aldrich, 13 December 1949; Constance Baker Motley to Current, 22 December 1949; Current to Aldrich, 24 February 1950; Current to William Cotter, 14 April 1950; Condensation of Great Neck Dispute (1950); resolutions of the Great Neck branch, 21 November 1952; agendas for the Committee on Branches, 19 December 1952, 4 February 1953, 26 March 1953; also see the minutes of the board meetings, 8 December 1952, 5 January 1953, NAACP II Records A 136.

60. On the Philadelphia branch, see NAACP Records II C 169: esp. Walter White to Roy Wilkins et al., 4 February 1949; undated report of the Special Committee, Philadelphia Branch; Gloster Current to White et al., 5 October 1950; Special Committee, Philadelphia Branch, to the NAACP board of directors, 6 November 1950; minutes of the meeting of the Committee on Branches, 10 November 1950; Gloster Current to Reverend E. T. Lewis, 15 November 1950; Current to Daniel E. Byrd, 16 November 1950; Current to Theodore Spaulding, 24 November 1950; Current to E. T. Lewis, 3 January 1951, NAACP Records II C 170.

61. On the Berkeley chapter, see NAACP Records II E 69: esp. Noah Griffin to Lucille Black, 1 April 1949; Black to Griffin, 26 April 1949; Ruby Hurley to Caroline Southard, 16 June 1949; undated memorandum "Berkeley California Chapter Situation"; Robert I. Weil to James V. Clark, 17 October 1949; Griffin to Hurley, 18 and 27 October 1949; Clark to Hurley, 28 November 1949; NAACP Records II E 70: esp. Roy Wilkins to Noah Griffin, 5 January 1950; Griffin to Gloster Current, 28 March 1950; minutes of the meeting of the board of directors, 10 April 1950.

62. On the Cornell chapter, see NAACP Records II E 85: esp. Ruby Hurley to James Gibbs, 21 September 1950; Gibbs to Hurley, 24 September 1950; Gibbs to Hurley, 14 March 1951; Hurley to Gibbs, 21 March 1951; Gibbs to Hurley, 8 April 1951; Gloster Current to Gibbs, 9 April 1951; Janet Morand to Hurley, 5 November 1951; Herbert Wright to Morand, 28 November 1951.

63. On the University of Wisconsin, Madison, chapter, see NAACP Records II E 100: esp. NAACP Newsletter, University of Wisconsin, 19 October 1950: "Are Communists Harming the NAACP?"; Newsletter, 4 December 1950; Ruby Hurley to Dick Weiner, 11 January 1951; Weiner to Hurley, 9 February 1951; Edith Davis to NAACP, 22 September 1953; Herbert Wright to Edith Davis, 13 October 1953; Wright to Wilbur Halyard, 13 October 1953; Jacquelyne Johnson to Wright, 14 October 1953; Wright to Johnson, 29 October 1953.

64. See the newspaper clipping "Are Communists Taking Over the Galveston NAACP?" 2 August 1947, NAACP Records II A 201; Clarence Mitchell to Walter White, 28 June 1950, NAACP Records II C 329; Nolan, *Communism versus the Negro*, 178–81.

65. HUAC, "The Negro and the Communist Party," 22 December 1954, in NAACP Records II A 202. On the Civil Rights Congress, see Horne, *Communist Front?* Horne's book is well documented, but extremely biased. Everything the CRC says or does is accepted at face value and solely motivated by pure idealism. Communists only figure as heroic fighters for social justice, while anticommunism is dismissed as "one of the major scourges of modern times and a major impediment to social progress" (10).

66. Milton Kaufman to Ruby Hurley, 29 March 1946; Thurgood Marshall to Kaufman, 23 April 1946; Roy Wilkins to Walter White, 7 May 1946; Wilkins to D. E. Byrd, 25 May 1946; NAACP press release (Wilkins's letter), 23 November 1949; Thurgood Marshall to William Patterson, 9 June 1950, 22 November 1950; White to Patterson, 9 November 1951; Patterson to White, 10 November 1951, all in NAACP Records II A 369. On the Civil Rights Mobilization, see the articles by Henry Lee Moon, "Mobilizing for Civil Rights," and Roy Wilkins (untitled), which both stress the anticommunist character of the gathering, NAACP Records II A 186. On the Scottsboro campaign, see chapter two.

67. See Horne, *Communist Front?*, 29 (CRC membership), 137–45 ("civil rights giants"), 204–5, 216–17, 223–24.

68. Hoover's estimate for the U.S. Senate according to *U.S. News and World Report*, 23 June 1950, 30 March 1951, cited in Nolan, *Communism versus the Negro*, 206.

69. See Fried, *Communism in America*, esp. 227–47, 315–16, 334–36; Hutchinson, *Blacks and Reds*, 185. NAACP leaders rarely missed a chance to remind their audiences of these facts. See NAACP press release (Wilkins's open letter to William Patterson), 23 November 1949; Roy Wilkins, "Stalin's Greatest Defeat," *American Magazine* (December 1951): 21, 107–10; Herbert Hill, "Communist Party—Enemy of Negro Equality," *Crisis* 58 (June–July 1951): 365–71, 421–24.

70. On the "white chauvinism" campaigns, see Hutchinson, *Black and Red*, 60–68, 195 (number of black Communist Party members), 223–33; also see the interesting case study by Gerald Zahavi, "Passionate Commitments."

71. Zieger, *The CIO*, 375–76. Zieger otherwise stresses the racial egalitarianism that communist activists practiced within the CIO. On the recent historiography on the CPUSA, see Kazin, "The Agony and Romance of the American Left," esp. 1491–94, 1503–9. The dependency of the CPUSA on the Soviet Union is now broadly documented in Klehr et al., *The Soviet World of American Communism*.

72. See, e.g., Roy Wilkins, "Stalin's Greatest Defeat," *American Magazine* (December 1951): 21, 107–10; Roy Wilkins, "Communists and Negroes," *ADA Magazine* (December 1951): 5, copies in NAACP Records II A 68, where many other sources of the same kind can be found.

73. See Roy Wilkins's circular letter to the NAACP branches, 18 October 1951, NAACP Records II A 201; see the appeals for solidarity by William Patterson and Doxey Wilkerson to Walter White, 15 and 16 June 1951; White to Gloster Current, Thurgood Marshall, Roy Wilkins, 19 June 1951, NAACP Records II A 202. However, in *Dennis v. United States*, 341 U.S. 494 (1951), the U.S. Supreme Court upheld the 1940 Smith Act, which criminalized the violent overthrow of any governments in the United States and on which the convictions of the Communist Party leaders were based.

74. See Otto Spaeth (ADA) to Walter White, 20 October 1952; Henry Lee Moon's

memorandum on the ADA request, 22 October 1952, NAACP Records II A 415; resolutions of the NAACP annual conference, 23–28 June 1953, Arthur B. Spingarn Papers, box 26; Alfred Baker Lewis to the NAACP Committee on Administration, 26 April 1954; brochures and other material against "McCarthyism," all in NAACP Records II A 415.

75. Fairclough, *Race and Democracy,* xviii; see also Fairclough, *Better Day Coming,* 215–16, for a skeptical assessment of a broad-based center-left coalition, including the CPUSA. For a detailed account of the efforts by southern racists to red-bait the NAACP, see Woods, *Black Struggle, Red Scare,* 43–84.

76. Schrecker, *Many Are the Crimes,* 395.

Chapter 6. "Aren't You an American Citizen?" The NAACP Voter Registration Campaigns in the South, 1940–1962

1. See H. E. Fauntleroy to Thurgood Marshall, 23 April 1937, NAACP Records I C 285; Luther P. Jackson to Walter White, 13 September 1942, NAACP Records II A 473.

2. Smith and Horton, *Historical Statistics of Black America,* 2:1606; J. E. Perkins to Thurgood Marshall, 26 November 1943, NAACP Records II B 217.

3. Henry Lee Moon to Reverend James Hinton, 14 August 1952; Hinton to Moon, 20 August 1952, NAACP Records II A 453; memorandum by Moon to Walter White, 20 August 1952; memorandum by Moon to White, 4 May 1952; Moon, "The Southern Negro Vote, 1943–1953. Paper presented July 10, 1953, at Tenth Annual Institute of Race Relations, Fisk University," all in NAACP Records II A 452.

4. For other figures that reflect the general trend, see Lawson, *Black Ballots,* 134; Rosenberg, *The Hollow Hope,* 61; Smith and Horton, *Historical Statistics of Black America,* 2:1303.

5. Roy Wilkins to Emory Jackson, 12 December 1949, BWC 1102.3

6. "League Begins Drive to Register Virginia Voters," *Richmond Journal and Guide,* 12 July 1941, NAACP Records II A 479; "Right to Vote Drive Spreads Throughout the South As NAACP Organizes Forces," NAACP press release, 24 May 1940; Luther P. Jackson to Walter White, 13 September 1942; "Drive to Register Voters Continues in Baltimore," NAACP press release, 6 August 1943, all in NAACP Records II A 473.

7. See the report by A. P. Tureaud, 1 September 1944, NAACP Records II B 212; on *Smith v. Allwright,* see chapter three.

8. Moon, "The Southern Negro Vote, 1943–1953," footnote 5; also see the memorandum by Palmer Weber to Walter White, 8 November 1948, NAACP Records II A 452.

9. McAdam, *Political Process and the Development of Black Insurgency,* 103–6; also see chapter four.

10. Interview by the author with Mr. W. C. Patton, Birmingham, Alabama, 20 October 1994.

11. See the unsigned report to the board of directors, 7 October 1942, Arthur B. Spingarn Papers, box 26.

12. St. James, *National Association for the Advancement of Colored People,* 73–76; see the interview with Ruby Hurley, the longtime regional secretary for the Southeast, RJBOHC, interview no. 122.

13. Resolutions of the NAACP annual conference in Washington, D.C., 24–29 June

1947, quoted in the NAACP Manual on Registration and Voting Campaign, undated (late 1947), NAACP Records II A 452; Walter White's memorandum to all branches and state conferences, 24 September 1946, NAACP Records II A 472.

14. Like many adherents to the balance of power theory, Moon considerably inflated the strength and strategic position of black voters. See Moon, *Balance of Power,* esp. 197–214.

15. Moon, "What NAACP Political Action Can Accomplish," delivered on 24 June 1948 to the NAACP annual conference, copy in NAACP Records II A 452.

16. Interview by the author with Mr. W. C. Patton, Birmingham, Alabama, 20 October 1994; undated flyer (1949 or 1950) of the Birmingham NAACP, NAACP Records II B 209.

17. Moon, "What NAACP Political Action Can Accomplish," delivered on 24 June 1948 to the NAACP annual conference, copy in NAACP Records II A 452; see also Moon, "Organizing for Effective Political Action," NAACP Political Action Institute, Clark College, Atlanta, 19 April 1952, copy in NAACP Records II A 478.

18. See the NAACP Manual on Registration and Voting Campaign, undated (late 1947), NAACP Records II A 452.

19. Interview by the author with Mr. W. C. Patton, Birmingham, Alabama, 20 October 1994.

20. Myrdal, *An American Dilemma,* 875; on the role of the churches in the civil rights movement, see Morris, *The Origins of the Civil Rights Movement,* 4–12.

21. Maynard Jackson, "The Role of the Church in Encouraging Registration and Voting," address delivered at the NAACP Political Action Institute, Clark College, Atlanta, 19 April 1952, copy in NAACP Records II A 477; on the relationship between the churches and the NAACP, see also the interview with Lucille Black, the longtime NAACP membership secretary, RJBOHC, interview no. 70.

22. See Charles Gommillion of the Tuskegee Institute to Emory Jackson, 16 April 1949, BWC 1102.117; on the difficult position of black teachers, see Fairclough, *Teaching Equality,* esp. 58–67; Tushnet, *Making Civil Rights Law,* 20–26, 151–52.

23. Luther P. Jackson to Walter White, 13 September 1942, NAACP Records II A 473; on the relationship between the NAACP and the voter leagues, see Lawson, *Black Ballots,* 125–27; interview with W. C. Patton, RJBOHC, interview no. 406; Patton to Walter White, 26 January 1954, NAACP Records II A 453.

24. See the undated report (June–July 1950) by Morrow, NAACP Records II A 453; on the attacks on Pepper, see Egerton, *Speak Now against the Day,* 530.

25. See the undated report (June–July 1950) by Morrow, NAACP Records II A 453 (quote); on "Operation Dixie," see Zieger, *The CIO,* 227–41.

26. See, e.g., the affidavit by Mr. Deacon Smith of Perry, Florida, Concerning Attempts to Register and Vote, undated (summer 1946), NAACP Records II B 211; Robert Carter to U.S. Assistant Attorney General Theron L. Caudle, 6 August 1946; Cornelius Maiden, president of Labor's League for Political Education, Birmingham, to U.S. Attorney General Howard McGrath, 17 January 1950, BWC 1102.1.17.

27. Lawson, *Black Ballots,* 132.

28. NAACP press release, 16 September 1948; memorandum by A. T. Walden to

Henry Moon, 5 November 1948; NAACP press release, 24 November 1948, all in NAACP Records II B 212; memorandum by Franklin Williams to Moon, 26 November 1948; Thurgood Marshall to U.S. Attorney General Tom Clark, 1 December 1948; Assistant Attorney General Alexander Campbell to Marshall, 22 March 1949, all in NAACP Records II B 211.

29. Memorandum by Franklin Williams to Moon, 26 November 1948; memorandum by Madison Jones for the files, 3 March 1949, NAACP Records II B 211.

30. Franklin Williams to A. T. Walden, 25 October 1948; Roy Wilkins to Walter White, 3 November 1948; A. T. Walden to Moon, 5 November 1948, all in NAACP Records II B 212; memorandum by Madison Jones for the files, 3 March 1949; excerpt from Committee of Branches meeting, 4 March 1949; Madison Jones to Dover Carter, 15 March 1949, all in NAACP Records II B 211.

31. Memorandum to the board by Madison Jones, 5 July 1949; Dover Carter to Jones, 14 September 1949; Jones to Carter, 21 September 1949, all in NAACP Records II B 211.

32. On the Belzoni violence, see Wilkins, *Standing Fast*, 222–23; Dittmer, *Local People*, 53–54; Payne, *I've Got the Light of Freedom*, 36–40; interview with Gus Courts, RJBOHC, interview no. 160.

33. See NAACP press release, 5 April 1956, "Mississippi Victim Tells of NAACP Aid"; Gloster Current to Roy Wilkins, 26 September 1956; Wilkins to Earl Dickerson, 20 March 1957, all in NAACP Records III A 230.

34. Gus Courts to Roy Wilkins, 18 April 1957; Wilkins to Courts, 26 April 1957, NAACP Records III A 230; interview with Gus Courts, RJBOHC, interview no. 160.

35. See the folders "Mississippi Pressure Cases," NAACP Records III A 230 and 231; John Morsell to James Gilliam, 10 October 1961, NAACP Records III A 230; interview by the author with Mr. W. C. Patton, Birmingham, Alabama, 20 October 1994.

36. See the budget figures for 1948 to 1952 in St. James, *National Association for the Advancement of Colored People*, 87–91.

37. See folder "Lasker Fund Reports," NAACP Records II A 477.

38. Walter White to Loula Davis Lasker, 25 January 1952, NAACP Records II A 477.

39. Memorandum by Henry Moon to Walter White, 13 February 1952, NAACP Records II A 477.

40. "Consensus of Opinion of Staff at a Conference on Registration and Voting in the South," 13 March 1952, NAACP Records II A 477; Roy Wilkins to Dr. J. M. Tinsley, 1 April and 6 July 1955, NAACP Records II A 453. Perhaps Loula Lasker made another contribution, but this is not clear from the record.

41. NAACP press release, 27 March 1952; memorandum by Henry Moon to Walter White, 24 March 1952, NAACP Records II A 477.

42. Walter White to Mrs. S. W. Tucker, 10 April 1952, NAACP Records II A 476; see the talks given by Walter White, "The Negro's Stake in the 1952 Elections"; Moon, "Organizing for Effective Political Action," both in NAACP Political Action Institute, Clark College, Atlanta, 19 April 1952, NAACP Records II A 478; NAACP press release, 21 April 1952, NAACP Records II A 477.

43. See the undated memorandum by W. C. Patton, "Voter Registration Activities in

Alabama"; memorandum by Ruby Hurley to Henry Moon, 9 April 1952, NAACP Records II A 476.

44. Memoranda by Moon to Walter White, 20 August 1952, 4 May 1953, NAACP Records II A 452. See table 2.

45. Memorandum by Moon to Walter White, 4 May 1953, NAACP Records II A 452.

46. See Black's "Report of Activity in Branches, State Conferences and Regional Conferences—re: Registration and Voting," 24 November 1953, NAACP Records II A 452.

47. See J. E. Pierce, "A Report of Negro Voting in Alabama by Counties," 4 April 1953, NAACP Records II A 453. The report also gave a much lower total for Alabama (30,000), than Moon's estimate of August 1952 (50,000). See table 2.

48. See Patton's reports to Walter White, 26 January 1954, 10 and 15 February 1954; NAACP press release, 9 April 1954, all in NAACP Records II A 453; White to Loula Lasker, 6 May 1954, NAACP Records II A 452.

49. See Moon's memorandum to Walter White, 6 April 1954, NAACP Records II A 452.

50. On the purge of the registration books in Mississippi, see the circular letter by Clifford R. Field, county registrar of Natchez, undated (summer 1955); Roy Wilkins to U.S. Attorney General Herbert Brownell, 4 August 1955; Joseph Rauh, Americans for Democratic Action, to Brownell, 25 August 1955; Roy Wilkins to the leadership of the Democratic Party, undated (fall 1955), all in NAACP Records II A 453; on the violence in Mississippi in the summer of 1955, see the NAACP brochure "M Is For Mississippi And Murder," NAACP Records III A 232. On the radicalization of white racism after *Brown*, see Bartley, *The Rise of Massive Resistance*; McMillen, *The Citizens' Council*; Klarman, "How *Brown* Changed Race Relations."

51. For the estimated registration figures of 1956, see Lawson, *Black Ballots*, 134; Rosenberg, *The Hollow Hope*, 61.

52. On the legal attacks by the southern states, see Woods, *Black Struggle, Red Scare*, 43–83; Tushnet, *Making Civil Rights Law*, 283–300; Morris, *Origins of the Civil Rights Movement*, 30–35; "Historical Sketch: Alabama State Coordinating Association for Registration and Voting" by W. C. Patton, undated, NAACP Records III C 299; interview with W. C. Patton, RJBOHC, interview no. 406.

53. See the report by Clarence Laws, regional officer for the Southwest, 28 May 1956, NAACP Records III C 177; annual report for 1956 by Ruby Hurley, regional officer for the Southeast; Wilkins to Hurley, 7 June 1956, NAACP Records III C 174.

54. Annual report for 1956 by Ruby Hurley, NAACP Records III C 177; reports by Medgar Evers, 14 November 1957 and 11 December 1957, NAACP records III C 246. On the Civil Rights Act of 1957, see chapter eight.

55. Memorandum by Current to Walter White, 5 September 1957; Current, "NAACP Conference on Registration and Voting," undated working paper, NAACP Records III A 266.

56. See the minutes of the Atlanta conference, 15–17 November 1957; "Statement of the NAACP Conference on Registration and Voting," 17 November 1957, NAACP Records III A 266; memorandum by Clarence Mitchell to Wilkins, 3 January 1958; min-

utes of the meeting of the Implementation Committee on Registration and Voting, 7 January 1958, NAACP Records III A 267.

57. Minutes of the NAACP board of directors meeting, 10 February 1958, Arthur B. Spingarn Papers, box 44; W. C. Patton to Wilkins, 25 July 1956, NAACP Records III A 268; report by the NAACP Voter Registration Committee 1958–1960, NAACP Records III A 266; memorandum by Roy Wilkins for the Taconic Foundation, "Structure and Activities of NAACP in Voter Registration," undated (1961), SNCC Papers, box 9; interview by the author with Mr. W. C. Patton, Birmingham, Alabama, 20 October 1994.

58. Medgar Evers to Wilkins, 1 April 1958, NAACP Records III C 246; Brooks's reports of 22 April 1958, 5 May 1958, 2 June 1958, 30 June 1958; 3 September 1958, 3 October 1958; Brooks to Wilkins, 14 October 1958; Wilkins to Brooks, 20 October 1958, all in NAACP Records III A 266; Wilkins to Gloster Current, 4 December 1958, NAACP Records III C 237.

59. Roy Wilkins to Mrs. Albert Hussey, 9 January 1958, NAACP Records III A 271; report by Donald Simmons and Dr. H. W. Williamson from the Oklahoma NAACP conference of branches, 28 November 1958, NAACP records III A 266.

60. See Brooks's reports of 22 April 1958, 5 May 1958, 2 June 1958, 30 June 1958, 3 September 1958, 3 October 1958, 4 November 1958, all in NAACP Records III A 266; Wilkins to Gloster Current, 4 December 1958, NAACP Records III C 237; W. C. Patton's circular letter to NAACP leaders, 28 January 1959, NAACP Records III C 299.

61. See Brooks's memorandum to Roy Wilkins, 23 May 1958; Brooks to Wilkins, 4 November 1958; report by Brooks, 3 April 1959, NAACP Records III A 266.

62. Annual report for 1958 by Medgar Evers, NAACP Records III C 246; see Brooks's undated analysis and figures, NAACP Records III A 266.

63. Jesse Turner, chairman of the Memphis NAACP executive committee, to Roy Wilkins, 31 March 1958; reports by Brooks, 2 June 1958, 18 August 1958, NAACP Records III A 266; report by W. C. Patton, 4 August 1958, NAACP Records III A 268; annual report for 1958 by Ruby Hurley, NAACP Records III C 174; report by W. C. Patton, 28 May 1959, NAACP Records III C 299.

64. Report by Patton, 21 August 1959; memorandum by Patton to Gloster Current, 10 September 1959, 18 August 1960, NAACP Records III C 299; report by the NAACP Voter Registration Committee, 22 December 1959, NAACP Records III A 266; Patton's report for Brooks, 17 November 1960, NAACP Records III A 269.

65. See the reports by Patton, 1 September 1960, 10 October 1960, 19 October 1960, 16 November 1960, NAACP Records III C 299.

66. See the reports by Patton, 21 August 1959, 16 June 1960, 18 August 1960, 19 October 1960, NAACP Records III C 299; 23 May 1960, NAACP Records III A 266; 11 July 1960, Patton to Brooks, 17 November 1960 (quote), 23 January 1961, NAACP Records III A 269.

67. Patton's report, 20 January 1960, NAACP Records III C 299; 14 March 1960, 27 April 1960, NAACP Records III A 269; annual report for 1959 by Brooks, 22 December 1959; John Brooks to Roy Wilkins, 5 April 1960, NAACP Records III A 266.

68. Memorandum by Patton to Brooks, 17 November 1960, NAACP Records III A

269; report of the NAACP Voter Registration Committee 1958–1960, NAACP Records III A 266.

69. 1961 annual report of the NAACP Voter Registration Committee, NAACP Records III A 266; annual report for 1961 by W. C. Patton, NAACP Records III A 269.

70. Wilkins to John Brooks, 18 June 1959; Brooks to John Morsell, 16 April 1963, NAACP Records III A 266; Patton to Wilkins, 24 January 1963; Patton to John Morsell, 16 May 1963, NAACP Records III C 299; interview by the author with Mr. W. C. Patton, Birmingham, Alabama, 20 October 1994.

71. Brooks's budget proposal, 28 November 1961; John Morsell to the presidents of the NAACP branches and state conferences, 19 October 1962, NAACP Records III A 267; see the annual budgets from 1958 to 1960, Arthur B. Spingarn Papers, box 44; on the fund-raising returns for 1959, see the annual report for 1959 by Brooks, 22 December 1959, NAACP Records III A 266; also see the proposed budget for a drive in Tampa, Florida, for 1958, NAACP Records III C 188.

72. John Morsell to the presidents of the NAACP branches and state conferences, 19 October 1962, NAACP Records III A 267.

73. Patton's circular letter, April 1962, NAACP Records III A 269; Patton's report on Arkansas, September 1960, NAACP Records III C 299; Patton's annual report for 1961, NAACP Records III A 269; reports by Clarence Laws, NAACP regional secretary for the Southwest, on violence against black voters in Louisiana, September 1962; annual report for 1962, NAACP Records III C 177; Rev. J. H. Scott to Roy Wilkins, 30 June 1963, NAACP Records III A 270; report by Medgar Evers, 20 January 1961, NAACP Records III C 247; campaign proposal for Mississippi by Patton, 8 May 1961; reports by Patton, 16 March 1962, 11 November 1962, NAACP Records III C 299.

74. Patton's annual report for 1961, NAACP Records III A 269; Brooks to Wilkins, 26 October 1960; for similar complaints, see Brooks to Wilkins, 22 August 1960, 27 April 1961; report by Brooks, 26 May 1961, NAACP Records III A 269.

75. Roy Wilkins to John Brooks, 12 November 1959; report by the NAACP Voter Registration Committee, 22 December 1959, NAACP Records III A 266.

76. Wilkins to Brooks, 19 June 1959; Brooks to Wilkins, 24 June 1959, 17 September 1959, NAACP Records III A 266.

Chapter 7. Voter Registration or Nonviolent Direct Action?

1. Brown v. Board of Education of Topeka, Kansas, 347 U.S. 483 (1954); on the history and consequences of Brown, see Kluger, Simple Justice; Patterson, Brown v. Board of Education. On the radicalization of white racism after Brown, see Bartley, The Rise of Massive Resistance; McMillen, The Citizens' Council; Klarman, "How Brown Changed Race Relations."

2. Roy Wilkins to Whitney Young, 5 December 1958, NAACP Records III A 212.

3. John Brooks to Wilkins, 4 November 1958; Wilkins to Brooks, 4 December 1958, NAACP Records III A 266.

4. The literature on the Montgomery Bus Boycott, Martin Luther King Jr., and the SCLC, respectively, is voluminous. See esp. the following standard accounts: Garrow, The Walking City; King, Stride toward Freedom; Ward and Badger, The Making of Martin Luther

King and the Civil Rights Movement; Fairclough, *To Redeem the Soul of America*; Branch, *Parting the Waters*.

5. The standard account of SNCC's organizational history remains Carson, *In Struggle*; from a contemporary perspective, see Zinn, *SNCC*; on the local origins of the 1960 sit-ins, see Chafe, *Civilities and Civil Rights*; on CORE, see Meier and Rudwick, *CORE*.

6. For statements expressing the will to cooperate with and their respect for the NAACP, see Martin Luther King Jr.'s letter to Roy Wilkins, 16 December 1957, NAACP Records III A 213; Marion Barry and Jane Stembridge of SNCC to Roy Wilkins, 9 August 1960, SNCC Papers, box 114; address by CORE leader James Farmer at the 52nd NAACP annual convention, 11 July 1961, NAACP Records III A 201.

7. Second Report—Special Committee on Strategy, 28 March 1962; also see Roy Wilkins to Barbee William Durham, 3 November 1961, NAACP Records III A 201.

8. See the memorandum by Roy Wilkins for Robert Ming, 20 September 1960; memorandum by Henry Lee Moon for Wilkins, 22 September 1960, Arthur Spingarn Papers, box 26.

9. See, e.g., the letter by Roy Wilkins to Dr. W. W. Plummer, 27 May 1958; Juanita Mitchell to Whitney Young, 21 February 1962; Young's reply, 2 March 1962, NAACP Records III A 212. On Whitney Young's role in the civil rights movement, see Weiss, *Whitney M. Young, Jr., and the Struggle for Civil Rights*, esp. 99–124.

10. See the letter by Abernathy, 20 May 1959; also see the report by Herbert Hill and James Farmer on attacks on the NAACP made by SCLC representative Bernard Lee, 3 March 1960, NAACP Records III A 213.

11. See the report by Brooks, 1 June 1959, NAACP Records III A 266.

12. Wilkins to Benjamin Mays, 19 May 1960, NAACP Records III A 213.

13. See the memorandum by Gloster Current to the field staff, 23 August 1957, including the editorial in the *Pittsburgh Courier* to be published the next day, NAACP Records III A 213.

14. Medgar Evers to Wilkins, 11 March 1957; Wilkins to Evers, 2 April 1957; Evers to Martin Luther King Jr., 20 August 1957; Evers to Ruby Hurley, 24 January 1958; Wilkins to SCLC director Wyatt Tee Walker, 1 March 1962, all in NAACP Records III A 213.

15. Garrow, *Bearing the Cross*, 95–96; memorandum by Gloster Current to Roy Wilkins, 9 January 1958; Roy Wilkins to Robert Saunders, 21 January 1958; address by Martin Luther King Jr. at the 50th NAACP convention, 17 July 1959, all in NAACP Records III 177.

16. Wilkins himself obtained the reports in 1979 under the Freedom of Information Act and kept them in his files. See J. Edgar Hoover to President Johnson, 30 November 1964; Cartha DeLoach to Mr. Mohr, 27 November 1964; memorandum by A. Jones to DeLoach on Wilkins's various contacts with the FBI, 16 March 1965, all in Roy Wilkins Papers, box 24. On the FBI campaign against King and the civil rights movement at large, see Garrow, *The FBI and Martin Luther King, Jr.*; O'Reilly, *"Racial Matters,"* esp. 144–46, on DeLoach's questionable credibility.

17. See Wilkins's weekly syndicated column, 13 April 1968, Roy Wilkins Papers, box 44; on the NAACP's position on the Vietnam War, see Berg, "Guns, Butter, and Civil Rights"; also see chapter nine.

18. See the exchange of letters between Reverend James Lawson and Roy Wilkins, 9 May 1960 and 13 May 1960; Wilkins to Benjamin Mays, 19 May 1960, in NAACP Records III A 213; Wilkins to James Farmer, 18 June 1963, NAACP Records III A 202.

19. See the letter by Marion Barry and Jane Stembridge to the national NAACP office, 14 June 1960, NAACP Records III A 214; Barry and Stembridge to Thurgood Marshall (quote), 9 August 1960, SNCC Papers, box 114.

20. Memorandum by John Morsell to Wilkins, 8 November 1961, NAACP Records III A 214.

21. Farmer, *Lay Bare the Heart*, 194–95; Wilkins to Farmer, 18 June 1963; G. L. Harris of CORE to Wilkins, 1 July 1963; John Morsell to Harris, 18 July 1963, all in NAACP Records III A 202.

22. Rudwick and Meier, "Integration vs. Separatism," 249; NAACP press release, 10 January 1964, NAACP Records III A 233; Wilkins's speech of 31 October 1964, quoted in a memorandum by Gloster Current to Henry Moon, 2 November 1964, NAACP Records III C 216.

23. See the minutes of a phone conversation between Gloster Current and P. B. Walker, 18 April 1961; memorandum by Herbert Wright to Wilkins and Current, 3 May 1961, NAACP Records III A 201.

24. SNCC quote in Zinn, *SNCC*, 220–21; King on *Meet the Press*, 17 April 1960, transcript in NAACP Records III A 177. The philosophical and historical roots of nonviolent resistance and civil disobedience cannot be discussed here at length. For a useful introduction, see Perry, "Civil Disobedience"; also see King, *Civil Rights and the Idea of Freedom*, 131–37. On the evolution of Martin Luther King Jr.'s thinking on nonviolent action, see the documents in Washington, ed., *A Testament of Hope*, 5–72.

25. See the report by R. S. Whitehouse and R. A. Watkins of the Birmingham Police Department on the passionate appeals by Martin Luther King Jr., Andrew Young, Ralph Abernathy, and others at a mass meeting at the 16th Street Church in Birmingham, 7 May 1963, Eugene T. Connor Papers, 13–14.

26. See Farmer's speech at the 52nd annual convention of the NAACP in Philadelphia, 11 July 1961, NAACP Records III A 201.

27. Meier and Rudwick, "The Origins of Nonviolent Direct Action in Afro-American Protest," esp. 308–9, 381–89.

28. Patterson, *Grand Expectations*, 348.

29. Kennedy quoted in Wilkins, *Standing Fast*, 291; on the frustratingly inconclusive Albany campaign, see Fairclough, *To Redeem the Soul of America*, 80–109.

30. Undated CORE paper (early 1960) by James R. Robinson, "The Meaning of the Sit-Ins," copy in NAACP Records III A 214.

31. *Boynton v. Virginia*, 364 U.S. 454 (1960). The decision resulted from a lawsuit brought by the LDF. See Tushnet, *Making Civil Rights Law*, 307–9.

32. Martin Luther King Jr. on NBC television's *The Nation's Future*, 26 November 1960, transcript in NAACP Records III A 177.

33. Martin Luther King Jr., "Civil Rights No. 1: The Right to Vote," in Washington, *A Testament of Hope*, 182–88; for the SCLC voting rights rhetoric, see, e.g., SCLC press release, 5 October 1957; SCLC, "Crusade for Citizenship," 15 May 1958; circular letter by

Martin Luther King Jr., 19 December 1961, all in NAACP Records III A 213; Marion Barry and Jane Stembridge to Wilkins, 17 June 1960; Wilkins's reply, 14 July 1960; see also Robert Moses' circular letter from SNCC's voter registration campaign in Greenwood, Mississippi, 15 September 1963, all in NAACP Records III A 214.

34. Undated letter by James Farmer to Wiley Branton (late 1961), CORE Papers, box 78 B; see the two CORE statements, 9 August 1964, NAACP Records III A 202. On the anti-Goldwater mobilization, see chapter eight.

35. Martin Luther King Jr. on NBC television's *The Nation's Future,* 26 November 1960, transcript in NAACP Records III A 177.

36. See chapter one; Wilkins, *Standing Fast,* 132–36.

37. Branch, *Parting the Waters,* 120–42; Meier and Rudwick, "The Origins of Nonviolent Direct Action in Afro-American Protest," 373–74; also see the literature listed in footnote 7.4, above.

38. On the sit-ins in Wichita and Oklahoma, see Eick, *Dissent in Wichita,* 1–11.

39. See the resolutions of the 47th NAACP annual convention, 26 June 1956, NAACP Records III A 2; resolutions of the 51st NAACP annual convention, 26 June 1960, NAACP Records III A 11; resolutions of the 52nd NAACP annual convention, 15 July 1961, NAACP Records III A 13.

40. See Farmer's speech before the NAACP annual convention, 11 July 1961, NAACP Records III A 201.

41. See the report by James Farmer on a meeting between NAACP representatives and SNCC students at Fisk University, 10 June 1960, NAACP Records III A 214; "Going to Jail Is Only Half the Battle," *Cleveland Call and Post,* 17 June 1961, copy in NAACP Records III 201.

42. See the fund-raising letter by James Farmer, 26 February 1962, NAACP Records III A 201; resolutions of the 51st NAACP annual convention, 26 June 1960, NAACP Records III A 1; John Morsell to Aaron Henry, 8 October 1965, NAACP Records III A 231; also see the interview with Roy Wilkins, RJBOHC, interview no. 550.

43. John Brooks to Wilkins, 20 April 1960; NAACP Records III A 213; Wilkins to Ed King, 1 September 1961, NAACP Records III A 214; Wilkins to Barbee William Durham, 3 November 1961, NAACP Records III A 201; Medgar Evers's report, 12 October 1961, NAACP Records III A 231.

44. NAACP press release, 3 June 1963, NAACP Records III A 232; Dittmer, *Local People,* 155–65; Moody, *Coming of Age in Mississippi,* 261–87. The assassin, a white supremacist by the name of Byron De La Beckwith, was twice acquitted on a hung jury and finally convicted in 1994.

45. NAACP press releases, 1 and 3 June 1963, NAACP Records III A 232; Dittmer, *Local People,* 164; Special Committee on Strategy, 28 March 1962, NAACP Records III A 201.

46. Resolutions of the 52nd NAACP annual convention, 15 July 1961, NAACP Records III A 13; see the leaflet by the NAACP-sponsored Jackson Area Boycott Movement, "To The Jackson Businessman," undated (early January 1963); United Front, Inc., "Unamerican [sic] Activities of Negro Organization in Jackson," March 1964, NAACP Records III A 232.

47. On the internal strife, see, e.g., the letter by Archie Jones of the Natchez NAACP to Martin Luther King Jr. demanding the withdrawal of SCLC activist Reverend Albert R. Sampson, 19 October 1965, NAACP Records III A 177; on the exasperation of the national office with the Natchez campaign, see John Morsell to Aaron Henry, 8 October 1965, NAACP Records III A 231; on the Natchez campaign, also see Dittmer, *Local People*, 353–62.

48. See Moon's memorandum to editors and columnists, including the text of the Natchez agreement, 8 December 1965; memorandum by Gloster Current to Roy Wilkins et al., 30 November 1965; NAACP press releases, 9 and 16 October 1965, NAACP Records III A 232; Dittmer, *Local People*, 360–61.

49. John Morsell to Aaron Henry, 8 October 1965, NAACP Records III A 231. On the civil rights legislation of 1964–65 and the splitting up of the civil rights movement, respectively, see chapters eight and nine.

50. See the interview with Roy Wilkins, RJBOHC, interview no. 550; Gloster Current to the NAACP branch presidents in large cities, 15 April 1965, warning against demonstrations in northern metropolitan cities, NAACP Records III A 177.

51. Circular letter by James Farmer et al., 27 February 1965, NAACP Records III A 267; SNCC Papers, box 165; fund-raising letter by Martin Luther King Jr., October 1965; Wilkins to Benjamin McAdoo, 14 December 1964, NAACP III A 214.

52. See Moses' undated memo (1963), "Memo to Workers in the Voter Education Project," SNCC Papers, box 23; see, however, the complaint by CORE worker David Dennis about the "lies" in the NAACP registration complaints, Dennis to James McCain, 30 July 1962, CORE Papers, box 81. My general assessment is based on the following archival sources: SCLC Papers, boxes 138–42, 165–69; SNCC Papers, boxes 16, 22–23, 103–4, 114; CORE Papers, boxes 77, 78A and B, 81–82; MFDP Papers, boxes 23–24.

53. John Brooks to Roy Wilkins, 27 February 1962, NAACP Records III A 266. On the NAACP Voter Registration Committee, see chapter six.

54. Stern, *Calculating Visions*, 56–57, 63–69; Branch, *Parting the Waters*, 478–82; see VEP director Wiley Branton to Russel Lynes of *Harper's Magazine*, 31 May 1962, SRC Papers, series 6 (Voter Education Project), reel 172.

55. Carson, *In Struggle*, 39–44; memorandum by SNCC worker Charles Dew, 14 August 1961, NAACP Records III A 214; SNCC prospectus for the VEP, 6 April 1962, SNCC Papers, box 23.

56. Memorandum by the SRC for the meeting scheduled for 23 August 1961, NAACP Records III A 267; memorandum by Henry Lee Moon to Roy Wilkins, 28 August 1961, NAACP Records III A 266; Leslie Dunbar to the representatives of the various groups, 13 September 1961, NAACP Records III A 271.

57. For very skeptical replies, see the memoranda by Brooks, 22 September 1961; Patton, 25 September 1961; Current, undated; Mitchell, 27 September 1961; Ruby Hurley, 25 September 1961; for cautious approval, see John Morsell, 27 September 1961; Clarence Laws, 26 September 1961; Kelly Alexander, 27 September 1961, all in NAACP Records III A 271.

58. Wilkins to Dunbar, 17 October 1961; Dunbar to Stephen Currier of the Taconic

Foundation, 10 November 1961; Dunbar to Wilkins, 10 November 1961; Wilkins to Dunbar, 22 November 1961, all in NAACP Records III A 271.

59. See the SRC press release, 29 March 1962, NAACP Records III A 271; on the budget and the registration figures, see Watters and Cleghorn, *Climbing Jacob's Ladder*, 26–27, 44–50; for Branton's administrative and mediation work, see, e.g., his letters to Andrew Young of SCLC, 19 and 21 March 1964, 14 April 1964, SCLC Papers, box 138; Branton to James Forman, 4 May 1962, SNCC Papers, box 22; Branton to Marvin Rich of CORE, 28 January 1964, CORE Papers, box 78B; see also the account by Branton, RJBOHC, interview no. 371.

60. See the circular letter by John Morsell, 19 October 1962; Brooks's memorandum, 28 October 1961, NAACP Records III A 267; Brooks to Wilkins, 27 February 1962; report by Brooks, 6 November 1963; reply by John Morsell, 13 November 1963, all in NAACP Records III A 266.

61. See the first quarterly report by the VEP, SCLC Papers, box 138; Roy Wilkins to Branton, 3 March 1963 (quote), NAACP Records III A 271; for the procedural aspects, see Branton to Morsell, 29 March 1963, 11 April 1963; Branton to Wilkins, 3 April 1963; Wilkins to Branton, 24 April 1963, all in NAACP Records III A 214; memorandum by Branton, 20 February 1963, SRC Papers, series 6, 177.

62. Wiley Branton to W. C. Patton, 11 May 1964, NAACP Records III A 214; for the cooperation and disagreements between Branton and the NAACP, see their correspondence in NAACP Records VI, series 1 (Voter Education Project), box 3 (Wiley Branton); SRC Papers, series 6, 172, 173, 177, 178.

63. For the reassignments by Branton, see Branton to the NAACP, 8 October 1962; Branton to James McCain (CORE), 28 September 1963, NAACP Records VI I 3; on the need to go into the rural areas, see the memorandum by Moses and Tom Gaither (CORE), 27 January 1962, NAACP Records III A 271; Elizabeth Wyckoff to Branton, 7 December 1962, SNCC Papers, box 23; on the founding of COFO, see Dittmer, *Local People*, 118–19.

64. See, e.g., the report by Robert Moses on his joint work with Amzie Moore, NAACP president of Bolivar County, Mississippi, undated (1964), NAACP Records III A 214; Gloster Current to Charles Evers, 5 February 1964, NAACP Records III C 245; Patton's report, 30 March 1963, NAACP Records III 269; Patton to Branton, 21 October 1963, NAACP Records VI I 3; Branton to Henry and Moses, 12 November 1963, SNCC Papers, box 23.

65. On the "freedom" registration and elections, see Dittmer, *Local People*, 200–207; MFDP Papers, box 14 (Mississippi Freedom Vote); SNCC Papers, box 98; NAACP press release, 12 October 1963, NAACP Records III A 232; report by John Brooks, 14 July 1964, NAACP Records III A 266; interview with Althea Simmons, RJBOHC, interview no. 574. On the MFDP's stand at the Atlantic City Democratic convention, see chapter eight.

66. On the disintegration of COFO, see Dittmer, *Local People*, 341–44; Brooks to Wilkins, 14 May 1965, NAACP Records III A 266; Wilkins's statement to the *New York Times*, 21 April 1965, NAACP Records III C 1; NAACP press release, 7 May 1965, NAACP Records III A 267.

67. See the proposal by Paul Anthony (SRC) to John Morsell, 26 October 1965; Morsell's reply, 3 December 1965, NAACP Records III A 214; on the political background,

see the memorandum by Thurgood Marshall to President Johnson, 14 January 1966, CRLBJ, part 1, reel 2; memorandum by U.S. Attorney General Nicholas Katzenbach, 2 November 1965, CRLBJ, part 1, reel 9; memorandum by Louis Martin (Democratic National Committee) to Lee White, 23 December 1965, CRLBJ, part 1, reel 13; on the procedural arrangements, see Vernon Jordan to Roy Wilkins, 9 March 1966; John Brooks to Wilkins, 14 March 1966, NAACP IV A 62.

68. See the summary by the NAACP on grants and results within the VEP framework for the period from January to October 1966; reports by Vernon Jordan, 5 December 1966, 8 December 1967; John Morsell to Jordan, 15 December 1967, all in NAACP Records IV A 64; Patton's speech, 5 October 1967, NAACP Records IV A 62; also see the accounts by Vernon Jordan, RJBOHC, interview no. 130/405. On the radicalization of SNCC and CORE, see chapter nine.

69. On the details of the Voting Rights Act, see chapter eight; see the memoranda by the Civil Service Commission to President Johnson, 19 August 1965, 31 January 1966, 25 April 1968, all in CRLBJ, part 1, reel 9.

70. See the study by the VEP, "The Effects of Federal Examiners and Organized Registration Campaigns on Negro Registration," July 1966, NAACP Records IV A'50; telegrams by Charles Evers to President Johnson, 9 August 1965; Charles Evers to U.S. Attorney General Katzenbach, 10 August 1965, NAACP Records III C 245; Patton to Katzenbach, 21 March 1966, NAACP Records IV 62.

71. See memoranda by Current, 8 and 11 February 1965; NAACP press release, 7 May 1965, all in NAACP Records III A 267.

72. See the two extensive reports on the summer project, 17 and 23 July (quote from Clarksdale Press Register) 1965, NAACP Records III A 268.

73. See the final report, 11 September 1965, NAACP Records III A 268; also see Patton's report, undated, "NAACP Alabama Summer Project," NAACP Records III C 299.

74. See the undated NAACP memorandum, "A Proposal for Expanded Voter Education Programs in the Southern States," NAACP Records IV A 64; John Morsell to Brooks, 24 March 1966; NAACP press release, 2 July 1966 (quote); Althea Simmons to Gloster Current, 10 January 1966, all in NAACP Records IV A 62.

75. See the article by Patton in the *Birmingham Times*, 4 November 1966; report by the New Orleans NAACP youth chapter on their registration in June 1967, NAACP Records IV A 62; report by Wilfred Aubert, 20 July 1967, NAACP Records IV A 63.

76. See the undated report by Morsell to Gilbert Jonas, "Interim Report on 1967–68 NAACP Voter Registration Activity"; Patton's undated report, "Political Action, November, December 1968"; "Progress Reports," April to October 1968, all in NAACP Records IV A 63; "Partial List of Registration Campaigns"; Patton to Wilkins, 20 December 1968, NAACP Records IV A 62.

77. See John Morsell to Brooks, 24 May 1968; Morsell to Brooks and Patton, 16 April 1969, NAACP Records IV A 62; memorandum by Morsell, 14 October 1968, NAACP Records IV C 55.

78. Roy Wilkins's syndicated column, "After the Vote," 15 August 1965, Roy Wilkins Papers, box 39.

79. Patton to Ralph McGill of the *Atlanta Constitution*, 5 September 1967, NAACP Records IV A 62; interview by the author with Mr. W. C. Patton, Birmingham, Alabama, 20 October 1994; interview with W. C. Patton, RJBOHC, interview no. 406. The names of W. C. Patton and John Brooks are rarely found in the indices of books on the history of the civil rights movement.

80. For the modernization of southern society after World War II, see Bartley, *The New South*; Goldfield, *Black, White, and Southern;* Watters and Cleghorn, *Climbing Jacob's Ladder, 115*.

81. NAACP press release, 7 May 1966, NAACP Records IV A 63; on Lurleen Wallace's candidacy, see Carter, *Politics of Rage*, 272–93. The state constitution prohibited George Wallace from seeking direct reelection.

Chapter 8. The Politics of Civil Rights

1. See chapter five.

2. Roy Wilkins's circular letter to the NAACP officers, 25 August 1952, NAACP Records II A 452; NAACP press release, 22 June 1952, "NAACP leads Negro Opinion," NAACP Records II A 477; Walter White's statement before the Resolutions Committee of the Democratic National Convention, 17 July 1952, NAACP Records II A 225. The southern registration drive fell far short of the 2 million goal, though. See chapter six.

3. White's speech before the NAACP Political Action Institute, 19 April 1952, NAACP Records II A 478; White's statement, 24 July 1952, NAACP Records II A 452; Wilkins's memorandum, 8 September 1952, on his interview with Stevenson, NAACP Records II A 477.

4. Clarence Mitchell to Walter White, 1 August 1952; Henry Lee Moon to Walter White, 29 September 1952; White to Wilson Wyatt, 30 September 1952, all in NAACP Records II A 225.

5. Walter White to Roderick Stevens, 16 May 1952, NAACP Records II A 248; Wilkins's memorandum, 8 September 1952, on his interview with Eisenhower; White's speech before the Ohio NAACP conference of branches, 21 September 1952, both in NAACP Records II A 477.

6. "Survey of the Negro Vote in the 1952 Presidential Elections," December 1952, NAACP Records II A 452; NAACP press release, 6 November 1952, NAACP Records II A 477; election results according to Diamond, ed., *Congressional Quarterly's Guide to U.S. Elections*, 358.

7. Daisy Lampkin to White, 29 October 1952; NAACP press release, 28 November 1952, both in NAACP Records II A 477.

8. Wilkins to White, 16 January 1953, NAACP Records II A 248; for the "Civil Rights under the GOP" conference, see the invitations, 18 November 1953; the minutes and the statement of the conference, 4 December 1953, all in NAACP Records II A 453.

9. Excerpts from Nixon's remarks before the NAACP annual convention in Atlantic City, 26 June 1955, NAACP Records II A 458; Eisenhower's address to the 1956 NAACP convention, 26 June 1956, NAACP Records III A 2; Wilkins's speech, 1 July 1956, NAACP Records III A 245; Wilkins, *Standing Fast*, 222; on Ike's racial views, see Burk, *The Eisenhower Administration and Black Civil Rights*, esp. 15–16; much more critical is O'Reilly, *Nixon's Piano*, 165–68.

10. Krock cited in a circular letter by Senator Paul Douglass (D-Ill.), 18 September 1956, NAACP Records III A 70; on the behavior of southern Democrats in the Senate, see the classical account by V. O. Key, *Southern Politics in State and Nation*, 345–68.

11. See the text of the "Southern Manifesto" in Martin, ed., *Brown v. Board of Education*, 220–23; resolution of the Republican State Central Committee of California, 15 August 1956, NAACP Records III A 246.

12. On the origins of the 1957 Civil Rights Act, see Lawson, *Black Ballots*, 140–202; Burk, *The Eisenhower Administration and Black Civil Rights*, 204–26.

13. *The Public Papers of the Presidents of the United States: Dwight D. Eisenhower: 1957*, 17–30; Roy Wilkins's statement to the *New York Post*, 1 February 1957, NAACP Records III A 177; telegrams by the SCLC to Eisenhower, Nixon, and Brownell, 14 February 1957, copies in NAACP Records III 213; see the testimony by Austin T. Walden of Atlanta and the Reverend W. D. Ridgeway of Hattiesburg, Mississippi, before the Senate Subcommittee on Constitutional Rights, 28 February 1957; letter by Clarence Mitchell to the committee chairman, Senator Thomas Hennings, 28 February 1957, all in NAACP Records III A 73. On the fate of Gus Courts, see chapter six.

14. See the open letter by Brownell, published by the DoJ, 3 June 1957, copy in NAACP Records III A 71.

15. See the memoranda by NAACP legal counsel Francis Pohlhaus, 18 April 1957, NAACP Records 1993 addition box 18; Pohlhaus to Wilkins, 7 June 1957, NAACP Records III A 72; undated memorandum from the legal department to the branches, "Analyzing the 'Jury Trial' Amendment," NAACP Records III A 68; resolutions of the 48th annual convention of the NAACP, 29 June 1957, NAACP Records III A 5.

16. Lawson, *Black Ballots*, 177–99; Burk, *The Eisenhower Administration and Black Civil Rights*, 221–27; Cohodas, *Strom Thurmond and the Politics of Southern Change*, 294–98.

17. See Roy Wilkins's memorandum to the states conference presidents, 12 July 1957, NAACP Records III A 68; NAACP press release, 1 August 1957, NAACP Records III A 73; Dirksen's letter to Wilkins, 30 July 1957, NAACP Records III A 69; Wilkins's memorandum, 13 August 1957, NAACP Records III A 68; Wilkins, *Standing Fast*, 245–46.

18. See numerous critical letters to the NAACP leadership, e.g., Cecil Moore to Wilkins, 16 August 1957; Elmer Carter to Channing Tobias, 16 August 1957; Wilkins's reply to Carter, 5 September 1957, all in NAACP Records III A 71; resolutions of members of the New Orleans NAACP branch, 16 August 1957; Wilkins's reply, 21 August 1957; Morris Henderson, NAACP branch St. Louis County, Missouri, to Wilkins, 5 September 1957; Arthur Johnson, NAACP branch Detroit, to Wilkins, 20 September 1957, all in NAACP Records III A 68; Wayne Morse to Roy Wilkins, 18 September 1957, NAACP Records III A 69; Paul Douglas to Arthur Spingarn, 6 September 1957, NAACP Records III A 70; NAACP press release, 12 September 1957, NAACP Records III A 73.

19. Wilkins, *Standing Fast*, 246.

20. Wilkins's letter to Rogers, 12 December 1957, NAACP Records III A 145; see the letters by Clarence Mitchell to Assistant Attorney General Wilson White, 7 February 1958, 28 May 1958, 13 June 1958, all in NAACP Records III A 145; Mitchell's memoranda for Wilkins, 19 March 1958, 25 March 1958; Mitchell's memorandum for the Civil Rights Commission, 12 June 1958; Wilkins to Attorney General Rogers, 11 December 1958, all in

NAACP Records III A 66; Mitchell to Wilkins, 15 January 1959, NAACP Records III A 145; on the activities of the DoJ, see Lawson, *Black Ballots*, 206–12.

21. U.S. Commission on Civil Rights, *Hearings Held in Montgomery, Alabama: Voting*; U.S. Commission on Civil Rights, *Hearings Held in Montgomery, Alabama: Report*, esp. 140–42; on the work of the commission during the crucial years of civil rights legislation, see Dulles, *The Civil Rights Commission: 1957–1965*, esp. 31–41, 82–85.

22. On the "referee" plan, see Lawson, *Black Ballots*, 233–34; Burk, *The Eisenhower Administration and Black Civil Rights*, 243–44; telegram by Wilkins to Attorney General Rogers, 4 February 1960; response by Assistant Attorney General Joseph Ryan, 10 February 1960, NAACP Records III A 145; letter by Wilkins to C. B. Powell of the *Amsterdam News*, 19 February 1960; memorandum by Robert Carter to Wilkins, 4 March 1960, both in NAACP Records III A 71.

23. See the summary of the law, in *Congressional Quarterly*, 8 April 1960, copy in NAACP Records III A 71; see Douglas's long press release on the bill and the legislative struggle, copy in NAACP III A 70; Wilkins's telegram to the NAACP branches, 30 March 1960, NAACP Records III A 68.

24. See the undated (1960) report by the Non-Partisan Crusade to Mobilize Negro Voters, NAACP Records III A 268.

25. On Nixon's membership status, see Roy Wilkins to Gertrude Gorman, 9 October 1956; John Morsell to Cynthia Hubbard, 22 October 1956; Wilkins to Nixon, 21 April 1959, all in NAACP Record III A 239.

26. Schlesinger, *History of American Presidential Elections*, 4:3541–45; for the standard accounts of JFK's civil rights policies, see Brauer, *John F. Kennedy and the Second Reconstruction*; Stern, *Calculating Visions*; for a very critical portrait, see O'Reilly, *Nixon's Piano*, 189–237; also very critical is Niven, *The Politics of Injustice*; for an analysis of JFK's stand on the jury trial amendment, see Shaffer, "Senator John F. Kennedy and the Liberal Establishment."

27. On the 1958 controversy between Wilkins and Kennedy, see the following documents: JFK to Roy Wilkins, 6 May 1958; Roy Wilkins to Peter Arlos, 16 May 1958; Wilkins to JFK, 29 May 1958; JFK to Wilkins, 6 June 1958, 18 July 1958 (quote); Roy Wilkins to Herbert Tucker (quote), 16 October 1958; JFK to Wilkins, 28 October 1958; JFK to Kivie Kaplan, 22 June 1959, all in NAACP III A 176; see also Wilkins, *Standing Fast*, 272–74.

28. On Johnson's attitude toward civil rights, see Stern, *Calculating Visions*, 115–59; on the development of LBJ's image among key NAACP leaders, see the interviews in Civil Rights during the Johnson Administration, 1963–1969 (CRLBJ), Part 3: Oral Histories: Thurgood Marshall, Clarence Mitchell, Charles Evers, Roy Wilkins, all in reel 3; Aaron Henry, reel 2; Wilkins, *Standing Fast*, 276.

29. See the letters by Henry Lee Moon to the press secretaries of both campaigns, 6 September 1960; letters by Moon to the three television networks, 19 September 1960; answer by the Nixon campaign, 14 September 1960; answer by NBC, 27 September 1960, all in NAACP III A 246; for a detailed account of the phone call to Mrs. King and the publication of the "No Comment Nixon versus a Candidate with a Heart" brochure, see Wofford, *Of Kennedys and Kings*, 11–28; see the letter by Roy Wilkins to Emmette Whitman, 29 September 1960, NAACP Records III A 72.

30. On black voting behavior in 1960, see Lawson, *Black Ballots*, 256–58.

31. Wilkins to Theodore Sorenson, 7 February 1961, NAACP III Records A 176 (quote); Wilkins, *Standing Fast*, 279–83; see the memorandum by the National Urban League to JFK, 29 December 1960, and the study by the Southern Regional Council, January 1961, "The Federal Executive and Civil Rights," both in Civil Rights during the Kennedy Administration (CRJFK), Part 1: The White House Central Files and Staff Files and the President's Office Files, reel 1.

32. Wilkins to William T. Coleman, 28 February 1961; speech by Bishop Stephen G. Spottswood, chairman of the NAACP board of directors, 12 July 1961, at the White House meeting, both in NAACP III Records A 176; Wilkins, *Standing Fast*, 284 (quote).

33. Handwritten note by Harris Wofford to a memorandum for Kenneth O'Donnell, 18 July 1961; memorandum by Louis Martin to O'Donnell, 20 June 1961; memorandum by Frank Reeves to JFK, 5 May 1961; memorandum by Wofford to O'Donnell, 4 October 1961, all in CRJFK, part 1, reel 1; Wofford, *Of Kennedys and Kings*, 136–39.

34. On the black appointments early in the administration, see the undated "Summary of Civil Rights Progress, January 20–October 1961," CRJFK, part 1, reel 1; also see Weisbrot, *Freedom Bound*, 49–50; Wilkins's telegram to JFK, 22 June 1961, NAACP III A 176.

35. Wilkins, *Standing Fast*, 280 (quote); also see Wilkins's sixty-one-page memo on behalf of the Leadership Conference on Civil Rights, CRJFK, part 1, reel 1; letter by White House adviser Lee C. White to the NAACP Staten Island Branch, March 1963, CRJFK, part 1, reel 2; for a copy of the "Ink for Jack" call, see Kenney, *John F. Kennedy*, 103.

36. See Robert Kennedy's report for JFK, 24 January 1963, in Belknap, *Civil Rights, the White House, and the Justice Department, 1945–1968*, vol. 15, *Voting Rights*, 118–24; also see Lawson, *Black Ballots*, 267–83; Wofford, *Of Kennedys and Kings*, 223–27; on the Voter Education Project, see chapter seven.

37. Farmer quoted in Wofford, *Of Kennedys and Kings*, 151; on the political strategy behind nonviolent direct action, see chapter seven.

38. On the Birmingham campaign, see the comprehensive study by Eskew, *But for Birmingham*; on the international impact, see Dudziak, "Birmingham, Addis Ababa, and the Image of America"; for JFK's 11 June 1963 speech, see *The Public Papers of the Presidents: John F. Kennedy: 1961–1963*, 468–71; Wilkins, *Standing Fast*, 290.

39. *The Public Papers of the Presidents: John F. Kennedy: 1961–1963*, 483–94; on the extremely complicated legislative history of the Kennedy civil rights bill and the ensuing 1964 Civil Rights Act, see Graham, *Civil Rights and the Presidency*, 46–86.

40. Wilkins, *Standing Fast*, 290–94; on the March on Washington, see Weisbrot, *Freedom Bound*, 76–85; Pfeffer, *A. Philip Randolph*, 240–80; circular letter to the NAACP branch presidents, 30 July 1963, NAACP Records III A 228.

41. See the comments by Edward P. Morgan of ABC, 29 August 1963; speeches by the march leaders and many more materials in NAACP Records III A 228; Stern, *Calculating Visions*, 105.

42. NAACP press release, 13 September 1963, NAACP Records III A 68; memorandum by Gloster Current to the NAACP branch presidents, 24 September 1963; memoranda by Roy Wilkins to the branch presidents, 18 October 1963 and 20 November 1963,

all in NAACP Records III A 67; Bishop Spottswood to Robert Kennedy, 14 October 1963, NAACP Records III A 145.

43. On the "K.O. the Kennedys!" signs, see the protest telegram by Mississippi NAACP president Aaron Henry to Governor Ross Barnett, 30 November 1963, NAACP Records III A 177; on the reaction to JFK's death among white supremacists, see Rorabaugh, *Kennedy and the Promise of the Sixties*, 228–29.

44. For the origins of Johnson's concept of a Great Society, see his speech at the University of Michigan in May 1964, *The Public Papers of the Presidents: Lyndon B. Johnson: 1964*, 704–6; for a general account, see Patterson, *Grand Expectations*, 524–92; even in O'Reilly's, *Nixon's Piano*, a book that is highly critical of virtually every president's racial policies and attitudes, Johnson receives relatively good marks (see 239–76).

45. See Wilkins's obituary, 24 January 1973, Roy Wilkins Papers, box 47; Clarence Mitchell interview in Civil Rights During the Johnson Administration, 1963–1969, Part 3: Oral Histories. Also see similar praise by other the NAACP leaders, including Wilkins, Aaron Henry, Charles Evers, Thurgood Marshall, ibid.

46. Wilkins, *Standing Fast*, 295–96; NAACP press release, 2 December 1963, NAACP Records III A 68; for affirmative public statements on the civil rights bill by LBJ, see *The Public Papers of the Presidents: Lyndon B. Johnson: 1963–1964*, 8–10, 11–12; 112–18; Wilkins to Johnson, 3 March 1964, NAACP Records III A 175.

47. Quote in Wilkins, *Standing Fast*, 299–300; Johnson, *The Vantage Point*, 157–58.

48. Humphrey quoted in Graham, *Civil Rights and the Presidency*, 79, 77–86; Wilkins, *Standing Fast*, 301; Johnson, *The Vantage Point*, 158–60; Stern, *Calculating Visions*, 169–86.

49. Memoranda by Roy Wilkins to the NAACP branches, 20 March 1964, 10 April 1964, NAACP records III A 67; NAACP press release, 24 January 1964, NAACP Records III A 68.

50. See the resolutions of the 55th annual convention of the NAACP, 22–27 June 1964, NAACP Records III A 17; Wilkins, *Standing Fast*, 299; on the NAACP membership in 1963–64, see Marger, "Social Movement Organizations and Response to Environmental Change," 23.

51. NAACP press release, 22 May 1964, NAACP Records III A 247; on Wallace's 1964 campaign, see Carter, *The Politics of Rage*, 195–225.

52. Telegram by Wilkins to Goldwater, 13 May 1964, NAACP Records III A 247; resolutions of the 55th annual convention of the NAACP, 22–27 June 1964, NAACP Records III A 17; see the *Wall Street Journal* report, 30 July 1964, "Many Gary [Indiana] Democrats Who Supported Wallace to Vote for Goldwater," copy in NAACP Records III A 247.

53. See the memorandum by Henry Lee Moon for John Morsell et al., 14 July 1964, NAACP Records III A 247; see the NAACP endorsement of Rep. William McCulloch (R-Ohio), 28 October 1964, NAACP Records III A 67; Roy Wilkins to Juanita Stout, 22 October 1964, NAACP Records III A 69; Roy Wilkins to the New York City branches, 31 July 1964, NAACP Records III A 268.

54. See Patton's report, 27 November 1964, NAACP Records III A 269; NAACP press releases, 21 August 1964 and 3 October 1964, NAACP Records III A 247; memorandum by Calvin Banks to Roy Wilkins, 5 November 1964, NAACP Records III A 268.

55. Memorandum by Johnson aide Lee C. White, 6 July 1964, CRLBJ, part 1, reel 2; Wilkins's telegram to Martin Luther King Jr. et al., 22 July 1964; statement by civil rights leaders, 29 July 1964, NAACP Records III A 247; CORE statement, 9 August 1964, NAACP Records III A 202; Wilkins, *Standing Fast*, 303–4.

56. On the origins of the MFDP, see Dittmer, *Local People*, 200–207; also see chapter seven.

57. Resolutions of the 55th annual convention of the NAACP, 22–27 June 1964, NAACP Records III A 17; memo by Arnold Aronson of the LCCR to cooperating organizations, 13 August 1964, NAACP Records III A 206; Wilkins's circular letter to the NAACP branch presidents, 12 August 1964, NAACP Records III A 232; letter by Wilkins to the New Jersey NAACP state board, 18 August 1964, NAACP Records III A 247.

58. The tug-of-war at Atlantic City has been told in great detail by many historians and participants. See, e.g., Dittmer, *Local People*, 280–32; Weisbrot, *Freedom Bound*, 116–23; on Fannie Lou Hamer, see the biography by Mills, *This Little Light of Mine*, esp. 111–13.

59. Wilkins's statement before the Resolutions and Platform Committee, 19 August 1964, NAACP Records III A 247; Wilkins, *Standing Fast*, 304–6; interview with Fannie Lou Hamer, RJBOHC, interview no. 282; Mills, *This Little Light of Mine*, 128.

60. See the letter by Theresa Del Pozzo, 19 September 1964, NAACP Records III A 247.

61. See the summary of the NAACP registration campaign, undated, NAACP Records III C 245; Moon, "How We Voted and Why," *Crisis* 72 (January 1965): 26–31; Wilkins's telegram to Johnson, 5 November 1964, NAACP Records III A 175.

62. Patterson, *Grand Expectations*, 560–61; Stern, *Calculating Visions*, 211–15.

63. Wilkins, *Standing Fast*, 306.

64. See Garrow, *Protest at Selma*, 37–38; Lawson, *Black Ballots*, 307.

65. NAACP press release, 12 March 1965, NAACP Records III A 270; see Wilkins's weekly syndicated column, "Lesson from Selma," 14 March 1965, in Roy Wilkins Papers, box 39. On the events during the Selma campaign, see Garrow, *Protest at Selma*, 39–95; Weisbrot, *Freedom Bound*, 127–49, Fairclough, *To Redeem the Soul of America*, 225–51.

66. Johnson, *The Vantage Point*, 162–63; Johnson quoted by Katzenbach in Raines, *My Soul Is Rested*, 337.

67. For a summary of the bill, see Graham, *Civil Rights and the Presidency*, 94–95.

68. Dirksen quoted in Lawson, *Black Ballots*, 309; Wilkins, *Standing Fast*, 307; Johnson, *The Vantage Point*, 164–66; *The Public Papers of the Presidents: Lyndon B. Johnson: 1965*, 281–87; Wilkins's telegram to LBJ, 16 March 1965, NAACP Records III A 175.

69. See the circular memorandum by Gloster Current to the NAACP branches, 23 February 1965, NAACP Records III A 267; for more material on these activities, see NAACP Records III C 306, folder: "Selma Demonstrations Branch Support"; Wilkins, *Standing Fast*, 308; Gloster Current to the NAACP branch presidents, 15 April 1965, NAACP Records III A 177.

70. See the joint declaration, 27 February 1965, NAACP Records III A 267; SNCC Papers, box 165 (emphasis in the original); see the memorandum by presidential aide Lee C. White for LBJ, 4 March 1965, in Belknap, *Civil Rights, the White House, and the Justice Department, 1945–1968*, vol. 15, *Voting Rights*, 152–55.

71. See the various drafts for amending the voting rights bill, NAACP Records III A 267; Clarence Mitchell to Wilkins, 22 July 1965, Roy Wilkins Papers, box 7; Watson, *Lion in the Lobby*, 650–58; also see chapter four on the anti–poll tax campaign of the 1940s.

72. Graham, *Civil Rights and the Presidency*, 97–98; *Harper v. Virginia State Board of Elections*, 383 U.S. 663 (1966); Roy Wilkins column, "The Poll Tax Decision," 9 April 1966, Roy Wilkins Papers, box 39; see also chapter four.

73. Watson, *Lion in the Lobby*, 639–45; Lawson, *Black Ballots*, 314–21; Graham, *Civil Rights and the Presidency*, 96–98; *The Public Papers of the Presidents: Lyndon B. Johnson: 1965*, 840–43.

74. Moses' speech at the *National Guardian* dinner, 24 November 1964, copy in MFDP Papers, box 23 (emphasis in the original); on the 1964 "freedom elections," see Dittmer, *Local People*, 320–24.

75. Dittmer, *Local People*, 338–41; Lawson, *Black Ballots*, 322–28; see presidential aide Lee C. White to SNCC leader John Lewis, CRLBJ, part 1, reel 9.

76. See Morsell's circular letter to the branches, 22 March 1965, and the attached memorandum by legal counsel Francis Pohlhaus, NAACP Records III A 232; Marvin Rich to David Dennis, 11 January 1965, on the LCCR meeting, CORE Papers, box 81.

77. MFDP statement, 10 February 1965, SNCC Papers, box 169; circular letter by the Washington Bureau of the MFDP, 29 March 1965, SNCC Papers, box 165; statement by John Lewis, 17 May 1965, SNCC Papers, box 169; Hamer quoted in the circular letter by Lawrence Guyot, 28 September 1965, SNCC Papers, box 169; on the vote in the House, see Dittmer, *Local People*, 351–52.

78. See, e.g., the circular letter by Lawrence Guyot, 19 May 1965, which leaves out the NAACP from the MFDP's list of supporting groups, SNCC Papers, box 169; on the registration figures, see Smith and Horton, *Historical Statistics of Black America*, 2:1312–13; also see chapter seven; on the massive resistance against the Voting Rights Act in Mississippi, see Parker, *Black Votes Count*, 34–77; on the issue of minority vote dilution, see the conclusion of this book.

79. *South Carolina v. Katzenbach*, 383 U.S. 301 (1966).

80. See LBJ's telegram to John A. Nixon, president of the Alabama NAACP, 2 September 1965, CRLBJ, part 1, reel 2; Weiss, "Creative Tensions in the Leadership of the Civil Rights Movement."

Chapter 9. Black Power—White Backlash

1. Washington, *A Testament of Hope*, 197; Wilkins to Anthony Lewis of the *New York Times*, 4 February 1960, NAACP Records III A 267.

2. Stone, *Black Political Power in America*, 247; on the riots, see Feagin and Hahn, *Ghetto Revolts*; Blum, *Years of Discord*, 253–64.

3. Rudwick and Meier, "Black Violence in the Twentieth Century"; National Advisory Commission on Civil Disorders, *Report*, 1, 2, 10 (quotes), summary 1–29.

4. For an introduction to the various strands of black nationalism, see Van Deburg, *Modern Black Nationalism*; for the NAACP's conflicts with Garvey, see chapter two.

5. Goldman, *The Death and Life of Malcolm X*; Samuels, "Two Ways," 40.

6. See, e.g., Malcolm X to Roy Wilkins, 1 August 1963; reply by Wilkins, 5 August 1963; statement by Wilkins on Malcolm X to *U.S. News and World Report*, 17 March 1964; NAACP press release on Malcolm X's death, 26 February 1965, all in NAACP Records III A 227; Wilkins, "The Violent Ones," 3 January 1965, copy in Roy Wilkins Papers, box 39.

7. Wilkins, "The Negro Mood," 21 February 1965, copy in Roy Wilkins Papers, box 39; Wilkins's speech is quoted in a memorandum by Gloster Current to Henry Moon, 2 November 1964, NAACP Records III C 216; Henry Lee Moon to Wilkins, 21 July 1965, NAACP Records III A 66.

8. For Johnson's speech at Howard University, 4 June 1965, see *The Public Papers of the Presidents: Lyndon B. Johnson: 1965*, 636; for Johnson's State of the Union message, 12 January 1965, see *The Public Papers of the Presidents: Lyndon B. Johnson: 1965*, 3–10; Wilkins's telegram to LBJ, 13 January 1966, NAACP Records IV A 35.

9. Letter by Sergeant Robert L. Hollis to the NAACP, 9 June 1966; Wilkins's reply, 1 July 1966, NAACP Records IV A 86. The author has written elsewhere on the NAACP's attitude toward the Vietnam War in more detail. See Berg, "Guns, Butter, and Civil Rights."

10. Telegram by Irene Smith, president of the New Jersey state conference of NAACP branches, to Wilkins, 14 March 1966; Wilkins's response, 20 May 1966, NAACP Records IV A 86; on the resolution by the Greenwich Village branch, see the memoranda by Gloster Current, 14 April 1966 and 6 May 1966, NAACP Records IV A 87. For the general context of racial discrimination in Vietnam, see Westheider, *Fighting on Two Fronts*. He argues that the protests by black soldiers during the war had a profound impact on the racial attitudes of the U.S. military.

11. King quoted in Garrow, *Bearing the Cross*, 429–30; Wilkins, "Sidetrack," 18 July 1965, Roy Wilkins Papers, box 39; "Mississippi Negroes Being Urged to Dodge Draft," *New York Times*, 31 July 1965, copy in NAACP Records III A 232; statement by the MFDP, 31 July 1965, SNCC Papers, box 169.

12. Wilkins, "Negroes and the Draft," 29 August 1965, Roy Wilkins Papers, box 39; SNCC declaration, 6 January 1966, printed in Taylor, *Vietnam and Black America*, 258–60. For more documentation of radical black opposition to the war, see ibid., passim.

13. Wilkins, "SNCC's Foreign Policy," 16 January 1966, Roy Wilkins Papers, box 39; on the meeting with Humphrey, see Humphrey's memorandum for Joe Califano, 22 January 1966, CRLBJ, part 1, reel 2.

14. See the minutes of the meeting of 23 March 1966, memorandum by Enid Baird of the NUL to Wilkins, 30 March 1966, Roy Wilkins Papers, box 7; SNCC press release, 23 March 1966, copy in NAACP Records IV A 50; for the deliberations on the Vietnam resolution, see CRLBJ, part 4, reels 9, 12 (CORE resolution), 13, 14, and 15 (resolution adopted).

15. For more details, see Berg, "Guns, Butter, and Civil Rights," 221–26.

16. On the founding of the LCFO, see Carson, *In Struggle*, 162–66, 200 (Carmichael quote).

17. NAACP press release, 23 April 1966, NAACP Records IV A 63; Wilkins, "Boycott the Ballot?" 1 May 1966, Roy Wilkins Papers, box 39; NAACP press release, 7 May 1966, NAACP Records IV A 63.

18. "Racist Label Rejected by SNCC Head," *Washington Post*, 30 May 1966, copy in NAACP Records IV A 50; Wilkins, "SNCC's New Road," 4 June 1966, Roy Wilkins Papers, box 39; memorandum by Current, 31 May 1966, NAACP Records IV A 50.

19. On the change in SNCC's leadership in 1966 and the conflict during the Meredith March, see Carson, *In Struggle*, 200–207; Wilkins, *Standing Fast*, 314–16; Weisbrot, *Freedom Bound*, 197–98; also see Wilkins's memorandum for the delegates of the 1966 NAACP annual convention, 5 July 1966, NAACP Records IV A 79. In his memoirs, the late Stokely Carmichael reflected that he and his associates said "some hard and stupid things" (see Carmichael and Thelwell, *Ready for Revolution*, 497).

20. For varying accounts of the march, see King, "Where Do We Go from Here?" in Washington, *A Testament of Hope*, 569–74; Fairclough, *To Redeem the Soul of America*, 315–19; Carson, *In Struggle*, 206–11; Weisbrot, *Freedom Bound*, 199–204.

21. Wilkins, "The March in Retrospect," 2 July 1966, Roy Wilkins Papers, box 39; Carmichael's letter to Wilkins, 4 July 1966, NAACP Records IV A 18; Wilkins's memorandum for the delegates of the 1966 NAACP annual convention, 5 July 1966, NAACP Records IV A 79; Wilkins quoted in "Roy Wilkins Warns NAACP of Extremists," unidentified newspaper clipping, 6 July 1966, copy in NAACP Records IV A 16.

22. Resolutions of the 1966 NAACP annual convention, 5–9 July 1966, NAACP Records IV A 3.

23. Carmichael and Hamilton, *Black Power*, preface; Hamilton, "An Advocate of Black Power Defines It," 154.

24. For the various ideological trends within the Black Power movement, see Van Deburg, *New Day in Babylon*; for a (retrospective) Marxist critique, see Marable, *Race, Reform, and Rebellion*, 96–99.

25. Wilkins, "The Battle Is Here," 3 October 1970," Roy Wilkins Papers, box 40; interview with Clarence Mitchell, RJBOHC, interview no. 351; Wilkins to Adam Clayton Powell, 30 August 1966, NAACP Records IV A 16.

26. Wilkins, "Sidetrack," 18 July 1965, Roy Wilkins Papers, box 39; Eldridge Cleaver, "The Black Man's Stake in Vietnam," printed in Taylor, *Vietnam and Black America*, 276.

27. See, e.g., the resolutions of the 1966 NAACP annual convention, 5–9 July, 1966, NAACP Records IV A 3; resolutions of the 1967 NAACP annual convention, 10–15 July 1967, NAACP Records IV A 5; NAACP Special Contribution Fund circular letter, 17 October 1966, NAACP Records IV A 16; Wilkins, "SNCC's New Road," 4 June 1966, Roy Wilkins Papers, box 39.

28. John Morsell to Michael G. Bradley, 6 September 1966; Wilkins to Powell, 30 August 1966, NAACP Records IV A 16; Arnold, "There Is No Rest for Roy Wilkins," 334; interview with Gloster Current, RJBOHC, interview no. 167.

29. On Williams, see the biography by Tyson, *Radio Free Dixie*. Tyson argues persuasively for a strong tradition of self-defense among southern blacks. On Williams's expulsion from the NAACP and reactions from the membership, see the material in NAACP Records III A 333. For a new synthesis of black armed resistance that stresses the differences between southern self-defense against white terrorism and the infatuation of northern radicals with militant and macho-like behavior, see Wendt, *The Spirit and the Shotgun*.

30. "CORE Director Speaks on Black Power," *Boston Correspondent,* 21 July 1966; "A Black Manifesto—CORE," 31 July 1967, copies in NAACP Records IV A 43; Carson, *In Struggle,* 295–96.

31. Letter by Roy Wilkins to Adam Clayton Powell, 31 August 1966, NAACP Records IV A 58; for statements of the Black Panthers on violence, see Foner, *The Black Panthers Speak,* 19–20, 41 (quote), and passim; also see Stern, "The Call of the Black Panthers," 230–42; National Advisory Commission on Civil Disorders, *Report,* 7–9; Feagin and Hahn, *Ghetto Revolts,* 31–55.

32. Resolutions of the 1967 NAACP annual conference, 10 to 15 July 1967, NAACP Records IV A 5; speech by Roy Wilkins, 6 August 1966, at the kick-off of the Louisiana summer project, NAACP Records IV A 63; press conference by NAACP voter registration director W. C. Patton, 5 October 1967, NAACP Records IV A 62; Wilkins, *Standing Fast,* 313–14.

33. Resolutions of the 1967 NAACP annual conference, 10 to 15 July 1967, NAACP Records IV A 5; also see Wilkins's syndicated columns, "Boycott the Ballot?" 1 May 1966, "SNCC's New Road," 4 June 1966, Roy Wilkins Papers, box 39.

34. Carmichael and Hamilton, *Black Power,* 58–84 (esp. 79–80), 98–120, 118–19 (quote).

35. Wilkins columns, "Negro Frontlash," 14 November 1966; "A Change in Mississippi" (quote), 26 November 1966, Roy Wilkins Papers, box 39; also see Jack Newfield, "Running Scared," *Village Voice,* 15 December 1966, copy in NAACP Records IV A 50.

36. "Black Lawmakers," 21 November 1970; see also "The Winners," 14 November 1970, Roy Wilkins Papers, box 40; Wilkins to Representative Charles Diggs, 3 May 1972, Roy Wilkins Papers, box 9; Wilkins's untitled column on Bradley's election, 16 June 1973, Roy Wilkins Papers, box 48; on Bradley's election and its implications for interracial electoral politics, see Sonenshein, *Politics in Black and White.*

37. See the undated (1967) manifesto "Black Power—Chicago Base," NAACP Records IV A 16; for a critique of the inconsistencies of Black Power's concept of the role of whites, see Sonenshein, *Politics in Black and White,* 275–81; "The New Left Conference," 23 September 1967, Roy Wilkins Papers, box 39.

38. See Wilkins's untitled column on the founding of the Black Caucus, 12 February 1973, Roy Wilkins Papers, box 47.

39. "Negroes and the Draft," 29 August 1965, Roy Wilkins Papers, box 39; Wilkins, *Standing Fast,* 324–25; Arnold, "There Is No Rest for Roy Wilkins," 329. The suspected would-be assassin, Herman Ferguson, belonged to a splinter group that wanted to establish a separate state in the South (see the interview with Ferguson, RJBOHC, interview no. 575).

40. See the interview with Henry Lee Moon, RJBOHC, interview no. 71; "Racist Label Rejected by SNCC Head," *Washington Post,* 30 May 1966, copy in NAACP Records IV A 50; Carson, *In Struggle,* 252–57.

41. Roy Wilkins to *LOOK Magazine,* 7 September 1967, NAACP Records IV A 81.

42. See the interview with Current, RJBOHC, interview no. 167; for similar statements, see the interview with Kelly Alexander, RJBOHC, interview no. 399; resolutions of the 1967 NAACP annual conference, 10 to 15 July 1967, NAACP Records IV A 5.

43. For the estimated number of branches in 1966, see the interview with Gloster Current, RJBOHC, interview no. 167; for the membership figures, see Marger, "Social Movement Organizations and Response to Environmental Change," 23, table 1; Rudwick and Meier, "Integration vs. Separatism," 249. Membership figures for SNCC are not available.

44. The first resolution of an NAACP branch against the Vietnam War dates back to April 1965. See the memorandum by Gloster Current, 22 April 1965, NAACP Records III A 328; also see the resolution by the Astoria, Long Island, branch of May 1965, NAACP Records IV C 55. For correspondence from members and external criticism, see NAACP Records IV A 16, folder: Black Power, and NAACP Records IV A 87, folder: "Vietnam Correspondence, 1967." Each of these folders contains about one hundred letters.

45. See the "Open Letter to the Convention Delegates" by the "Young Turks," 12 July 1967, NAACP Records IV A 12; on the "Young Turk" rebellion, see the recent in-depth treatment by Eick, *Dissent in Wichita,* esp. 91–94, 102–5, 114–17, 125–29, 153–57, passim; also see Rudwick and Meier, "Integration vs. Separatism," 254–57.

46. Chester Lewis's speech before the Colorado-Wyoming state conference of branches, 1967, quoted in Eick, *Dissent in Wichita,* 12–29; see "The NAACP's Young Turk Movement," sent as a memorandum by Gloster Current to Wilkins, 4 March 1968, NAACP Records IV A 80; interview with Celes King, a leader of the "Young Turks" and president of the Los Angeles NAACP branch, RJBOHC, interview no. 420; resolutions of the 1968 NAACP annual conference, 30 June 1968, NAACP Records IV A 7; "The New Orthodoxy," *Washington Post,* 10 July 1968, copy in NAACP Records IV A 43.

47. Wilkins quote about Chester Lewis in Eick, *Dissent in Wichita,* 156; Gloster Current to Morsell and Wilkins, 3 July 1968, both in NAACP Records IV C 55; Roy Wilkins's circular letter to NAACP officers, 24 July 1968, NAACP Records IV A 80; Wilkins to Current, 24 October 1968, NAACP Records IV A 12.

48. Wilkins, *Standing Fast,* 341; Harris poll, 19 December 1966, copy in NAACP Records IV A 19; on the election of Carmichael, see Carson, *In Struggle,* 200–206.

49 See, e.g., Carmichael and Hamilton, *Black Power,* 53–56. Its middle-class character had always been a staple tenet of the NAACP's critics (see Myrdal, *An American Dilemma,* 831–36); Frazier, *Black Bourgeoisie,* 88–91; for internal views, see Current to Wilkins, 19 September 1967, NAACP Records IV A 80; interview with Arthur Spingarn, RJBOHC, interview no. 165; memorandum by Daniel Wright to Gloster Current, "A Study of the NAACP Branch Presidents, Secretaries and Treasurers," 30 October 1967, NAACP Records IV C 55.

50. Interview with Gloster Current, RJBOHC, interview no. 167; also see the interviews with Theodore Henry (NAACP youth council leader of Mississippi), RJBOHC, interview no. 485; Ruby Hurley (secretary of the NAACP South East Regional Office), RJBOHC, interview no. 122; Rudwick and Meier, "Integration vs. Separatism," 258–59; newsletter by Ruby Hurley, 12 October 1967, NAACP Records IV C 35; letter by Johns Hopkins sociologist Louis C. Goldberg to Roy Wilkins, 6 March 1966, NAACP Records IV C 52; "A Black Manifesto—CORE, " 31 July 1967, copy in NAACP Records IV A 43.

51. Stone, *Black Political Power in America,* 9; "Picketing Threat By CORE Hit," *Phila-*

delphia Inquirer, 6 January 1965; James O. Williams to Roy Wilkins, 7 January 1965, NAACP Records III A 202; Rudwick and Meier, "Integration vs. Separatism," 248 and 254; Carson, *In Struggle,* 236–43; on the role of whites in the NAACP, see Berg, "Activists, Leaders, and Supporters."

52. Malcolm X quoted in Samuels, "Two Ways," 40; interview with Lucille Black, RJBOHC, interview no. 70; interview with Gloster Current, RJBOHC, interview no. 167; Rudwick and Meier, "Integration vs. Separatism," 257.

53. Jackie Robinson, "Taking off on the NAACP," *Amsterdam News,* 14 January 1967, copy in NAACP Records IV A 79; on the development of the external income of the various civil rights organizations, see Marger, "Social Movement Organizations and Response to Environmental Change," 23, table 1; Haines, "Black Radicalization and the Funding of Civil Rights," 31–43, 36, table 1; Haines, *Black Radicals and the Civil Rights Mainstream,* esp. 93–94.

54. See the widely distributed fund-raising letter by Roy Wilkins, 17 October 1966, NAACP Records IV A 16; Haines, *Black Radicals and the Civil Rights Mainstream,* 84.

55. See the aggregated data of polls taken in 1963, 1966, and 1969 in Smith and Horton, *Historical Statistics of Black America,* 2:1259. In contrast, NAACP director of publications Henry Lee Moon, in 1971, claimed an approval rate of 91 percent for the association among blacks. See the interview with Henry Lee Moon, RJBOHC, interview no. 71.

56. Wilkins to Adam Clayton Powell, 30 August 1966; Gloster Current to John Morsell, 29 June 1967, NAACP Records IV A 16; "Wilkins Opposes Black Separatism," *Washington Post,* 6 July 1968; copy of speech by Whitney Young, 6 July 1968; John Morsell to Roy Wilkins, 9 July 1968, all in NAACP Records IV A 43.

57. Current to Roy Wilkins and John Morsell, 19 September 1967; Current to Wilkins et al., 29 May 1968, NAACP Records IV A 80; Current to Wilkins, 9 March 1967; Current to Wilkins and Morsell, 3 July 1968, NAACP Records IV C 55; Wilkins to Current, 24 October 1966, NAACP Records IV A 12; Roy Wilkins to Charles C. Diggs, 3 May 1972, Wilkins Papers, box 9; for a similar line of argument against ghetto romanticism, see John Morsell to Roy Wilkins, 9 July 1968, NAACP Records IV A 43.

58. Carmichael and Hamilton, *Black Power,* 175–77; Lawson, *Running for Freedom,* 136, 143; for the backlash thesis, see esp. Edsall and Edsall, *Chain Reaction,* 4–5, 47–73; McAdam, *Political Process and the Development of Black Insurgency,* 192–97, 214–16.

59. Sugrue, *The Origins of the Urban Crisis;* also see the contributions to a *Journal of American History* roundtable of 1995: Hirsch, "Massive Resistance in the Urban North"; Sugrue, "Crabgrass-Roots Politics"; Gerstle, "Race and the Myth of the Liberal Consensus"; Wallace quoted in a study by the American Jewish Committee, "Elections, 1963 (Civil Rights and White Reactions)," December 1963, copy in NAACP Records III A 65.

60. Ralph, *Northern Protest,* 114–30; Fairclough, *To Redeem the Soul of America,* 279–309; also see the annual report of the NAACP's Washington Bureau, 19 December 1966, NAACP Records IV A 89; Graham, *Civil Rights and the Presidency,* 127–29.

61. Blum, *Years of Discord,* 270; Wilkins column, "Negro Frontlash," 14 November 1966, Roy Wilkins Papers, box 39; also see the annual report of the NAACP's Washington Bureau, 19 December 1966, NAACP Records IV A 89.

62. Louis Goldberg to Roy Wilkins, 6 March 1967, NAACP Records IV C 52; Wilkins's call to the local branches, 17 June 1967; Walter McClane to Wilkins, 18 July 1967, NAACP Records IV A 64; W. C. Patton's circular letter, 26 July 1967, NAACP records IV A 62; interview with Gloster Current, RJBOHC, interview no. 167; "Dirksen and Carmichael," 4 February 1967, Roy Wilkins Papers, box 39; untitled column by Wilkins, 5 October 1968, Roy Wilkins Papers, box 45.

63. Blum, *Years of Discord*, 310–11; on Wallace's campaign, see Carter, *The Politics of Rage*, 324–70; O'Reilly, *Nixon's Piano*, 278–87.

64. Wilkins, *Standing Fast*, 330–31; NAACP press release, 30 May 1968, NAACP Records IV C 55; staff memorandum by W. C. Patton, September 1968; standardized draft of speech for registration workers by Patton, undated; Patton's report on "Political Action, November and December 1968," all in NAACP Records IV A 63; Wilkins's column, untitled, 21 September 1968, Roy Wilkins Papers, box 44.

65. Schlesinger, *History of American Presidential Elections*, 4:3753–80, 3770–71; on the pledge to seat an integrated delegation from Mississippi, see chapter eight.

66. Diamond, ed., *Congressional Quarterly's Guide to U.S. Elections*, 461–62; Lawson, *Running for Freedom*, 136.

67. Wilkins, *Standing Fast*, 332–34; Roy Wilkins column, "Death Is White," 16 May 1970, Roy Wilkins Papers, box 40; Wilkins to Charles Diggs, 3 May 1972, Roy Wilkins Papers, box 9; DeBenedetti, *An American Ordeal*, 286.

68. Untitled column by Wilkins, 20 November 1971, Roy Wilkins Papers, box 8; Roy Wilkins column, "Not so Benign," 14 March 1970, Roy Wilkins Papers, box 40; on the clashes at the 1972 NAACP convention, see the speeches by Bishop Spottswood and NAACP labor secretary Herbert Hill and other pertaining materials in *Civil Rights During the Nixon Administration: 1969–1974* (CRRN), part 1, reel 4; untitled column by Wilkins, 18 November 1972, Roy Wilkins Papers, box 47; Wilkins to Clarence Mitchell, 29 November 1972, Roy Wilkins Papers, box 9.

69. Roy Wilkins column, "A Haynsworth Parallel," 29 November 1969, Roy Wilkins Papers, box 40; Clarence Mitchell to Wilkins, 24 November 1969, NAACP Records IV A 88; on the Parker fight, see chapter two.

70. Nixon's civil rights policy is highly controversial among historians. For accounts that depict it as a mix of hidden racism and opportunism, see O'Reilly, *Nixon's Piano*, 289–329; Blum, *Years of Discord*, 332–41; Weisbrot, *Freedom Bound*, 278–87; for a revisionist interpretation that stresses Nixon's achievements, see Hoff, *Nixon Reconsidered*, 77–114; for an in-depth study of the bureaucratic infighting and struggles that led to many paradoxical and unintended results, see Graham, *The Civil Rights Era*, 301–449; also see Greene, *The Limits of Power*, 36–47, on busing and school integration.

71. On the extremely complex legislative history of the 1970 Voting Rights Act, see Lawson, *In Pursuit of Power*, 130–57; Graham, *The Civil Rights Era*, 346–65. On the original stipulations, see chapter eight.

72. See the memorandum by Raymond K. Price for Nixon, 18 June 1970, CRRN, part 1, reel 21; in fact, the Supreme Court struck down the federal voting age, which prompted the Twenty-sixth Amendment to be passed in record time. On the background, see Berg,

"Soldiers and Citizens," 211–14; on the further development of the Voting Rights Act, see the conclusion of this book.

73. Edsall and Edsall, *Chain Reaction*, 4–7, passim; on the legacy of George Wallace, see the somewhat alarmist assessment by Carter, "Legacy of Rage"; on the ways that the rights revolution has shaped the American regulatory state, see Graham, *The Civil Rights Era*, 454–76.

74. Wilkins to *LOOK Magazine*'s Leonard Rubin, 7 September 1967, NAACP Records IV A 81; on the continuity of Black Power as a cultural concept, see Van Deburg, *New Day in Babylon*, 306–9.

Conclusion: The Ticket to Freedom?

1. Edward Muse to Roy Wilkins, 9 July 1968, NAACP Records IV A 80.

2. Interview with NAACP assistant secretary John Morsell, RJBOHC, interview no. 72.

3. Interview with Aaron Henry, RJBOHC, interview no. 326; for a general overview of the economic agenda of civil rights organizations, see Hamilton and Hamilton, *The Dual Agenda*; also see chapters two, four, and five.

4. For a summary of my argument, also see Berg, "Individual Right and Collective Interest."

5. In 1936, e.g., the New York–based Proportional Representation Campaign Committee invited NAACP secretary Walter White to join, arguing that proportional representation would improve the chances of black candidates. White, however, declined. See the letter by the committee to White, 3 October 1936, NAACP Records I C 392. On the marginal significance and low acceptance of proportional representation in the American tradition, see Argersinger, "Electoral Processes," 494–95; for a recent argument that proportional representation would solve many problems related to minority representation, see Keyssar, *The Right to Vote*, 298–302. Keyssar, however, is also rather skeptical that reforms would be politically feasible.

6. This and the following information is based on my interview with Mr. Joseph Madison on 20 September 1994 in Washington, D.C.; on W. C. Patton's work, see chapter six.

7. Leonard Carter to John Morsell and Gloster Current, 1 November 1965, NAACP Records III A 214; interview with Mr. Joseph Madison, Washington, D.C., 20 September 1994.

8. For the registration and voting figures, see Tate, *From Protest to Politics*, 184, table 9.1. The NAACP's approach to voter education and registration in the late 1980s and early 1990s was described to the author by Mr. Clifford Collins in a phone conversation on 6 May 1994. Mr. Collins was then the director of the NAACP voter education department.

9. John H. McCray speech, 16 March 1947, quoted in Cohodas, *Strom Thurmond and the Politics of Southern Change*, 102.

10. See chapter six, table 2.

11. Lawson, *In Pursuit of Power*, 256–59; on the transformation of southern politics and society, see Goldfield, *Black, White, and Southern*, 174–87; Bartley, *The New South*, 417–54; for Carter's early appeals to black voters, see his speech to the African-American Georgia Voters League, 20 August 1966, SCLC Papers, box 166.

12. On the registration figures, see Lawson, *In Pursuit of Power,* 297, table 1; see the reports by NAACP registration director John Brooks on his registration campaigns in Virginia, 17 May 1966, 14 July 1966, 18 October 1966, 6 September 1967, 14 November 1967, all in NAACP Records IV A 62; the numbers of black elected officials are according to Lawson, *Running for Freedom,* 126; Morris, "Black Electoral Participation and the Distribution of Public Benefits," 280–81, table 12–3.

13. On the return of the two-party system, see Black and Black, *Politics and Society in the South,* 259–316; Goldfield, *Black, White, and Southern,* 241–44.

14. Handley and Grofman, "The Impact of the Voting Rights Act on Minority Representation," 344. The article is part of a volume edited by political scientists Chandler Davidson and Bernard Grofman, entitled *Quiet Revolution in the South.* Mostly, the book's findings stress the positive changes since the enactment of the Voting Rights Act.

15. For an introduction to the numerous analytical, empirical, and constitutional issues related to minority vote dilution, see Davidson, ed., *Minority Vote Dilution;* Grofman and Davidson, *Controversies in Minority Voting;* Grofman et al., *Minority Representation and the Quest for Voting Equality;* on the massive resistance against the Voting Rights Act in Mississippi, see Parker, *Black Votes Count,* 34–77.

16. *Allen v. State Board of Elections,* 393 U.S. 544 (1969); on the number of preclearance reviews, see Davis and Graham, *The Supreme Court, Race, and Civil Rights,* 235; *White v. Regester,* 412 U.S. 755 (1973).

17. *Beer v. United States,* 425 U.S. 130 (1976); *City of Mobile v. Bolden,* 446 U.S. 55 (1980); for an overview of the decisions and debates about voting rights cases in this period, see Davidson, "The Voting Rights Act."

18. *Thornburgh v. Gingles,* 478 U.S. 30 (1996); on the extensions of the Voting Rights Act, see Grofman et al., *Minority Representation and the Quest for Voting Equality,* 29–60; Lawson, *In Pursuit of Power,* 288–92.

19. On the 1992 election results, see Tate, *From Protest to Politics,* 198–200.

20. The most important rulings are: *Shaw v. Reno,* 509 U.S. 630 (1993); *Holder v. Hall,* 512 U.S. 874 (1994); *Miller v. Johnson,* 515 U.S. 900 (1995); *Shaw v. Hunt,* 517 U.S. 899 (1996); *Bush. v. Vera,* 517 U.S. 952 (1996); *Abrams v. Johnson,* 521 U.S. 74 (1997).

21. On Clarence Thomas and the general conservative turn of the Supreme Court, see Savage, *Turning Right,* esp. 423–50; *Holder v. Hall,* 512 U.S. 874 (1994); Cooper and Biskupic, "Thomas's Unwelcome Opinion."

22. NAACP Washington Bureau chief Wade Henderson quoted in Biskupic, "Court Rejects Race-Based Voting District"; Kousser, *Colorblind Injustice,* 465–66, passim; see also Parker, "The Court's Blind Eye on Voting Rights."

23. On the 1996 elections, see Fletcher, "New Tolerance in the South or Old Power of Incumbency?"; for the numbers of black congressional and state legislative representation, see the Congressional Research Service Report, *Black Members of the United States Congress, 1789–2001,* esp. table 4, www.senate.gov/reference/resources/pdf/RL30378.pdf (18 March 2003); Joint Center for Political and Economic Studies, *Black Elected Officials,* esp. tables 1 and 2, www.jointcenter.org/publications/BEO/BEO-01.html (7 January 2004); on the limited impact of the Supreme Court on social change, see Rosenberg, *The Hollow Hope;* Klarman, "How *Brown* Changed Race Relations"; Klarman, "Is the

Supreme Court Sometimes Irrelevant?"; also see chapter three on the white primary cases.

24. Tate, *From Protest to Politics*, 200–201; Whitby, *The Color of Representation*, 113–33; Williams, "Blacked Out in the Newt Congress"; for an argument against equating black representation with black representatives, see Swain, *Black Faces, Black Interests*; John Lewis, "Why Republicans Are in Love with the Voting Rights Act," www.house.gov. johnlewis/voting_rights.html (21 July 2003); *Georgia v. Ashcroft*, 195 F. Supp. 2d 25, www.supremecourtus.gov/opinions/02pdf/02-182.pdf

25. For an influential critique of extending the Voting Rights Act, see Thernstrom, *Whose Votes Count?*; Thernstrom and Thernstrom, *America in Black and White*, 462–92; also see Swain, *Black Faces, Black Interests*; for a position in support of color-conscious remedies as a way toward the goal of color-blindness, see the conclusions in Grofman et al., *Minority Representation and the Quest for Voting Equality*, 129–37.

26. For Guinier's views and proposals, see the collection of her essays *The Tyranny of the Majority*; the quote is from her essay "Voting Rights and Democratic Theory: Where Do We Go from Here?" 292. On the nomination, see her preface to *The Tyranny of the Majority*, vii–xx.

27. On the figures, see Joint Center for Political and Economic Studies, *Black Elected Officials*, 8 and table 8; on the problems of black mayors in large cities, see Lawson, *Running for Freedom*, 164–82.

28. On the poverty figures, see the press release of Bureau of the Census, 2 October 2003, "Poverty, Income See Slight Changes," www.census.gov/Press-Release (2 October 2003); on the decline of the black family, see Thernstrom and Thernstrom, *America in Black and White*, 437–41; also see Patterson, "Broken Bloodlines."

29. Bell, *Faces at the Bottom of the Well: The Permanence of Racism*, 9; for other influential texts based on the paradigm of structural racism, see Hacker, *Two Nations*; Smith, *Racism in the Post–Civil Rights Era*. For a summary and analysis of the debate on the black underclass, see my own essay, Berg, "Struktureller Rassismus oder pathologisches Sozialverhalten? Die Debatte über die Black Underclass in den USA."

30. See Wilson's books, *The Declining Significance of Race*; *The Truly Disadvantaged*; *When Work Disappears*; *The Bridge over the Racial Divide*.

31. For several influential texts of this conservative critique, see Murray, *Losing Ground*; Mead, *Beyond Entitlement*; D'Souza, *The End of Racism*.

32. Thernstrom and Thernstrom, *America in Black and White*, 530–45, 533; Patterson, *The Ordeal of Integration*, 4, 171 (quotes).

33. See, e.g., Sowell, *Civil Rights*; Conti and Stetson, *Challenging the Civil Rights Establishment*; Steele, *The Content of Our Character*; Steele, "The Age of White Guilt and the Disappearance of the Black Individual"; McWorther, *Losing the Race*; also see Swain, *The New White Nationalism in America*, who argues that white resentment is often based on understandable frustration over political correctness and affirmative action.

34. Marable, *Black Leadership*; also see Smith, *We Have No Leaders*.

35. On these meetings, see Walters, "Serving the People"; Merida, "Black Leaders Convene Meeting in Baltimore"; for a background report on the crisis at the NAACP, see Duke, "What's Gone Wrong at the NAACP?"

36. Williams, "Blacked Out in the Newt Congress"; White, "Let's Scrap the NAACP."

37. Goodstein, "On the NAACP Agenda."

38. On Mfume's election, see Fletcher and Merida, "Mfume Is Chosen to Lead NAACP"; Harris and Fletcher, "In Mfume, NAACP Hires a Veteran of the Public Arena"; Fletcher, "Mfume Takes NAACP Helm Today"; also see Mfume's autobiography, *No Free Ride*.

39. Interview with Mr. Joseph Madison, Washington, D.C., 20 September 1994.

Bibliography

Manuscript Collections, Microforms, and Oral History Collections

Birmingham World Correspondence. Birmingham Public Library, Birmingham, Alabama.

Ralph J. Bunche Oral History Collection. Moorland-Spingarn Research Center, Howard University, Washington, D.C.

Civil Rights During the Kennedy Administration. Frederick, Md.: University Publications of America, 1986. Part 1: The White House Central Files and Staff Files.

Civil Rights During the Johnson Administration. A Collection from the Holdings of the Lyndon Baines Johnson Library, Austin, Texas. Bethesda, Md.: University Publications of America, 1984. Part 1: The White House Central Files. Part 3: Oral Histories.

Civil Rights During the Nixon Administration 1969–1974. Black Studies Research Sources. Bethesda, Md.: University Publications of America, undated. Part 1: The White House Central Files.

Congress of Racial Equality Papers. Martin Luther King, Jr., Center for Nonviolent Social Change, Atlanta, Georgia.

Eugene T. Connor Papers. Birmingham Public Library, Birmingham, Alabama.

The Crisis: A Journal of the Darker Races. New York, 1910 to 1970.

Mississippi Freedom Democratic Party Papers. Martin Luther King, Jr., Center for Nonviolent Social Change, Atlanta, Georgia.

National Association for the Advancement of Colored People. Annual Reports. New York, 1911 to 1970.

National Association for the Advancement of Colored People Records. Library of Congress, Manuscript Division, Washington, D.C.

Part I:

Series A: Board of Director File, 1909–1959.

Series B: Annual Conference File, 1913–1939.

Series C: Administrative File, 1906–1940.

Series D: Legal File, 1910–1940.

Series G: Branch File, 1913–1939.

Part II:

Series A: General Office File, 1940–1955.

Series B: Branch File, 1940–1955.

Part III:

Series A: Administrative File, 1956–1965.

Series C: Branch File, 1956–1965.

Part IV:

Series A: Administrative File, 1966–ca. 1969.

Series C: Branch File, 1966–ca. 1970.

1993 Addition Files (since 1997 renamed Part V).

Part VI:

Series I: Voter Education Project.

President Truman's Committee on Civil Rights. Black Studies Research Sources. Bethesda, Md.: University Publications of America, 1984.

Southern Christian Leadership Conference Papers. Martin Luther King, Jr., Center for Nonviolent Social Change, Atlanta, Georgia.

Southern Regional Council Papers. Library of Congress, Manuscript Division, Washington, D.C.

Arthur B. Spingarn Papers. Library of Congress, Manuscript Division, Washington, D.C.

Joel E. Spingarn Papers. Moorland-Spingarn Research Center, Howard University, Washington, D.C.

Moorfield Storey Papers. Library of Congress, Manuscript Division, Washington, D.C.

Student Nonviolent Coordinating Committee Papers. Martin Luther King, Jr., Center for Nonviolent Social Change, Atlanta, Georgia.

Roy Wilkins Papers. Library of Congress, Manuscript Division, Washington, D.C.

Books and Articles

Agnew, Jean-Christophe, and Roy Rosenzweig, eds. *A Companion to Post-1945 America.* Malden, Mass.: Blackwell Publishing, 2002.

Anderson, Carol. "From Hope to Disillusion: African Americans, the United Nations, and the Struggle for Human Rights, 1944–1947." *Diplomatic History* 20 (1996): 531–63.

———. *Eyes off the Prize: African Americans, the United Nations, and the Struggle for Human Rights, 1944–1955.* New York: Cambridge University Press, 2003.

Aptheker, Herbert, ed. *W.E.B. Du Bois: The Correspondence of W.E.B. Du Bois.* 3 vols. Amherst: University of Massachusetts Press, 1978.

———, ed. *Writings by W.E.B. Du Bois in Periodicals Edited by Others.* 4 vols. Millwood, N.Y.: Kraus-Thomson Organization Limited, 1982.

———, ed. *Newspaper Columns by W.E.B. Du Bois.* 2 vols. White Plains, N.Y.: Kraus-Thomson Organization, 1986.

———, ed. *Pamphlets and Leaflets by W.E.B. Du Bois.* White Plains, N.Y.: Kraus-Thomson Organization, 1986.

Argersinger, Peter H. "Electoral Processes." Jack P. Greene, ed. *Encyclopedia of American*

Political History: Studies of the Principal Movements and Ideas. 3 vols. New York: Charles Scribner's Sons, 1984, 2:489–512.

Arnold, Martin. "There Is No Rest for Roy Wilkins." August Meier, John Bracey, and Elliott Rudwick, eds. *Black Protest in the Sixties.* New York: Markus Wiener Publishing, 1997, 325–338.

Avery, Sheldon. *Up from Washington: William Pickens and the Negro Struggle for Equality, 1900–1954.* Newark: University of Delaware Press, 1989.

Bartley, Numan V. *The Rise of Massive Resistance: Race and Politics in the South during the 1950s.* Baton Rouge: Louisiana State University Press, 1969.

———. *The New South, 1945–1980.* Baton Rouge: Louisiana State University Press, 1995.

Bates, Beth T. "A New Crowd Challenges the Agenda of the Old Guard in the NAACP, 1933–1941." *American Historical Review* 102 (1997): 340–77.

Belknap, Michael R., ed. *Civil Rights, the White House, and the Justice Department, 1945–1968.* Vol. 15, *Voting Rights.* New York: Garland Publishing, 1991.

Bell, Derrick. *Faces at the Bottom of the Well: The Permanence of Racism.* New York: Basic Books, 1992.

Berg, Manfred. "Soldiers and Citizens: War and Voting Rights in American History." David K. Adams and Cornelis A. van Minnen, eds. *Reflections on American Exceptionalism.* Keele: Ryburn Publishing of Keele University Press, 1994, 188–225.

———. "Black Power: The National Association for the Advancement of Colored People and the Resurgence of Black Nationalism during the 1960s." Knud Krakau, ed. *The American Nation—National Identity—Nationalism.* Münster: LIT Verlag, 1997, 235–62.

———. "Guns, Butter, and Civil Rights: The National Association for the Advancement of Colored People and the Vietnam War, 1964–1968." David K. Adams and Cornelis van Minnen, eds. *Aspects of War in American History.* Keele: Ryburn Publishing of Keele University Press, 1997, 213–38.

———. *The Ticket to Freedom: Die NAACP und das Wahlrecht der Afro-Amerikaner.* Frankfurt/M.: Campus, 2000.

———. "Activists, Leaders, and Supporters: On the Role of Whites in the NAACP." Larry E. Jones, ed. *Crossing Boundaries: The Exclusion and Inclusion of Minorities in Germany and America.* Providence, R.I.: Berghahn Books, 2001, 193–210.

———. "Individual Right and Collective Interest: The National Association for the Advancement of Colored People and the American Voting Rights Discourse." Manfred Berg and Martin H. Geyer, eds. *Two Cultures of Rights. The Quest for Inclusion and Participation in Modern America and Germany.* New York: Cambridge University Press, 2002, 33–57.

———. "Schwarze Bürgerrechte und liberaler Antikommunismus: Die NAACP in der McCarthy-Ära." *Vierteljahreshefte für Zeitgeschichte* 51 (2003): 363–84.

———. "Struktureller Rassismus oder pathologisches Sozialverhalten? Die Debatte über die Black Underclass in den USA." Winfried Fluck and Welf Werner, eds. *Wie viel Ungleichheit verträgt die Demokratie? Armut und Reichtum in den USA.* Frankfurt/M.: Campus, 2003.

Berman, William C. *The Politics of Civil Rights in the Truman Administration.* Athens: Ohio University Press, 1970.

Biskupic, Joan. "Court Rejects Race-Based Voting District." *Washington Post,* 30 June 1995: A1, A18.

Black, Earl, and Merle Black. *Politics and Society in the South.* Cambridge and London: Harvard University Press, 1987.

Blum, John M. *Years of Discord: American Politics and Society, 1961–1974.* New York: Norton, 1991.

Boris, Eileen. "'The Right to Work Is the Right to Live!' Fair Employment and the Quest for Social Citizenship." Manfred Berg and Martin H. Geyer, eds. *Two Cultures of Rights: The Quest for Inclusion and Participation in Modern America and Germany.* New York: Cambridge University Press, 2002, 121–41.

Borstelmann, Thomas. *The Cold War and the Color Line: American Race Relations in the Global Arena.* Cambridge: Harvard University Press, 2001.

Bott, Alexander J. *Handbook of United States Election Laws and Practices: Political Rights.* New York: Greenwood Press, 1990.

Boylan, James. *The New Deal Coalition and the Election of 1946.* New York: Garland Publishing, 1981.

Boyle, Kevin. *Arc of Justice: A Saga of Race, Civil Rights, and Murder in the Jazz Age.* Boston: Henry Holt, 2004.

Bracey, John H., and August Meier. "Allies or Adversaries? The NAACP, A. Philip Randolph and the 1941 March on Washington." *Georgia Historical Quarterly* 75 (1991): 1–17.

Branch, Taylor. *Parting the Waters: America in the King Years, 1954–63.* New York: Simon and Schuster, 1988.

———. *Pillar of Fire: America in the King Years, 1963–1965.* New York: Simon and Schuster, 1998.

Brauer, Carl M. *John F. Kennedy and the Second Reconstruction.* New York: Columbia University Press, 1977.

Brooks, Roy L. *Integration or Separation? A Strategy for Racial Equality.* Cambridge, Mass., and London: Harvard University Press, 1996.

Bunche, Ralph J. "A Critical Analysis of the Tactics and Programs of Minority Groups." *Journal of Negro Education* 4 (1935): 308–20.

———. *The Political Status of the Negro in the Age of FDR.* Chicago and London: University of Chicago Press, 1973.

Bureau of the Census. "Poverty, Income See Slight Changes." www.census.gov/Press-Release (2 October 2003).

Burk, Robert F. *The Eisenhower Administration and Black Civil Rights.* Knoxville: University of Tennessee Press, 1984.

Carmichael, Stokely, and Charles V. Hamilton. *Black Power: The Politics of Liberation in America.* New York: Random House, 1967.

Carmichael, Stokely, and Ekwueme M. Thelwell. *Ready for Revolution: The Life and Struggles of Stokely Carmichael (Kwame Ture).* New York: Scribner's, 2003.

Carson, Clayborne. "Civil Rights Movement." Jack P. Greene, ed. *Encyclopedia of Ameri-*

can Political History: Studies of the Principal Movements and Ideas. New York: Charles Scribner's Sons, 1983, 218–32.

———. "Civil Rights Reform and the Black Freedom Struggle." Charles W. Eagles, ed. *The Civil Rights Movement in America.* Jackson and London: University Press of Mississippi, 1986, 19–32.

———. "Martin Luther King, Jr.: Charismatic Leadership in a Mass Struggle." *Journal of American History* 74 (1987): 448–54.

———. *In Struggle: SNCC and the Black Awakening of the 1960s.* Cambridge, Mass.: Harvard University Press, 1995.

Carter, Dan T. *Scottsboro: A Tragedy of the American South.* Baton Rouge and London: Louisiana State University Press, 1979.

———. *The Politics of Rage: George Wallace, the Origins of the New Conservatism, and the Transformation of American Politics.* New York: Simon and Schuster, 1995.

———. "Legacy of Rage: George Wallace and the Transformation of American Politics." *Journal of Southern History* 62 (1996): 3–26.

Caute, David. *The Great Fear: The Anti-Communist Purge under Truman and Eisenhower.* New York: Simon and Schuster, 1978.

Chafe, William H. *Civilities and Civil Rights: Greensboro, North Carolina, and the Black Struggle for Freedom.* New York: Oxford University Press, 1980.

———. "The End of One Struggle, the Beginning of Another." Charles W. Eagles, ed. *The Civil Rights Movement in America.* Jackson and London: University Press of Mississippi, 1986, 126–48.

Cohodas, Nadine. *Strom Thurmond and the Politics of Southern Change.* New York: Simon and Schuster, 1993.

Congressional Research Service Report. *Black Members of the United States Congress, 1789–2001.* www.senate.gov/reference/resources/pdf/RL30378.pdf (18 March 2003).

Conti, Joseph G., and Brad Stetson. *Challenging the Civil Rights Establishment: Profiles of a New Black Vanguard.* Westport, Conn.: Praeger, 1993.

Cooper, Kenneth, and Joan Biskupic. "Thomas's Unwelcome Opinion: Justice Stokes Fires of Foes with Arguments in Voting Rights Case." *Washington Post,* 22 July 1994: A3.

Cortner, Richard C. *A Mob Intent on Death: The NAACP and the Arkansas Riot Cases.* Middletown, Conn.: Wesleyan University Press, 1988.

Cronon, David E. *The Story of Marcus Garvey and the Universal Negro Improvement Association.* Madison: University of Wisconsin Press, 1969.

Daniels, Roger. *The Decision to Relocate the Japanese Americans.* Malabar, Fla.: Krieger, 1986.

Davidson, Chandler, ed. *Minority Vote Dilution.* Washington, D.C.: Howard University Press, 1984.

———. "The Voting Rights Act: A Brief History." Bernard Grofman and Chandler Davidson, eds. *Controversies in Minority Voting: The Voting Rights Act in Perspective.* Washington, D.C.: Brookings Institution, 1992, 7–51.

Davidson, Chandler, and Bernard Grofman, eds. *Quiet Revolution in the South: The Impact of the Voting Rights Act, 1965–1990.* Princeton, N.J.: Princeton University Press, 1994.

Davis, Abraham L., and Barbara L. Graham, eds. *The Supreme Court, Race, and Civil Rights*. Thousand Oaks, Calif.: Sage Publications, 1995.

DeBenedetti, Charles. *An American Ordeal: The Antiwar Movement of the Vietnam Era*. Syracuse: Syracuse University Press, 1990.

Diamond, Robert A., ed. *Congressional Quarterly's Guide to U.S. Elections*. Washington D.C.: Congressional Quarterly, 1985.

Diner, Hasia. *In the Almost Promised Land: American Jews and Blacks, 1915–1935*. Baltimore and London: Johns Hopkins University Press, 1995.

Dittmer, John. *Local People: The Struggle for Civil Rights in Mississippi*. Urbana and Chicago: University of Illinois Press, 1994.

D'Souza, Dinesh. *The End of Racism: Principles for a Multiracial Society*. New York: Free Press, 1995.

DuBois, Ellen C. *Feminism and Suffrage: The Emergence of an Independent Women's Movement in America*. Ithaca and London: Cornell University Press, 1978.

Du Bois, W.E.B. *Dusk of Dawn: A Essay toward an Autobiography of a Race Concept*. New Brunswick, N.J., and London: Transaction Publishers, 1984.

———. *The Souls of Black Folk*. New York: Penguin Books, 1989.

Dudziak, Mary L. "Desegregation as a Cold War Imperative." *Stanford Law Review* 41 (1988): 61–120.

———. "Josephine Baker, Racial Protest, and the Cold War." *Journal of American History* 81 (1994): 543–70.

———. *Cold War Civil Rights: Race and the Image of American Democracy*. Princeton, N.J., and Oxford: Princeton University Press, 2000.

———. "Birmingham, Addis Ababa, and the Image of America: International Influence on U.S. Civil Rights Politics in the Kennedy Administration." Brenda G. Plummer, ed. *Window on Freedom: Race, Civil Rights, and Foreign Affairs, 1945–1988*. Chapel Hill and London: University of North Carolina Press, 2002, 181–99.

Duke, Lynne. "What's Gone Wrong at the NAACP?" *Washington Post Magazine*, 18 December 1994: 8–23.

Dulaney, W. Marvin. "Whatever Happened to the Civil Rights Movement in Dallas, Texas?" W. Marvin Dulaney and Kathleen Underwood, eds. *Essays on the American Civil Rights Movement*. College Station: Texas A&M University Press, 1993, 66–95.

Dulles, Foster Rhea. *The Civil Rights Commission: 1957–1965*. East Lansing: Michigan State University Press, 1968.

Eagles, Charles W. "The Civil Rights Movement." John B. Boles, ed. *A Companion to the American South*. Malden, Mass.: Blackwell Publishers, 2002, 461–73.

Edsall, Thomas B., and Mary D. Edsall. *Chain Reaction: The Impact of Race, Rights, and Taxes on American Politics*. New York: Norton, 1991.

Egerton, John. *Speak Now against the Day: The Generation Before the Civil Rights Movement in the South*. Chapel Hill: University of North Carolina Press, 1994.

Eick, Gretchen Cassel. *Dissent in Wichita: The Civil Rights Movement in the Midwest, 1954–72*. Urbana and Chicago: University of Illinois Press, 2001.

Elliott, Ward E. Y. *The Rise of Guardian Democracy: The Supreme Court's Role in Voting Rights Disputes, 1845–1969*. Cambridge, Mass.: Harvard University Press, 1974.

Ellis, Mark. "W.E.B. Du Bois and the Formation of Black Opinion in World War I: A Commentary on the 'Damnable Dilemma.'" *Journal of American History* 81 (1995): 1584–90.

Eskew, Glenn T. *But for Birmingham: The Local and National Movements in the Civil Rights Struggle.* Chapel Hill: University of North Carolina Press, 1998.

Fairclough, Adam. *To Redeem the Soul of America: The Southern Christian Leadership Conference and Martin Luther King, Jr.* Athens and London: University of Georgia Press, 1987.

———. "Historians and the Civil Rights Movement." *Journal of American Studies* 24 (1990): 387–98.

———. *Martin Luther King, Jr.* Athens and London: University of Georgia Press, 1995.

———. *Race and Democracy: The Civil Rights Struggle in Louisiana, 1915–1972.* Athens and London: University of Georgia Press, 1995.

———. *Better Day Coming: Blacks and Equality, 1890–2000.* New York: Viking Penguin, 2001.

———. *Teaching Equality: Black Schools in the Age of Jim Crow.* Athens and London: University of Georgia Press, 2001.

———. "Segregation and Civil Rights: African American Freedom Strategies in the Twentieth Century." Melvyn Stokes, ed. *The State of U.S. History.* Oxford and New York: Berg Publishers: 2002, 155–75.

Farmer, James. *Lay Bare the Heart: An Autobiography of the Civil Rights Movement.* New York: Arbor House, 1985.

Feagin, Joe R., and Harlan Hahn. *Ghetto Revolts: The Politics of Violence in American Cities.* New York: Macmillan, 1973.

Finch, Minnie. *The NAACP: Its Fight for Justice.* Metuchen, N.J.: Scarecrow Press, 1981.

Fletcher, Michael A. "Mfume Takes NAACP Helm Today." *Washington Post,* 15 February 1996: A3.

———. "New Tolerance in the South or Old Power of Incumbency?" *Washington Post,* 23 November 1996: A1, A6.

Fletcher, Michael A., and Kevin Merida. "Mfume Is Chosen to Lead NAACP," *Washington Post,* 10 December 1995: A1 and A25.

Foner, Eric. *Reconstruction: America's Unfinished Revolution, 1863–1877.* New York: Harper and Row, 1988.

Foner, Philip S., ed. *The Black Panthers Speak.* New York: Da Capo Press, 1995.

Foner, Philip S., and Herbert Shapiro, eds. *American Communism and Black Americans: A Documentary History, 1930–1934.* Philadelphia: Temple University Press, 1990.

Franklin, John Hope, and August Meier, eds. *Black Leaders of the Twentieth Century.* Urbana and Chicago: University of Illinois Press, 1982.

Frazier, E. Franklin. *Black Bourgeoisie: The Rise of a New Middle Class in the United States.* New York: Collier Books, 1962.

Fried, Albert, ed. *Communism in America: A History in Documents.* New York: Columbia University Press, 1997.

———, ed. *McCarthyism: The Great American Red Scare. A Documentary History.* Oxford and New York: Oxford University Press, 1997.

Fried, Richard M. *Nightmare in Red: The McCarthy Era in Perspective*. New York and Oxford: Oxford University Press, 1990.

Gardner, Michael R. *Harry Truman and Civil Rights: Moral Courage and Political Risks*. Carbondale and Edwardsville: Southern Illinois University Press, 2002.

Garrow, David J. *Protest at Selma: Martin Luther King, Jr., and the Voting Rights Act of 1965*. New Haven, Conn.: Yale University Press, 1978.

———. *The FBI and Martin Luther King, Jr.: From "Solo" to Memphis*. New York: Norton, 1981.

———. *Bearing the Cross: Martin Luther King, Jr., and the Southern Christian Leadership Conference*. New York: Morrow, 1986.

———, ed. *The Walking City: The Montgomery Bus Boycott, 1955–1956*. New York: Carlson Publishing, 1989.

Gavins, Raymond. "The NAACP in North Carolina during the Age of Segregation." Armstead L. Robinson and Patricia Sullivan, eds. *New Directions in Civil Rights Studies*. Charlottesville and London: University Press of Virginia, 1991, 105–25.

Gerstle, Gary. "Race and the Myth of the Liberal Consensus." *Journal of American History* 82 (1995): 579–86.

Goings, Kenneth W. *The NAACP Comes of Age: The Defeat of Judge John J. Parker*. Bloominton and Indianapolis: Indiana University Press, 1990.

Goldfield, David R. *Black, White, and Southern: Race Relations and Southern Culture 1940 to the Present*. Baton Rouge and London: Louisiana State University Press, 1990.

Goldman, Peter. *The Death and Life of Malcolm X*. Urbana and Chicago: University of Illinois Press, 1979.

Goodstein, Laurie. "On NAACP Agenda: A Capital Trip." *Washington Post*, 20 February 1995: A4, A6.

Graham, Hugh D. *The Civil Rights Era: Origins and Development of National Policy*. New York: Oxford University Press, 1990.

———. *Civil Rights and the Presidency: Race and Gender in American Politics, 1960–1972*. New York: Oxford University Press, 1992.

Greenberg, Jack. *Crusaders in the Courts: How a Dedicated Band of Lawyers Fought for the Civil Rights Revolution*. New York: Basic Books, 1994.

Greene, John R. *The Limits of Power: The Nixon and Ford Administrations*. Bloomington and Indianapolis: Indiana University Press, 1992.

Grofman, Bernard, et al. *Minority Representation and the Quest for Voting Equality*. New York: Cambridge University Press, 1992.

Grofman, Bernard, and Chandler Davidson, eds. *Controversies in Minority Voting: The Voting Rights Act in Perspective*. Washington, D.C.: Brookings Institution, 1992, 7–51.

Guinier, Lani. "Voting Rights and Democratic Theory: Where Do We Go from Here?" Bernard Grofman and Chandler Davidson, eds. *Controversies in Minority Voting. The Voting Rights Act in Perspective*. Washington, D.C.: Brookings Institution, 1992, 283–92.

———. *The Tyranny of the Majority: Fundamental Fairness in Representative Democracy*. New York: Free Press, 1994.

Hacker, Andrew. *Two Nations: Black and White, Separate, Hostile, Unequal.* New York: Charles Scribner's Sons, 1992.

Haines, Herbert H. "Black Radicalization and the Funding of Civil Rights: 1957–1970." *Social Problems* 32 (1984): 31–43.

———. *Black Radicals and the Civil Rights Mainstream, 1954–1970.* Knoxville: University of Tennessee Press, 1988.

Hamby, Alonzo. *Beyond the New Deal: Harry S. Truman and American Liberalism.* New York: Columbia University Press, 1973.

Hamilton, Charles V. "An Advocate of Black Power Defines It." August Meier et al., eds. *Black Protest in the Sixties.* New York: Wiener, 1991, 154–68.

Hamilton, Dona C., and Charles V. Hamilton. *The Dual Agenda: Race and Social Welfare Policies of Civil Rights Organizations.* New York: Columbia University Press, 1997.

Handley, Lisa, and Bernard Grofman. "The Impact of the Voting Rights Act on Minority Representation: Black Officeholding in Southern State Legislatures and Congressional Delegations." Chandler Davidson and Bernard Grofman, eds. *Quiet Revolution in the South: The Impact of the Voting Rights Act, 1965–1990.* Princeton, N.J.: Princeton University Press, 1994, 335–50.

Harlan, Louis R. *Booker T. Washington: The Making of a Black Leader, 1856–1901.* New York: Oxford University Press, 1972.

———. *Booker T. Washington: The Wizard of Tuskegee, 1901–1915.* New York: Oxford University Press, 1983.

Harris, Hamil R., and Michael A. Fletcher. "In Mfume, NAACP Hires a Veteran of the Public Arena." *Washington Post,* 11 December 1995: A14.

Harris, Jacqueline L. *History and Achievement of the NAACP.* New York: Franklin Watts, 1992.

Harris, Robert L., Jr. "Racial Equality and the United Nations Charter." Armstead L. Robinson and Patricia Sullivan, eds. *New Directions in Civil Rights Studies.* Charlottesville and London: University Press of Virginia, 1991, 126–48.

Heale, Michael J. *American Anticommunism: Combatting the Enemy Within, 1830–1970.* Baltimore and London: Johns Hopkins University Press, 1990.

Hill, Robert A., ed. *The FBI's Racon: Racial Conditions in the United States during World War II.* Boston: Northeastern University Press, 1995.

Hine, Darlene C. *Black Victory: The Rise and Fall of the White Primary in Texas.* New York: KTO Press, 1979.

Hirsch, Arnold R. "Massive Resistance in the Urban North: Trumbull Park, Chicago, 1953–1966." *Journal of American History* 82 (1995): 522–50.

Hixson, Walter B. *Moorfield Storey and the Abolitionist Tradition.* New York: Oxford University Press, 1972.

Hoff, Joan. *Nixon Reconsidered.* New York: Basic Books, 1994.

Horne, Gerald. *Black and Red: W.E.B. Du Bois and the Afro-American Response to the Cold War.* Albany: State University Press of New York, 1986.

———. *Communist Front? The Civil Rights Congress, 1946–1956.* London and Toronto: Associated University Presses, 1988.

―――. *Black Liberation/Red Scare: Ben Davis and the Communist Party.* London and Toronto: Associated University Presses, 1994.

―――. "Commentary: Who Lost the Cold War? Africans and African Americans." *Diplomatic History* 20 (1996): 613–26.

Hughes, Langston. *Fight for Freedom: The Story of the NAACP.* New York: Norton, 1962.

Hutchinson, Earl O. *Blacks and Reds: Race and Class in Conflict, 1919–1990.* East Lansing: Michigan State University Press, 1995.

Janken, Kenneth R. *White: The Biography of Walter White, Mr. NAACP.* New York: New Press, 2003.

Johnson, James W. *Along This Way: The Autobiography of James Weldon Johnson.* New York: Viking Penguin, 1990.

Johnson, John W. *American Legal Culture, 1908–1940.* Westport, Conn.: Greenwood Press, 1981.

Johnson, Lyndon B. *The Vantage Point: Perspectives of the Presidency, 1963–1969.* New York: Holt, Rinehart and Winston, 1971.

Joint Center for Political and Economic Studies. *Black Elected Officials: A Statistical Summary 2001.* www.jointcenter.org/publications/BEO/BEO-01.html (7 January 2004).

Jordan, William. "'The Damnable Dilemma': African-American Accommodation and Protest During World War I." *Journal of American History* 81 (1995): 1562–83.

Kazin, Michael. "The Agony and Romance of the American Left." *American Historical Review* 100 (1995): 1488–1512.

Kelley, Robin D. G. *Hammer and Hoe: Alabama Communists during the Great Depression.* Chapel Hill and London: University of North Carolina Press, 1990.

Kellogg, Charles F. *NAACP: A History of the National Association for the Advancement of Colored People, 1909–1920.* Baltimore: Johns Hopkins University Press, 1967.

Kenney, Charles. *John F. Kennedy: The Presidential Portfolio. History as Told through the Collection of the John F. Kennedy Library and Museum.* New York: BBS Public Affairs, 2000.

Key, V. O. *Southern Politics in State and Nation.* Knoxville: University of Tennessee Press, 1984.

Keyssar, Alexander. *The Right to Vote: The Contested History of Democracy in the United States.* New York: Basic Books, 2000.

Kirby, John B. *Black Americans in the Roosevelt Era: Liberalism and Race.* Knoxville: University of Tennessee Press, 1980.

King, Martin Luther, Jr. *Stride toward Freedom: The Montgomery Story.* London: Victor Gollancz, 1959.

King, Richard. *Civil Rights and the Idea of Freedom.* New York and Oxford: Oxford University Press, 1992.

Klarman, Michael J. "How *Brown* Changed Race Relations: The Backlash Thesis." *Journal of American History* 81 (1994): 81–118.

―――. "Is the Supreme Court Sometimes Irrelevant? Race and the Southern Criminal Justice System in the 1940s." *Journal of American History* 89 (2002): 119–53.

Klehr, Harvey, et al. *The Soviet World of American Communism.* New Haven, Conn.: Yale University Press, 1998.

Kluger, Richard. *Simple Justice: The History of Brown v. Board of Education and Black America's Struggle for Equality*. New York: Knopf, 1975.

Korstad, Robert, and Nelson Lichtenstein. "Opportunities Found and Lost: Labor, Radicals, and the Early Civil Rights Movement." *Journal of American History* 75 (1988): 786–811.

Kousser, J. Morgan. *The Shaping of Southern Politics: Suffrage Restriction and the Establishment of the One-Party South, 1880–1910*. New Haven, Conn., and London: Yale University Press, 1974.

———. *Colorblind Injustice: Minority Voting Rights and the Undoing of the Second Reconstruction*. Chapel Hill: University of North Carolina Press, 1999.

Laville, Helen, and Scott Lucas. "The American Way: Edith Sampson, the NAACP, and African American Identity in the Cold War." *Diplomatic History* 20 (1996): 565–90.

Lawson, Steven F. *Black Ballots: Voting Rights in the South, 1944–1969*. New York: Columbia University Press, 1976.

———. *In Pursuit of Power: Southern Blacks and Electoral Politics, 1962–1982*. New York: Columbia University Press, 1985.

———. *Running for Freedom: Civil Rights and Black Politics in America since 1941*. Philadelphia: Temple University Press, 1991.

Levine, Lawrence W. "Marcus Garvey and the Politics of Revitalization." John Hope Franklin and August Meier, eds. *Black Leaders of the Twentieth Century*. Urbana and Chicago: University of Illinois Press, 1982, 105–37.

Levy, Eugene. "James Weldon Johnson and the Development of the NAACP." John Hope Franklin and August Meier, eds. *Black Leaders of the Twentieth Century*. Urbana and Chicago: University of Illinois Press, 1982, 85–104.

Lewis, David L. *King: A Critical Biography*. Chicago: University of Illinois Press, 1978.

———. "Parallels and Divergences: Afro-American and Jewish Elites from 1910 to the Early 1930s." *Journal of American History* 71 (1984/85): 543–64.

———. *W.E.B. Du Bois: Biography of a Race, 1868–1919*. New York: Holt, 1993.

———. *W.E.B. Du Bois: The Fight for Equality and the American Century*. New York: Holt, 2000.

Lewis, John. "Why Republicans Are in Love with the Voting Rights Act." www.house.gov.johnlewis/voting_rights.html (21 July 2003).

Lisio, Donald J. *Hoover, Blacks, and Lily-Whites: A Study of Southern Strategies*. Chapel Hill and London: University of North Carolina Press, 1985.

Logan, Rayford W., ed. *The Attitude of the Southern White Press toward Negro Suffrage*. Washington, D.C.: Foundation Publishers, 1940.

———. *The Negro and the Post-War World: A Primer*. Washington, D.C.: Minorities Publishers, 1945.

Lunardini, Christine A. *From Equal Suffrage to Equal Rights: Alice Paul and the National Woman's Party, 1910–1928*. New York: New York University Press, 1986.

Marable, Manning. *W.E.B. Du Bois: Black Radical Democrat*. Boston: Twayne Publishers, 1986.

———. *Race, Reform, and Rebellion: The Second Reconstruction in Black America, 1945–1990*. Jackson and London: University Press of Mississippi, 1991.

——. *Black Leadership*. New York: Columbia University Press, 1998.

Marger, Martin N. "Social Movement Organizations and the Response to Environmental Change: The NAACP, 1960–1973." *Social Problems* 32 (1984): 16–31.

Martin, Waldo E., ed. *Brown v. Board of Education: A Brief History with Documents*. Boston and New York: Bedford/St. Martin's, 1998.

McAdam, Doug. *Political Process and the Development of Black Insurgency, 1930–1970*. Chicago: University of Chicago Press, 1982.

McMillen, Neil R. *The Citizens' Council: Organized Resistance to the Second Reconstruction, 1954–64*. Urbana and Chicago: University of Illinois Press, 1994.

McNeil, Genna R. *Groundwork: Charles Hamilton Houston and the Struggle for Civil Rights*. Philadelphia: University of Pennsylvania Press, 1983.

McPherson, James M. *The Abolitionist Legacy: From Reconstruction to the NAACP*. Princeton, N.J.: Princeton University Press, 1975.

McWhorter, John. *Losing the Race: Self-Sabotage in Black America*. New York: Free Press, 2000.

Mead, Lawrence. *Beyond Entitlement: The Social Obligation of Citizenship*. New York: Free Press, 1986.

Meier, August. *Negro Thought in America, 1880–1915: Racial Ideologies in the Age of Booker T. Washington*. Ann Arbor: University of Michigan Press, 1963.

——. "On the Role of Martin Luther King." *New Politics* 4 (1965): 1–8.

——. "Booker T. Washington and the Rise of the NAACP." August Meier and Elliot Rudwick, eds. *Along the Color Line: Explorations in the Black Experience*. Urbana and Chicago: University of Illinois Press, 1976, 74–93.

——. "Epilogue: Toward a Synthesis of Civil Rights History." Armstead L. Robinson and Patricia Sullivan, eds. *New Directions in Civil Rights Studies*. Charlottesville and London: University Press of Virginia, 1991, 211–24.

Meier, August, and John H. Bracey. "The NAACP as a Reform Movement, 1909–1965: 'To Reach the Conscience of America.'" *Journal of Southern History* 59 (1993): 3–30.

Meier, August, and Elliot Rudwick. *CORE: A Study in the Civil Rights Movement, 1942–1968*. Urbana: University of Illinois Press, 1975.

——. *Along the Color Line: Explorations in the Black Experience*. Urbana and Chicago: University of Illinois Press, 1976.

——. "Attorneys Black and White: A Case Study of Race Relations within the NAACP." August Meier and Elliot Rudwick, eds. *Along the Color Line: Explorations in the Black Experience*. Urbana and Chicago: University of Illinois Press, 1976, 128–73.

——. "The Origins of Nonviolent Direct Action in Afro-American Protest: A Note on Historical Discontinuities." August Meier and Elliot Rudwick, eds. *Along the Color Line: Explorations in the Black Experience*. Urbana and Chicago: University of Illinois Press, 1976, 307–404.

Merida, Kevin. "Black Leaders Convene Meeting in Baltimore." *Washington Post*, 13 June 1994, A1, A10.

Mfume, Kweisi, and Ron Stodghill. *No Free Ride: From the Mean Streets to the Mainstream*. New York: One World, 1996.

Mills, Kay. *This Little Light of Mine: The Life of Fannie Lou Hamer.* New York: Dutton, 1993.

Moody, Ann. *Coming of Age in Mississippi: An Autobiography by Anne Moody.* New York: Dell Publishing, 1968.

Moon, Henry Lee. *Balance of Power: The Negro Vote.* Westport, Conn.: Greenwood Press, 1977.

Morris, Aldon D. *The Origins of the Civil Rights Movement: Black Communities Organize for Change.* New York: Free Press, 1984.

Morris, Milton D. "Black Electoral Participation and the Distribution of Public Benefits." Chandler Davidson, ed. *Minority Vote Dilution.* Washington, D.C.: Howard University Press, 1984, 271–85.

Murray, Charles. *Losing Ground: American Social Policy, 1950–1980.* New York: Basic Books, 1984.

Myrdal, Gunnar, et al. *An American Dilemma: The Negro Problem and Modern Democracy.* New York: Harper and Row, 1962.

Nalty, Bernard C. *Strength for the Fight: A History of Black Americans in the Military.* New York: Free Press, 1986.

National Advisory Commission on Civil Disorders. *Report.* New York: Dutton, 1968.

National Association for the Advancement of Colored People, ed. *Thirty Years of Lynching in the United States, 1889–1919.* New York: Negro Universities Press, 1969.

Newton, Michael, and Judy Ann Newton. *Racial and Religious Violence in America: A Chronology.* New York and London: Garland Publishing, 1991.

Niven, David. *The Politics of Injustice: The Kennedys, the Freedom Rides, and the Electoral Consequences of Moral Compromise.* Knoxville: University of Tennessee Press, 2003.

Nolan, William A. *Communism versus the Negro.* Chicago: Regnery, 1951.

Norrell, Robert J. *Reaping the Whirlwind: The Civil Rights Movement in Tuskegee.* New York: Knopf, 1985.

Oates, Stephen B. *Let the Trumpet Sound: The Life of Martin Luther King, Jr.* New York: Harper and Row, 1982.

O'Reilly, Kenneth. *"Racial Matters": The FBI's Secret File on Black America, 1960–1972.* New York: Free Press, 1989.

———. *Nixon's Piano: Presidents and Racial Politics from Washington to Clinton.* New York: Free Press, 1995.

Ovington, Mary W. *The Walls Came Tumbling Down: The Autobiography of Mary White Ovington.* New York: Schocken, 1970.

Parker, Frank R. *Black Votes Count: Political Empowerment in Mississippi after 1965.* Chapel Hill: University of North Carolina Press, 1990.

———. "The Court's Blind Eye on Voting Rights." *Focus* (1993): 7–8.

Patterson, James T. *Grand Expectations: The United States, 1945–1974.* New York: Oxford University Press, 1996.

———. *Brown v. Board of Education: A Civil Rights Milestone and Its Troubled Legacy.* New York: Oxford University Press, 2001.

Patterson, Orlando. *The Ordeal of Integration: Progress and Resentment in America's "Racial" Crisis.* Washington, D.C.: Counterpoint, 1997.

———. "Broken Bloodlines: Gender Relations and the Crisis of Marriage and Families among Afro-Americans." Orlando Patterson. *Rituals of Blood: Consequences of Slavery in Two American Centuries*. Washington, D.C.: Civitas, 1998, 3–167.

Payne, Charles M. *I've Got the Light of Freedom: The Organizing Tradition and the Mississippi Freedom Struggle*. Berkeley and Los Angeles: University of California Press, 1995.

Perman, Michael. *Struggle for Mastery: Disfranchisement in the South, 1888–1908*. Chapel Hill and London: University of North Carolina Press, 2001.

Perry, Lewis. "Civil Disobedience." Jack P. Greene, ed. *Encyclopedia of American Political History: Studies of the Principal Movements and Ideas*. 3 vols. New York: Charles Scribner's Sons, 1983, 1:210–217.

Pfeffer, Paula F. *A. Philip Randolph: Pioneer of the Civil Rights Movement*. Baton Rouge and London: Louisiana State University Press, 1990.

Plummer, Brenda G. *Rising Wind: Black Americans and U.S. Foreign Affairs, 1935–1960*. Chapel Hill and London: University of North Carolina Press, 1996.

Porter, Kirk H. *A History of Suffrage in the United States*. Chicago: University of Chicago Press, 1918.

Powers, Richard G. *Not Without Honor: The History of American Anticommunism*. New York: Free Press, 1995.

Proceedings of the National Negro Conference 1909. New York: Arno Press and the New York Times, 1969.

The Public Papers of the Presidents of the United States: Franklin D. Roosevelt: 1933–1945. Washington, D.C.: Government Printing Office, 1963–1964.

The Public Papers of the Presidents of the United States: Harry S. Truman: 1945–1953. Washington, D.C.: Government Printing Office, 1963–1964.

The Public Papers of the Presidents of the United States: Dwight D. Eisenhower: 1953–1961. Washington, D.C.: Government Printing Office, 1963–1964.

The Public Papers of the Presidents of the United States: John F. Kennedy: 1961–1963. Washington, D.C.: Government Printing Office, 1963–1964.

The Public Papers of the Presidents of the United States: Lyndon B. Johnson: 1963–1968/69. Washington, D.C.: Government Printing Office, 1965–1970.

Raines, Howard, ed. *My Soul Is Rested: Movement Days in the Deep South Remembered*. New York: Penguin, 1983.

Ralph, James R. *Northern Protest: Martin Luther King, Jr., Chicago and the Civil Rights Movement*. Cambridge, Mass.: Harvard University Press, 1993.

Ransby, Barbara. *Ella Baker and the Black Freedom Movement: A Radical Democratic Vision*. Chapel Hill and London: University of North Carolina Press, 2003.

Record, Wilson. *The Negro and the Communist Party*. Chapel Hill: University of North Carolina Press, 1951.

———. *Race and Radicalism: The NAACP and the Communist Party in Conflict*. Ithaca, N.Y.: Cornell University Press, 1964.

Reed, Christopher R. "Organized Racial Reform during the Progressive Era: The Chicago NAACP, 1910–1920." *Michigan Historical Review* 14 (1988): 75–99.

———. *The Chicago NAACP and the Rise of Black Professional Leadership, 1910–1966*. Bloomington: Indiana University Press, 1997.

Reed, Merl E. *Seedtime for the Modern Civil Rights Movement: The President's Committee on

Fair Employment Practice, 1941–1946. Baton Rouge: Louisiana State University Press, 1991.

Rorabaugh, William J. *Kennedy and the Promise of the Sixties*. Cambridge, U.K., and New York: Cambridge University Press, 2002.

Rosenberg, Gerald. *The Hollow Hope: Can Courts Bring About Social Change?* Chicago: University of Chicago Press, 1991.

Rosenstone, Steven J., and John M. Hansen. *Mobilization, Participation and Democracy in America*. New York: Macmillan, 1993.

Ross, B. Joyce. *J. E. Spingarn and the Rise of the NAACP, 1911–1939*. New York: Atheneum, 1972.

Rudwick, Elliot, and August Meier. "Black Violence in the Twentieth Century: A Study in Rhetoric and Retaliation." August Meier and Elliot Rudwick, eds. *Along the Color Line: Explorations in the Black Experience*. Urbana and Chicago: University of Illinois Press, 1976, 224–37.

———. "Integration vs. Separatism: The NAACP and CORE Face Challenge from Within." August Meier and Elliot Rudwick, eds. *Along the Color Line: Explorations in the Black Experience*. Urbana and Chicago: University of Illinois Press, 1976, 238–63.

———. "The Rise of the Black Secretariat in the NAACP, 1909–1935." August Meier and Elliot Rudwick, eds. *Along the Color Line: Explorations in the Black Experience*. Urbana and Chicago: University of Illinois Press, 1976, 94–127.

Samuels, Gertrude. "Two Ways: Black Muslim and NAACP." August Meier et al., eds. *Black Protest in the Sixties*. New York: Wiener, 1991, 37–45.

Savage, David G. *Turning Right: The Making of the Rehnquist Supreme Court*. New York: Wiley and Sons, 1992.

Schlesinger, Arthur M., Jr. *The Vital Center: The Politics of Freedom*. Boston: Houghton Mifflin, 1949.

———, ed. *History of American Presidential Elections 1787–1968*. 4 vols. New York: Chelsea House, 1971.

Schneider, Mark R. *Boston Confronts Jim Crow, 1890–1920*. Boston: Northeastern University Press, 1997.

———. *We Return Fighting: The Civil Rights Movement in the Jazz Age*. Boston: Northeastern University Press, 2002.

Schrecker, Ellen. *The Age of McCarthyism: A Brief History with Documents*. Boston and New York: Bedford Books of St. Martin's Press, 1994.

———. *Many Are the Crimes: McCarthyism in America*. Boston: Little, Brown, 1998.

Scott, William R. *The Sons of Sheba's Race: Afro-Americans and the Italo-Ethiopian War, 1935–1941*. Bloomington: Indiana University Press, 1993.

Senechal, Roberta. *The Sociogenesis of a Race Riot: Springfield, Illinois, in 1908*. Urbana, Ill.: University of Illinois Press, 1990.

Shaffer, William R. "Senator John F. Kennedy and the Liberal Establishment: Presidential Politics and Civil Rights Legislation in 1957." Paul Harper and Joann P. Krieg, eds. *John F. Kennedy: The Promise Revisited*. New York and Westport, Conn.: Greenwood Press, 1988, 225–35.

Sherman, Richard B. *The Republican Party and Black America: From McKinley to Hoover, 1896–1933*. Charlottesville: University Press of Virginia, 1973.

Shklar, Judith N. *American Citizenship: The Quest for Inclusion*. Cambridge, Mass.: Harvard University Press, 1991.

Sitkoff, Harvard. "Racial Militancy and Interracial Violence in the Second World War." *Journal of American History* 58 (1971): 661–81.

———. *A New Deal for Blacks: The Emergence of Civil Rights as a National Issue*. New York: Oxford University Press, 1978.

Smith, Jessie C., and Carrell P. Horton, eds. *Historical Statistics of Black America*. 2 vols. New York: Gale Research, 1995.

Smith, Robert C. *Racism in the Post–Civil Rights Era: Now You See It, Now You Don't*. Albany: State University of New York Press, 1995.

———. *We Have No Leaders: African Americans in the Post–Civil Rights Era*. Albany: State University of New York Press, 1996.

Sonenshein, Ralph J. *Politics in Black and White: Race and Power in Los Angeles*. Princeton, N.J.: Princeton University Press, 1993.

Sowell, Thomas. *Civil Rights: Rhetoric or Reality?* New York: Morrow, 1984.

Steele, Shelby. *The Content of Our Character: A New Version of Race in America*. New York: St. Martin's Press, 1990.

———. "The Age of White Guilt and the Disappearance of the Black Individual." *Harper's Magazine* (November 2002): 33–42.

Stein, Judith. *The World of Marcus Garvey: Race and Class in Modern Society*. Baton Rouge and London: Louisiana State University Press, 1986.

Stern, Mark. *Calculating Visions: Kennedy, Johnson, and Civil Rights*. New Brunswick, N.J.: Rutgers University Press, 1992.

Stern, Sol. "The Call of the Panthers." August Meier, John Bracey, and Elliott Rudwick, eds. *Black Protest in the Sixties*. New York: Markus Wiener Publishing, 1991, 230–42.

Stevens, Edward W. *Literacy, Law, and Social Order*. DeKalb, Ill.: Northern Illinois University Press, 1988.

St. James, Warren D. *The National Association for the Advancement of Colored People: A Case Study in Pressure Groups*. New York: Exposition Press, 1958.

Stone, Chuck. *Black Political Power in America*. Indianapolis and New York: Bobbs-Merrill, 1968.

Sugrue, Thomas J. "Crabgrass-Roots Politics: Race, Rights, and the Reaction against Liberalism in the Urban North, 1940–1964." *Journal of American History* 82 (1995): 551–78.

———. *The Origins of the Urban Crisis: Race and Inequality in Postwar Detroit*. Princeton, N.J.: Princeton University Press, 1996.

Sullivan, Patricia. *Days of Hope: Race and Democracy in the New Deal Era*. Chapel Hill and London: University of North Carolina Press, 1996.

Swain, Carol M. *Black Faces, Black Interests: The Representation of African Americans in Congress*. Cambridge, Mass., and London: Harvard University Press, 1993.

———. *The New White Nationalism in America: Its Challenge to Integration*. New York: Cambridge University Press, 2002.

Tate, Katherine. *From Protest to Politics: The New Black Voters in American Elections.* Cambridge, Mass., and London: Harvard University Press, 1994.

Taylor, Clyde, ed. *Vietnam and Black America: An Anthology of Protest and Resistance.* Garden City: Anchor, 1973.

Thernstrom, Abigail M. *Whose Votes Count? Affirmative Action and Minority Voting Rights.* Cambridge, Mass., and London: Harvard University Press, 1987.

Thernstrom, Stephan, and Abigail Thernstrom. *America in Black and White: One Nation Indivisible.* New York: Simon and Schuster, 1997.

Topping, Simon. "'Supporting Our Friends and Defeating Our Enemies': Militancy and Nonpartisanship in the NAACP, 1936–1948." *Journal of African American History* 89 (2004): 17–35.

To Secure These Rights: The Report of the President's Committee on Civil Rights. Washington, D.C.: Government Printing Office, 1947.

Tuck, Stephen G. N. *Beyond Atlanta: The Struggle for Racial Equality in Georgia, 1940–1980.* Athens: University of Georgia Press, 2001.

———. "Black Protest during the 1940s: The NAACP in Georgia." Patrick B. Miller et al., eds. *The Civil Rights Movement Revisited: Critical Perspectives on the Struggle for Racial Equality in the United States.* Münster: LIT Verlag, 2001, 63–79.

Tushnet, Mark V. *The NAACP's Legal Strategy against Segregated Education, 1925–1950.* Chapel Hill: University of North Carolina Press, 1987.

———. *Making Civil Rights Law: Thurgood Marshall and the Supreme Court, 1936–1961.* New York and Oxford: Oxford University Press, 1994.

———. *Making Constitutional Law: Thurgood Marshall and the Supreme Court, 1962–1991.* New York and Oxford: Oxford University Press, 1997.

Tyson, Timothy B. *Radio Free Dixie: Robert F. Williams and the Roots of Black Power.* Chapel Hill: North Carolina University Press, 1999.

U.S. Commission on Civil Rights. *Hearings Held in Montgomery, Alabama: Report.* Washington, D.C.: Government Printing Office, 1959.

———. *Hearings Held in Montgomery, Alabama: Voting.* Washington, D.C.: Government Printing Office, 1959.

U.S. Department of Commerce. Bureau of the Census, ed. *Historical Statistics of the United States: Colonial Times to 1970.* 2 vols. Washington, D.C.: Government Printing Office, 1975.

Valelly, Richard M. "National Parties and Racial Disenfranchisement." Paul E. Peterson, ed. *Classifying by Race.* Princeton, N.J.: Princeton University Press, 1995, 188–216.

Van Deburg, William L. *New Day in Babylon: The Black Power Movement and American Culture, 1965–1975.* Chicago and London: University of Chicago Press, 1992.

———, ed. *Modern Black Nationalism: From Marcus Garvey to Louis Farrakhan.* New York: New York University Press, 1997.

Villard, Oswald Garrison. *Fighting Years: Memoirs of a Liberal Editor.* New York: Harcourt, Brace, 1939.

von Eschen, Penny M. "Commentary: Challenging Cold War Habits: African Americans, Race, and Foreign Policy." *Diplomatic History* 20 (1996): 627–38.

————. *Race against Empire: Black Americans and Anticolonialism*. Ithaca: Cornell University Press, 1996.

Walling, William E. "The Race War in the North." *Independent* 65 (1908): 529–34.

Walters, Ronald. "Serving the People: African-American Leadership and the Challenge of Empowerment." Billy J. Tidwell, ed. *The State of Black America, 1994*. New York: National Urban League, 1994.

Ward, Brian, and Tony Badger, eds. *The Making of Martin Luther King and the Civil Rights Movement*. London: Macmillan, 1996.

Washington, Booker T. *Up from Slavery*. New York: Penguin Books, 1986.

Washington, James M., ed. *A Testament of Hope: The Essential Writings and Speeches of Martin Luther King, Jr.* San Francisco: HarperCollins, 1991.

Watson, Denton L. *Lion in the Lobby: Clarence Mitchell, Jr.'s Struggle for the Passage of Civil Rights Laws*. New York: Morrow, 1990.

Watters, Pat, and Reese Cleghorn. *Climbing Jacob's Ladder: The Arrival of Negroes in Southern Politics*. New York: Harcourt, Brace and World, 1967.

Weber, Max. *Wirtschaft und Gesellschaft: Grundriß der verstehenden Soziologie*. Tübingen: J.C.B. Mohr, 1972.

Weisbrot, Robert. *Freedom Bound: A History of America's Civil Rights Movement*. New York and London: Norton, 1990.

Weiss, Nancy J. *The National Urban League 1910–1940*. New York: Oxford University Press, 1974.

————. *Farewell to the Party of Lincoln: Black Politics in the Age of FDR*. Princeton, N.J.: Princeton University Press, 1983.

————. "Creative Tensions in the Leadership of the Civil Rights Movement." Charles W. Eagles, ed. *The Civil Rights Movement in America*. Jackson and London: University Press of Mississippi, 1986, 39–55.

————. *Whitney M. Young, Jr., and the Struggle for Civil Rights*. Princeton, N.J.: Princeton University Press, 1989.

Wendt, Simon. *The Spirit and the Shotgun: Armed Resistance and the Radicalization of the African American Freedom Movement*. Ph.D. thesis: Free University of Berlin, 2004.

Westheider, James E. *Fighting on Two Fronts: African Americans and the Vietnam War*. New York: New York University Press, 1997.

Whitby, Kenny J. *The Color of Representation: Congressional Behavior and Black Interests*. Ann Arbor: University of Michigan Press, 1997.

White, Jack E. "Let's Scrap the N.A.A.C.P." *Time*, 13 February 1995: 70.

White, Walter F. *A Rising Wind*. Westport, Conn.: Negro Universities Press, 1945.

————. *A Man Called White: The Autobiography of Walter White*. Athens and London: University of Georgia Press, 1995.

Wilkins, Roy, with Tom Mathews. *Standing Fast: The Autobiography of Roy Wilkins*. New York: Da Capo Press, 1994.

Williams, Juan. "Blacked Out in the Newt Congress." *Washington Post*, 20 November 1994: C1, C4.

Wilson, William J. *The Declining Significance of Race: Blacks and Changing American Institutions*. Chicago: University of Chicago Press, 1978.

———. *The Truly Disadvantaged: The Inner City, the Underclass, and Public Policy.* Chicago and London: University of Chicago Press, 1987.

———. *When Work Disappears: The World of the New Urban Poor.* New York: Knopf, 1996.

———. *The Bridge over the Racial Divide: Rising Inequality and Coalition Politics.* Berkeley and Los Angeles: University of California Press, 1999.

Wofford, Harris. *Of Kennedys and Kings: Making Sense of the Sixties.* New York: Farrar, Straus and Giroux, 1980.

Wolters, Raymond. *Negroes and the Great Depression: The Problem of Economic Recovery.* Westport, Conn.: Greenwood Publishing, 1970.

Woods, Jeff. *Black Struggle, Red Scare: Segregation and Anticommunism in the South, 1948–1968.* Baton Rouge, Louisiana State University Press, 2004.

Wright, George C. "The Civil Rights Movement in Kentucky, 1900–1970." W. Marvin Dulaney and Kathleen Underwood, eds. *Essays on the American Civil Rights Movement.* College Station: Texas A&M University Press, 1993, 44–65.

Wynn, Neil A. *The Afro-American and the Second World War.* New York: Holmes and Meier, 1993.

Zahavi, Gerald. "Passionate Commitments: Race, Sex, and Communism at Schenectady General Electric, 1932–1954." *Journal of American History* 83 (1996): 514–48.

Zangrando, Robert L. *The NAACP Crusade against Lynching, 1909–1950.* Philadelphia: Temple University Press, 1980.

———. "Manuscript Sources for Twentieth Century Civil Rights Research." *Journal of American History* 74 (1987/88): 243–51.

Zieger, Robert. *The CIO, 1935–1955.* Chapel Hill: University of North Carolina Press, 1995.

Zinn, Howard. *SNCC: The New Abolitionists.* Boston: Beacon Press, 1964.

Court Cases

Abrams v. Johnson, 521 U.S. 74 (1997).

Allen v. State Board of Elections, 393 U.S. 544 (1969).

Beer v. United States, 425 U.S. 130 (1976).

Boynton v. Virginia, 364 U.S. 454 (1960).

Breedlove v. Suttles, 302 U.S. 277 (1937).

Brown v. Board of Education of Topeka, Kansas, 347 U.S. 483 (1954).

Buchanan v. Warley, 245 U.S. 60 (1917).

Bush. v. Vera, 517 U.S. 952 (1996).

City of Mobile v. Bolden, 446 U.S. 55 (1980).

Dennis v. United States, 341 U.S. 494 (1951).

Georgia v. Ashcroft, 195 F. Supp. 2nd 25 539 U.S.—(2003) www.supremecourtus.gov/opinions/02pdf/02-182.pdf.

Giles v. Harris, 189 U.S. 475 (1903).

Giles v. Teasley, 193 U.S. 146 (1904).

Grovey v. Townsend, 295 U.S. 45 (1935).

Guinn v. United States, 238 U.S. 347 (1915).

Harper v. Virginia State Board of Elections, 383 U.S. 663 (1966).

Holder v. Hall, 512 U.S. 874 (1994).
Lane v. Wilson, 307 U.S. 268 (1939).
Miller v. Johnson, 515 U.S. 900 (1995).
Missouri ex rel. Gaines v. Canada, 305 U.S. 337 (1938).
Moore v. Dempsey, 261 U.S. 86 (1923).
Nixon v. Condon, 286 U.S. 73 (1932).
Nixon v. Herndon, 273 U.S. 536 (1927).
Plessy v. Ferguson, 163 U.S. 537 (1896).
Shaw v. Hunt, 517 U.S. 899 (1996).
Shaw v. Reno, 509 U.S. 630 (1993).
Shelley v. Kramer, 334 U.S. 1 (1948).
Smith v. Allwright, 321 U.S. 649 (1944).
South Carolina v. Katzenbach, 383 U.S. 301 (1966).
Terry v. Adams, 345 U.S. 461 (1953).
Thornburgh v. Gingles, 478 U.S. 30 (1996).
United States v. Classic, 313 U.S. 299 (1941).
White v. Regester, 412 U.S. 755 (1973).
Williams v. Mississippi, 170 U.S. 213 (1897).

Personal Interviews

Clifford Collins, telephone conversation, Baltimore, Maryland, 6 May 1994.
Joseph Madison, Washington, D.C., 20 September 1994.
W. C. Patton, Birmingham, Alabama, 20 October 1994.

Index

Page references under National Association for the Advancement of Colored People are mostly related to organizational matters. More references to the NAACP are to be found under proper names, e.g., Student Nonviolent Coordinating Committee, and terms, e.g., Voter registration.

Abernathy, Ralph, 146, 168
ACLU. See American Civil Liberties Union
Addams, Jane, 12, 19, 23, 33, 44
AFL. See American Federation of Labor
African Methodist Episcopal Church, 102
Afro-American Council, 15
Agricultural Adjustment Act, 64
Alabama State Coordinating Committee (Association) for Registration and Voting, 148, 155, 163
Alexander, Kelly, 110, 158, 181
Allen, Henry J., 54–55
Amenia conferences, 19 (1916), 60–61 (1932)
American Bar Association, 13
American Broadcasting Corporation (ABC), 206
American Civil Liberties Union (ACLU), 89, 105
American Dilemma, An, 94, 110–11
American Federation of Labor (AFL), 53, 105
American Fund for Public Service (Garland Fund), 76
American Independent Party, 245
American Jewish Congress, 206
American Labor Party, 109, 135
American Legion, 136
American Mercury, 27

American Negro Labor Congress, 62
American Newspaper Guild, 131
Americans for Democratic Action, 139
Anderson, Carol, 3, 118, 286n7
Anticommunism, 7, 116–18, 131–39. See also McCarthyism; National Association for the Advancement of Colored People
Anti-Defamation League, 184
Antilynching bills, 4, 56, 65, 67, 106, 124–25, 130; Dyer bill, 51, 68
Appeal to the World, An, 120–21, 125. See also National Association for the Advancement of Colored People
Arnall, Ellis, 104, 142
Associated Press, 141
Atkins, Jack, 83–84

Bagnall, Robert W., 38
Baird, David, 55
Baker, Ella, 2, 113, 167
Balance of Power: The Negro Vote (1948), 129, 143
Barry, Marion, 170
Bethune, Mary McLeod, 64, 109, 119, 169
Bilbo, Theodore, 91–92, 121
Birth of a Nation, The, 22–23, 175
Black, Hugo, 86

Black, Lucille, 110, 112, 155
Black churches, 146–47, 160, 232, 240
Black Congressional Caucus, 236, 264
Black elected officials, 255–56, 259–62
Black electorate: influenced by NAACP, 68,
   192; party affiliation, 43, 64, 66–67, 130,
   193, 202, 213, 243, 246; strength of, 41, 43,
   45, 46, 49–50, 56, 65, 95, 162, 190, 191–92,
   200, 234, 253–54
Black lawyers, 76, 85
Black nationalism (separatism), 2, 222–23,
   227–28, 230–31, 236–37, 240–43, 263. See
   also Black Power; Garvey, Marcus; Malcolm
   X; Nation of Islam
Black Panthers, 233
Black Power, 8, 222, 245; concept of, 230–31;
   and NAACP, 230–38, 242–43, 248–49,
   250
Black Power: The Politics of Liberation (1967),
   230
Black soldiers: in World War I, 24–25; in
   World War II, 95, 99–100, 102; in Vietnam
   War, 225–26
Black Star Line, 36–37
Black teachers, 147, 160
Boas, Franz, 17
Borah, William, 49, 51
Boston Guardian, 12
Bradley, Tom, 235
Branton, Wiley, 181–83, 185
Breckenridge, Sophonisba, 19
Breedlove v. Suttles (1937), 107
Brennan, William, 258
Brooke, Edward, 234, 245
Brooks, John M., 158–60, 162–64, 166, 168,
   176, 179, 182, 184, 189, 252
Brooks, William Henry, 12
Brotherhood of Sleeping Car Porters, 100
Brown, Hubert "Rap," 236
Brown v. Board of Education of Topeka,
   Kansas (1954), 5, 70, 92, 147, 156, 166,
   168, 194, 278n3
Brownell, Herbert, 195–96
Bryan, William J., 28
Buchanan v. Warley (1917), 74
Bunche, Ralph, 69, 110
Byrd, Harry, 159

Call, The, 12, 14, 16
Cannon, Poppy, 113
Capper, Arthur, 54
Cardozo, Benjamin, 81
Carmichael, Stokeley (Kwame Ture), 227–30,
   234, 236, 239
Carnegie Foundation, 241
Carson, Clayborne, 2
Carter, Dover, 149–52
Carter, James E., 255
Carter, Robert, 199
Catt, Carrie Chapman, 33–34
Chandler, Owen, 38
Charleston News and Courier, 32, 91
Chavis, Benjamin, 263
Chicago Defender, 128
Church, Robert, 47
CIO. See Congress of Industrial Organizations
City of Mobile v. Bolden (1980), 257
Civilian Conservation Corps, 64
Civil Rights Act of 1957, 157–58, 194–200,
   203, 214
Civil Rights Act of 1960, 199–200, 214
Civil Rights Act of 1964, 204–10, 213–14, 219,
   221, 244, 254
Civil Rights Congress, 136–37
Clansman, The, 23
Clark, Jim, 214, 234
Cleghorn, Reese, 190
Clinton, William J., 261
COFO. See Council of Federated Organiza-
   tions
Cold War, 3, 4, 7; and civil rights, 116–17, 121,
   131, 138–39
Colonialism, 98, 101–2; NAACP attitude to-
   ward, 116, 119, 122–23, 231–32
Communist International, 62
Communist Party of the United States
   (CPUSA), 55, 62, 103, 109, 117, 131; and
   NAACP, 62–63, 132–38; and Scottsboro tri-
   als, 63; and "white chauvinism," 137–38
Congress of Industrial Organizations (CIO),
   62, 99, 105, 126, 148–49, 153
Congress of Racial Equality (CORE), 1, 204,
   211, 216, 236–37, 241; radicalization of, 185,
   228–29, 232–33, 240–42; relations with
   NAACP, 8, 167–68, 171–72, 184; and Viet-

nam War, 227; and voter registration, 174, 176, 179, 183, 190

Connor, Eugene T., 173, 214

Coolidge, Calvin, 47–49

CORE. *See* Congress of Racial Equality

Council of Federated Organizations (COFO), 183–84, 186, 211

Courts, Gus, 150–52, 156, 195

Cox, James B., 46

Cox, William B., 203

CPUSA. *See* Communist Party of the United States

Crisis, The: cited, 20, 28, 31, 33, 37, 42, 43, 44, 45, 55, 79, 96, 98, 101, 127–28; finances of, 18, 20, 58–59, 152; as organ of NAACP, 14, 16, 33, 59, 97; sales figures of, 16, 24–25; segregation controversy, 57–58

Current, Gloster, 110, 112, 127, 157, 169, 175, 186, 227–28, 237, 242

Dabney, Virginius, 90

Darrow, Clarence, 72, 76

Daughters of the American Revolution, 136

Dawes, Charles G., 48

Delany, Hubert, 114

DeLoach, Cartha, 170

Democratic Party, 6, 28, 40, 50, 56, 65–66, 70, 106, 127, 184, 192, 199, 211–13, 254; in the South, 25, 66–67, 77, 80, 82, 93, 142, 156, 180, 184, 194, 211–13, 227, 236, 256

Dennis, David, 183

DePriest, Oscar, 41, 65

Dewey, John, 12

Dewey, Thomas, 130

Diggs, Charles, 243

Diner, Hasia, 17

Dirksen, Everett, 197, 208, 215

Disfranchisement, 4, 8, 12, 26, 28–30, 32, 34, 40, 64, 72, 82, 87, 107–9, 140, 142, 227, 251, 256, 259. *See also* Grandfather clause; Literacy tests; Minority Vote Dilution; Poll tax; Understanding clauses; Violence; White Primary

Dixon, Thomas, 23

Douglas, Paul, 198–99, 244

Douglas, William, 86

Douglass, Frederick, 43

Du Bois, W.E.B.: on Booker T. Washington, 15–16; as cofounder of NAACP, 12, 14, 21; as director of special research for NAACP, 119, 122; dismissal from NAACP in 1948, 123, 128–29; on economic reform, 60–61, as editor of *Crisis*, 14, 16, 18, 24, 29, 30–31, 43, 46, 49–50, 53; on elections, 44–45, 47–49, 68; on litigation, 69; and Marcus Garvey, 37–39; and Niagara Movement, 16; and Pan-Africanism, 96; on political education, 41, 51–52; on race relations in NAACP, 20–21; resignation from *Crisis* and NAACP in 1934, 59–60; on segregation, 24, 57–59, 113; Spingarn Medal, 169; and UN petition, 120–22, 125; on white primary, 77, 79; on woman suffrage, 33; and World War I, 24–25

Dunbar, Leslie, 180–81

Dyer, Leonidas, 51–52

Eagles, Charles, 1

Eastland, James, 96, 195, 203

Eighteenth Amendment (to U.S. Constitution), 32–33

Eisenhower, Dwight D., 129, 158, 191–96, 198, 202; administration of, 199–200

Elections:

—congressional elections: of 1910, 28; of 1934, 54; of 1942, 105; of 1946, 126–27; of 1966, 219, 244

—"freedom elections" (1963 and 1964), 183–84, 211, 217–18

—presidential elections: of 1908, 28; of 1912, 44; of 1916, 45; of 1920, 46, 77; of 1924, 40, 43, 48; of 1928, 50; of 1932, 55, 66; of 1936, 65–67; of 1940, 67; of 1948, 117, 130–31; of 1952, 191–93; of 1956, 202; of 1960, 161, 201–2; of 1964, 209–13, 243; 1968, 243, 246; of 1972, 243

See also White primary

Ervin, Sam, 195

Evers, Charles, 178, 229, 234

Evers, Medgar, 157–58, 160, 163, 169, 176–79, 204–5, 229

Evers-Williams, Myrlie, 263–64

Fairclough, Adam, 3, 4, 139

Fair Employment Practices Committee (FEPC), 100–101, 124–25, 130, 136, 192

Farmer, James, 171–72, 176, 204

Farrakhan, Louis, 263–64

FBI. *See* Federal Bureau of Investigation

Federal Bureau of Investigation (FBI), 102–3, 137, 169–70, 180, 204

FEPC. *See* Fair Employment Practices Committee

Fifteenth Amendment (to U.S. Constitution), 6, 13, 25, 28, 32, 33, 34, 40, 73, 86, 219; strict construction of, 30–31; and white primary, 77, 79, 81, 84, 89

Florida Progressive Voters League, 149

Folsom, James, 142

Ford, Henry, 62

Ford Foundation, 241

Ford Motor Company, 62

Fourteenth Amendment (to U.S. Constitution), 6, 13, 72–74, 258; NAACP campaign to enforce Section Two, 27–30; and poll tax, 107; and white primary, 79, 81, 84

Frankfurter, Felix, 76, 86, 90

Franklin, Pink, 72

Freedom rides. *See* Nonviolent direct action

Freedom Summer (1964), 184, 186, 214

Gallup polls, 67, 162

Gandhi, Mohandas, 172

Garland, Charles, 76. *See also* American Fund for Public Service

Garrison, Francis Jackson, 19

Garrison, William Lloyd, 12, 19

Garvey, Marcus, 6, 36–37, 57, 103; and NAACP, 37–39

Gerry, Elbridge, 258

Geyer, Lee, 105

Geyer-Pepper bill, 106–7. *See also* Poll tax

Glass, Carter, 31

Goldwater, Barry, 174, 209–11, 213, 256

Grandfather clause, 73, 77, 85–86, 251–52, 254. *See also Guinn v. United States; Lane v. Wilson*

Great Depression, 56, 59–62, 76, 83, 94

Great Migration, 22, 41

Green, William, 53

Griffith, D. W., 22

Grovey v. Townsend (1935), 84, 88–90, 92

Guinier, Lani, 261

Guinn v. United States (1915), 73–74, 82, 85, 87, 92

Hamer, Fanny Lou, 212, 217–18

Hamilton, Charles, 230, 234

Harding, Warren G., 46–48, 52

Harper v. Virginia State Board of Elections (1966), 108

Harris, Abram, 61

Hastie, William, 57, 85–86, 89

Hatch Acts (1939 and 1940), 107

Hays, William, 47, 64

Henry, Aaron, 178, 183

Hill, Arnold, 100

Hill, Robert A., 103

Hitler, Adolf, 97–99, 102, 106, 233

Holder v. Hall (1994), 259

Hollow Hope, The, 70

Holmes, Oliver Wendell, 79

Hoover, Herbert, 49–50, 52–56

Hoover, J. Edgar, 102–3, 137, 170, 204

Hopkins, Harry, 65

Horne, Gerald, 118, 137, 293n65

House Un-American Activities Committee (HUAC), 132, 136

Houston, Charles Hamilton, 85–86

Houston, William, 64

HUAC. *See* House Un-American Activities Committee

Hughes, Charles Evans, 45, 48

Humphrey, Hubert, 198, 200, 208, 217, 226, 245

Humphrey, John, 120

Hunton, Addie, 35

Hurley, Ruby, 157

Ickes, Harold, 64

ILD. *See* International Labor Defense

Independent, The, 10

International Labor Defense (ILD), 63, 136

Jackson, Jesse, Sr., 263

Jackson, Luther P., 142

Jackson, Maynard, Jr., 256

Jackson, Maynard, Sr., 146–47

Jackson Daily News, 91

Janken, Kenneth R., 3, 113

Jaybird Democratic Association (Fort Bend, Texas), 91

Jet, 156

Johnson, James Weldon: as executive secretary of NAACP, 19, 27, 37, 40, 41, 46–47, 49, 52, 61, 80; as field secretary of NAACP, 22

Johnson, Lyndon B., 142, 170, 184, 197–98, 200, 211, 243; administration of, 8, 227, 228, 246; and Civil Rights Act of 1964, 206–9; and Great Society, 207, 213, 222, 224, 226, 244–45, 251; and open housing bill, 229; and Voting Rights Act of 1965, 214–17, 221

Joint Center for Political and Economic Studies, 260

Jordan, Vernon, 184–85

Journal of Negro Education, 69

Kansas City Call, 113

Katzenbach, Nicholas, 214–15

Kefauver, Estes, 161

Kelley, Florence, 12, 33, 35–36

Kellogg, Charles, 1

Kennedy, John F., 173, 254; administration of, 180, 203–4; civil rights policy of, 203–7; and NAACP, 200–202

Kennedy, Robert F., 180, 201–6, 245

Kerner, Otto, 222

Kerner Report. *See* National Advisory Commission on Civil Disorders

King, Coretta, 201–2

King, Ed, 183

King, Martin Luther, Jr., 2, 113, 146–47, 167, 175, 177, 195, 200, 203, 206, 212, 235, 239; and nonviolent direct action, 172–73, 204–5, 211, 214–16, 244; relations with NAACP, 8, 168–71; and Vietnam War, 225, 227; on voter registration, 174, 179, 221

King, Martin Luther, Sr., 200

Klarman, Michael, 70–71

Knollenberg, Fred, 76, 81, 83–84

Kousser, J. Morgan, 259

Krock, Arthur, 194

Ku Klux Klan, 23, 27, 37, 48–49, 55, 77, 78, 126, 132, 150, 156, 215

Labor Youth League, 135

La Follette, Robert, Sr., 48–49

Lampkin, Daisy, 193

Landon, Alf, 65

Lane v. Wilson (1939), 86–87, 92

Lasker, Loula Davis, 153–54, 156

Layton, Caleb, 52

LDF. *See* NAACP Legal Defense and Education Fund

Leadership Conference on Civil Rights, 197, 218

League of Nations, 97

League of Women Voters, 35

Lee, George, 150–51, 156

Lewis, Alfred Baker, 98, 133

Lewis, Chester, 238–39

Lewis, David Lewering, 17–18, 37, 59, 125

Lewis, John, 205, 239, 260

Life Magazine, 131

Lincoln, Abraham, 11, 12, 67, 210, 217

Literacy tests, 25, 28, 30, 77, 85, 87, 104, 106, 185, 248; NAACP attitude toward, 31–32, 252

Literary Digest, 65

LOOK Magazine, 237

Lowndes County Freedom Organization (LCFO), 227, 234

Lovejoy, Elijah, 11

Lynching, 10, 23, 63, 64, 66, 253

Madison, Joseph, 252–53, 264

Majority-black districts, 256, 258–61

Malcolm X, 223, 240

Marable, Manning, 117, 263

Marcantonio, Vito, 109

March on Washington: 100–101 (1941); 205–6, 237 (1963)

Margold, Nathan, 76

Marshall, Louis, 17, 76, 79, 81

Marshall, Thurgood, 5, 85, 111–12, 124, 176, 203, 259, 278n3; on poll tax, 107–8, 217; in white primary cases, 88, 90, 92

Mays, Benjamin, 168

McAdam, Doug, 143

McCarthy, Eugene, 245

McCarthy, Joseph, 116, 139

McCarthyism, 116–18, 136, 139. *See also* Anti-communism

McCulloch, Roscoe, 54–55
McReynolds, James, 81
Meier, August, 1, 171–72, 237
Meredith, James, 228–29
Messenger, The, 38
Metcalf, George, 178
MFDP. *See* Mississippi Freedom Democratic
    Party
Mfume, Kweisi, 264
Milholland, John, 13
Miller v. Johnson (1995), 258–59
Minority vote dilution, 219, 256–62; at-large
    elections, 256–57; racial gerrymandering,
    256, 258
Mississippi Freedom Democratic Party
    (MFDP), 184, 216, 220, 227, 246; at Atlan-
    tic City convention, 211–13; and congres-
    sional challenge of 1965, 217–19; and Viet-
    nam War, 225–26
Mitchell, Arthur, 65
Mitchell, Clarence, 4, 111–12, 129, 132, 181,
    192, 197–98, 207–9, 217–18, 226, 248
Molotov, Vyacheslav M., 121–22
Montgomery, Alabama, Bus Boycott (1955–56),
    167, 175
Moody, Dan, 80
Moon, Henry Lee, 112, 129, 141, 143–45, 153–
    56, 178, 213, 224, 236
Moore, Harry T., 147, 149
Moore v. Dempsey (1923), 72
Morrow, Frederic, 148
Morse, Wayne, 198
Morsell, John, 163, 171, 178, 187–88, 218
Moses, Robert, 179, 183, 212, 217–18
Moskovitz, Henry, 12
Muse, Edward, 250
Myrdal, Gunnar, 94–95, 110, 115, 146

NAACP. *See* National Association for the Ad-
    vancement of Colored People
NAACP Legal Defense and Education Fund, 5,
    111, 137, 168, 241, 261
Nash, Roy, 23
Nation, The, 12
National Advisory Commission on Civil Disor-
    ders, 222, 246

National American Woman Suffrage Associa-
    tion (NAWSA), 33–35
National Association for the Advancement
    of Colored People (NAACP): abolitionist
    legacy in, 17, 19; anticommunism of, 7, 63,
    117–18, 131–39; antilynching campaign of,
    23, 27, 51–52, 62; articles of incorporation,
    21–22; balance-of-power strategy in elec-
    tions, 42–43, 46, 191–92, 234, 254; board
    of directors, 3, 19, 20, 21, 24, 29, 34, 35, 42,
    54, 59–61, 78, 98, 108, 112, 114, 119–20,
    122–23, 126–29, 132–36, 143–44, 150, 152,
    158–59, 181, 215, 239, 241, 264; Committee
    on Administration, 126, 128–29; Commit-
    tee on Political Domination, 133; commu-
    nist "infiltration" of, 131–36; finances of, 18,
    21, 25, 56, 83, 111, 152–53, 163, 241, 252,
    263–64; founding of, 1, 4, 10–15; historiog-
    raphy on, 1–2, 7, 9, 116–18; injunction
    against, 148, 157, 163, 196; and integration,
    6, 9, 19–20, 39, 222–23, 232, 240, 250–
    51, 254; and international affairs, 96–97;
    interracialism of, 18, 20–21, 39, 97, 254;
    Jews in, 17–18, 97, 240–41; legal committee
    of, 85–86; legal department of, 5, 150; legal-
    ism of, 2, 166, 174–75; litigation strategy of,
    6, 72, 74–75, 87; membership, 1, 7, 13, 19–
    20, 22–23, 39, 54, 109–11, 114, 137, 152–53,
    225, 232, 237, 251; middle-class orientation,
    17, 110, 146, 239–40, 250–51; national sec-
    retariat, 3, 5, 20, 21, 55, 74, 108, 110, 112,
    114, 133–36, 143, 152–53, 163, 182, 187, 239–
    40, 253; nonpartisanship of, 6, 42–43, 55,
    127, 134, 148, 164, 202; organizational
    structure, 13, 21, 25, 109–15, 237; and politi-
    cal education, 32, 42–43, 67–68, 191; pro-
    gram of, 6, 13–14, 60–62, 224, 237, 251;
    race relations in, 6, 18–21, 136; records of,
    2; regional offices, 143; state conferences of,
    2, 55, 110, 141, 143, 147, 149, 155, 159, 181,
    225; Voter Registration Committee, 7, 158–
    60, 179, 187, 252–53; Washington Bureau
    of, 4, 111–12, 129, 144, 181, 208, 259; whites
    in, 17–18, 19–21, 136, 232, 240–41; women
    in, 112–13; "Young Turks" in, 238–39, 241;
    youth groups of, 22

—annual conferences, 143; **1911**, 25, 72; **1920**, 22; **1924**, 48; **1926**, 42; **1932**, 60; **1933**, 96–97; **1935**, 61–62, 64; **1936**, 97; **1940**, 98–99; **1941**, 99; **1942**, 101; **1944**, 126; **1947**, 123; **1948**, 144; **1950**, 132–33, 136; **1955**, 194; **1956**, 175; **1957**, 196; **1959**, 169; **1960**, 175–76; **1961**, 175–77, 202–3; **1964**, 208; **1966**, 225, 230; **1967**, 234, 237; **1968**, 238, 245; **1972**, 247

—branches of NAACP, 2, 7, 21–22, 25, 45, 51–53, 55, 62, 74, 80, 90, 110, 133, 142–45, 157, 164, 177, 181–83, 210, 237–40, 242, 252–54, 259; Alston, Ga., 150; Baltimore, Md., 4, 22, 62, 142, 146; Baton Rouge, La., 110; Beaumont, Tex., 78; Belzoni, Miss., 150–52, 195; Birmingham, Ala., 145; Boston, Mass., 19, 22; Chicago, Ill., 19, 22, 62, 64; Detroit, Mich., 62, 110, 112; El Paso, Tex., 76, 78, 81; Fort Worth, Tex., 78; Great Neck, Long Island, 134–35; Greenwich Village, N.Y., 225; Greenwood, S.C., 74; Houston, Tex., 75, 78, 88; Key West, Fla., 22; Little Rock, Ark., 75; Memphis, Tenn., 160–61; Mobile, Ala., 35; Monroe, N.C., 232; New Orleans, La., 22, 87, 187; Philadelphia, Pa., 22, 135, 240; San Antonio, Tex., 78; San Francisco, Calif., 143; Shreveport, La., 22, 110; Tampa, Fla., 232; Waco, Tex., 75; Washington, D.C., 22, 42

—student chapters: 22, 133, 135, 171; Cornell University, 135; University of California, Berkeley, 135; University of Wisconsin, Madison, 135

—youth groups: Jackson, Miss., 177; Oklahoma City, 175; Wichita, Kans., 175

National Association of Colored Women, 35
National Black Political Convention (1972), 242–43
National Broadcasting Corporation, 172
National Committee to Abolish the Poll Tax (NCAPT), 105–6; and NAACP, 108–9
National Council of Negro Women, 102, 184
National Lawyers' Guild, 89
National Negro Business League, 15
National Negro Conference (1909), 12–13, 14, 16, 18, 28, 40
National Negro Congress, 120, 136

National Urban League (NUL), 1, 14, 100, 102, 166, 180, 202, 226, 228, 241, 250; and NAACP, 168, 247
National Woman's Party, 34–35
National Youth Administration, 64
Nation of Islam, 223, 263
NAWSA. *See* National American Woman Suffrage Association
Nazi Germany, 97–99, 177, 215, 227
NCAPT. *See* National Committee to Abolish the Poll Tax
Negro World, The, 37
Nerney, Mary Childs, 18
New Deal coalition, 117, 126–27, 248; and NAACP, 6, 63–67
Newsweek, 162
New York Evening Post, 12, 13, 41
New York Times, 194, 221
Niagara Movement, 16
Nineteenth Amendment (to U.S. Constitution, 33–35. *See also* Woman suffrage
Nixon, Edgar Daniel, 175
Nixon, Isaac B., 149–51
Nixon, Lawrence, 78, 80, 83
Nixon, Richard M., 194, 200, 202, 246–47, 256; administration of, 246–48; civil rights policy of, 247–48; southern strategy of, 245
Nixon v. Condon (1932), 81–84, 87, 90, 92
Nixon v. Herndon (1927), 79–80, 84, 87, 90, 92
Nonviolent direct action, 5, 70–71, 165, 167–68, 204, 254–55; and Black Power, 231–33; boycotts, 173, 177–78; demonstrations, 173, 177, 210–11, 214–16, 219; freedom rides (1961), 167, 172–73, 175, 180; and "jail, no bail," 175–77; NAACP and, 7, 171–72, 178–79; sit-in movement, 170, 175, 177; and voter registration, 5, 8, 166–68, 174, 176–77, 188–90, 191
Northeastern Federation of Women's Clubs, 33

O'Connor, Sandra Day, 258
Open housing bill, 229, 244
Ovington, Mary White, 17, 18, 22, 35, 60–62; as cofounder of NAACP, 12–14
Owens, Jesse, 97

Pan-African Congress (1919), 96
Parker, John J., 51, 52–55, 68, 82, 91, 247
Patterson, William L., 136
Patton, W. C., 145–46, 152, 155, 157–63, 179, 182–85, 187–89, 210, 252
Paul, Alice, 34–35
Pepper, Claude F., 105, 142, 148
Pickens, William, 19, 37–38, 49, 52, 54, 82
Pillsbury, Albert, 28, 30
Pittsburgh Courier, 102, 129, 193
Plessy v. Ferguson (1896), 73, 259
Poll tax, 4, 25, 28, 80, 87, 124–25, 130, 142, 145, 154, 160, 216–17, 252–54; and National Committee to Abolish the Poll Tax, 104–9
Porter, Kirk H., 26
Powell, Adam Clayton, 232
President's Committee on Civil Rights (1946), 124, 127
Progressive Party: of 1912, 44; of 1924, 48–49; of 1948, 117, 127–31
Prohibition, 32
Proportional representation, 252, 258, 261, 319n5
Public Works Administration, 64

Race Riots. *See* Violence
RACON. *See Survey of Racial Conditions in the United States*
Randolph, A. Philip, 38, 109, 120, 125, 169, 211; and March on Washington of 1941, 100–101; and March on Washington of 1963, 205
Rankin, John, 121
Reagan, Ronald, 252–53
Reapportionment, 28–30, 258
Reed, Stanley, 86, 90
Republican Party, 6, 28, 42, 46, 55, 65–66, 191, 193, 195, 199, 209–10, 256, 260; "lily-white" strategy in the South, 40, 44, 47, 50–51, 53–54, 71
Reuther, Walter, 238
Richmond Times Dispatch, 90
Roberts, Owen, 89
Robinson, Jackie, 241
Rockefeller Foundation, 241
Rogers, William, 198
Roosevelt, Eleanor, 56, 109, 121–22, 126

Roosevelt, Franklin D., 55–56, 64–68, 86, 89, 95, 100, 102, 119, 126; administration of, 63–64, 126; Black Cabinet, 64
Roosevelt, Theodore, 44
Roper, Elmo, 191–92
Rosenberg, Gerald, 70
Rosenwald, Julius, 17, 19
Rudwick, Elliot, 1, 171–72, 237
Russell, Richard, 196, 208
Rustin, Bayard, 205, 212

Schlesinger, Arthur M., Jr., 117, 131
Schneider, Mark R., 3
Schrecker, Ellen, 118
Schuyler, George, 129
SCLC. *See* Southern Christian Leadership Conference
Scottsboro trials, 63, 136
Shaw v. Reno (1993), 258–59
Shores, Arthur L., 147
Shuttlesworth, Fred L., 146
Simmons, Althea, 186–87
Sit-in movement. *See* Nonviolent direct action
Smith, Alfred E., 50
Smith, Ellison "Cotton Ed," 65
Smith, John David, 3
Smith, Lamar, 156
Smith, Lonnie, 89
Smith v. Allwright (1944), 88–93, 142
SNCC. *See* Student Nonviolent Coordinating Committee
Socialist Party, 45, 48, 50, 55
Soldier Vote Act (1942), 106
Souls of Black Folk, The, 15, 30
Southern Christian Leadership Conference (SCLC), 1, 113, 167, 216, 241, 244; relations with NAACP, 8, 147, 167–71, 178, 184; and voter registration, 174, 179, 190, 200
Southern Conference on Human Welfare, 105
Southern Manifesto, 194, 201
Southern Regional Council (SRC), 180–81, 184, 202
Sparkman, John, 156, 192
Spingarn, Arthur, 23, 128, 238, 240; as co-founder of NAACP, 17; legal work for NAACP, 76–77, 79, 85

Spingarn, Joel E., 23–24, 44, 61–62, 169; as chairman of the board of directors, 19, 58; as cofounder of NAACP, 17; as president of NAACP, 66
Spingarn Medal, 169
Spottswood, Stephen G., 206, 238, 247
Springfield (Illinois): race riot in, 10–11
SRC. *See* Southern Regional Council
Stalin, Joseph, 62, 121, 131
Stanton, Elizabeth Cady, 33
Steffens, Lincoln, 12
Stembridge, Jane, 170
Stevenson, Adlai, 192–93, 200–201
Stone, Harlan Fisk, 89
Storey, Moorfield: legal work for NAACP, 76, 79, 81; as president of NAACP, 13, 17, 28, 30, 44, 73
Strunsky, Anna, 10
Student Nonviolent Coordinating Committee (SNCC), 1, 113, 216–17, 234, 237, 241; on nonviolent direct action, 172–73, 180, 211; radicalization of, 185, 220, 227–28, 232–33, 239; relations with NAACP, 8, 167–68, 170–71, 178, 184, 226; and Vietnam War, 226–27; and voter registration, 174, 176, 179, 183, 186, 190
Sugrue, Thomas, 243
Sumner, Charles, 17
Survey of Racial Conditions in the United States (RACON), 103
Sweet, Ossian, 72

Taconic Foundation, 180–81
Taft, Robert, 131
Taft, William Howard, 28, 44, 47, 72; administration of, 73
Talbert, Mary B., 35
Terrell, Mary Church, 12, 33, 35
Terry v. Adams (1953), 91
Thomas, Clarence, 259
Thompson, William "Big Bill," 41
Thornburgh v. Gingles (1986), 258
Thurmond, J. Strom, 130, 197
Tinkham, George H., 29–30
Tobias, Channing, 124, 132
To Secure These Rights (1947), 124–25
Trotter, William Monroe, 12, 18

Truman, Harry S., 95, 108, 124–26, 129–30, 191–93, 254; administration of, 117, 122–23, 125–27, 191; Truman Doctrine, 134
Tureaud, A. P., 142
Tuskegee Normal and Industrial Institute (Alabama), 15–17, 18, 36
Twenty-fourth Amendment (to U.S. Constitution), 108. *See also* Poll tax

UAW. *See* United Automobile Workers
Understanding clauses, 87, 91, 106, 185
United Automobile Workers (UAW), 62, 184, 206, 238
United Nations: NAACP petition to, 119–23, 128
United States v. Classic (1941), 88–89, 92
Universal Negro Improvement Association, 36–38, 103. *See also* Marcus Garvey
Urban League. *See* National Urban League
U.S. Commission on Civil Rights, 198–99
U.S. Department of Justice, 124, 135–36, 185, 195–96, 199, 205, 208, 261; and majority-black districts, 257–58; and Voting Rights Act of 1965, 214–15; and voting rights cases, 74, 87, 89–90, 149–50, 198, 203–4
U.S. Department of State, 97, 119
U.S. Supreme Court, 5, 47, 53, 63, 69–72, 87–88, 112, 156–57, 166–67, 194, 223, 247, 293n73; on grandfather clause, 73–74, 86; on literacy tests, 30, 72–73; on majority-black districts, 258–60; on minority vote dilution, 257–58; on poll tax, 107–8, 217; on white primary, 77–85, 88–93, 142. *See also individual rulings*

Vietnam War, 8, 170, 231–32; and NAACP, 224–27, 237–38, 245–47
Villard, Oswald Garrison, 16, 17, 18, 23, 44, 72; as cofounder of NAACP, 12–13, 41
Violence: and Black Power, 224, 232–33, 236, 251; against black voters, 27, 35, 92, 149–52, 159–60; NAACP support for victims of racial violence, 150–52; race riots, 10–11, 23, 24, 94–95, 103–4, 175, 210, 221–22, 233, 240–43, 255
Virginia Voters League, 142, 147
Vital Center, The, 117

Vote, right to, 1, 25, 33, 195, 203, 251, 255. *See also* Fifteenth Amendment, Nineteenth Amendment

Voter Education Project (VEP), 8, 179–85, 204; achievements of, 182; and NAACP, 181–85

Voter registration: apathy as an obstacle to, 140, 142, 145, 245; campaigns by NAACP, 4, 5, 6, 7, 142–46, 152–55, 159–65, 184–88, 192, 200, 210, 245, 250–55; and economic reprisals, 161–62; estimates and figures on black voter registration, 88, 140–41, 154, 156–58, 160–64, 185, 188–89, 210, 219, 245, 248, 254–55; "freedom registrations" (1963), 183–84. *See also* Black electorate; Nonviolent direct action; Voter Education Project

Voting Rights Act (1965), 184–85, 188, 214–19, 221, 225, 244, 250, 254–55; extension in 1970, 247–48; extension in 1982, 257; and majority-black districts, 258–61; and minority vote dilution, 256–58

Wagner, Robert, 53

Walden, A. T., 147

Wallace, George C., 190, 204, 209–10, 214, 228, 243, 246–47

Wallace, Henry A., 117, 125–31

Wallace, Lurleen, 190, 228

Walling, William English: as cofounder of NAACP, 10–14, 42

Walters, Alexander, 12

Waring, Watis, 91

Warren, Earl, 219

Washington, Booker T., 19, 36; as advocate of accommodationism, 15, 57; and founding of NAACP, 15–17

Watters, Pat, 190

Weber, Max, 39

Weiss, Nancy, 67

Wells-Barnett, Ida, 12, 18, 33

White, Walter Francis, 2, 3, 19, 31, 51, 54, 75, 119, 261; as assistant secretary of NAACP, 27, 42, 46, 49–50, 52–53, 55, 56, 80; on communism, 131, 135; as executive secretary of NAACP, 58, 62–63, 65–66, 103, 106–7, 109, 111–13, 116, 193; and March on Washington (1941), 100–101; and Progressive

Party of 1948, 126–28; segregation controversy with Du Bois, 57–59; and Truman administration, 124–30, 192; and UN petition, 120–23; and voter registration, 153, 155–56

White backlash, 209, 211, 222, 243–46, 248–49

White Citizens' Councils, 156

White House Conference on Civil Rights (1966), 226–27

White primary, 7, 69, 74–75, 77, 109, 149, 252, 254; NAACP legal campaign against, 77–83, 88–93. *See also* Grovey v. Townsend; Nixon v. Condon; Nixon v. Herndon; Smith v. Allwright; Terry v. Adams

Wilcher, Helen, 177

Wilkins, Roy, 2, 119, 127, 261; as assistant secretary of NAACP, 58, 98, 103, 122, 126; and Black Power, 227–29, 231–37, 242, 244, 249; on Civil Rights Act of 1957, 197–99; on communism, 131, 134, 136, 138; as editor of *Crisis*, 103, 113–14; on Eisenhower administration, 192–94; as executive secretary of NAACP, 112–14, 166, 174, 204–5, 215, 222, 238–39, 245, 247; and John F. Kennedy, 200–203; and Lyndon B. Johnson, 207–9, 212–13, 216, 219; and Martin Luther King, Jr., 168–70; on nonviolent direct action, 175–77; on Vietnam War, 225–27; on voter registration, 142, 155, 157–59, 164, 179, 181, 184, 186, 188, 190, 221; on white backlash, 209–11, 239–42

Williams, Robert, 85–86

Williams, Robert F., 232

Williams v. Mississippi (1897), 73

Wilson, Woodrow, 33, 44–45, 48

Wofford, Harris, 203

Woman suffrage, 6, 26; NAACP attitude toward, 32–36

Workers Defense League, 89, 109

Works Progress Administration, 65

Young, Andrew, 235, 255

Young, Whitney M., Jr., 166, 168, 226, 229, 242

Younge, Sammy, 226

Zieger, Robert, 138

Manfred Berg is the executive director of the Center for U.S. Studies at the Leucorea Foundation of the Martin Luther University of Halle-Wittenberg. He is the author of numerous books and articles on German and American history.